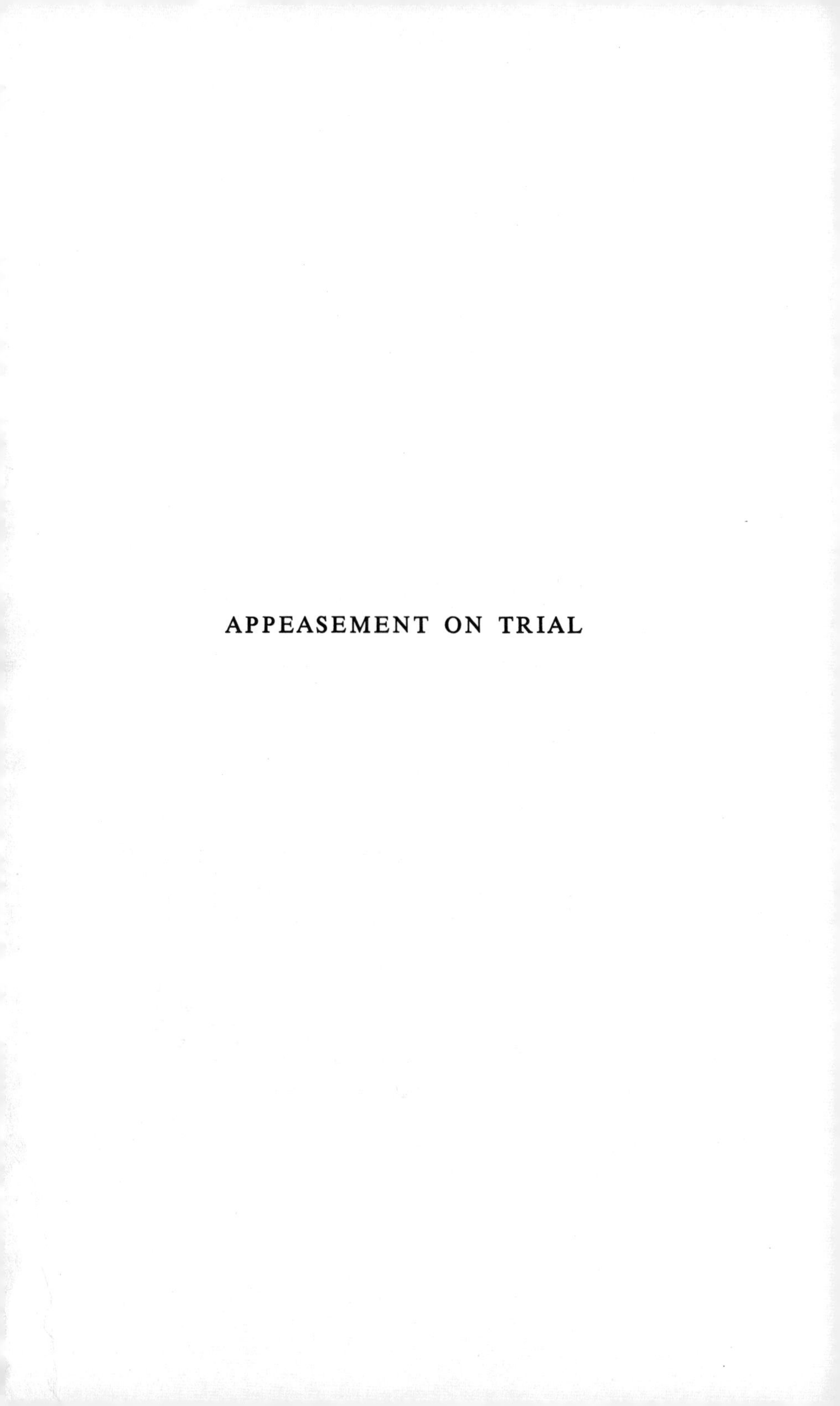

APPEASEMENT ON TRIAL

APPEASEMENT ON TRIAL

British Foreign Policy and Its Critics, 1938–1939

by

WILLIAM R. ROCK

ARCHON BOOKS

1966

Library of Congress Catalog Card Number: 66-19715
Printed in the United States of America

To

My Mother and Father

Contents

Preface

THE HISTORY of appeasement has been chronicled by writers of all kinds from many points of view. The origins of the policy have been much discussed; the attempts of British diplomats to implement the policy have been thoroughly traced; and its eventual collapse has been painstakingly recorded. The validity of the total policy is still heatedly debated. In all that has been written, however, there has been no systematic attempt to treat the opposition to appeasement and its effect on British foreign policy during the crucial years 1938–1939. The subject has been relatively ignored, largely on the basis of two widely-held assumptions: that there was no significant opposition to appeasement in Britain, aside from the prophetic warnings of Winston Churchill, and that what there was had no practical effect on the course of British policy. Both these assumptions are mistaken, and herein the primary concern of this work lies.

This study originated in and revolves around the sudden reversal of traditional British foreign policy which followed Germany's destruction of Czechoslovakia in March, 1939—a shift so significant that Prime Minister Neville Chamberlain explained to the House of Commons (April 3, 1939) that:

> Indeed, to have departed from our traditional ideas in this respect so far as I did on behalf of His Majesty's Government on Friday constitutes a portent in British policy so momentous that I think it safe to say it will have a chapter to itself when the history books come to be written.

The distinct suggestion, arising from early investigation, that increasing pressure from the critics of appeasement had played a significant role in the Government's change of policy indicated a need to examine the opposition to appeasement, to trace the course of its development, and to assess its relationship to the general trend of British foreign policy during 1938–1939. That is what this study purports to do. It is not intended as an exhaustive treatment of appeasement, nor is it a definitive account of British diplomacy during the last two prewar years. It attempts to provide a narrative of British policy sufficiently thorough to make the criticism of policy meaningful—and which, indeed, might serve as a convenient survey for those who find themselves lost in the myriad of works which touch upon some facet of this subject—but throughout emphasis is placed on criticism and the inter-relationship of criticism and policy.

The British diplomatic revolution which began with the guarantee to Poland was impelled in no small measure by a climactic outburst of public dissatisfaction with appeasement following the German seizure of Prague. This protest was by no means new; it had developed gradually through 1938 and the early months of 1939. Since Eden's resignation from the Foreign Office in February, 1938, over Chamberlain's "immoderate haste" to reach a general settlement of differences with Mussolini, there had emanated from certain sections of Parliament and the press explicit discontent with appeasement and a continued demand that it be abandoned in favor of a policy of collective defense against aggression. The Labor Party and press were undoubtedly motivated in part by partisan political considerations, but among appeasement's most avid critics were the Liberal Party and press, and a group of dissident Conservatives, including Churchill and Eden, who had little party capital to make by their actions. Moreover, as the tide of protest rose amid the fluctuating international scene, the opinions most forcefully expressed did not always follow party lines.

Though the demand for a new policy early took the form of a vague Labor-Liberal call for a return to "collective security" through support of the League of Nations, it assumed more definite form on March 14, 1938, when, after the German occupation of Austria, Winston Churchill proposed to the House of Commons his "grand alliance"—a number of nations gathered together in a solemn treaty for mutual defense against aggression.

Munich heightened the fears of those who opposed appeasement, though of course their warnings were dulled by the respite from war. Then Hitler's subjugation of Czechoslovakia raised the agitation for a more vigorous British foreign policy to meet the Nazi menace to fever heat—to a point where to ignore it might well have meant the collapse of the Chamberlain Government. This sustained agitation gave impetus to the resulting British attempt to construct an anti-aggression front in Europe during the summer of 1939.

In development, the British diplomatic revolution was a thing of fits and starts, of panic rushes and shy hesitations. And Britain's inability to reach an agreement with Russia, coupled with Chamberlain's ideological and military distrust of the Soviet Union, led to a reaction in July, 1939, when a final guarded approach was made to Germany. The approach yielded nothing, and as the Polish crisis reached a climax the temper of the British people was such as to make negotiations almost unthinkable.

The influence of that elusive force called public opinion on a government's foreign policy is difficult to measure. Seldom can it be proved by documentary evidence. Nevertheless, the growth of public interest in what was once the exclusive domain of a few Foreign Office experts has resulted in a strong force that most states, especially democratic ones, have had to recognize and deal with. This force is all the more powerful since government officials are by no means devoid of those sentiments which move the general public. For this reason—as well as for its pertinence to the continuing controversy over the validity of appeasement as a technique of foreign policy—the opposition to appeasement which developed in Britain during 1938–1939 is especially noteworthy.

This study originated as a dissertation written under the direction of the late Dr. E. Malcolm Carroll, James B. Duke Professor of History at Duke University. To him my debt is great. Financial aid from Duke University enabled me to prepare the study in its first form; grants from Bowling Green State University facilitated its revision and expansion. The courteous assistance given me by personnel of various libraries, including the Library of Congress, the Duke University Library, and the Bowling Green State University Library, was very helpful. I especially wish to express gratitude to my family, particularly to my wife Suzanne, and to unnamed friends for their constant encouragement and patience. Mrs. Phyllis Wulff has provided expert secretarial aid. Final responsibility for the work is, of course, mine, and in the event of omissions, misjudgments, or other deficiencies, I take refuge in Dr. Johnson's reply to a critic: the error is due only to my ignorance.

W. R. R.

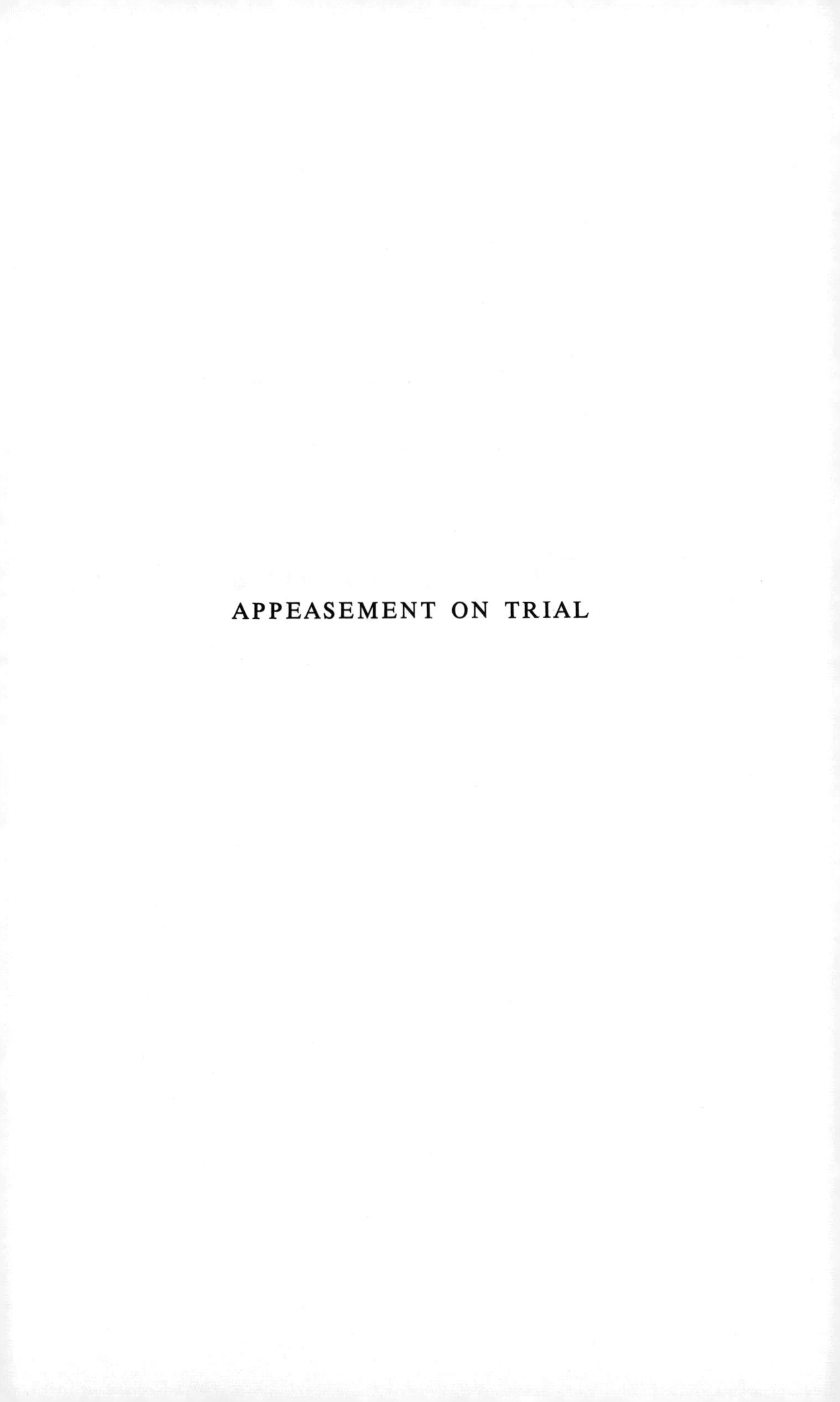

APPEASEMENT ON TRIAL

CHAPTER ONE

Prelude to Controversy

DURING THE DECADE of the 1930's a number of powers adopted profound changes of foreign policy which resulted in international havoc and led to the bitter ordeal of the Second World War. While the disgruntled powers resorted to policies of blustering, bullying, or outright aggression, the more satisfied powers abandoned the idea of collective security, constructed earlier upon support for the League of Nations, and substituted for it the policy of appeasement. The nations most closely associated with appeasement were Britain and France—and in affairs of concern to both nations Britain almost invariably assumed leadership. The man most closely connected with the policy was Neville Chamberlain. He was the one democratic statesman who sought to develop appeasement into a systematic approach to foreign affairs, and it was during his years as British Prime Minister (1937–1940) that appeasement reached its climax in response to German moves in central Europe. This is not to say that the idea of appeasement was original with Chamberlain; there are earlier instances of its use in international diplomacy. Nor does it mean that the appeasement policy of the 1930's was wholly Chamberlain's creation, for others certainly contributed to its development. It is merely to state that after he became Prime Minister in May, 1937, Chamberlain was appeasement's principal architect and primary exponent.[1]

Single factors seldom adequately explain historical episodes, and such is the case with appeasement. The motives, experiences,

1. The term appeasement had no agreed-upon definition—though all who used it seemed to have something quite definite in mind—and as time passed, it came to mean very different things to different people. A discussion of the semantics of appeasement appears in Appendix I. A volume by

and feelings which converted the British to appeasement—at least temporarily—were certainly complex. The policy sprang from various origins, some rather general in nature, others quite specific, ranging from a natural revulsion against war in the democracies and the impact of world-wide depression on European political life to the "do-little" character of the National Government formed in Britain in 1931, the military weakness of Britain, fear of Bolshevism, and the potent notion that perhaps Germany was only agitating for a long overdue revision of Versailles. Whatever the total causes of appeasement, this much is clear: once he assumed his nation's highest political office, Chamberlain pursued with single-minded determination efforts to lower the political temperature of Europe by assuring German and Italian leaders of the British desire to be friends. To convince them of this he offered something to each, in Hitler's case a general European settlement (with such things as reform of the League of Nations and Germany's return to it, "reasonable settlements" in central Europe, that is, Danzig, Austria, and Czechoslovakia, and the return of German colonies as possible means to that end), in Mussolini's the formal recognition of his new Abyssinian Empire.

To promote this end Chamberlain encouraged Lord Halifax, Lord President of the Council (and Master of the Middleton Foxhounds) to accept the invitation of Hermann Göring, Chief Huntsman of the Reich, to an international hunting exhibition in Berlin in November, 1937. Here was an excellent opportunity to establish personal contacts with the Nazi leaders, and yet the private and unofficial nature of the visit was such as would avoid both exaggerated hope and apprehension. It is not surprising, then, that Halifax ignored the slaughter of foxes and spent his time talking informally with Göring in Berlin and Hitler at Berchtesgaden.[2]

Martin Gilbert and Richard Gott, *The Appeasers* (London, 1963), examines in detail British policy toward Nazi Germany in the 1930's, showing "what the appeasers sought and what methods they were prepared to use in order to attain their ends." (Preface) Another recent study, by Margaret George, probes the motives and explains the behavior of the appeasers. *The Warped Vision: British Foreign Policy, 1933–1939* (Pittsburgh, 1965).

2. The memoirs of Lord Halifax and Foreign Secretary Anthony Eden

While Halifax's visit failed to produce any significant result other than to expose the wide gulf between Britain and Germany which had to be bridged if peace were to be assured, Chamberlain was satisfied. "The German visit was from my point of view a great success," he recorded in his diary, "because it achieved its object, that of creating an atmosphere in which it is possible to discuss with Germany the practical questions involved in a European settlement."[3]

There was nothing simple about the international problems which Chamberlain faced as British Prime Minister. He was confronted with a tense, combustible Europe. While Germany was quiescent at the time, she was menacing, having already decreed universal compulsory military service and remilitarized the Rhineland. Italy had been on a rampage for two years. In October, 1935, she had begun the invasion of Abyssinia, and since the outbreak of the civil war in Spain in July, 1936, had poured troops and supplies into the Nationalist camp despite her professed adherence to the Non-Intervention Agreement. Germany and Italy were linked by affinities of outlook and by similar forms of government. On the other hand, France was linked with Britain by common ideals of democracy, liberty, and Parliamentary government. Thus the problem, as Chamberlain saw it, was this:

> Are we to allow these two pairs of nations to go on glowering at one another across the frontier, allowing the feeling between the two sides to become more and more embittered, until at last the barriers are broken down and the conflict begins which many think would mark the end of civiliza-

---

give different impressions of the background of this visit, Halifax's version assigning Eden an active role in the promotion of the idea, but Eden's account in effect rejecting this interpretation. Lord Halifax, *Fullness of Days* (New York, 1957), pp. 185–86; Earl of Avon, *The Memoirs of Anthony Eden: Facing the Dictators, 1923–1938* (Cambridge, 1962), pp. 576–82. See also Viscount Templewood, *Nine Troubled Years* (London, 1954), pp. 281–82; John W. Wheeler-Bennett, *Munich: Prologue to Tragedy* (London, 1948), pp. 17–19; The Earl of Birkenhead, *Halifax: The Life of Lord Halifax* (London, 1965), pp. 365–74.

3. Keith Feiling, *The Life of Neville Chamberlain* (London, 1947), pp. 332–33.

> tion? Or can we bring them to an understanding of one another's aims and objects, and to such discussion as may lead to a final settlement?

If the four nations could be brought into friendly discussion, to a settling of their differences, Chamberlain believed that the peace of Europe would be saved "for a generation."[4] Russia was excluded because, in Chamberlain's view, her participation would be making 1914 over again, effecting the encirclement which might be Hitler's pretext for an early war.[5]

Thus it was that Chamberlain bent every effort "to arrive at what has sometimes been called a general settlement, to arrive at a position . . . when reasonable grievances may be removed, when suspicions may be laid aside, and when confidence may again be restored." This could be achieved, he told the House of Commons in December, 1937, "only . . . by a real understanding and effort to meet others' needs," and for that reason "any effort that we can make to promote harmony and to remove legitimate causes of grievances among the nations may well bring its own reward hereafter, if it should prove to have been a contribution to the general welfare."[6]

The hope of removing reasonable grievances and allaying suspicions had been in the minds of British statesmen and the British public since the end of the World War and was particularly evident in the British attitude toward the rest of Europe in the early 1930's. During those years British impatience with the apparent intransigence of France over reparations and disarmament produced a growing sympathy with Germany, who, after all, it was felt, had been wronged by the punitive provisions of the Versailles Treaty. Britain led the way to the abolition of reparations at the Lausanne Conference in June, 1932. Although the German withdrawal from the World Disarmament Conference in October, 1933, in effect dealt that conference a

4. Great Britain, *Parliamentary Debates, House of Commons,* Fifth Series, (hereinafter cited as *Parl. Debs., HC*), February 21, 1938, vol. 332, 64.

5. Feiling, *Life of Neville Chamberlain,* p. 325.

6. *Parl. Debs., HC,* December 21, 1937, vol. 330, 1804–07.

fatal blow, Britain held no grudge against Germany, and when there appeared in the German budget of March, 1934, a greatly expanded financial provision for armaments, the British, eager to seize any chance of satisfying Germany's legitimate claims in a general settlement that would ease European differences, condemned France's violent reaction. Germany's adoption of conscription in March, 1935, alarmed Britain, but in June of that year the two nations concluded a naval agreement which provided that the Reich would limit its fleet to 35 per cent of the British fleet, with the exception of submarines, which could be built up to parity with the whole Commonwealth. The agreement evoked a vigorous protest from Paris, but Britain maintained that it was better to have Germany voluntarily limit herself to a reasonable level of armaments than to adopt a high moral attitude towards treaty violation, or to refuse to discuss the matter and thus in effect to acquiesce in unlimited German rearmament. Within Britain it seemed that impatience with France and consequent sympathy with Germany had reached a point where the British saw themselves no longer as the ally of a wronged country against an aggressor, but as the mediator between two parties to a dispute in which faults were to be found on both sides.[7]

This attitude received confirmation in a far more serious crisis, the German remilitarization of the Rhineland in March, 1936. While the French considered mobilizing, London demurred—and whatever French resolution there may have been melted quickly away. The British felt a general measure of sympathy with the German move—after all, Germany was only occupying

7. These matters are treated at length in Arnold Wolfers, *Britain and France Between Two Wars: Conflicting Strategies of Peace Since Versailles* (New York, 1940) and W. M. Jordan, *Great Britain, France, and the German Problem, 1918–1939* (London, 1943). See also G. M. Gathorne-Hardy, *A Short History of International Affairs, 1920 to 1938* (London, 1939), *passim.* There had developed in Britain a small but rowdy organization known as the British Union of Fascists, led by Sir Oswald Mosley, which was quite sympathetic to Germany and Italy. See Robert Graves and Alan Hodge, *The Long Weekend: A Social History of Great Britain, 1918–1939* (London, n.d.), pp. 254, 311–12; Viscount Simon, *Retrospect: The Memoirs of The Rt. Hon. Viscount Simon* (London, 1952), pp. 215–16.

"her own back yard"—and believed that Germany had some ground for objecting to the encirclement implied by the Franco-Soviet mutual assistance pact signed in May, 1935.[8]

The British attitude reflects a rather curious trait of the British national character: indulgence in a guilt complex with regard to her past history. When other people make trouble for them, the British sometimes instinctively persuade themselves that it is they who have really been to blame. Thus misgivings as to the severity of the Versailles Treaty spread as Hitler began to assert himself. And this kind of doubt would later bedevil the British attitude toward Austria and Czechoslovakia.[9]

Chamberlain believed that the dictators had reason to ask the remedy of some grievances and he was prepared to recognize the "legitimate interests" of both Germany and Italy. The only condition he made was that necessary changes take place peacefully. The removal of political grievances which Hitler was exploiting, such as the existence of ten million Germans outside the Reich, might strengthen pacific elements in Germany, reduce the internal value of war propaganda, and allow the Nazi revolution to become respectable. Perhaps Hitler was only an astute man taking calculated risks, knowing when to stop. These possibilities surely raised Chamberlain's hopes.[10]

In any case, Chamberlain abhorred war, and this, along with his judgment, or as it turned out, misjudgment, of Hitler's aims, goes far toward explaining his commitment to appeasement—and the support which the policy received from his colleagues in the Cabinet and his followers in Parliament and among the electorate. "War," he once declared, "wins nothing, cures nothing, ends nothing. . . . There are no winners, but all are losers."[11]

8. P. A. Reynolds, *British Foreign Policy in the Inter-War Years* (London, 1954), pp. 33, 99–106.

9. On this point, see L. S. Amery, *My Political Life* (London, 1955), III, 247.

10. M. A. Fitzsimons, "The Masque of Uncertainty: Britain and Munich," *The Review of Politics,* XII (October, 1950), 497; W. N. Medlicott, "Neville Chamberlain," *British Prime Ministers: A Portrait Gallery* (New York, 1953), p. 173.

11. Feiling, *Life of Neville Chamberlain,* p. 320. "Mere pacifist clichés, ignorant and untrue," British historian A. L. Rowse calls these words of Chamberlain in his critical essay *Appeasement: A Study in Political Decline, 1933–1939* (New York, 1961), p. 104.

Not that this view set Chamberlain apart from other men. On the contrary, in his fundamental hatred of war Chamberlain was undoubtedly representative of an overwhelming majority of the British people, the very reason which made the view so potent. Like the people of western Europe and the United States, the British had by this time reached a stage of moral and social development at which war was no longer taken as a matter of course, but had come to be regarded as a barbarity incompatible with civilized life. Consequently, the avoidance of war was one of the highest ambitions of statesmanship, and it followed that to placate, yes, to appease, an adversary was a fundamental purpose of diplomacy, because it was a necessary condition of the civilized order which it was the purpose of that diplomacy to preserve and develop.[12]

The so-called "Peace Ballot" of 1935 had emphasized the already obvious fact that Britain stood for peace. Of approximately twelve million people canvassed, a crushing majority cast their ballots for British support of the League of Nations, an "all-around reduction of armaments," an "all-around abolition of military and naval aircraft," and the prohibition of the manufacture and sale of armaments for profit—all by international agreement. In addition, economic and non-military sanctions against an aggressor were overwhelmingly approved, while sanctions involving military measures received a large, though reduced majority. Whether this vote was a considered expression of national determination is open to debate; there can be little doubt of its accuracy as an expression of national desires.[13]

What finer achievement could there be for a minister than to bring about peace among Britain, France, Germany, and Italy, and to allay the suspicion and fear poisoning the life of Europe? But how? Chamberlain had no illusion about the League of Nations; in his view, the "collective security" for which it stood did not exist. The unsuccessful application of sanctions

12. Wheeler-Bennett, *Munich,* p. 3; Arnold Toynbee and Frank Ashton-Gwatkin (eds.), *The World in March 1939* (London, 1952), (vol. 1 of *Survey of International Affairs, 1939–1946*), pp. 34–36. For further discussion of the "logic of appeasement" see Charles L. Mowat, *Britain Between the Wars, 1918–1940* (Chicago, 1955), pp. 589–94.

13. Harold Nicolson, "British Public Opinion and Foreign Policy," *Public Opinion Quarterly,* I (January, 1937), 57–59.

against Italy after her invasion of Abyssinia had proved to Chamberlain that the hope of the League's supporters was "midsummer madness." It had become clear that the mechanism of collective security could not be operated by small states alone, that small states were inevitably reluctant to take any initiative in operations against powerful aggressors, and in fact, that if resort to aggressive war were to be checked, the burden would fall upon an increasingly limited number of great powers. Germany, Italy, Japan, and the United States had to be left out of the calculation, and Russia was a disputed quantity regarded with suspicion by conservative opinion in Britain. As the Conservatives saw it, everything therefore depended upon Britain and France. This meant that the two must march in step or that, if one held back, the other must resign herself to following suit, in view of the impracticality of taking on single-handed a task which might prove a real problem even for their united efforts.[14] Thus Chamberlain told the Commons on December 21, 1937: "In its present condition the League is unable to discharge some of the functions with which it was invested when it was first created." While Britain would continue to give the League "warmest support," she must "frankly . . . face the realities of the situation."[15]

But if Chamberlain discarded collective security, how were discussions looking toward peaceful change and the restoration of confidence to be held? He determined to see whether he could win peace by a direct approach to the dictators, relying upon personal contacts and appeals to their reason and moderation.

From the first Chamberlain was sure that he could influence Hitler and Mussolini. As a businessman in Birmingham—he did not enter Parliament until he was 49—Chamberlain had learned that the best way to settle business disputes was for the disputants to sit down, quietly discuss their problems, and arrive at a solution by compromise and conciliation. Appeasement in the business world, then, meant the removal of the causes of friction between

14. Toynbee and Ashton-Gwatkin, *The World in March 1939,* pp. 40–41; Feiling, *Life of Neville Chamberlain,* pp. 324–25; Halifax, *Fullness of Days,* pp. 232–33.

15. *Parl. Debs., HC,* December 21, 1937, vol. 330, 1810.

employers and employees. Since political appeasement meant to Chamberlain the methodical removal of the principal causes of friction between nations—by negotiation in the light of reason instead of resort to force—why could not the same method be used for dealing with international problems as had proved so successful in settling industrial disputes? To Chamberlain, the policy seemed so reasonable that he could not believe that even Hitler would repudiate it.[16]

Moreover, Chamberlain was unwilling to believe that the ruler of a state so close to the British Isles could have such an utterly different outlook on life from his own as to be determined to have a war for its own sake. Herein lies the other major factor behind his commitment to appeasement. Chamberlain took at face value Hitler's repeated declarations that his territorial aims were limited to securing the application of the principle of self-determination, which, the Führer once reminded Chamberlain, had not been formulated by Germany. Assuming, as he did, that Hitler's ambitions were limited to obtaining for Germany what might appear to be an overdue measure of justice, Chamberlain was unwilling to believe that disputes arising within this limited field could not be solved on the common-sense, give-and-take methods by which two businessmen would iron out some complication in the dealings between their respective firms.[17]

He was all the more bent on personal action because experience had led him to believe that approaches left to the normal channels of diplomacy had a habit of "running into the sand." The old-established machine of the Foreign Office did not seem to him to move quickly enough for the crisis threatening Europe. Classical methods of diplomacy by which Foreign Ministers interviewed ambassadors and dispatches passed between distant capitals seemed inadequate. Had the time not come, Chamberlain asked himself, when the Prime Minister should deal directly with those who controlled foreign policy in other countries?[18]

In order to avoid what seemed to him the tangled web of

16. Templewood, *Nine Troubled Years,* pp. 374, 378; Sir Nevile Henderson, *Water Under the Bridges* (London, 1945), p. 216.
17. Toynbee and Ashton-Gwatkin, *The World in March 1939,* pp. 37–38.
18. Templewood, *Nine Troubled Years,* p. 259.

the Foreign Office, Chamberlain began to employ special emissaries who established contacts outside the official channels of the Foreign Office. His confidants maintained close relations with the German and Italian Ambassadors in London. Their activities were co-ordinated by Sir Horace Wilson, upon whom Chamberlain fully relied for the carrying out of his policy.[19]

Wilson, Chief Industrial Adviser to His Majesty's Government, and later Official Head of His Majesty's Civil Service, was in every respect the orthodox, conscientious, and efficient civil servant. Chamberlain had earlier found his outstanding administrative talents particularly helpful in the Ministry of Health and the Treasury, and finding himself overwhelmed with domestic and foreign problems upon becoming Prime Minister, he called for Wilson's aid. When Wilson was installed in an office adjoining the Cabinet Room where the Prime Minister habitually worked, it was immediately assumed that a rival Foreign Office was being formed at 10 Downing Street. This quite naturally caused resentment in the Foreign Office, and when Chamberlain and Wilson, distrustful of the permanent Foreign Office officials, began to interfere with the details of policy execution, a serious lack of co-ordination in British administration of foreign affairs developed.[20]

The test case of the Abyssinian affair might reasonably have been held as ample evidence that the system for the regulation of international affairs that had grown out of the World War was now out of working order. In the circumstances of real international anarchy, there was a strong case for Chamberlain's decision not to hamper himself by action only through the League, which the aggressor powers had repudiated, but instead to seize any opportunity of persuading Hitler and Mussolini to

19. Felix Gilbert, "Two British Ambassadors: Perth and Henderson," in Gordon A. Craig and Felix Gilbert (eds.), *The Diplomats, 1919–1939* (Princeton, 1953), p. 550. See also Amery, *My Political Life,* III, 230–31; John Connell, *The Office: A Study of British Foreign Policy and Its Makers, 1919–1951* (London, 1958), p. 266.

20. Gilbert, "Two British Ambassadors," p. 550; Templewood, *Nine Troubled Years,* pp. 260–61. Connell writes somewhat caustically that in the last two and one half years of Chamberlain's premiership the Foreign Office was "as powerless as a branch Post Office." *The Office,* p. 282.

sit around a table with him, and of making it clear that, if they would cast aside resort to force and agree to peaceful change by conference methods, he would be prepared to go to the limit of justice, and perhaps even beyond, in his efforts to meet their demands. Would this approach "work"? Under what conditions should it be tried? How far should it be pursued? What should be considered a sufficient test of its validity? And what might follow if it proved unsuccessful? These were the unanswered questions which were later to be significant points of controversy.

Although avoidance of war was one of the highest ambitions of British statesmanship, the use of force, at least for purposes of self-defense, was still regarded as legitimate in all but strictly pacifist circles. Consequently a successful foreign policy had to oscillate between two apparently opposite poles. In this situation, statesman and ordinary citizen alike were left with the harrowing moral and political question of what limits they should set to the price they would be prepared to pay for peace—on the assumption that peace could always be purchased at one price or another. Should nations—even those which were members of the League—abide by the precept that whatever might be the moral law for individuals, a sovereign state was not its brother's keeper? Or should they, for the sake of exemption from the evil of war, be prepared to sacrifice interests, and even territories of their own, only drawing a line at throwing their neighbors to the wolves?

At the beginning of 1938 the British people were confused about these matters. In one camp, represented chiefly though certainly not exclusively by the Labor Party, there was a multitude who had not decided in their own minds whether they were first and foremost champions of the League of Nations and collective security or first and foremost pacifists. In the other camp, comprised mainly of Conservatives, the majority believed that appeasement and security were perfectly compatible, although there had sifted out a strong-minded minority which supported collective security with single-minded devotion.

Mainly inspired by Arthur Henderson, a former Foreign Secretary, the Labor Party officially adopted after 1931 the policy of collective security, that is, a League of Nations strong enough to deter any potential aggressor. Support for the policy necessarily entailed a British contribution toward the armed forces of the League, a rather sticky reality for the Laborites. The majority of the party approved such a contribution, but the remainder, headed by George Lansbury, the party leader, maintained a thoroughly pacifist attitude. Consequently, in debates on defense and on the Service Estimates, the Labor Party held that while willing that Britain contribute to collective security, it was opposed to purely national armaments. The rise of Hitler and the aggression of Mussolini in Abyssinia caused growing apprehension in the party, especially among the trade unions which had witnessed the destruction of social democracy in Germany, and, as a result, the party split on the issue of support for sanctions against Italy. Lansbury resigned as leader and was replaced by Clement Attlee.[21] While a number of Laborites were still undecided whether to cast out their pacifism in order to pursue a crusade for collective security or to renounce their allegiance to collective security to keep their pacifism inviolate, the resignation of Lansbury and the assumption of leadership by Attlee presaged increasing support for collective security. Attlee made this clear in the Commons on October 22, 1935, when he stated:

> When in office we supported and endeavoured to enhance the League of Nation's authority, and in Opposition we have unremittingly urged the government to make support of the League the whole basis of its policy. . . . We believe that in a state of the world so closely linked together as is the world of today, you must have some authority other than the will of individual powers.[22]

When, in early summer of 1936, the Baldwin Government announced its intention to advocate the termination of sanctions against Italy at the coming Assembly of the League, the Labor Party proposed a vote of censure. Attlee told the House that

21. Clement Attlee, *As It Happened* (New York, 1954), pp. 138–39. See also Lord Citrine, *Men and Work: An Autobiography* (London, 1964), pp. 349–51.

22. *Parl. Debs., HC,* October 22, 1935, vol. 305, 35.

the Government had "destroyed the League of Nations as an effective instrument for peace." Thereafter, Labor repeatedly made the charge, holding that the steady deterioration of the international situation was the result of the Government's "inept foreign policy." That view was unaffected by Chamberlain's replacement of Baldwin. At its annual conference in the autumn of 1937, the Labor Party adopted a comprehensive document calling for a government strongly equipped to defend the country and to play its full part in collective security.[23] Thus collective security was basic to the program of the party in the late 1930's—although many persons outside the party seriously questioned its understanding of what the term really meant and doubted its willingness to accept the realities that a bona fide policy of collective security might entail.

The policy of the Liberal Party, led by Sir Archibald Sinclair, was essentially the same as that of Labor. Ever since the Versailles Treaty, Liberals had advocated the maintenance of peace by collective security, general disarmament to lower levels but the retention of defense forces sufficient for "the needs of the times," and the use by the League of Nations of sanctions, economic or military, against any state which should defy its authority and engage in aggression.[24] Since that policy was so similar to Labor's, cooperation between the two parties in opposition to Chamberlain's new departure was easily effected.

Among the keenest critics of Chamberlain's policy was a group of dissident Conservatives, a small band of clear-sighted men stronger in quality than numbers, who temporarily broke with their party because they were greatly alarmed by Hitler's growing power in Germany. They believed that concessions to dictators only whetted their appetites and encouraged them to make ever larger demands. Consequently they held that Britain, in close cooperation with France, must stand firm in the face of the increasing truculence of the dictators: she must be prepared to

23. Attlee, *As It Happened,* pp. 142–45. A fuller account of Labor's position on foreign policy matters during this period, utilizing materials from Labor party conference reports, may be found in Elaine Windrich, *British Labour's Foreign Policy* (Stanford, 1952), pp. 98–137.

24. Viscount Samuel, *Memoirs* (London, 1945), p. 269.

resist aggression by force of arms and she must resist it by coming to the help of other victims without waiting until she herself was directly attacked. Since the Labor Opposition, though it protested appeasement in as loud a voice as the dissident Conservatives, was actually less willing than Chamberlain to rearm and face the grim possibility that national arms might have to be used, these Conservative opponents of Chamberlain were his most telling critics and his most worthy adversaries.

At the time of the general election in November, 1935, the foreign policy of the National Government was analagous to that of the Labor-Liberal Opposition: support for the League but no isolated action; forces adequate to meet British obligations; the closing of gaps in British armaments; the general limitation of all armaments; in the air, no inferiority to any power within striking distance. With particular reference to the League, a manifesto issued by the Baldwin Government declared: "The League of Nations will remain, as heretofore, the keystone of British foreign policy. . . . Our attitude . . . is dictated by the conviction that collective security by collective action can alone save us from a return to the old system which resulted in the Great War."[25] Thus it is not surprising that when Chamberlain denied the effectiveness of the League to maintain peace and announced his intention to pursue a policy of personal approaches to the dictators, he was at once subjected to acrid denunciations by the Labor-Liberal group for having gone back on the election pledge of the National Government.

From the beginning of Chamberlain's pursuit of appeasement he was thus faced with criticism from the Labor and Liberal Parties and from that minority of his own party which had made up its mind to sacrifice appeasement and to stand by collective security and the policy of the League of Nations as the best way to maintain peace in Europe. At first the debate was largely academic and turned as much on partisan politics as anything else, for whether Chamberlain's policy would ultimately bring sweet success or bitter disappointment and defeat none could say with certainty. There were indeed arguments

25. G. M. Young, *Stanley Baldwin* (London, 1952), p. 213; Samuel, *Memoirs*, p. 269 n.

which could be used to support both views, yet all either side could do was to "assess the probabilities." Furthermore, the terms "appeasement" and "collective security" were frequently used without any precise, much less agreed upon, definition of what they entailed—with the result that the opposing sides sometimes debated from wholly different frames of reference. As time passed and specific attempts to "apply" appeasement were made, the definitions, at least by implication, became clearer, the issues more pointed, the differences more vital, and the controversy more heated.

The internal political situation in Britain in the late 1930's was propitious for a strong-willed man like Chamberlain to pursue a personal foreign policy. Since 1931, the government had been in the hands of a coalition, the "National Government," which had in time grown essentially conservative. When Prime Minister Stanley Baldwin, a Conservative, forced a general election in November, 1935, the National Government was returned to office with a majority of approximately 250 seats, a majority so large as to be invincible unless, for some totally unexpected reason, there should be a profound shift of opinion among the Conservative members on the back benches. Neville Chamberlain inherited this majority when he succeeded Baldwin in May, 1937.[26]

The British tradition of rigid party discipline was beneficial to Chamberlain. The same might be said for the powerful role played by party leaders, especially in the Conservative Party, where it was generally accepted that the leader would exercise actual control, including exclusive responsibility for the formulation of party policy until, for one reason or another, he chose to resign or lost the confidence of his followers.[27]

But the explanation of Chamberlain's strength lies still deeper. In the late 1920's there had been serious divisions of opinion

26. See Appendix II for data on the parties represented in the House of Commons as of January 1, 1937, and the relative strength of each.

27. For a discussion of the Conservative leader's powers, see R. T. McKenzie, *British Political Parties: The Distribution of Power Within the Conservative and Labour Parties* (New York, 1955), pp. 62–68.

within the Conservative Party. At a most critical juncture (mid-1930), when "the party chairmanship might damn, or divert, the party fortunes," Chamberlain was asked to take the post. Convinced that he could "render a service which is possible to no one else" (though aware that it "might ultimately break me"), Chamberlain accepted.[28] For some months thereafter he devoted his businessman's talents to a major reorganization of the party machinery, consolidating and strengthening it, with the upshot that when he returned to Parliament in 1931, he had behind him a party organization sensitive to his touch. This was not necessarily a result of specific design, but was almost inevitable during this transitional moment in the history of the party. Nor did the matter rest there. Chamberlain's successes as Chancellor of the Exchequer, a post he assumed in late 1931, gave him considerable influence with contributors to the Conservative campaign funds, so that his personal influence in the party increased. As Baldwin began to tire of the turmoil of party activity Chamberlain took on more and more of the burdens, stimulating the work of research and publicity in the party's Central Office and arranging meetings of Conservative Ministers to underscore the independent identity of the party within the National Government.[29] By the election of 1935, many of the party's candidates were men personally familiar with and temperamentally sympathetic to Chamberlain. This does not mean that Conservatives outside the party organization were wholly devoted to Chamberlain—in fact, it is quite clear that many were not—but for a time at least, it was his Parliamentary support which was of greatest importance.

Ironically, four months after Chamberlain became Prime Minister the Western powers made one of their few resolute stands against totalitarian lawlessness, in the context of the Spanish Civil War. At the Nyon Conference, held in late summer, 1937,

28. See Feiling, *Life of Neville Chamberlain,* pp. 178–79.

29. See McKenzie, *British Political Parties,* pp. 44, 271–72; Marion L. Kenney, "The Role of the House of Commons in British Foreign Policy During the 1937–38 Session," in Norton Downs (ed.), *Essays in Honor of Conyers Read* (Chicago, 1953), p. 145.

in response to a mysterious outbreak of submarine piracy against British, French, and Russian shipping in the western Mediterranean (Italian submarines were suspected), the three injured powers agreed that submarines attacking any non-Spanish merchant vessel would be counter-attacked and destroyed by ships from the British and French fleets. Although Italy, as well as Germany, had declined to attend the conference because of the Soviet imputation that Italy was responsible for certain of the acts of piracy, the Italian Government was afterward persuaded to adhere and no further acts of piracy were reported.[30]

The Nyon Conference was largely a personal triumph for the British Foreign Secretary, Anthony Eden, who had long denounced Italian duplicity and disregard for international law. Italy's undoubted resentment at the British action did not provide a favorable background for the improvement of the Anglo-Italian atmosphere for which Chamberlain was determined to work. But the Prime Minister went ahead with his plan. Unheedful of the cautious views of Eden, who saw the dangers of placing trust in German and Italian pledges, unmoved by the Cassandra-like warnings of Winston Churchill, Chamberlain chose this moment, as he later told the House of Commons, to begin a general exploration for the basis "on which we might build up a general scheme of appeasement."[31]

The Halifax visit to Germany having achieved no significant result, Chamberlain momentarily abandoned his approach to the Reich and set out to win Italian friendship and good will. His methods brought him into conflict with his own Foreign Secretary, and the disagreement which ensued opened to national consideration the whole question of the validity of appeasement.

30. Winston S. Churchill, *The Gathering Storm* (Boston, 1948), pp. 245–46; Templewood, *Nine Troubled Years,* p. 256.

31. *Parl. Debs., HC,* February 21, 1938, vol. 332, 54.

CHAPTER TWO

Eden's Resignation

THE BRITISH FOREIGN SECRETARY conducts his affairs under the continuous scrutiny of the principal members of the Cabinet. This supervision is especially maintained by the Prime Minister, who is responsible for controlling, personally or through his Cabinet, the main course of foreign policy. Unless supported constantly by his chief, no Foreign Secretary can work effectively. An agreement between them on fundamentals, as well as a harmony of outlook and even to some extent of temperament, is essential if things are to go smoothly. If the Prime Minister devotes special attention to foreign affairs, this is all the more important.

Anthony Eden had served as Foreign Secretary under Stanley Baldwin, who took little active share in foreign policy. Neville Chamberlain, on the other hand, had strong views about foreign affairs, and from the moment he succeeded Baldwin, determined to assume a dominant position in the formulation of foreign policy.[1] Chamberlain's assumption of office, therefore, implied a delicate but perceptible change in the position of the Foreign Secretary.

Yet beyond the fact that the Foreign Secretary now had to accustom himself to the supervision of his leader (two of whose intimate advisers were Eden's immediate predecessors at the Foreign Office), differences in temperament and outlook—indeed in political philosophies—suggested that Chamberlain and Eden might not work together easily. Eden tended to apply moral

1. See Kenney, "The Role of the House of Commons in British Foreign Policy During the 1937–1938 Session," pp. 138–42.

values to political problems and was moved by a sense of idealism. Chamberlain considered himself more "practical," and in his dedication to the one great cause of peace was disinclined to allow ethical considerations to stand in his way. This was perhaps obvious from Chamberlain's first public incursion into foreign affairs in June, 1936, when, as Chancellor of the Exchequer, he told a meeting of the 1900 Club that the retention of sanctions against Italy was "the very midsummer of madness." Just days previously Eden had assured the Commons that there was no change contemplated in the Government's position on sanctions. Chamberlain's diary later revealed his thinking:

> I did it deliberately because I felt that the party and the country needed a lead, and an indication that the Government was not wavering and drifting without a policy. . . . I did not consult Anthony Eden, because he would have been bound to beg me not to say what I proposed. . . . He himself has been as nice as possible about it, though it is of course true that to some extent he has had to suffer in the public interest.[2]

During the latter half of 1937 divergence, both in method and in aim, grew between the Prime Minister and his Foreign Secretary. Chamberlain, imbued with a sense of a special and personal mission to come to friendly terms with the dictators of Italy and Germany, believed that conciliation and the avoidance of anything likely to offend them was the best method to achieve this end. Eden, quite to the contrary, had won his reputation at Geneva. A devoted adherent of the French Entente, he had insisted for some time on staff conversations. He favored closer relations with Russia. He feared the Nazi peril and was alarmed by the weakness of British armaments and the resulting impact on foreign affairs. More specifically, at the end of 1937 Chamberlain wished to recognize the Italian conquest of Abyssinia as part of a settlement of differences with Italy. At the same time he was disinclined to consider any great increase of British armaments or the necessity of close collaboration with France. Eden, on the other hand, seemed convinced—though Chamber-

2. Feiling, *Life of Neville Chamberlain,* p. 296.

lain's diary attributes to him, before mid-January, 1938, a "softer" attitude toward the *de jure* recognition of Italy's Abyssinian conquest than is noted elsewhere[3]—that any agreement with Italy must be part of a general Mediterranean settlement which must include Spain and be reached in close understanding with the French. Chamberlain consequently believed that the Foreign Office was obstructing his attempts to open discussions with Italy, as well as with Germany, while Eden felt that his chief was displaying immoderate haste in approaching the dictators, especially while British armaments were weak.[4]

While the question of conversations with Italy lay smouldering, the budding Chamberlain-Eden controversy was heightened by a new and separate issue: Chamberlain's now well-known rebuff of a proposal made by President Roosevelt. The Foreign Office received a telegram from Washington on January 12, 1938, in which Roosevelt, troubled by the deterioration of the international situation, proposed a conference in Washington of representatives of certain governments to consider the underlying causes of tension, with the hope of agreement on essential principles to be observed in the conduct of international relations. Without consulting Eden (who was vacationing in southern France) or other Cabinet colleagues, and against the advice of Sir Alexander Cadogan, the Permanent Under-Secretary, and Sir Ronald Lindsey, the British Ambassador in Washington, Chamberlain replied within twenty-four hours that the British Government hoped to secure agreements with Italy and Germany; for that reason Roosevelt should consider "whether there is not a risk of this proposal cutting across our efforts here."[5]

3. Iain Macleod, *Neville Chamberlain* (London, 1961), pp. 211–12. For Eden's own account, see *Facing the Dictators, 1923–1938,* pp. 646 ff.

4. Templewood, *Nine Troubled Years,* pp. 256–61; Churchill, *The Gathering Storm,* pp. 240–43. Churchill records an interview between Chamberlain and Eden in mid-November, 1937, in which the Foreign Secretary tried to convey his misgivings about the slowness of British rearmament. Chamberlain, after a while, refused to listen to him and advised him to "go home and take an aspirin." *Ibid.,* p. 250.

5. Message from the Prime Minister to the President, Jan. 14, 1938. *Foreign Relations of the United States: Diplomatic Papers, 1938* (hereinafter cited as *U.S. For. Rel., 1938*), I, 118–20. For Chamberlain's explanation of his views, as well as his independent action, see Macleod, *Neville Chamberlain,* p. 212.

Eden hurried back to England on the evening of January 15, urged to return by dismayed officials at the Foreign Office. He was "outraged" (his own word) at the way this opportunity had been handled and immediately telegraphed Washington attempting to minimize the effects of Chamberlain's chilling reply. Then, in a series of none-too-harmonious meetings of the Foreign Affairs Committee of the Cabinet,[6] Eden gained a considerable modification in Chamberlain's attitude. A cordial explanatory message was sent to Washington on January 20, in effect approving the President's initiative should he decide to go ahead with it. But Roosevelt never repeated his proposal.[7]

This incident widened the growing differences between Chamberlain and Eden. "For the first time," Eden records in his memoirs, "our relations were seriously at odds." Chamberlain believed the President's proposal vague and certain to fail. He

6. This committee was composed of "nine or ten of the principal Ministers" which Chamberlain summoned for advice on urgent international problems. It was in close touch with the Chiefs of Staff whose reports were always carefully considered. While the meetings of this group tended to short circuit the full Cabinet, the latter had the last word upon the more important questions. See Templewood, *Nine Troubled Years,* pp. 290–91.

7. This incident is described in many sources. The fullest treatment appears in Eden, *Facing the Dictators,* pp. 621–645. See also Macleod, *Neville Chamberlain,* pp. 212–13 (for Chamberlain's own account); Duff Cooper, *Old Men Forget: The Autobiography of Duff Cooper* (London, 1953), pp. 210–11; Churchill, *The Gathering Storm,* pp. 252–53; Templewood, *Nine Troubled Years,* pp. 271–72. Other accounts appear in Randolph S. Churchill, *The Rise and Fall of Sir Anthony Eden* (New York, 1959), p. 148; Lewis Broad, *Anthony Eden: The Chronicle of a Career* (New York, 1955), pp. 101–08; Alan Campbell-Johnson, *Sir Anthony Eden* (London, 1955), pp. 146–49; William L. Langer and S. Everett Gleason, *The Challenge to Isolation 1937–1940* (New York, 1952), pp. 27–28; Connell, *The Office,* pp. 259–64; Birkenhead, *Halifax,* pp. 376–77.

British opinion is, and probably will remain, divided upon the question of the significance of Chamberlain's rejection of Roosevelt's proposal. In Winston Churchill's view, it marked "the loss of the last frail chance to save the world from tyranny otherwise than by war." Writing in 1948, he found Chamberlain's "lack of all sense of proportion and even of self-preservation . . . appalling." *The Gathering Storm,* pp. 254–55. On the other hand, Viscount Templewood (Sir Samuel Hoare) and Lord Halifax minimize the significance of the event. Templewood explains that the British Government was deeply suspicious of American readiness to follow up inspiring words with practical action, and felt that, whatever Roosevelt's wishes might be, Congress would never approve any resolute intervention in European affairs. As for Chamberlain's independent action, Templewood feared that the dictators would pay no heed or else use this "line up of the democracies" as a pretext for a break. Eden preferred to risk that result rather than the loss of American good will; even if the proposal did fail, Britain would gain immeasurably from this first American intervention in Europe.[8] Beyond this difference of opinion, it was the Prime Minister's method of handling the affair, of course, which was so ominous for the relationship between the two men.

In early February, 1938, Chamberlain received through his sister-in-law[9] a message from Mussolini in which the Duce expressed a desire for an early Anglo-Italian agreement covering all points in dispute between the two countries. Chamberlain took up the idea with renewed vigor.[10] Evidence of his determination is found in a February 17 diary entry which, though full of false assumptions, reveals his sense of personal responsibility for averting European catastrophe:

> To intimate now that this was not the moment for conversations would be to convince Mussolini that he must consider

argues that it would have been very difficult to arrange a meeting of the Foreign Policy Committee during the recess. *Nine Troubled Years,* pp. 263–71. Halifax terms it "legend" to assert that Chamberlain's reply amounted to "a rebuff which had grave consequences for the world." In his view it is impossible to maintain the argument that Roosevelt's proposal, if differently handled, might have had the effect of preventing the war. *Fullness of Days,* pp. 196–97. L. S. Amery, later one of the group of dissident Conservatives in Parliament, also questions Churchill's view. *My Political Life,* III, 232. But A. L. Rowse calls Roosevelt's proposal "a life-buoy thrown to a drowning man." *Appeasement,* p. 67.

8. Eden, *Facing the Dictators,* pp. 628–29; Feiling, *Life of Neville Chamberlain,* p. 336. In defending Chamberlain's action, both Halifax and Templewood deny that Roosevelt felt resentment at the reception accorded his proposal. *Fullness of Days,* pp. 196–97; *Nine Troubled Years,* p. 274. But no resentment was a poor outcome of an offer which might have brought the United States into a position of some responsibility in the affairs of Europe.

9. Lady Chamberlain, widow of Sir Austen, who spent much time in Italy and was a personal friend of Mussolini. For an explanation of this contact, see Macleod, *Neville Chamberlain,* p. 213. See also Eden, *Facing the Dictators,* pp. 635, 637, 650, 658.

10. According to the United States Chargé in London, Chamberlain had the support of the armed service departments. They believed it essential to detach at least one member of the German, Italian, Japanese anti-Comintern combination. Johnson to the Secretary of State, London, Feb. 15, 1938. *U.S. For. Rel., 1938,* I, 137.

talks with us off, and act accordingly. . . . Italian public opinion would be raised to a white heat against us. There might indeed be some overt act of hostility, and in any case the dictatorships would be driven closer together, the last shred of Austrian independence would be lost, the Balkan countries would feel compelled to turn towards their powerful neighbours, Czechoslovakia would be swallowed, France would either have to submit to German domination or fight, in which case we should almost certainly be drawn in. I could not face the responsibility for allowing such a series of catastrophes.[11]

Conversations with Great Britain had become an urgent matter for Italy. The German blow of February 15 to Austrian independence (Hitler's demand that three Nazi sympathizers be named at once to the Austrian Cabinet) had been delivered in a manner which surprised even the Italian Government. Consequently, Count Ciano, the Italian Foreign Minister, wrote a letter to Ambassador Grandi in London instructing him to attempt to reach quickly a full and final agreement with Great Britain. In Ciano's view, transactions could take place "today" in the normal give-and-take of diplomacy:

but tomorrow, should the Anschluss be an accomplished fact, should Greater Germany by then press on our frontiers with the weight of its whole seventy million, then it would become increasingly difficult for us to reach an agreement or even talk with the English, since it would be impossible to prevent the entire world interpreting our policy of rapprochement with London as a journey to Canossa under German pressure.[12]

Grandi had met with Eden several times during the early part of February in order to discuss Anglo-Italian problems, but by mid-month the normal channels of diplomacy were neither sufficiently swift nor effective for Mussolini or Chamberlain. It was

11. Feiling, *Life of Neville Chamberlain,* pp. 337–38.

12. Letter to the Italian Ambassador to London, Count Dino Grandi, Rome, Feb. 16, 1938. *Ciano's Diplomatic Papers,* edited by Malcolm Muggeridge, (London, 1948), pp. 161–62.

then that Grandi sought and obtained, against the wishes of Eden, an interview with Chamberlain himself. This meeting took place, with Eden present, at Downing Street on February 18. Exactly how it was arranged is uncertain, but it appears that Grandi first declined an invitation from Eden to come to the Foreign Office on February 17—presumably to discuss events in Austria—fearful lest such a visit be exploited as having occurred on Italian initiative; then he assented to the meeting the next morning when informed by a confidential agent[13] that it would be inopportune to avoid the conversation inasmuch as Chamberlain would probably take part.[14]

Grandi's account of his interview with Chamberlain and Eden —the only detailed report available except for that in Eden's recently-published *Facing the Dictators,* which does little to alter the substance of Grandi's account—presents a startling picture of a Prime Minister using a foreign diplomat to confute and discomfit his own Foreign Secretary.[15] Allowing for the author's desire to enhance the dramatic nature of the conflict between the two British officials and to magnify the importance of his own influence, it is yet a revealing diplomatic document. Eden insisted upon discussing Austria, which Grandi declined to do on the grounds that it had no connection with the projected Anglo-Italian conversations, while Chamberlain assured the Italian Ambassador that he understood his refusal. When Eden moved to refute Grandi's charge that the course of events in Austria was the direct consequence of Anglo-French policy during the past

13. The background of this unconventional approach, according to Templewood, was a long-standing contact between an unnamed official in the Conservative Party Office and a subordinate member of the Italian Embassy. Chamberlain used this method of contacting Grandi because of the apparent deadlock between the Foreign Office and the Italian Embassy. *Nine Troubled Years,* p. 278. The agent is identified elsewhere as Sir Joseph Ball. See Amery, *My Political Life,* III, 230–31; Macleod, *Neville Chamberlain,* pp. 218–19.

14. See Report of the Ambassador to London, Grandi, to the Minister of Foreign Affairs, Ciano, Italian Embassy, London, Feb. 19, 1938. *Ciano's Diplomatic Papers,* pp. 165–67; Templewood, *Nine Troubled Years,* pp. 277–78; Macleod, *Neville Chamberlain,* p. 214; Eden, *Facing the Dictators,* p. 656.

15. Grandi to Ciano, London, Feb. 19, 1938. *Ciano's Diplomatic Papers,* pp. 165–83.

three years, Chamberlain intervened by stating that this was not the moment to begin a discussion of responsibility. The Foreign Secretary's insistence on a full discussion of the Spanish situation was cut off by Chamberlain's avowals that it was useless to continue with "polemics of this sort." On the question of a site for Anglo-Italian conversations, Grandi insisted on Rome and won Chamberlain's quick approval with his intimation that the conduct of the negotiations there might well influence their result. Throughout the interview Chamberlain gave evidence of "irritation and disappointment" with Eden, and more than once interrupted the Foreign Secretary's remarks "with an air of being thoroughly annoyed."

The apparent antagonism between Chamberlain and Eden was graphically summarized by Grandi in his report to Ciano:

> Chamberlain and Eden were not a Prime Minister and a Foreign Secretary discussing with the Ambassador of a Foreign Power a delicate situation of an international character. They were—and revealed themselves as such to me in defiance of all established convention—two enemies confronting each other, like two cocks in true fighting posture.[16]

Grandi reported that the questions addressed to him by Chamberlain were intentionally asked with the aim of producing replies which would contradict and overthrow the arguments on which Eden based his "miserable anti-Italian and anti-Fascist policy." He reasoned that Chamberlain expected detailed answers which would be used as ammunition against Eden.[17]

That Grandi's account "loses nothing in the telling" is acknowledged by Eden himself,[18] but this does not alter the essential fact that the tension between Chamberlain and Eden was great,

16. *Ibid.*, p. 182.

17. Grandi's story that Chamberlain later sent his confidential agent to meet him (in a public taxi) to express appreciation for his statements appears to be untrue. See Templewood, *Nine Troubled Years,* pp. 278–79; Amery, *My Political Life,* III, 231 fn. Macleod gives a cogent explanation of the taxi idea. *Neville Chamberlain,* pp. 219–20.

18. Eden, *Facing the Dictators,* p. 663. Templewood considers the report greatly exaggerated (*Nine Troubled Years,* pp. 278–79) and Chamberlain's biographer Macleod terms it a "highly colored fiction" spun from "the bare threads of truth" (*Neville Chamberlain,* p. 220).

so great that, after Grandi's departure, the Prime Minister became quite vehement and—according to his own account—simply "could not refrain from reproaches." "I told A. E. [Eden]," Chamberlain later wrote in his diary, "that he had missed one opportunity after another of advancing towards peace; he had one more chance, probably the last, and he was wanting to throw it away."[19]

Doubtless alarming to Eden was Grandi's assertion (again according to Grandi's account) that:

> Up to the present moment the attitude of Great Britain has been deliberately hostile to Italy. The entire Italian people is aware of this and convinced that it is true; moreover, Britain's actions and initiative go to confirm it daily. Events in Austria have undoubtedly introduced an increased tempo into the European drama. No country can wait longer. Italy . . . can wait no more and demands to know immediately, and once for all, in deeds and not in words, if England intends to remain an enemy country or if it has decided to conclude a chapter in Anglo-Italian relations which has lasted for three years, and to come to an overall, conclusive agreement—an agreement without any obscurities or cause for future friction or differences with Fascist Italy. . . . I require that there should be a conclusion and that rapidly; since, should new delays again be caused, Italy would have no alternative and the Duce would definitely have to direct Italian policy in a spirit of frank, open, unshakable hostility towards the Western Powers.[20]

But Chamberlain's mind was set, and he declared that at the Cabinet meeting next day he would request permission to announce that the Anglo-Italian conversations had officially begun. In an effort to win unanimous Cabinet support he proposed

19. Macleod, *Neville Chamberlain,* p. 215. Or as Eden records it in his memoirs: "Anthony, you have missed chance after chance. You simply cannot go on like this." *Facing the Dictators,* p. 662.

20. Grandi to Ciano, London, Feb. 19, 1938. *Ciano's Diplomatic Papers,* pp. 171–72. Eden's memoirs relate that when Chamberlain asked Grandi to speak of Anglo-Italian relations, the Italian "did his stuff admirably." *Facing the Dictators,* p. 661.

to elicit, through Grandi, Mussolini's support for the British formula put forward in the Non-Intervention Committee concerning belligerency and volunteers in Spain.[21]

The Cabinet convened in special session on February 19. Eden's memoirs reveal in detail what transpired there.[22] In the course of a long discussion on the proposed Anglo-Italian conversations, it became evident that a majority of the Cabinet, particularly the older members, agreed with the Prime Minister (Chamberlain's diary notes that "14 supported me without qualification . . . 4 with some qualification or reserve"). According to Eden, few seemed to know what benefits the immediate opening of conversations could bring, and some imagined that any positive step, however fruitless, was worthwhile—reminding the Foreign Secretary of Lord Melbourne's remark that when a colleague said "we must do something," he always knew that he wanted "to do something damned silly." When, at length, Chamberlain summed up the discussion and firmly announced that he proposed to go ahead, Eden revealed his intention to resign. A few moments of shocked silence apparently followed; several ministers expressed concern and dismay; then Chamberlain let the Cabinet see that the alternative to Eden's resignation might be his own, later recording in his diary: "I thought it necessary to say clearly that I could not accept any decision in the opposite sense." Adjournment followed.[23]

The remainder of that afternoon was spent in efforts—perhaps sincere, perhaps not[24]—to induce the Foreign Secretary to change

21. The British formula of July 14, 1937, proposed recognition that both sides in Spain were juridically in a position which allowed them to exercise the rights of belligerents at sea, and withdrawal of volunteers.

22. *Facing the Dictators,* pp. 667 ff.

23. *Ibid.;* Feiling, *Life of Neville Chamberlain,* p. 338; Macleod, *Neville Chamberlain,* p. 216.

24. Much remains uncertain concerning Chamberlain's attitude. He appeared to his Cabinet at the time, and to his biographer Feiling later, as trying to go as far as his principles permitted to retain Eden. But serious doubt is cast upon his sincerity by Grandi's report to Rome on February 19. This led Duff Cooper to conclude in his memoirs that Chamberlain was "deliberately playing a part" and "had in reality determined to get rid of [Eden]." *Old Men Forget,* pp. 214–15. Some recent writers, including Connell (*The Office,* p. 270) and Campbell-Johnson (*Anthony Eden,* p. 156), have accepted this conclusion, the latter declaring that "from what

his mind. By the time the Cabinet met on the following day, all efforts had failed. It had become clear that the difference between Chamberlain and Eden was not confined to the means of handling the immediate issue; there were deeper differences of outlook which made it difficult for them to work together. The break had come with shocking suddenness, probably because during the preceding months Eden had not made his doubts and resentments explicit and Chamberlain had ignored his Foreign Secretary's mute discomfort and accepted unquestioningly his polite reassurances. Chamberlain reported that he had received private assurances from Grandi (significantly, no word had come through the Foreign Office) that the British formula in regard to Spain had been accepted by Mussolini. But that was of no consequence in respect to Eden's action.

After that Cabinet meeting Duff Cooper, First Lord of the Admiralty, wrote in his diary:

> My own belief is that [Eden] means to go because he doesn't want to make terms with Italy, and he feels that he will never be allowed to pursue his own policy with the P.M. at his shoulder. If he goes it will certainly be a body-blow for the National Government. There were crowds in Downing Street last night and tonight, and when he drove off there were loud cheers. This I am afraid will stiffen his attitude, because he will feel that he has popular opinion behind him, which indeed he has.[25]

---

we now know Eden's decision to resign can only have forestalled by a matter of hours Chamberlain's obvious resolve to remove him." Yet, as Randolph Churchill aptly points out (*The Rise and Fall of Sir Anthony Eden,* p. 145), Eden's blameless reputation and popularity made him an undoubted "disinfectant." For this reason his continued presence in the Cabinet could have been of some value to Chamberlain. Eden himself records that "the pressure to reach some accommodation was very strong." Yet he admits he had not been reassured by Chamberlain's February 7 denial that there was a plan to "kick him upstairs" if he did not follow the wishes of the Prime Minister and his small group of advisers in foreign affairs. Perhaps the nearest thing to the truth is revealed in the clumsy attempt by Sir John Simon, one of Chamberlain's closest associates, to persuade Eden to leave immediately for a six months' holiday in order to restore his health. *Facing the Dictators,* pp. 654, 664–65, 674. In that way, Eden need not resign, but he would be out of Chamberlain's way.

25. Duff Cooper, *Old Men Forget,* p. 213. Eden's memoirs note the

Late Sunday evening, February 20, the Cabinet met once more. A letter from Eden told of his inability to accept any of the compromises suggested in a meeting with a smaller group of ministers and his determination to resign. With Eden went his Under-Secretary of State, Lord Cranborne, who agreed with the Foreign Secretary both on the immediate issue and in general outlook.[26]

"I have won through," Chamberlain wrote a friend, "but it has only been with blood and tears."[27]

Eden's resignation touched off an acrid and lengthy debate in the House of Commons. In his statement there before a full House, Eden agreed that Britain must be ready to negotiate with all countries in order to promote international understanding, but she must be very careful that she was in fact strengthening, not undermining, the foundations upon which international confidence rests. The attitude of the Italian Government toward international problems in general, and Britain in particular, was not yet in his opinion such as to justify the opening of official conversations. Italian propaganda against Britain—and against Eden personally for his part in imposing sanctions on Italy several years earlier—was still rife, and little progress had been made toward solving the Spanish problem. Furthermore, it was never right to depart from the traditional method of diplomacy because one party to the negotiations intimated that it was "now or never." Rather, "in the light of the present interna-

---

friendly crowds in Downing Street during this series of critical meetings. *Facing the Dictators,* pp. 667, 673, 680.

26. Eden, *Facing the Dictators,* pp. 672 ff.; Templewood, *Nine Troubled Years,* pp. 279–80; Duff Cooper, *Old Men Forget,* pp. 212–13; Halifax, *Fullness of Days,* p. 197; Feiling, *Life of Neville Chamberlain,* p. 338; Macleod, *Neville Chamberlain,* p. 216; Birkenhead, *Halifax,* pp. 376–80. For secondary accounts of Eden's resignation also see Broad, *Anthony Eden,* pp. 114–16; Campbell-Johnson, *Anthony Eden,* pp. 145, 148–51; Connell, *The Office,* pp. 268–70.

Rumor in London on February 20 had half a dozen other Cabinet members ready to follow Eden, but rumor was ahead of fact.

27. Feiling, *Life of Neville Chamberlain,* p. 338.

tional situation . . . this is a moment for this country to stand firm." His immediate difference with the Prime Minister, Eden explained, was not an isolated issue; on the contrary, the difference had been "fundamental" a few weeks before upon an important decision of foreign policy which did not concern Italy at all.[28] Had he not resigned, he would have had to tell the Commons that he believed the Prime Minister's policy would succeed. That he could not do.

Viscount Cranborne's language was less reserved, particularly on one point. Whereas Eden had interpreted Italy's attitude to be "now or never," Cranborne saw Britain's entrance into official conversations with Italy at that moment as "surrender to blackmail."

This interpretation Chamberlain indignantly denied. While he found Eden's resignation "especially painful," he was convinced that a rebuff to the Italian desire for the immediate initiation of conversations would confirm their suspicion that Great Britain did not want conversations at all, but was rather engaged in a "Machiavellian design" to lull the Italians into inactivity while Britain completed her rearmament. Chamberlain was, in short, "never . . . more completely convinced of the rightness of any course that I have had to take than I am today. . . ."

That was too much for Clement Attlee, who rose to denounce Chamberlain's "nonsense" and his "abject surrender to the dictators." Eden and Cranborne had stood for definite principles in international relations, but Chamberlain's "extremely amateur methods" rejected all principle and betrayed the cause of peace and security. Sir Archibald Sinclair thundered along the same line, showing special concern that in every crisis in recent years Great Britain had retreated before the bluff and threats of the dictators, and none of these retreats had brought peace.

Criticism of Chamberlain's position was not restricted to the Opposition leaders. Laborite F. J. Bellenger considered the Prime Minister's policy a gamble which would probably lose Britain more friends than it would gain. His fellow party member, R. T. Fletcher, thought it "time to cease running after dictators" and

28. This referred to Roosevelt's proposal of January 12, 1938.

time to make friends with those who held similar views on peace and international decency. It was time to recreate the policy of collective security which would provide far more security than any negotiation with a dictator. Harold Nicolson, National Labor member, considered Chamberlain's whole proposal "a splendid bit of give-and-take. We give and they take." And from the Liberal bench Geoffrey Mander termed it a "terribly humiliating situation—the most popular man in Great Britain driven from office by a dictator, joy all over the dictator countries, and the British Government sitting smug-faced, pleased and delighted, glad to see him go."

Nor were all Conservative members pleased with the Prime Minister's action. Though more restrained than the Opposition, Major J. W. Hills asserted that peace lay in Britain's taking a "quite different line" from Chamberlain's, and P. V. Emrys-Evans saw Eden's policy as the only way Britain could keep her friends and maintain her ideals.

Several Conservatives spoke for the Prime Minister. Following his reasoning, they emphasized that an agreement with Italy was certain to have a soothing effect on the strained international situation. And Chamberlain himself, apparently sensing the depth of Parliament's misgivings, rose again to ask the Commons not to assume that the moment Britain entered into conversations with Italy she was committed to do whatever Italy asked. Britain was "not prepared to make peace at any price."[29]

The next day Arthur Greenwood, deputy leader of the Labor Party, introduced a motion of no-confidence in the Government's conduct of foreign affairs. Deploring the absence of any reference to the League of Nations or collective security in Chamberlain's outlook, he saw "very bleak prospects" for settled peace coming from "this policy of truck and scuttle." Liberty could not be maintained by a relapse to the standards of the jungle; rather, "firmness is of the essence of statesmanship." Whereas Eden had stood for faith and works, the Prime Minister stood for blind faith.

Again Chamberlain contended that if the Government meant

29. *Parl. Debs., HC,* February 21, 1938, vol. 332, 45–155.

to have real conversations with Italy, it could not lay down conditions beforehand. Charging the Opposition with clinging to meaningless phrases, he argued that he should have failed in his duty had he refused to take the action he had.

It remained for Winston Churchill to point the moral to the tale. In expressing deep sympathy for Eden, "whose policy I admired" and whose going would be an "irreparable loss to the Government," he warned that Britain should not set herself unduly against the duty which sometimes falls upon nations and individuals of standing up boldly in defense of "the right," even when attended by risk. The day would come when at some point or other, on some issue or other, Britain would have to take a stand, and it was his hope that when that day arrived, Britain would not find that through an unwise policy she was left to make her stand alone.

Lloyd George, the former Prime Minister, caustically charged that the dictators were determined to drive Eden out of office because he was the only man in the British Government who would stand up to them. Chamberlain had played along with their game. If the Prime Minister was "as dovelike in his innocence" as to believe all of Mussolini's promises, "he is really not fit to deal with the Machiavellian dictators. He is only fit for a stained glass window." Britain lived under the "cowering peace of the white flag, retreating from one position after another," but the moment would come, he proclaimed, and soon, when the British people would insist on once more unfurling their own flag and getting men who would stand by it.

An Independent Labor member, James Maxton, considered it "absolutely necessary" that the Chamberlain Government be put out of office. A Labor government might make mistakes, but he could not conceive of it "crawling in front of Fascist Powers." Stimulated by that remark, someone shouted from the floor: "The Labor Party has no guts." "Then God help this country," Maxton retorted, "because it has been amply demonstrated that the present Government has no guts." On that point Herbert Morrison of the Labor Party wished to elaborate. Eden had been "stabbed in the back with an Italian dagger" by his own ministerial colleagues at a time when the Prime Minister, instead of rushing into negotiations, should have bided his time and awaited the point at which Mussolini would have had to push for an agreement. That would have made British bargaining power infinitely greater.

Dissatisfied Conservatives then gained the floor. J. R. Cartland wished to make it clear that in all questions of foreign policy "right should always come before expediency." Chamberlain had been forced into the initiation of these conversations by fear. He had made use of opportunities and was employing methods which were not in keeping with British traditions and which, even if successful, would spoil Britain's good name. A. C. Crossley regarded Chamberlain's action "an ostensible sign of weakness in face of the world." If the day came when the British were unwilling to pay the price for the liberty they cherished, they would be unworthy of their great possessions in the world. The sharpest Conservative attack was delivered by Vyvyan Adams, who could not understand how, in logic, it was possible to be magnanimous to people who were bullying you. "It seems about as logical as asking people to be magnanimous to a man-eating tiger or to a raging forest fire." The substantial effect of what had happened was that decency and respect for international obligations, for which Eden stood, had momentarily collapsed.

In spite of the drama of the debate, political anti-climax had by this time set in. Rumors of schisms or "middle parties" gave way to the steady acquiescence of whip-led majorities, and the debate was finally closed on behalf of the Government by W. S. Morrison, the Minister of Agriculture, whose perfunctory summary stated: the Government is pushing conciliation as far as possible in an effort to give "realistic form to that idealistic conception which we all in our hearts desire." When the House divided on Greenwood's motion, 168 members favored it, 330 opposed. Chamberlain's opening of conversations with Italy was thereby vindicated.[30]

During the course of the debate, twenty-five speakers voiced dissatisfaction with Chamberlain's plan of action. While the brunt of the attack was carried by the Labor and Liberal Opposition,

30. *Ibid.*, February 22, 1938, vol. 332, 209–332.

six Conservatives, in addition to Eden and Cranborne, were among them. This was no well-planned and coordinated attack. Indeed, Chamberlain's timing of the approach to Italy had taken the Parliament by at least as much surprise as it had the Cabinet. Criticism was rather in the form of a series of individual reactions to the Prime Minister's initiative, a hodge-podge of opinions which, though frequently similar in substance, emanated from a variety of individuals. Most Labor-Liberal critics, of course, spoke from a traditional party point of view, but in their reactions, as well as in those of Conservative and independent members, was real alarm at increasing totalitarian power and a genuine concern for the rule of law in international relations. There was fear for Britain's good name, and perhaps most important when compared with the Government's attitude on this point, Britain's own security. There was, in short, already evident a broad concern for both principle and practicality which would characterize the emerging opposition to appeasement. Just how far could a government go in subverting "right" to expediency, especially when there was no real evidence, much less a guarantee, that the line of policy deemed expedient would provide significant gain for Britain and the cause of European peace and security? It was their similar approaches to this kind of question which, more than anything else, brought Churchill and Attlee, Cartland and Maxton, Adams and Fletcher—usually far apart in their general political philosophies—together on this occasion.

Throughout the debate a faint air of academicism seemed to pervade that area of the hall occupied by back-bench Conservatives. Was the issue after all that important? Certainly conversations with Italy involved no direct threat to British security or vital interests; what, then, did Britain have to lose in pursuing them? This approach was both misleading and ambiguous, for the Prime Minister's attitude was far more positive. It really did matter to him. The issue was important. So, while those who opposed the Government's proposal in this instance may have done so for varying reasons, it is also likely that some who supported the Government's proposal did so for reasons other than those of the Prime Minister.

Much may be said for Chamberlain's view that the matter

was important—though indeed in a very different way. In the chronicling of appeasement in general, the appeasement of Italy has frequently been slighted in view of the ultimately more important and consequential appeasement of Germany. But from the point of view of the principle of appeasement itself, the approach to Italy was every bit as debatable as the approach to Germany. Italian Fascists had already shown themselves to be as unscrupulous in their international dealings as German Nazis. Their fulminations against Britain were far more abusive and irritating than German propaganda, for Hitler had long since seen the advantage of working with Britain in international affairs—on his own terms, of course. Italian lawlessness in connection with the Ethiopian crisis and the Spanish Civil War was already legendary. In short, at the beginning of 1938, there was as much or more reason to consider Italy, rather than Germany, the primary threat to European peace, and the British Government's decision to seek an accommodation by appeasement with Italy in these circumstances was fraught with political implications. The appeasement of Germany, after all, was pushed most vigorously when force of circumstances made it, according to the later explanations of Chamberlain spokesmen, absolutely essential. There seemed to be more freedom of choice involved in the approach to Italy. Thus those who, caught largely unaware by the Government's initiative, labored to translate the whole issue into one of major principle and to criticize it from that point of view, were not unrealistic in their calculations. And their attempt to make a major issue out of what many were inclined to consider not so important after all, was not unreasonable. It cannot, however, be said that this fact was generally appreciated.

When the vote on the motion was taken, only one Conservative, Vyvyan Adams, voted for it; significantly, however, about fifty Government supporters abstained.[31] The fact that this vote involved a motion of censure which, if passed, would have meant the fall of the Government probably masked the real feeling of

31. Among those abstaining, in addition to Eden and Cranborne, were Churchill, Harold Macmillan, Brigadier-General E. L. Spears, and J. P. L. Thomas.

still more Conservative members and ensured that the voting followed orthodox party lines. In his memoirs L. S. Amery admits that he "had doubts as to what Chamberlain really wanted to achieve, even more as to whether it was not already too late for his policy to achieve anything. But I thought it only right to support him and keep our Party together."[32]

It is characteristic of the British system that increasing dissatisfaction with the Government sometimes has the practical effect of diminishing restraints upon the Prime Minister within his own party. When confronted by a potential trend against the Government, or a sticky issue which might cause the Government to lose face, few Government supporters wish to risk losing their seats by failing to sustain a vote of confidence and so bringing on a general election. This does not mean that they are entirely selfish; frequently they harbor sincere doubts about the policies of the Opposition. This factor was certainly potent in early 1938, for it is quite clear that the average Government supporter in the Commons, even if he had begun to doubt the complete wisdom of Chamberlain's course, was far more doubtful of the Labor Party's ability to deal realistically with the dangers threatening Britain and Europe. Nor did he take comfort in the possibility that a group of dissident Conservatives might win control of party policy. Consequently, though a number of young Conservatives heartily cheered Eden,[33] and some regular Government supporters backed an amendment deploring the circumstances in which Eden had been obliged to resign,[34] they did not endorse the motion of no-confidence. The final result was that Chamberlain's large majority was not endangered.

When Eden's resignation occupied the House of Lords on February 24, Lord Addison questioned whether it was "good business" to open negotiations with a man who had consistently

32. Amery, *My Political Life,* III, 235.

33. *Western Mail* (Cardiff), Feb. 22, 1938.

34. *The Times,* Feb. 23, 1938. This group included Brigadier-General E. L. Spears, Harold Nicolson, A. C. Crossley, Godfrey Nicholson, Major J. W. Hills, Brigadier-General Ernest Makins, Captain J. R. Macnamara, R. H. Turton, R. A. Carey, P. T. Eckersley, R. A. Pilkington, Captain D. W. Gunston, Mark Patrick, Colonel Bernard Cruddas, P. V. Emrys-Evans, Harold Macmillan, and J. R. Cartland.

violated his contracts in the past without any effective guarantee of good faith. Chamberlain's policy seemed only short-sighted expediency, grasping at the advantage of a day to the destruction of confidence among Britain's friends. Addison was joined in these sentiments by Viscount Cecil of Chelwood, long-time exponent of the League of Nations, who believed peace could not be obtained either by running away from the dictators or by running after them. Still sharper criticism, especially of the Government's disregard for its election pledge to support the League, came from Lord Strabolgi: "The Roman legions were withdrawn from Britain . . . in the year 411 A.D. Since then we have not taken our orders from Rome, and we have no intention of taking orders from Rome." Although the remarks of Lord Strabolgi, like Lord Addison a former Labor M. P., had a distinctly partisan ring, there was none of that in what Lord Addison or Viscount Cecil, a former Conservative M. P., had to say. Thus their expressions of concern cannot properly be dismissed as nothing but partisan needling of the Government.

The Chamberlain view was defended by Lord Halifax, soon to be named Eden's successor in the Foreign Office. He believed progress in conversations with Italy improbable if "made dependent on the acceptance in advance of a period of probationary discipline," and explained: "We refuse to fold our hands and merely drift along on dangerous tides, making warlike noises to encourage the passengers." A few others briefly replied to the critics of Chamberlain's "new approach"—but the discussion soon succumbed to monotony.[35]

Meanwhile, Germany had reason to look upon the turn of events in Britain with satisfaction. She was assured by the Italian Embassy in Berlin that the negotiations with Britain would not be allowed to impair the Axis; in fact, Italy would make no agreement unless it was "in fullest harmony with Germany." Further, R. A. Butler, soon to assume the post of Parliamentary Under-Secretary of State in the Foreign Office, told Woermann, the

35. Great Britain, *Parliamentary Debates, House of Lords,* Fifth Series, (hereinafter cited as *Parl. Debs., HL*), February 24, 1938, vol. 107, 888–944.

German Chargé d'Affaires in London, that the Eden crisis meant the decline of the old pro-French foreign service and the ascendency of the "new generation of men" like Sir Horace Wilson, who were decidedly pro-German.[36]

Widely varying opinions on Eden's resignation were expressed in the British press.[37] On February 21, the reaction was fairly temperate on both sides. The pro-Government *Times* saw in Eden's departure no abrupt reorientation of British foreign policy or any fundamental change in British aims. The Conservative *Daily Telegraph,* recognizing merit on both sides, felt the decisive consideration was the "unwisdom of delay." If an agreement were to be reached with Italy, it were best done quickly. To the Conservative *Daily Mail,* Eden's going was a "relief"; his policy during two years in office had produced "uncertainty at home and bewilderment abroad." But the *Daily Herald,* official organ of the Labor Party, charged that with Eden went the last pretence that the British Government cared for ideals of international justice. Chamberlain was prepared "to concede everything in which British public opinion believes, and to which the peace-loving democracies of the world look." He had come out nakedly on the side of power politics; the Italian press had demanded that "Eden must go," and Eden had gone. A real peace policy, as Labor viewed it, would consist of building a more vital and effective League of Nations.

The independent *Glasgow Herald* was concerned lest the world be given an excuse for believing that Eden shared the fate of Delcassé,[38] while the Unionist Cardiff *Western Mail,* though confident that the Government would continue to defend the chief principles of foreign policy for which Eden had worked, feared a relaxation of pressure upon Italy to withdraw from Spain. The Liberal *Liverpool Daily Post* deplored that at such a critical

36. Memorandum by the Foreign Minister, Berlin, Feb. 23, 1938; Memorandum, London, Feb. 25, 1938. *Documents on German Foreign Policy, 1918–1945,* Series D (hereinafter cited as *G.D.*), I, 212, 223–25.

37. Some basic data (including proprietors and editors) on each of the newspapers and periodicals utilized in this study may be found in Appendix III.

38. Théophile Delcassé was the anti-German French Foreign Minister ousted in 1905 in an effort to facilitate Franco-German negotiations.

moment a division of opinion on foreign policy should be published to the world. "Unless the Premier has a strong defence to offer, it will be a bad day for the Government," proclaimed the Liberal *Manchester Guardian.* Of stronger conviction at the moment was the Liberal Bradford *Yorkshire Observer,* which considered Eden's resignation "a calamity." Opportunism had achieved a great triumph over principle. The Foreign Secretary had been abandoned because he would not consent to a one-sided bargain. The country would thus demand that Chamberlain had been given some substantial security for peace by Mussolini that could not possibly have been obtained by any other means.

With few exceptions, British newspapers regretted Eden's departure. Irrespective of political affiliation, they generally regarded him as a young man of great vigor and ability. In this way the press reflected Eden's unquestionably enthusiastic following among the British public. Even to "Chamberlain men" his blameless reputation, his charm and his glamor, had made him, in the words of Randolph Churchill, "an emblem, a symbol, a mascot, an insurance policy."[39]

In the days following Eden's explanation in the Commons, the comments of the press became more animated. The *Daily Telegraph* (Feb. 22) thought Eden should have acquiesced in the Anglo-Italian conversations, for his prescription of standing firm and demanding not promise but achievement had not been conspicuously successful in the past. The Conservative *Financial Times* (Feb. 22), though admitting that Eden would be missed, felt Chamberlain was "entitled to expect the support of Parliament, business, and the public generally in his efforts to promote European appeasement." Eden's resignation, in the opinion of *The Times* (Feb. 23), was "an event which means no more at bottom than that the British Government . . . will devote new energy to a thorough test of what may be done by a more positive diplomacy for the elimination of the causes of international suspicion and hostility." His action was liable to "make mischief abroad," said the independent *Observer* (Feb. 27), but otherwise there was no reason to regret his departure. As for Eden's Par-

39. R. S. Churchill, *The Rise and Fall of Sir Anthony Eden,* p. 145.

liamentary indictment of the Government's conduct of foreign affairs, the Cardiff *Western Mail* (Feb. 23) found it "utterly unconvincing."

The Liberal *News Chronicle* (Feb. 22), however, insisted that Eden was right. Twice Mussolini had "pulled the wool over the eyes of the British Government, and each time they have come back for more." Common sense dictated that any further agreement with Italy must be preceded by proof of sincerity. Though Chamberlain denied there had been a threat of "now or never," the situation was serious when two responsible ministers interpreted the language used as a threat. Eden's contention that this was the moment for Britain to stand firm was heartily endorsed. In like manner the *Manchester Guardian* (Feb. 23) wondered whether Chamberlain, if he felt it so urgent to reach an agreement, would not also feel bound by his own logic to make one concession after another. It reasoned:

> Chamberlain said it was humiliating to impose conditions on a Great Power as the price of friendship. But what is Italy doing to Britain? Chamberlain's policy does more credit to his character than to his intelligence. The Christian principles of faith, hope and charity are a noble pattern for human conduct, but they do not seem an adequate basis for foreign policy in the twentieth century.

Urging, during the next two days, that public opinion, "the only serious check on the Government," be given full vent on the issue, the *Guardian* claimed already to have received a vast volume of anti-Government correspondence.[40]

The *Liverpool Daily Post* (Feb. 23) could not think of the Prime Minister's new course "without some uneasiness." Bitter experience had shown that German and Italian policies abroad could not be trusted, and Chamberlain had doubtless shocked feeling in many countries by parting with Eden on an issue which involved the honorable regard for international undertakings. Chamberlain was willing to rely on precarious independent bar-

40. One letter told of a group of 150 Oxford and Cambridge students who went to London to protest the change in foreign policy and actually met with two Cabinet members, Sir Thomas Inskip and Walter Elliot.

gains contrived with dictators, lamented the Bradford *Yorkshire Observer* (Feb. 23). No wonder Britain must accept, instead of make, conditions. To placate Mussolini the Prime Minister was making "almost indecent haste," but worse still, he was prepared to let the dictators kill the League of Nations as an instrument of British foreign policy.

Anxiety over Chamberlain's policy also appeared in the non-partisan *Spectator* (Feb. 25), which found it "impossible to think he has made a good bargaining." The radical *New Statesman and Nation* (Feb. 26) bitterly alleged that Chamberlain viewed foreign affairs "with a simplicity so gross that it can only mean indifference." The whole concept of compromise with Italy demanded resolute opposition. The independent *Economist* (Feb. 26) saw public sentiment deeply moved and confidence in the Government greatly shaken, for to weaken the confidence among peace-loving peoples in the hope of a temporary relaxation of tension with Italy would be disastrous.

Press reaction to the proposed Anglo-Italian conversations and Eden's resignation generally followed party lines. The Labor and Liberal press denounced Chamberlain's action and the general policy it implied; the Conservative press supported it as a move toward peace and the easing of international tension; and the independent organs, while showing skepticism, usually took a reserved position on neutral ground—perhaps more reserved than neutral. Most papers conceded that a man who sacrificed his position for reason of conviction deserved great respect.

All of this was quite natural. The *Daily Herald,* official organ of the Labor Party, and *The Times,* long-established supporter of the Government in power, could hardly have been expected to share one view. After all, the specific issues at stake were still quite unclear; the arguments on all sides were still largely theoretical and beyond immediate "proof"; the probabilities of success or failure for appeasement necessarily hinged on the turn of future events, which no one, of course, could predict with certainty. The debate was still couched in terms of principle, and principle is always open to varying interpretations. Appeasement was still an untested idea and it was reasonably doubtful that its proponents would abandon it without giving it a trial. But, on the other hand, there was skepticism and open opposition in the press, vigorously and in some instances effectively stated. It appeared in some London and provincial newspapers alike, in some of great influence and circulation, in some of lesser import. As in Parliament, there was concern for Britain's reputation and security, the rule of law, and the impact of the Government's action on other nations. This appeared primarily in organs likely to be critical of the Chamberlain Government in any circumstances, but it is nonetheless significant for the light it sheds on the extent to which appeasement, even in its early stages, was questioned in Britain. (And the shifting positions of other organs of the press, *The Times* included, as the years 1938–1939 wore on, is one significant indicator of changing attitudes toward appeasement.)

It is perhaps surprising that so little reference was made to Eden's conduct in the House of Commons, even by those journals most antagonistic toward appeasement. Eden had spoken with evident (and many would later say excessive[41]) reserve. He had barely skimmed over the surface of the differences which divided him from Chamberlain and the rest of the Cabinet, and in so doing had showed his loyalty to his leader and his party to be above reproach. But was not something more required? Since he believed the policy he deplored inimical to his country's interests, was it not his duty to denounce appeasement openly as being destructive of Britain's safety? Should he not have devoted his power and prestige to organizing opposition to a course which he considered to be disastrous? At the time few critics of appeasement asked such questions, perhaps because they respected Eden's wide popularity, perhaps because they did not want to risk alienating a potential ally, perhaps because in the heat of the moment they did not look that far ahead. At any rate, they concentrated largely on the question of principle for which Eden stood.

41. One of his biographers asserts that many Conservatives would have followed Eden's lead had he chosen to give one, and the resulting effect on British policy might have been significant. Broad, *Anthony Eden,* pp. 107–08. Connell holds the view that Eden could have broken the Chamberlain Government had he challenged it. *The Office,* p. 270. But both agree that he was not the man even to contemplate such a step.

Indeed, Eden had resigned on a vital point of principle. He could not agree that the Prime Minister's steps to implement appeasement were in the best interests of the country. He was unconvinced of Italian good faith and unwilling to negotiate with Italy on the basis of "now or never"—an interpretation of Grandi's statement which appears quite justified. As his memoirs suggest, "it was neither timing nor temperament nor the gap in years, nor any other of the minor influences which have from time to time been attributed," which made it impossible for him to continue as Chamberlain's Foreign Secretary. "The differences which divided us were about matters which are decisive to the successful conduct of foreign affairs at any time."[42]

It might be argued, as some of Eden's critics did both at the time and later, that there were other issues of greater significance on which Eden might, with advantage to the nation and himself, have chosen to separate himself from his colleagues—for example, the question of national defense. However that may be, the pertinent fact is that Eden's resignation was the first open move of significance in opposition to Chamberlain's plan. It provided the first real opportunity for the critics of appeasement, and those who, while perhaps not thorough-going critics, had their reservations about the policy, to speak out on a specific issue. And although their criticism had no immediate effect on British policy, it marked the beginning of a tide of protest which, some thirteen months later, would swell to proportions of great consequence. Taken together with the Nazi annexation of Austria it constituted the first major blow to the general popular confidence which Chamberlain had hitherto enjoyed.

42. *Facing the Dictators,* pp. 678–79. Eden includes on these pages some noteworthy reflections on the "lessons to be drawn" from his difference with Chamberlain.

CHAPTER THREE

The Impact of the Anschluss

EDEN AND CRANBORNE spoke in their respective constituencies shortly after resigning their Foreign Office positions. As young Conservatives unwilling to jeopardize their future political careers, neither indulged in factious opposition to the Government. Both pursued the arguments submitted earlier to the House and expressed the need for National Government.[1] Labor, on the other hand, showed little reserve. Taking the opportunity to make political capital out of Chamberlain's approach to Italy, Attlee lashed at the Government's "betrayal of democracy" in successive public appearances in Eastleigh and Gosport. He also joined with Herbert Morrison and Sir Stafford Cripps in addressing a demonstration arranged by the London Labor Party at Kingsway Hall "to protest against the circumstances which have resulted in the resignation of Mr. Eden and to condemn the new developments apparent in the Government's foreign policy."[2]

In the meantime Eden and Cranborne were succeeded at the Foreign Office by Lord Halifax and R. A. Butler.[3] The appointment of Halifax resulted in Chamberlain's further involvement in the day-to-day details of foreign affairs in the House of Commons. With the Foreign Secretary in the Lords, the Prime Minister was

1. *The Times,* Feb. 26, 28, 1938.
2. *Ibid.,* Feb. 28, Mar. 1, 1938.
3. For a good general account of Halifax's outlook and attitudes toward his work in the Foreign Office, see Birkenhead, *Halifax,* pp. 417–26. Halifax's appointment was questioned in the House of Commons on constitutional grounds, but in the end the Opposition argument that the Foreign Secretary is by tradition a member of the Commons—an argument which had little basis in fact—was riddled, and Halifax was confirmed as Eden's successor. *Parl. Debs., HC,* February 28, 1938, vol. 332, 882–84.

forced to answer scores of questions in the Commons and had to bear the brunt of the Opposition attacks. The effect of these responsibilities was to underline further the differences between Chamberlain's own ideas and those of his critics.[4]

Halifax had barely taken office when, on March 12, 1938, German troops streamed into Austria and absorbed Hitler's native land. Though the British Government and people alike were shocked, there had been indications that trouble was brewing. The Austrian Chancellor, Kurt von Schuschnigg, had been summoned to Berchtesgaden a month before by Hitler, who sharply attacked Schuschnigg's policy as unfriendly to the Reich, reminded the Austrian Chancellor of his "historic mission,"[5] and boasted of his personal popularity and the power of Germany. He concluded: "Who is not with me will be crushed." Hitler gave Schuschnigg a written ultimatum demanding amnesty for all imprisoned Nazis, the appointment of Nazi sympathizers as Minister of Justice and Minister of Security, and full political freedom for Austrian Nazis.[6]

The British knew of all this but remained relatively unmoved. Their apathy is attested by a February 20 entry in Duff Cooper's diary:

> The past week has been a busy one, full of events. The full significance of Hitler's summons to Schuschnigg appeared gradually. It was nothing less than the end of Austria's independence: a portentous event in European history about which nobody here seems to think or care.[7]

This attitude was even conveyed to Hitler by Nevile Henderson, the British Ambassador in Berlin. While developments in Austria had caused concern and would unavoidably hamper a general settlement, he informed the Führer on March 3 (upon instructions from the Foreign Office), "the British Government is not yet in a position properly to assess the consequences of the agreements

4. Templewood, *Nine Troubled Years,* p. 281.
5. This was probably a reference to Hitler's idea of incorporating all Germans in the Reich. See footnote 3, chapter V.
6. Kurt von Schuschnigg, *Austrian Requiem* (New York, 1946), pp. 12–19.
7. Duff Cooper, *Old Men Forget,* p. 216.

recently reached between Austria and the German Reich." These consequences must necessarily depend on the manner in which both parties implemented the various obligations and arrangements. Henderson himself had often advocated *anschluss* and assured Ribbentrop, the Foreign Minister, that the complaint by the British Minister in Vienna of German pressure on Austria "did not necessarily represent the views of the British Government."[8]

Among those people in Britain concerned about the ominous German demands upon Austria was Laborite Arthur Henderson. In the Commons, March 2, he urged Chamberlain to endorse a declaration made earlier by Yvon Delbos, the French Foreign Minister, that the independence of Austria was an essential element of European peace. This, Henderson felt, would give great moral encouragement to the Austrians in their struggle to maintain independence. Chamberlain was unmoved, replying that it was too early to estimate the effect of the arrangements between Austria and Germany, and the matter should be "left alone for the present."[9]

Although Britain warned the Germans on March 10–11 that a solution of the Austrian question by force might result in a large-scale conflict involving Britain,[10] the matter largely had been "left alone" when a German ultimatum demanding, among other things, the resignation of the Chancellor, his replacement by the Minister of Interior, and a new Cabinet to be two-thirds Nazi was delivered to Austria late in the afternoon of March 11. Subsequently, Nevile Henderson, acting upon instructions from Halifax, told Göring and wrote von Neurath, the acting German Foreign Minister, that if the report of the ultimatum received in Britain were true, the British Government would feel "bound to register

8. The German Foreign Minister to the British Ambassador in Germany, Berlin, Mar. 4, 1938. *G. D.*, I, 240–49.

9. *Parl. Debs., HC,* March 2, 1938, vol. 332, 1247–50.

10. Halifax had spoken in these terms to Ribbentrop, who was visiting in London at the time, and Henderson had done likewise to the German Foreign Office. Memorandum, Mar. 10, 1938; Memorandum by the Foreign Minister, London, Mar. 11, 1938. *G. D.*, I, 253–61, 272–73. Henderson to Halifax, Berlin, Mar. 11, 1938. *Documents on British Foreign Policy, 1919–1939,* Third Series (hereinafter cited as *B. D.*), I, 8.

protest in strongest terms against such use of coercion, backed by force, against an independent state in order to create a situation incompatible with its national independence." This conditional protest was lightly dismissed by von Neurath, who replied in effect that no third power had any concern with the relations between Germany and Austria.[11] Eventually, the British Government contented itself with "taking note" of assurance given Henderson by Göring that the German troops would be withdrawn from Austria as soon as the situation was stable, after which free elections would be held without intimidation. Halifax agreed with Henderson that nothing short of a direct threat of force could have altered the course of events in Austria.[12] Thus for the British Government, unwilling even to contemplate the use of force, the *Anschluss* was an accomplished fact.

The immediate reaction of all sections of the British press to Germany's act was unqualified condemnation. It was universally recognized that the mailed fist had seldom struck with such dramatic effect as in Austria between dawn and dusk on March 12. Some newspapers let it go at that. Others, including the Conservative *Daily Mail* (Mar. 12, 14), the Liberal *Liverpool Daily Post* (Mar. 14), and the independent *Sunday Pictorial* (Mar. 13),

11. Henderson to Halifax, Berlin, Mar. 12, 1938. *B. D.*, I, 23–24, 30–32. When the news of the seizure of Austria reached Britain, Ribbentrop was in London officially taking leave of the British Government at the end of his mission as German Ambassador. In fact, a farewell luncheon in his honor was underway in Downing Street when the telegram arrived. Cadogan, the Permanent Under-Secretary of State for Foreign Affairs, read it and handed it to Halifax, who in turn showed it to Chamberlain. The three of them left the dining room, taking Ribbentrop with them. When they told him the news, he appeared completely taken aback. Halifax was convinced (so Templewood records; Halifax does not mention it in his memoirs) that either he knew nothing of the *coup,* or that, if he did, he was a most successful liar in concealing it. Whichever was the case, the luncheon finished in an atmosphere of icy coldness. Templewood, *Nine Troubled Years,* p. 282. Ribbentrop claims that he had no report of the events in Austria, that it was not until he saw Hitler in Vienna that he realized that the Führer had thoughts of actual *anschluss.* Joachim von Ribbentrop, *Zwischen London und Moskau: Erinnerungen and letze Aufzeichnungen* (Leoni, Germany, 1954), pp. 134–36. For other accounts of the luncheon incident see Churchill, *The Gathering Storm,* pp. 271–72; Fritz Hesse, *Das Spiel um Deutschland* (Munich, 1953), p. 103.

12. Halifax to Henderson, F. O., Mar. 12, 1938. *B. D.*, I, 32, 33.

drew the conclusion that Britain's safety now lay in pushing rearmament to the fullest extent of her capacity. Still other papers emphasized their distrust of Germany. "Whatever faith remained in the pacific assurances of Hitler has been shattered beyond redemption," asserted the Unionist Cardiff *Western Mail* (Mar. 14). The governments of Europe would now know what to expect from Germany, warned the Liberal *Manchester Guardian* (Mar. 12); they could no longer plead ignorance of her methods or intentions.

In the opinion of several influential organs, vastly increased armaments were not enough since everyone in Europe was rearming. Rather, the British Government must adopt a new policy. Only through some form of collective understanding among the peace-loving nations of Europe could a means of restraint against future aggressors be constructed, the *Manchester Guardian* (Mar. 13) stated. The democratic nations stood in the "Valley of Decision," warned the Liberal *News Chronicle* (Mar. 12); what had happened in Austria was the kind of thing which must be expected if governments continued to act on the principle of yielding to every threat. Even more emphatic was the Labor *Daily Herald* (Mar. 12): will the British Government learn from this experience, it asked, or is it too blind to read the writing on the Viennese wall? What use was there to make an agreement when there could be no confidence that it would be honored beyond the minute when it had served the purpose of those signatories whose ultimate interest seemed to lie in getting their own way through the lawless threat of force? "There is no escape from danger save by working with redoubled power . . . for the reconstruction of the collective system." The *Sunday Times* (Mar. 1) summarized this sentiment concisely and with a bluntness which struck the heart of the issue: "To proceed now with the Berlin talks about appeasement would be a mockery."

Once more prominent Labor leaders, in public addresses, urged Chamberlain to "think again" about foreign affairs, to seek an associated effort of the nations which wanted peace and security, and to make it clear that they would not tolerate continued acts of aggression. Attlee at Hull, Morrison at Northampton, Greenwood at Liverpool, Shinwell at Grimsby, and Cripps at Inverness all bitterly criticized the Government's policy, alleging that it was now reaping what it had sown during the past six years. The essence of these speeches was contained in Greenwood's acid remark: "Red Riding Hood Chamberlain better return to the shelter of the League of Nations and collective security."[13]

Chamberlain explained the Government's attitude toward the *Anschluss* in the House of Commons on March 14. Germany's methods, he declared, called for "severest condemnation" and could not fail to prejudice the Government's hope of removing misunderstandings between nations. But Britain was under no commitment to take any action with regard to Austria; she was pledged only to consultation with the French and Italian Governments, and that pledge had been fully discharged. As a result, the French addressed protests to Germany; the Italians made no reply. Nothing, the Prime Minister avowed, could have arrested the German action except force. As a salve to widespread anxiety, Chamberlain proclaimed that Britain's defense program was "flexible," and a fresh review would be made to see what further steps it might be necessary to take.

No one argued with Chamberlain's contention that only force could have stopped the German thrust in Austria. What his critics found so disconcerting was his apparent unconcern for the future. Neither Attlee nor Sinclair found the Prime Minister's remarks at all satisfying. What Britain needed, Attlee urged, was not an attempt to build peace by separate bargains with dictators but a return to League principles and policy. Unless she stood firm, all Europe would be thrown "into the melting pot"; admission of the rule of force only made war inevitable. Sinclair agreed: "If we cannot rally against aggression all the forces of the potential victims, they will be sacrificed one by one, till it comes our turn." France, Poland, and the United States were among those nations toward whom Britain should draw closer immediately in an effort to base international relationships on moral law rather than on the shifting sands of power politics.

Undoubtedly the most stimulating speech of the day, judging

13. The *Sunday Times,* Mar. 13, 1938.

from the future references it provoked, was delivered by Winston Churchill. It was on this occasion that he proposed the "grand alliance." Why not make a stand while there was still a good company of powerful countries to share Britain's dangers and aspirations? Why delay until confronted with a general landslide of the small countries passing over to the overwhelming power of the Nazi regime because they had no other choice?

> If a number of States were assembled around Great Britain and France in a solemn treaty for mutual defence against aggression; if they had their forces marshalled in what you may call a grand alliance; if they had their staff arrangements concerted; if all this rested, as it can honourably rest, upon the Covenant of the League of Nations, agreeable with all the purposes and ideals of the League of Nations; if that were sustained, as it would be, by the moral sense of the world; and if it were done in the year 1938—and, believe me, it may be the last chance there will be for doing it—then I say that you might even now arrest this approaching war. . . . Before we cast away this hope . . . let those who wish to reject it ponder well and earnestly upon what will happen to us if, when all else has been thrown to the wolves, we are left to face our fate alone.[14]

Among those greatly impressed with Churchill's proposal was Admiral of the Fleet Sir Roger Keyes (Conservative), who urged that Churchill be taken into the Cabinet at once because of his "vision, foresight, energy, determination and drive, as well as great knowledge and experience in all matters pertaining to preparations for and prosecution of war." That in itself constituted a demand that the Government revise the direction of its foreign policy.

The cause of collective security and a return to the principles and policy of the League of Nations received support from all sides of the House. From the Labor benches F. J. Bellenger, Lieutenant-Commander R. T. Fletcher, A. V. Alexander, and J. C. Ede insisted upon the absolute necessity of such a course.

14. *Parl. Debs., HC,* March 14, 1938, vol. 333, 100.

Ede in particular was vehement: unless the Government was prepared to take a much bolder line in facing the dictators, Britain would soon find herself left to face the bully alone and to "take the thrashing that our own cowardice will have well merited." The Laborites were joined in this sentiment by Liberal Geoffrey Mander, Liberal Nationalist E. L. Granville, and Communist William Gallacher. Nor did all Conservative members stand aloof; ardent in their support were the Duchess of Atholl and Vyvyan Adams, the former a constant and fervid Chamberlain critic. The Duchess, Mander, and Gallacher suggested the inclusion of Russia in the scheme of collective security, while Mander and Fletcher emphasized closer ties with the United States. All openly stated or apparently assumed that it was Britain's duty to form the backbone of such a coalition. The Duchess, indeed, believed the fact that Britain had always been the center of such coalitions was "the proudest thing in British history."[15]

The moral Vyvyan Adams drew from Germany's action in Austria was that it was right for Britain to use her power to "terrify" Hitler. He translated the idea of collective security into a plan of action: Britain should join with France and the other members of the League in guaranteeing the independence and integrity of Czechoslovakia. The consequence of failing to do so would be a procession of aggressions further strengthening the aggressors and leading to the day when Britain would be in virtual isolation, faced not only with war but with defeat.

R. A. Butler, the new Under-Secretary of State for Foreign Affairs, in replying maintained that it was the general policy of the Government to make collective security a reality "if it could be made so [but] the more we examine the possibility of summoning the League at the present moment . . . the more we see the difficulties that would arise from this particular solution of the problem."[16]

Butler's closing remark pointed out a basic difference in the interpretation of "collective security" between the Government

15. The Duchess of Atholl spoke frequently in public on the theme of collective security during 1938–1939. See Katherine, Duchess of Atholl, *Working Partnership* (London, 1958), pp. 219–31.

16. *Parl. Debs., HC,* March 14, 1938, vol. 333, 47–168.

and those who urged a new foreign policy upon it—a difference which was to last throughout 1938. When the Government spoke of collective security, it spoke in terms of the existing League of Nations. Having reached the conclusion that the League was ineffectual, it believed little could be accomplished through it. On the other hand, the Laborites, Liberals, and dissident Conservatives who called for collective security in opposition to the Government's policy of appeasement, thought in terms of a new, rebuilt, revitalized League, or of Churchill's grand alliance: a number of nations gathered together in a solemn treaty for mutual defense against aggression, having no necessary relation to the existing League except that it would be based on League principles. But the Government, and Chamberlain in particular, looked upon the Opposition's cry for collective security only as an undefined shibboleth with which to attack those in authority, apparently incognizant of the fact that some of the most avid supporters of the collective scheme were Liberals and Conservatives who had little motive of making party capital by their action.

In any event, the debate of March 14 showed that a number of members were convinced that something more definite and vigorous than Chamberlain's policy of kind words to the dictators was necessary if peace and security in Europe were to be preserved. It must also be acknowledged that some of the critics, like the communist Gallacher and the vitriolic Duchess of Atholl, were not among the Commons' most temperate and beloved members—indeed, some would hardly have considered them "decent"—and the very fact of their support for a new approach in foreign affairs undoubtedly helped to prejudice the issue.

That no sharp definition of differing Labor, Liberal, and Conservative positions of opposition emerged in the debate suggests that no sharp distinctions existed. Once again, this was much more of a spontaneous expression of concern for the general drift in foreign policy, which happened to catch up members of differing political affiliations, than it was the presentation of well-defined party positions. Any debate which found Gallacher, the Duchess of Atholl, Churchill, Bellenger, and Mander in essential agreement necessarily involved some issue which transcended usual partisan politics. These members were in agreement that British foreign policy was in urgent need of revision. That the direction this should take lacked precise definition—although certainly the proposals of Churchill and Adams were clear enough—indeed detracted from the force of certain critics' arguments. But, inasmuch as their comments were made in reaction to the Prime Minister's statement of policy, which itself left much to be desired in the way of precision and clarity, perhaps little more was to be expected.

Following the Commons debate a group of members representing all parties, along with a number of other prominent Englishmen, issued a manifesto entitled "A Stand Against Aggression." It declared that the British Government must take the lead in rallying all nations which had demonstrated their willingness to abide by their treaty obligations to stand firm and resolute against any further act of aggression, whether in western, central, or eastern Europe. Conspicuous among the signatories were Sir Norman Angell, G. D. H. Cole, Wickham Steed, and Professors Ernest Barker, J. M. Keynes, Gilbert Murray, and Arnold Toynbee.[17] Thus endorsed by men of stature in English intellectual circles—some of whom were not closely associated with any one particular political bias—this manifesto bore testimony that "thinking men" as well as professional politicians were gravely concerned about where the pursuit of appeasement would lead.

The House of Lords, sitting on March 16, reacted only slightly more vigorously to the *Anschluss* than to the Eden-Chamberlain controversy several weeks before. Still, sentiment favoring the revitalization of the League was expressed by Lord Snell, Viscount Sankey, Viscount Cecil of Chelwood, and Lord Strabolgi. The latter, not content to let the matter rest there, declared that the time had come when Britain must say: "Here we fight." The Government should reverse the Chamberlain policy and do everything possible to strengthen resistance to the dictators. The only

17. Other signatories included the following Members of Parliament: the Duchess of Atholl, Vyvyan Adams, R. Acland, Lt.-Cmdr. R. Fletcher, G. Mander, Harold Nicolson, and J. Wedgwood. *The Times,* Mar. 16, 1938. Within this group, Conservative, Labor, and Liberal viewpoints were all represented.

alternative was to try to buy off the aggressors, but "this country was nearly ruined by trying to buy off the Danes a thousand years ago, and we should have no better fortune today."[18]

The *Anschluss* touched off a commotion in the British press which did not quickly subside, and the debate in the Commons on March 14 provided additional material for comment. A few newspapers were satisfied with Chamberlain's statement. The Conservative *Daily Telegraph* (Mar. 15) thought he had been "as firm as the nation would wish him to be." Pursuing an isolationist line, the *Daily Mail* (Mar. 18) proclaimed that under Chamberlain's "vigorous and realistic" leadership Britain had entered a new era of rearmament endeavor and non-entanglement in the affairs of other countries. Though Hitler's action had momentarily shaken *The Times* (Mar. 12) into believing it "more than doubtful whether appeasement is possible in a continent exposed to the visitations of arbitrary force," its confidence had been restored by March 14, when it argued that while no precaution could be deemed irrelevant, the Government would not be deflected from the "broad lines of policy" laid down by the Prime Minister.

A far greater number of newspapers evidenced extreme anxiety about the future. The independent *Glasgow Herald* (Mar. 15) and the Conservative *Financial Times* (Mar. 15) both deplored Chamberlain's vagueness, the former calling for "a firmness which rejects the idea of peace at any price," then (Mar. 18) urging that a line be drawn beyond which the aggressor forces would not be permitted to press, the latter noting that although it was dangerous to make hasty decisions, it was often more dangerous not to make any decisions at all.

More specifically, a system of collective security—such as the Churchillian plan for mutual defense—gained solid support in the press. Denouncing the "smash-and-grab" technique of the dictators, the Liberal Bradford *Yorkshire Observer* (Mar. 15) heartily endorsed Churchill's scheme, asserting (Mar. 17) that the British nation was now ripe for such a plan since few could see any hope of peace in the "drifting sands of ineffective isolation" which appeared to be the Chamberlain-Halifax attitude

18. *Parl. Debs., HL,* March 16, 1938, vol. 108, 132–76.

toward Europe. Of like sentiment were the *Liverpool Daily Post* (Mar. 15) and the Cardiff *Western Mail* (Mar. 15), the latter terming "most tragic" the attempt to renew faith in the integrity of the dictators and induce them to pursue appeasement. Clearly there was only one course for Britain: to intensify rearmament and hasten reform of the League. The independent *Financial News* (Mar. 14) emphasized that British foreign policy must begin all over again. The new departure initiated by Chamberlain had already been "an immediate fiasco." The same newspaper also found it hard to think of any occasion in recent history when the failure of an official policy more obviously called for the resignations of those responsible: "The present is a time for men of realism and determination and not for amiable conversationalists." The *Manchester Guardian* (Mar. 15) believed the British Government could confer a "great service on humanity" if it set out honestly to rebuild a collective system. Chamberlain's policy, it declared (Mar. 18), was compatible with neither national interests nor democracy. The Prime Minister was in fact evading any definition of policy at all, so the Liberal and Labor Parties should take the initiative and head a united campaign for a rebuilt collective system.

With reference to still more precise immediate needs—and with keener insight into the future than was revealed by the Government—some journals openly advocated support for Czechoslovakia against future German aggression. The *Manchester Guardian* (Mar. 18) proposed a strong British warning against any interference in Czech affairs, while the *Financial News* (Mar. 15) contended that the maintenance of Czech independence was the one guarantee against German hegemony in central Europe and the one guarantee, consequently, of the safety of the British Empire. In proclaiming any future undertaking with Germany "worthless and irrelevant," the non-partisan *Spectator* (Mar. 18) intimated that the best service Britain could render to the peace of Europe was to make it clear that if Czechoslovakia were attacked, Britain would stand by her. That view was shared by the radical *New Statesman and Nation* (Mar. 19). The independent *Economist* (Mar. 19) suggested that Britain and France might first discuss with Czechoslovakia the status of the Sudeten German minority, then, having satisfied themselves that justice was being done, say to Hitler: "Hands off! Resort to force at your own peril. We draw the line *here*." It also lent strong support to Churchill's plan. Wickham Steed, writing in the *Contemporary Review,* emphasized the importance of an independent Czechoslovakia to British security: "If Czechoslovakia goes down, we and France shall assuredly be called upon either to submit to Hitler's demands or to fight in what may be a forlorn hope."[19] The *Statist* (Mar. 19), while making no direct reference to Czechoslovakia, recommended a plain statement of British intentions as the greatest deterrent to final disaster, concluding:

> Sectional attempts at appeasement are useless unless the conditions of security exist prior to them. If peace is to be kept it must be organised, and that organisation must now take the form of a military welding together of all States who consider themselves threatened with aggression.

To be sure, these expressions of anxiety for the future, support for a system of mutual defense, and aid for Czechoslovakia should she be the victim of aggression, emanated largely from journals of opposition affiliation or independent sentiment. But they appeared in great number nonetheless and in some organs of considerable influence. The momentary doubts about appeasement expressed by *The Times* on March 12, though quickly subdued, suggest an interesting distinction between candid immediate reaction and more politically-tempered second thoughts. Yet the Conservative press as a whole is difficult to judge on this count since its reaction was not particularly vigorous in any direction, except in deprecating Germany's action. Whether this was more or less calculated, the simple result of indecision, or a reflection of willingness to await a lead from the Prime Minister is hard to say, although the latter two explanations seem more likely.

The threatening international situation alarmed Russia. On March 17 Maxim Litvinov, Commissar for Foreign Affairs,

19. Wickham Steed, "British Interests," *Contemporary Review,* CLIII (April, 1938), 387–88.

released to the press in Moscow a statement declaring Russia's willingness to "commence immediately together with other States in the League of Nations or outside of it the discussion of practical measures called for by the present circumstances." A copy was sent at once to Halifax through Ivan Maisky, the Soviet Ambassador in London. It met with little warmth.[20] Halifax did not acknowledge Maisky's communication until five days later and did not reply until March 24. Then his response was very cool. Assuming the Soviet proposal to mean that arrangements should be made for an immediate discussion among interested powers of practical measures required to check further aggression, the British would welcome an international conference at which all European states would be represented; but a conference attended by only some powers, and designed less to secure the settlement of outstanding problems than to organize concerted action against aggression "would not necessarily, in the view of His Majesty's Government, have such a favourable effect upon the prospects of European peace."[21] The guarded Russian initiative, therefore, died in infancy. And in retrospect, another wave broke in the sea of suspicion which separated Russia from the democracies of the West.

The British press was surprisingly quiet. The silence was broken by a few papers such as the Cardiff *Western Mail* (Mar. 18) which, in an editorial "Russia Invites the Powers," proposed to let the world know that Britain, in cooperation with other states, would not fail to resist further aggression directed against a League member. But the press in general either shared the Government's coolness toward the Russian proposal for one reason or another, suffered from a lack of information about it, or doubted whether so nebulous an approach was worthy of serious consideration. Since later sources are disappointingly silent on the issue, it is difficult to tell which factor was predominant.

Yet support for the idea of collective action had by no means faded. On March 20 the Labor Party concluded in London a

20. Soviet Ambassador in London to Halifax, London, Mar. 17, 1938. *B. D.*, I, 62–64.

21. Halifax to the Soviet Ambassador in London, F. O., Mar. 24, 1938. *Ibid.*, I, 101.

special campaign for "peace and security." At the last of three big meetings Attlee, speaking in the Cambridge Theater, completely denied the validity of Chamberlain's policy. Peace could be maintained only by supporting the League of Nations and being prepared to resist aggression.[22] Several days later the "Council of Action for Peace and Reconstruction" ran an "Eden policy test ballot" in four selected constituencies: Bradford North, Manchester Exchange, Cambridge Borough, and Clapham. In answer to the question, "Do you approve of Mr. Eden's stand for good faith in international affairs and his demand for the re-establishment of peace and security through the League of Nations?", the ratio of "yesses" to "noes" was ten to one.[23]

Chamberlain made an anxiously-awaited statement in the House of Commons on March 24. A masterpiece of obfuscation, it left wholly uncertain the essential issues involved in the new situation in Europe. While it clarified what Britain would not do, it left quite unclear what she might do in certain contingencies. The Prime Minister proclaimed his belief in the League as an effective instrument for preserving peace profoundly shaken, though he conceded that Britain should "nurse it back to health." He quickly dismissed the Soviet proposal for a conference since there could be no expectation that all European powers would be represented and because it envisaged primarily "a concerting of action against an eventuality which has not yet arisen." In regard to Spain, the Government placed "full reliance upon the intentions of the Italian Government to make good their assurances." On the vital question of Czechoslovakia, the Government simply felt unable to make any commitment—although Chamberlain did at length admit, in very guarded phraseology, the probability of Britain's becoming involved should France go to war in honoring her obligations to the Czechs. He also explained, perhaps in an attempt at something constructive, that the fundamental basis of British foreign policy was "the maintenance and preservation of peace and the establishment of a sense of confidence that peace will, in fact, be maintained." But this was far more an aim, both old

22. *The Times,* Mar. 21, 1938.

23. *The Times,* Mar. 24, 1938. In all, 60,000 persons were polled. The basis on which the constituencies were selected is undetermined.

and obvious, than a policy—a distinction which Chamberlain never quite seemed able to make in his own mind.

In the debate which followed Chamberlain was severely criticized for his negative attitude. Particularly distasteful to his critics was the absence of any promise of support for the democratic forces throughout Europe. How could Chamberlain continue negotiation with persons who had shown their belief in force even while the Prime Minister was negotiating with them, Attlee wanted to know? What possible reason was there for placing reliance upon the Italian Government? The Prime Minister showed "amazing credulity," and his policy meant at best "only a postponement of war." Sinclair pursued the case for rallying the peace-loving powers in a system of mutual assistance, and Laborite Major James Milner proposed a definite defensive alliance with all who would join Britain in guaranteeing mutual security.

The inadequacy of the Government's response to the German threat was further exposed by Churchill, who saw Britain attempting "to bridge a 12-foot stream with an 8-foot plank." Britain should make it crystal-clear that if Germany marched on Czechoslovakia without submitting the Sudeten problem to the League or some other body, she would feel committed to join France in resisting that act. Churchill also showed special interest in building up a Danubian bloc, to include Yugoslavia, Rumania, Bulgaria, and possibly Greece and Turkey, as a deterrent on aggressors. Was Britain really going to let these tremendous possibilities fall away without a concerted effort of any kind he asked. If she did not stand up to the dictators now, she would have to do so later under far more adverse conditions.

A group of Labor members then took up the charge. James Griffiths, John McGovern, Arthur Henderson, Ben Riley, and P. J. Noel-Baker each in turn urged that only through a revitalization of the League and a stand behind the "rule of law" could peace be maintained. Britain must act, not drift. She must organize a peace front of all countries outside the Rome-Berlin axis. Riley stated the point concisely: "We have had enough attitude . . . and want more policy."[24] The usual and oft-expressed Labor viewpoint, not especially telling in the eyes of Government sup-

24. *Parl. Debs., HC,* March 24, 1938, vol. 333, 1399–1494.

porters in part because the danger to Britain herself was still far from widely recognized, this appeal nonetheless gave voice to the need for a more positive statement of British policy in the changed circumstances caused by the *Anschluss*.

Disappointment with Chamberlain's statement appeared in the press on March 25. The Bradford *Yorkshire Observer* and the *Financial News* abhorred the absence of any constructive concept of armed collective guarantees among the powers mentioned earlier by Churchill. The *Manchester Guardian* assailed the negative approach to the League, as did the *Economist* (Mar. 26), which ventured to note that if the Prime Minister believed in the virtues of the League half as much as he appeared to believe in the gentlemanliness and honesty of Mussolini, the League would soon be in a very different position. In view of British policy a little more than a year later, the *Economist's* conclusion was noteworthy: "Though the Prime Minister won the day, it does not require a great gift of prophecy to foresee that it is Mr. Churchill's policy that will win the campaign." Though various critical journals chose to emphasize different aspects of Chamberlain's statement, the underlying mood was one of disappointment with the vague and negative character of the Prime Minister's pronouncement.

Disappointment was by no means universal. Duff Cooper, who six months later was to join Churchill and Eden in the dissident Conservative camp, thought it a "great success." Without saying so definitely, the Prime Minister had implied that if France went to war, Britain would go too, and in Duff Cooper's view, it was wiser in the long run to imply this than to state it openly, "for British public opinion was reluctant to accept the unpleasant necessity."[25] In view of France's later surrender of initiative in foreign affairs to Britain, the implication Duff Cooper drew from Chamberlain's remarks was certainly not worth much. This was not yet obvious, at least to most observers, and Duff Cooper's attitude seemed to typify that of the British Government and of many average citizens as well.

25. Duff Cooper, *Old Men Forget*, p. 218.

What had happened to Churchill's "grand alliance"? Chamberlain revealed that in a letter to his sister on March 20:

> The plan of the 'Grand Alliance' as Winston calls it, had occurred to me long before he mentioned it. . . . I talked about it to Halifax and we submitted it to the Chiefs of Staff and F. O. experts. It is a very attractive idea; indeed, there is almost everything to be said for it until you come to examine its practicability. From that moment its attraction vanishes. You have only to look at the map to see that nothing France or we could do could possibly save Czechoslovakia from being overrun by the Germans, if they wanted to do it. . . . I have, therefore, abandoned any idea of giving a guarantee to Czechoslovakia, or the French in connection with her obligations to that country.[26]

The idea of Russian collaboration was either ignored or quickly dismissed.

The British Government and people alike deplored the German occupation of Austria, but at no time was there any demand that Britain go to war, with or without allies, to undo what had been done. Though for several years prior to the *Anschluss* Britain had given Austria assurances of support in her struggle against Hitler,[27] she was in no position to save her in March, 1938. Many Englishmen reasoned that the case against Hitler was not yet cast-iron.[28] Austria was German and many Austrians were whole-

26. Feiling, *Life of Neville Chamberlain,* pp. 347–48.

27. Sir Walford Selby, *Diplomatic Twilight, 1930–1940* (London, 1953), p. 96. Selby had been the British Minister to Vienna before his transfer to Lisbon in October, 1937.

28. Writing in April, 1938, R. B. Mowat claimed that most Englishmen, after the event had occurred, seemed of the opinion that a close union of Germany and the Austrian Germans was inevitable. "The Crisis in Central Europe," *Nineteenth Century,* CXXIII (Apr., 1938), pp. 399–401. As shown earlier, Nevile Henderson openly favored *anschluss.* In fact, during the Nuremburg trials von Neurath testified that Lord Halifax, during his November, 1937, visit to Berchtesgaden, had stated: "People in England would never understand why they should go to war only because two German countries wish to unite." International Military Tribunal, *Trial of the Major War Criminals Before the International Military Tribunal* (Nuremberg, 1948), XVI, 636.

heartedly in favor of union with the Reich. In fact, there were great demonstrations in Austria in Hitler's honor, especially in Vienna where the Führer received, according to an American newspaperman, "the outstanding tribute of his life."[29]

Britain could hardly show herself more Austrian than the Austrians. Furthermore, no support could have been expected from France. When the Germans marched into Vienna, France was actually without a government; Camille Chautemps had resigned on March 10, and the second Leon Blum Cabinet was not formed until three days later.

The German subjugation of Austria was for Britain like the gentle shaking of a soundly sleeping man. While insufficient to awake him, it nevertheless disturbed his slumber; it caused certain of his members to twitch; it even stimulated a bad dream, a subconscious appreciation that the expansion of British defenses must be pushed forward with new energy and that Britain must bear her part in a joint effort to avert a European war. Whether the dream would ultimately end in awakening, or fly in the face of deepening slumber, at the moment none could say.

Churchill testified at the time that it was generally realized now that Britain could play her proper role in European affairs only by strength and not by weakness, by firmness and not by deference.[30] This may have been as much hope as belief. Yet it was in these circumstances that further suspicion was thrown on the practicability of appeasement. And from these circumstances the demand for concerted diplomatic action and firmer policy toward the dictators gradually drew increasing strength. This was certainly not yet in an amount sufficient to have significant impact upon the Government's policy, but in the long run the cumulative effect would be telling.

The effect of the *Anschluss* upon Chamberlain is difficult to assess. He was, apparently, not wholly unaffected by what had happened. He wrote his sister that it was now "perfectly evident" that force was the only argument Germany understood. It was

29. Frederick T. Birchall, *The Storm Breaks* (New York, 1940), p. 286.
30. Winston S. Churchill, *Step by Step, 1936–1939* (New York, 1939), pp. 192–93.

also obvious, he admitted, that force and determination are most effectively mobilized by alliances, adding: "Heaven knows, I don't want to get back to alliances, but if Germany continues to behave as she has done lately, she may drive us to it."[31] Still, Chamberlain was deeply concerned lest for any reason the Germans should get the impression that the British were something less than gracious and understanding, perhaps even sympathetic. The Government even kept a watchful eye on the relations of British corporations with German business, and when one firm (Lewis's) broke off its contacts with some fourteen buyers in various parts of Germany in protest against the *Anschluss,* the head of that company was summoned to 10 Downing Street, told that the Prime Minister strongly disapproved of his action, and informed that he had no right to interfere in this manner in the foreign policy of the country.[32]

In any event, Chamberlain realized that for the moment the idea of conversations with Germany would have to be abandoned, rearmament accelerated, and conversations with Italy quietly and steadily pursued.[33] To the latter task he now directed his attention.

31. Feiling, *Life of Neville Chamberlain,* pp. 341–42.
32. The Earl of Woolton, *The Memoirs of the Rt. Hon. The Earl of Woolton* (London, 1959), pp. 130–32.
33. Feiling, *Life of Neville Chamberlain,* p. 342.

CHAPTER FOUR

Britain, Italy, and Spain (1938)

UNDETERRED BY THE repercussions of Eden's resignation, the British Government proceeded with the Italian conversations. Lord Perth, the ambassador in Rome who was to conduct the talks on the British side, visited London, consulted with Chamberlain, Halifax, and other members of the Cabinet, then returned to Rome on March 6. Official conversations with Count Ciano began two days later.[1]

Significantly, however, Perth announced at the first meeting that British opinion would have to be taken into account in the negotiations. The British people attached great importance to the evacuation of volunteers from Spain, so concrete progress must be made in this regard as soon as possible.[2] This seemed to indicate that the Government was more than a little concerned about the charge, with which both Parliament and the press had rung at the time of Eden's resignation, that there was no basis for belief in Italian good faith—a charge based largely on the continued existence of Italian troops in Spain in spite of Italy's participation in the Non-Intervention Committee.

The Perth-Ciano talks continued for nearly six weeks. Of the eleven points which constituted the agenda,[3] the question of Spain

1. Arnold J. Toynbee, *Survey of International Affairs, 1938* (London, 1941), I, 138–39.

2. Conversation with the British Ambassador, Rome, Mar. 8, 1938. *Ciano's Diplomatic Papers,* p. 188.

3. Spain; confirmation of the Mediterranean agreement of 1937; extension of the articles concerning the status quo in the Mediterranean to other Mediterranean powers; Italian forces in Libya; exchange of military information; naval treaty; Palestine; Syria; Arabia; propaganda; and Abyssinia.

remained most acute. Late in March, Perth produced a memorandum requesting permission for his Government to announce that Italy had renewed her promise to withdraw all volunteers and war materials from Spain at the end of the war. Such a statement, it was believed, would help to dispel the distrust which many Members of Parliament felt toward Italy and would create an atmosphere favorable to the conclusion of an Anglo-Italian agreement.[4]

This memorandum probably was prompted by the debate in the Commons on March 16, in which the Government's policy of appeasement was obliquely attacked through acid criticism of its pursuance of non-intervention in Spain. Six members of the Labor-Liberal Opposition (Attlee, Sinclair, James Maxton, Frederick Seymour Cocks, Harold Nicolson, and Arthur Greenwood) had let loose with unusual bitterness, denouncing non-intervention as a "farce" and a "sham." While Britain assiduously adhered to non-intervention, Italy contemptuously supplied troops and materials to the Nationalist side. While Chamberlain held out the hand of friendship to Italy, Maxton complained, he was being "kicked right in the solar plexus." Seymour Cocks took up the strain: "This is the first time in English history that an English Prime Minister has had . . . to send his Ambassador to lay a wreath on the tomb of the Unknown Pirate." Greenwood thought the Prime Minister was "clucking like a bewildered hen trying to cross a busy road"; his only policy was "kiss and be friends."

These were hardly terms calculated to win supporters from the Government but they could provide sufficient irritation to make the Government squirm, and that, in the circumstances, was about all that Labor could hope to accomplish. Chamberlain, of course, held firmly to non-intervention, believing the fact that war had

4. Conversation with the British Ambassador, Rome, Mar. 26, 1938. *Ciano's Diplomatic Papers,* pp. 197–98. Despite the terms of Perth's request, Britain had not withdrawn her demand for a "proportional evacuation" of Italian troops from Spain during the war. In fact, provision for such evacuation formed an integral part of the Anglo-Italian Agreement signed three weeks later. See P. A. M. van der Esch, *Prelude to War: The International Repercussions of the Spanish Civil War (1936–1939)* (The Hague, 1951), pp. 130–31. What Perth apparently wanted in this instance was assurance that Italy would not try to exert political influence in Spain after the war.

not spread beyond Spain a "remarkable tribute" to that policy[5]—a position which sheds much light on the Government's criteria for judging the British non-intervention policy successful.

Though the British memorandum made no mention of it, the validity of non-intervention was undergoing serious questioning in many sections of the British press also, and not only in Opposition journals. The independent *Glasgow Herald* (Mar. 17) foresaw that if the situation in Spain continued unchanged, some effort to redress the balance of military power there might become necessary. If the "external dictators" plundered Spain as they had Austria, observed the Unionist Cardiff *Western Mail* (Mar. 17), Britain would have no choice but to resort to drastic counter-intervention. In language wholly unreserved, the Liberal *Manchester Guardian* (Mar. 16) proclaimed: "The least that could be done is to confess that non-intervention is a criminal pretence and should immediately be abandoned." In like manner, the independent *Economist* (Mar. 12) and the radical *New Statesman and Nation* (Mar. 19) spelled out their belief in the naivety of British non-intervention in Spain when Italy's aim of aggrandizement in the western Mediterranean was clear to all who would open their eyes. This latter view found clear expression in the non-partisan *Spectator* (Apr. 2), which charged Chamberlain and Halifax with trying the "Nelson touch"—putting their spy-glasses up to their blind eyes whenever compelled to train them on Italy's activities in Spain. It also drew support from a rash of signed articles in the periodical press, including those by Air-Commodore L. E. Charlton in the *Fortnightly*[6]; Robert Dell, who felt an agreement with Mussolini "not worth the ink on which it is written," in the *New Statesman and Nation*[7]; and Maxwell Garnett (Secretary of the League of Nations Union), who argued in the *Contemporary Review* that promises without guarantees of fulfillment were all that Britain could be sure of obtaining "in return for

5. *Parl. Debs., HC,* March 16, 1938, vol. 333, 491–537.

6. Air-Commodore L. E. Charlton, "The Mischief in the Mediterranean," *Fortnightly,* CXLIX (March, 1938), 282–90.

7. Robert Dell, "Abyssinia Unconquered," *New Statesman and Nation,* XV (April 9, 1938), 597–98.

Danegeld."[8] Once again critics of various hues chose to emphasize different aspects of non-intervention, but the basic implication was the same: was it not ridiculous for Britain to proceed with the projected appeasement of Italy when the Italian violation of her pledged word in Spain was so obvious for all to see?

When foreign affairs occupied the House of Lords on March 29, Lord Snell, Viscount Cecil, and Lord Strabolgi, three constant critics of the Government's policy, opened fire again. Strabolgi warned that a victorious Franco regime in Spain was a "terrible gamble" for Britain in view of the likelihood that it would need foreign help to hold the country if it did win. Halifax replied only that to scrap the non-intervention policy would be doing "something very dangerous" to European peace.[9]

At the instigation of Arthur Greenwood, who moved a vote of censure, the Commons again echoed with criticism on April 4. To sacrifice liberty was not the way to peace, nor could peace "be bought at Woolworth's," Greenwood bitterly observed. The Soviets had proposed a union of non-Fascist powers against aggression, Cordell Hull had declared the faith of the United States in law, order, and justice, but Britain remained silent on the big issues of the day—"the Prime Minister is too busy with Signor Mussolini." What was an alliance with Italy worth anyway? In his own defense, Chamberlain argued that his policy had won the approval of the entire country, possibly even of the whole world. This suggestion carried little weight with the Opposition. Sinclair and six Labor members followed Greenwood's lead, all clamoring for a return to the policy of the League and denying there could be any value whatever in an agreement with Italy. Two speakers loathed the Prime Minister's "childlike, implicit confidence in the dictators." But when the House divided on Greenwood's motion, Chamberlain's overwhelming majority remained intact: ayes, 152; noes, 359.[10]

In referring to this vote, the *Manchester Guardian* (Apr. 5)

8. Maxwell Garnett, "The Future of the League," *Contemporary Review,* CLIII (April, 1938), 404–07.

9. *Parl. Debs., HL,* March 29, 1938, vol. 108, 436–77.

10. *Parl. Debs., HC,* April 4, 1938, vol. 334, 39–156.

asked rather sardonically: "Since when has the capacity of the Tory party in the House to stick together . . . proved anything about the mind of the country?" While this question smacked of "sour grapes," it is likely that the unimpaired majority which followed the Government did not reflect similarly overwhelming support for the Government's policy throughout the country. Quite clearly, in fact, many people were profoundly disturbed by its implications, though most of them not to the point of voting the Labor Party into power.

Yet there occurred at this juncture an event heartening to the Labor Opposition. In early April a by-election in traditionally Conservative West Fulham produced a thousand-vote Labor victory, whereas in the previous election there the Conservatives had gained a 3,483 vote majority.[11] Foreign policy had been a major issue; during the campaign Chamberlain had endorsed the Conservative candidate in a public letter which focused attention on the Government's foreign policy. Indeed, partly as a result of this, the election had attracted nation-wide interest and was closely watched by leaders of both parties. The result was, of course, variously interpreted both by party officials and in the press. The Opposition hailed it as a clear-cut victory with significant foreign policy implications; the Conservatives dismissed it as "indecisive." Yet insofar as any by-election is fought on a single major issue and the outcome implies a perceptible change in one direction or another, the West Fulham vote was anything but comforting to the Chamberlain Government.

The completed Anglo-Italian Agreement was signed by Ciano and Perth at Rome on April 16. Covering the wide range of interest conflicts between the two countries, it gave Italy a free hand in Abyssinia and in effect Spain, in return for the imponderable value of Italian good will in central Europe. Both countries disclaimed any desire to modify the status quo in the Mediterranean. The agreement was to take effect on such a date as the two Governments should determine, its coming into force to depend on the fulfillment of two conditions: the recognition of Italy's Abyssinian empire by Britain, and the clarification of Italy's attitude toward Spain (a "settlement of the Spanish ques-

11. *The Times*, Apr. 7, 1938.

tion" as it came to be called).[12] While Chamberlain earlier had rejected Eden's view that some positive Italian act in the form of a withdrawal of Italian troops from Spain ought to precede the opening of Anglo-Italian negotiations, he was nevertheless a sufficiently good "Edenite" to insist that the agreement must remain in suspense until a "settlement of the Spanish question" had been reached.

Foreign Office officials were skeptical of the whole transaction. "You should have seen the draft [of the agreement] put to me by the F. O.," Chamberlain wrote in a private letter; "it would have frozen a Polar bear."[13] Churchill and Eden shared these misgivings.[14] The German Government, on the other hand, fully informed by Italy, hailed the agreement as a product of Chamberlain's "realism." Germany stood to gain by the lessened danger of being drawn into a war by Italy. Far more important, Britain had abandoned the doctrine of non-recognition of conquests made by force of arms.[15]

The British press gave a varied reception to the Anglo-Italian Agreement. The Conservative *Sunday Times* (Apr. 17) regarded it "a most auspicious beginning" for the policy of appeasement. The pro-Government *Times* (Apr. 18), though recognizing the importance of a settlement in Spain, was pleased with "the new atmosphere of confidence and good will." While admitting that everything depended on the spirit in which the agreement was carried out, the Conservative *Daily Telegraph* (Apr. 18) termed it "a good augury for peace"; even if it failed it was a worthwhile experiment. Tribute was paid to Chamberlain's "tenacity and realism" by the Conservative *Daily Mail* (Apr. 18). The Cardiff *Western Mail* (Apr. 18) saw in the agreement the hope of restoring mutual confidence and ending years of distrust; the result justified Chamberlain's confidence. The independent *Observer* (Apr. 17) was most enthusiastic, calling the agreement "a first

12. Great Britain. *Agreement Between the United Kingdom and Italy, Consisting of a Protocol with Annexes and Exchange of Notes, Rome, April 16, 1938.* Command Paper 5726 (London, 1938).

13. Feiling, *Life of Neville Chamberlain*, p. 350.

14. Churchill, *The Gathering Storm*, pp. 283–84.

15. The German Foreign Ministry to the German Legation in Czechoslovakia, Berlin, Apr. 19, 1938; Unsigned Memorandum, Apr. 27, 1938. *G. D.*, I, 1079–80, 1100–01.

big step towards European reconciliation." Its beneficent range was unlimited. "The nightmare is past. . . . Goodwill, common sense, and hard diplomacy have at last undone the historic blunder" (sanctions on Italy in 1935).

Some journals assumed an attitude of limited hope. The Liberal *Liverpool Daily Post* (Apr. 18) conceded that if the agreement made a substantial contribution to the large purpose Chamberlain had in view, it could be accepted with reasonably good grace despite its unpleasant implications. "A treaty in suspense" was the description propounded by the *Glasgow Herald* (Apr. 18); the bargain with Italy seemed good, "but some will prefer to wait till they are quite sure it is true before indulging in immoderate jubilation." The Liberal Bradford *Yorkshire Observer* (Apr. 18) considered it a document of promise rather than fulfillment, to be welcomed for what it was and not made to carry exaggerated expectations.

Unlimited condemnation emanated from other newspapers. To the *Manchester Guardian* (Apr. 18) the agreement marked Britain's decision to return to pre-war, pre-League diplomacy, where policy had nothing to do with right and wrong, but only with expediency. Chamberlain had achieved a momentary lessening of Anglo-Italian friction, but at the expense of other countries. The Labor *Daily Herald* (Apr. 18) struck a similar chord. Chamberlain had sealed the betrayal of Abyssinia and Spain and had struck another blow at the League. All he had obtained was the friendship of Mussolini—"a man who has betrayed friends and causes unhesitatingly whenever it served his purpose or his ambition." The agreement condoned aggression in Abyssinia and Spain, lamented the Liberal *News Chronicle* (Apr. 18). What existed was an armistice, not peace, and it could be followed by friendship only after Italy had given proof of good faith by sustained good actions. Similar sentiments were echoed in the *Economist* (Apr. 23) and the *New Statesman and Nation* (Apr. 23) which, like the *Manchester Guardian,* pursued the argument that the agreement marked a rejection of the concept of international justice and an unashamed return to power politics. For the *Fortnightly* (Apr.) the agreement merely lighted up the chasm of humiliation into which Britain had fallen. By dislodging the

"Eden boulder," Chamberlain had set in motion a "long, perilously poised avalanche."

There had been very little shift in opinion on this issue since the occasion of Eden's resignation. Those organs which had favored Chamberlain's initiative then supported the newly-signed agreement; those which had opposed the Chamberlain position earlier criticized the agreement; those which had fallen somewhere in the neutral "let's wait and see" category continued in that position. The three categories were composed mainly of Conservative and a few independent journals; Labor, Liberal, and some independent journals; and some Liberal and independent papers respectively. In short, party lines were still followed rather assiduously.

That there was little change of position is not surprising. The issue in April was essentially the same as that in February; it was simply a matter of translating a stated policy into practice. What had happened on the international scene had had the effect of encouraging those who favored the approach to Italy. Was this not the opportunity, in view of Italy's surprised and adverse reaction to the *Anschluss,* to seek to detach Mussolini from the Axis?—a possibility which Chamberlain seems to have contemplated for some time.

It is noteworthy that many of the journals which either accepted the agreement or did not openly reject it, gave it only qualified approval. Much remained to be ascertained about Italy's behavior, and final judgment on the treaty must be postponed accordingly. This sort of reservation was not unnatural, but it might be taken to suggest that the circle of skeptics was widening, albeit very slowly and cautiously.

Anti-Government sentiment found an additional outlet in Queen's Hall, London, April 23, when eighteen hundred delegates "of all classes and parties" (so the *Manchester Guardian* reported) met in a "National Emergency Conference" to condemn the Government's Spanish policy. Professor Gilbert Murray addressed the group and, with particular reference to the recently signed agreement, damned the notion that "the land which once held the Mother of Parliaments" had come to such a pass that it could complacently disregard the destruction of a democratic Parliament in a friendly country [Spain] and try to derive some temporary profit from the disaster.[16]

Not until two weeks after the signing of the Anglo-Italian Agreement did the House of Commons, having been recessed for Easter, meet to consider the pact. In his motion for approval, Chamberlain optimistically asserted that the clouds of mistrust and suspicion between Britain and Italy had already cleared away. Explaining that full effect would not be given to the agreement until Britain could regard the Spanish question as settled and found herself, consequently, in a position to recognize the Italian conquest of Abyssinia, he was at once interrupted by Attlee, who demanded a definition of "a settlement" in Spain. Chamberlain preferred not to give a definition, for "at this stage it would be wrong to try to define the circumstances in which one could say that a settlement had been arrived at." Much disturbed, Attlee retorted:

> The right honorable Gentleman is asking the House to approve a treaty that is to come into force on the specific terms that there should be a settlement in Spain, and now he says that he cannot tell the House what a settlement is. It is ridiculous. The House is entitled to know.

Ignoring Attlee's outburst, Chamberlain went on to claim, somewhat vainly, that the world had received the agreement with an "almost universal chorus of praise." For Italy and Britain it marked "the beginning of a new Era."[17]

Labor did not share the Prime Minister's optimism. Herbert Morrison made this quite explicit when he blasted Chamberlain as an "admirer of the Mussolini regime with all its tyranny, murders and assassinations," and moved an amendment to Chamberlain's motion:

> This House cannot approve an agreement made with a state actively engaged in wanton aggression in Spain, which in exchange for illusory promises sacrifices the people of Abyssinia, violates the spirit of the Covenant of the League

16. *Manchester Guardian,* Apr. 25, 1938.
17. *Parl. Debs., HC,* May 2, 1938, vol. 335, 533–45.

> of Nations, and substitutes for the principle of collective security a policy of alliances and armament rivalries which so far from bringing general appeasement will intensify the danger of world war.

The Prime Minister had been forced to make an agreement, Morrison charged; to have failed to do so would have ruined him politically.[18]

Sir Archibald Sinclair, always an ardent Chamberlain critic, was on this occasion more vehement than usual. What was the settlement in Spain going to be, he asked—"whatever Mussolini and Hitler are able to impose upon the Spanish people?" Britain was always restraining someone in order to keep peace, but the people she restrained were always the victims of aggression. If the agreement were ratified, he concluded, Britain will have sold Spain and the Mediterranean to Mussolini and Hitler.

Lloyd George then took up the attack. Is the Prime Minister actually going to recognize "this theft, this robbery, this piratical enterprise" in Abyssinia, he asked incredulously, and even in the name of general appeasement? Chamberlain said tension had been relieved? Where? All Europe resounded with talk of war. This "abject, dishonourable, cowardly surrender" to Italy would only strengthen Germany's conviction that Britain would not fight. Until Britain had a government that would make it quite clear where it would make a stand, there would be no peace in Europe.

The Duchess of Atholl, flanked by Laborites F. J. Bellenger and John McGovern, pursued the matter further. She protested Chamberlain's continuance of negotiations while possessing information indicating the arrival of Italian and German reinforcements in Spain throughout February, March, and early April. That he was aware of this she was certain—she had sent him the information. Waxing more prophetic than he perhaps realized,

18. *Ibid.*, vol. 335, 546–61. Exaggerated as the latter charge might seem, a Halifax conversation with Joseph Kennedy a month before had underscored the same point. "Halifax realizes, and said so," Kennedy reported to Washington, "that Britain must bring in successful negotiation with Italy to save their political faces. . . ." Kennedy to the Secretary of State, London, Mar. 23, 1938. *U.S. For. Rel.*, 1938 I, 40.

McGovern pronounced war a certainty, whether "this year or next year." If Chamberlain believed the word of Mussolini, he "is about the only responsible man I know in this country who does."

Before the debate closed, Attlee again pressed for a definition of "a settlement" in Spain, charging that in refusing to tell what he meant by the term, the Prime Minister was treating the House "with a contempt which is absolutely unparalleled." But the division made it evident that the Opposition's vigorous censure had gone for naught. Morrison's amendment was defeated 110 to 332; Chamberlain's motion prevailed 316 to 108.[19]

The conditional signing of the Anglo-Italian Agreement was thereby endorsed by the Commons. It is a notable fact that even in those circles where Chamberlain's policy was strongly approved, there was no great elation. The Government's intention to recognize, even though on conditions, Italian sovereignty over Abyssinia seemed to set the seal on Italy's diplomatic victory over Britain in the struggle of recent years. Even most appeasers, if the realists they claimed to be, could not be purblind to diplomatic defeat. And the vigor with which the Labor Opposition rubbed salt into this wound could not help but make it more painful.

In accordance with the promise made to Italy in the Anglo-Italian Agreement, the British Government sent a note to the Secretary-General of the League of Nations on April 9, 1938, requesting that the matter of according *de jure* recognition of Italian sovereignty over Abyssinia be placed on the agenda of the forthcoming meeting of the Council. Technically, it sought clarification of the "anomalous situation" arising from the fact that some League members, including five of the states represented on the Council (Belgium, Ecuador, Latvia, Poland, and Rumania), had already recognized Italian sovereignty or had taken action implying recognition, whereas other League members had not done so.[20]

19. *Parl. Debs., HC,* May 2, 1938, vol. 335, 533–666.
20. Letter, Dated April 9, 1938, From the United Kingdom Government

The Council met at Geneva on May 9. The Abyssinian question came into the open three days later, when Halifax proposed that the recognition of "Italy's position in Ethiopia" be considered by the Council as "one which every member of the League must be held entitled to decide for itself in the light of its own situation and its own obligations." He carefully explained that the British Government did not approve the method by which the Italian position in Abyssinia had been obtained, nor did it abandon in any way the principles of the League. But, he argued in a manner both illogical and vain, the greatest end which the League existed to serve was peace, and, assuming that the course he advocated would serve the cause of peace, it involved no question of principle. The Council was, he admitted, on the horns of a moral dilemma, but where the ideal of devotion to some high purpose conflicted with a practical victory for peace, the latter, in his view, was the stronger claim.[21]

Emperor Haile Selassie was given a chance to state Abyssinia's case; then the representatives of France, Russia, Rumania, Poland, Sweden, Belgium, Peru, China, New Zealand, Ecuador, Bolivia, and Iran aired their views—Russia, China, New Zealand, and Bolivia supporting Abyssinia, the others upholding Great Britain. The chairman of the Council, Vilhelms Munters of Latvia, at length observed that no formal decision had been requested. Yet on the showing of the debate, it was his opinion that "a great majority of the members of the Council considered that it lay with the divers members of the League to decide on their attitude individually in the light of their own situation and obligations."[22]

The avoidance of a formal decision at Geneva did not diminish the effect of what had happened there. Britain had freed herself, and all the other members of the League, to recognize Italian sovereignty over Abyssinia whenever she chose—and this with reference only to what was expedient. The action was the subject of much comment in the British press. Even before the debate

---

to the Secretary-General, London, Apr. 9, 1938. *League of Nations, Official Journal, 1938* (London, 1938), XIX, pt. 1, 535.

21. *Ibid.*, XIX, pt. 1, 333–35.

22. *Ibid.*, XIX, pt. 1, 335–47.

in the Council the *Daily Mail* (May 10) referred to Britain's "common-sense move which has been dictated by hard facts." *The Times* (May 13) took as its own the arguments used by Halifax: "a practical step towards a wider settlement is more valuable than a vain idealism which refuses to face facts." In a rather reluctant display of "realism," the Cardiff *Western Mail* (May 10, 13), the *Liverpool Daily Post* (May 10), and the *Glasgow Herald* (May 11) agreed that the proceedings at Geneva were distasteful, but it was perhaps wise to liquidate a failure that could not conceivably be retrieved. The Bradford *Yorkshire Observer* (May 10) settled for a reference to Britain's "humiliating position."

Other journals heaped unqualified abuse on the Government's action. Britain was back again with the pre-League mind in the pre-war era, snapped the *Manchester Guardian* (May 9), back to the time when the great powers maneuvered unceasingly for position and those who could not protect themselves by their own arm went to the wall. For reasons of political expediency the Government was determined to break its pledges and to violate the law of the League to which it still professed adherence, charged the *Daily Herald* (May 13). It labeled as "fantastic" the claim that the betrayal of Abyssinia and the Covenant was a "practical victory for peace," adding: to the "big crimes of our times" the Government meant to be blind, and it was inviting the other League states to emulate its blindness. The *Spectator* (May 20) and the *New Statesman and Nation* (May 14) contended that history could show, in the words of the latter, "few more shameful, or more ominous spectacles" than the meeting of the League Council. The *Economist* (May 21) described "taking the sense of the meeting" as a strange inversion of the constitution of the League to circumvent the unanimity rule. The critical journals were again those which usually attacked the Chamberlain policy, but the point of their thrust, emphasizing as it did a kind of moral debasement, must have stung all but the most insensitive Conservatives.

The British action at Geneva did not provoke a full-fledged debate in the Commons, but it certainly did not go unnoticed. On May 18 Arthur Henderson voiced his conviction that Britain had "inflicted the greatest humiliation on the League since its inception. . . . Never was there a greater betrayal of moral and legal responsibility." Then digressing momentarily from the principle involved, he claimed that Italy's conquest of Abyssinia was far from effective, and challenged the Government to produce conclusive proof that it was. How then could the Italian Government be entitled to recognition as the *de jure* government?[23]

Next day Wedgwood Benn (Labor) took up where Henderson had left off, reiterating that the Government had made no effort to determine whether Italy was in complete control of Abyssinia. He doubted the value of Italy's word: "The history of the Great War is a sharp reminder of how the Italians decide on great issues at critical moments." It was a "rather curious thing," he aptly observed, that in negotiations with Italy the two moments at which the Italian Government had shown the most active spirit of cooperation were not the times when the British Prime Minister was writing affectionate letters to the Duce, but when the British and French Governments met at Nyon and when the swastika appeared at the Brenner Pass. Wedgwood Benn received warm support from Ellen Wilkinson (Labor), who had attended the meeting of the League Council. In her view, Halifax had gone there with the distinct purpose of making League machinery do something it was never meant to do: sanction what was really an "old-fashioned imperialist deal." It was in Britain's moral leadership that her greatest contribution to collective peace lay, but the Government had now discarded that priceless asset for nothing.[24]

Although the issue had long since been decided, the Opposition took one more jab at the Genevan action on May 20, when P. J. Noel-Baker (Labor) told the Commons that he had never seen anything "so half-hearted, so tepid, so frigid" as the reception given the Anglo-Italian Agreement there. It certainly was not approved in the legal sense, and hardly in the moral sense either. Most distressing was the fact that Britain had failed to use this

23. *Parl. Debs., HC,* May 18, 1938, vol. 336, 502–12. R. A. Butler, the Under-Secretary of State, replied that Henderson's information was simply incorrect; the Italians were in virtually complete control of Abyssinia.

24. *Ibid.,* May 19, 1938, vol. 336, 704–20.

opportunity to strike a blow for the maintenance of international law by recognizing that non-intervention in Spain should not be continued and that there was now an overwhelming case for giving the Spanish Government its rights under international law to purchase arms.[25] This kind of criticism was too rambling, ill-timed, and obtuse to be particularly effective, but the Labor Opposition lost no opportunity to express its real dissatisfaction with the Chamberlain foreign policy.

British policy toward Italy was subjected to further criticism in the House of Lords on May 18. Lord Snell described millions of British people as "perplexed and humiliated by the unrighteous compacts and by the un-English devices by which we are attempting to secure temporary respite from threats and from acts of aggression." Is every crime to be tested by its success? he asked. "Is the burglar to be recognized because he has gotten away with the swag?" Referring to Abraham Lincoln's "House Divided" speech, and substituting totalitarian and free for slave and free, the Lord Bishop of Durham postulated that unless "this conflict of fundamental idiosyncrasies, this dissidence in the elementary rights of our civilised world" could be exorcised, "our civilisation will have to become totalitarian or remain free." By conceding now this point and now that the immediate conflict could be postponed, thereby only making it certain that when the inevitable strife did at last occur, the strategic points would all have been conceded to the adversaries, thus ensuring the destruction of free civilization. Addressing the Lords as "practical people looking coldly at the world and weighing facts calmly in the scales of reason," was it reasonable to trust the words of the dictators, he asked.

The Marquess of Crewe, Viscount Cecil, and Lord Strabolgi joined in these critical sentiments. They were concerned mainly with two points: doubt as to whether Italy's occupation of Abyssinia was complete or effective, and still graver doubt as to the value of Mussolini's word. It was still not too late, they believed, to use the machinery of the League, not for encircling one nation or dividing Europe into two camps of differing ideologies, but

25. *Ibid.*, May 20, 1938, vol. 336, 778–89.

in trying to form a league of friendly states who believed in and were willing to stand for the same things as Britain. Halifax's response was a long defense of the Government's policy utilizing the usual argument: the action Britain had taken was a step toward peace.[26]

It is obvious by this point that in the Lords' debates the criticism of Government policy emanated in the main from three or four peers, Snell, Cecil, and Strabolgi among them. This may well be taken to mean that, while the volume of criticism seemed great, it represented the views of only a handful of peers. On the other hand, few debates in the Lords stimulated wide popular participation, and in view of the frequent absence of enthusiasm in the remarks of Government supporters, as well as the tendency of at least a few peers to look to Snell (a former Labor M. P. and a member of the Council of the Royal Institute of International Affairs), Cecil (one-time Conservative M. P. and champion of the League), and Strabolgi (Opposition Chief Whip) to vocalize their particular point of view, the criticisms of these three are not to be dismissed lightly. In any event, they gave testimony to the fact that there *was* an opposing point of view, a definite and distinct one, even though perhaps not widely held.

Two influential newspapers commented on the course of the debate in the Lords, and their views were diametrically opposed. The Conservative *Daily Telegraph* (May 20) saw the real division between Halifax and his critics to be that the latter, in misapplied loyalty to the League, wanted to resort to measures which would jeopardize peace, the one thing which the League existed to promote. "Policy must consent to adapt means to ends, and not persist with means which would only frustrate ends." The Liberal *News Chronicle* (May 20) could see in Halifax's speech only one useful purpose: it revealed the object of the Government's policy—"peace at any price." Disastrous as war might be, there were things more disastrous for civilization. To yield continually to foreign pressure until Britain's liberties were suppressed, her democratic institutions uprooted, her native culture supplanted, her self-respect gone—and gone without a blow

26. *Parl. Debs., HL,* May 18, 1938, vol. 109, 108–216.

being struck—that was a far worse disaster than war. But that was the philosophy which inspired the Government's policy.

This difference of opinion between two great newspapers points up the essential question which divided the Government from its critics on this issue. It was the age-old query: does the end justify the means? In the light of its action at Geneva, and the defense of that action as stated officially by its spokesmen, the Government obviously cast its vote "yes"; the Opposition chose to take the other view. In looking back, the Government seems to have had the weaker position, especially since there existed little tangible evidence to suggest that the means it used would necessarily result in the end it sought. Yet most Englishmen, outside the ranks of the usual critics, seemed to accept the Government's action, certainly not with enthusiasm, but as unpleasant practical necessity. Some would say this made them "realists"; others are led to the distressing conclusion that even the most principled of peoples, in certain contingencies and especially when ill-informed, subvert their ideals to the hope of more tangible immediate gain. Nevertheless, the effect of this harrowing moral question on the minds of those who accepted the less idealistic course as unpleasant realism necessarily weighed heavily in the "fury of patient men" who, some months later, found their hopes dashed by the course of European events.

After Halifax's success at Geneva, it appeared that only a settlement in Spain remained in the way of final accord between London and Rome. But Mussolini, speaking at Genoa on May 14, did not appear duly grateful. In a speech calculated to soothe any German sensitiveness over the signing of the Anglo-Italian Agreement[27] and to assert Italo-German solidarity following Hitler's recent visit to Rome (May 2-7), the Duce extolled the collaboration between the Nazi and Fascist revolutions, which

27. When the Italian Ambassador in Berlin transmitted a copy of the Anglo-Italian Agreement to the German Foreign Office on April 16, he included a draft of this speech, the obvious intent being to forestall German sensitiveness. Minute (Weizsäcker), Berlin, Apr. 16, 1938. *G. D.*, I, 1074–75.

were "destined to leave their imprint on this century." He referred to the sanctions of 1935–1936, "which we have not yet forgotten." In speaking of the agreement with Britain, he observed that "the last speech pronounced by the British Prime Minister[28] was an attempt to escape from the tangle of commonplaces and to recognize Fascist Italy in all its majesty and might." Finally, he blatantly voiced the Italian hope for a Franco victory in Spain, threatening that if the "so-called great democracies" were really preparing an ideological war, the totalitarian states would "immediately form a bloc and march together to the end."[29]

This was hardly an auspicious beginning for the "new era" of Anglo-Italian friendship of which Chamberlain had recently spoken. As Kingsley Griffith (Liberal) remarked in the Commons on May 19: " 'We have not forgotten sanctions' was a rather curious way of showing how much [Mussolini's] heart had been won over to friendship for the British people. He has not forgotten sanctions, but we are supposed to have forgotten the occasion for sanctions."[30] The British Government did, in time, mildly protest Mussolini's outburst, Lord Perth conveying to Ciano on May 18 a message notable for its reference to Chamberlain's critics:

> The British Government now felt it its duty to let it be known that the expressions used by the Duce were not those which had been expected in London. . . . It must not be forgotten that Chamberlain has encountered very serious parliamentary difficulties in order to bring about the agreement with Italy and that even today the opposition has not been disbanded.[31]

Mussolini's attitude was sufficient to hinder the fulfillment of the second condition for the entry into force of the April agreement—a settlement of the Spanish problem. Nevertheless, by

28. Presumably Chamberlain's May 2 speech in the Commons. See above pp. 74–5.
29. *New York Times,* May 15, 1938.
30. *Parl. Debs., HC,* May 19, 1938, vol. 336, 715.
31. Conversation with the British Ambassador, Rome, May 18, 1938. *Ciano's Diplomatic Papers,* p. 217.

early June, Ciano was insisting that Italy had fully met her obligations under the agreement and that all conditions for its operation had been fulfilled. Troops were being withdrawn from Libya, propaganda in regard to Arabia had been discontinued, and Italy had long since accepted the British proposal for the withdrawal of volunteers from Spain in the Non-Intervention Committee. On the other hand, Britain was now free from her obligations to Geneva on the question of Abyssinia.[32]

Yet the British still regarded the definition of a settlement in Spain as the one remaining obstacle. And the Government felt compelled to proceed cautiously, an official British note of June 20 explained, in consideration of British public opinion. The bombings of the last two weeks had produced an especially unfavorable reaction. The Government, therefore, could not consider as a settlement Italy's acceptance of the British plan in the Non-Intervention Committee. Rather, three alternatives existed: execution of the plan; the unilateral withdrawal of Italian volunteers based on the Italian acceptance of the plan; or the arrangement of an armistice in Spain. Ciano and Mussolini dismissed the first and third alternatives as "impractical," the second as "out of the question."[33]

The bombings referred to in the British note, and the consequent British action—or inaction—they evoked, were a major bone of contention between the British Government and its critics throughout the summer of 1938. Since the outset of the Spanish war, non-Spanish ships which called at Spanish ports to unload their cargoes had been liable to suffer damage during air raids. Beginning in early 1938, the Nationalists, who held superiority in the air, concentrated their attacks upon the harbor areas in Republican ports, presumably in the hope of frightening away foreign ships, thus cutting off the importation of essential supplies by their opponents. Despite Eden's warning in early February that the British Government could not continue to deal with such attacks on British ships solely by protests and claims for compensation, and that it reserved the right to take appropriate

32. The German Ambassador in Italy to the German Foreign Ministry, Rome, June 22, 1938. *G. D.*, I, 1138.

33. *Ibid.*, I, 1138–39.

retaliatory action,[34] the Nationalist campaign increased in intensity. By June scarcely a day passed without a report of damage suffered by some ship flying the British flag in a Spanish port.[35]

It was a generally accepted fact, acknowledged by the British Government, that most of the planes involved in these attacks, as well as their crews, were Italian. This was a serious impediment to the attempt to bring the Anglo-Italian Agreement into force, both because it prohibited any "settlement" of the Spanish question, and because of the violent protest against the Government's policy of non-intervention and inaction which it provoked in Parliament and in the press. How could the Government contemplate bringing the agreement with Italy into force when British ships were being sunk and the lives of British sailors were being taken by Italian airmen? For the sake of appeasement the Government was dealing with violent attacks on British lives and property by means of peaceable protests. To many Englishmen this was intolerable.

Led by the Labor and Liberal newspapers, including the influential *Manchester Guardian, Daily Herald,* and *News Chronicle,* as well as the independent weeklies, the *Economist* and the *New Statesman and Nation,* the protest against the bombing of British ships and the demand for positive action on the part of the British Government became very heated in all sections of the press in June and July, 1938. Indicative of the intensity of feeling were the comments of several papers which normally were pro-Government and which just two months before had been among those giving staunchest support to the Anglo-Italian Agreement. The *Daily Mail* (June 13) asserted: "The public demand strong and vigorous measures to put an end to assaults on British property and the lives of British sailors." The *Daily Telegraph* (June 6) declared: "It is surely to the interest of all civilised nations to bring the atrocity of indiscriminate aerial bombardment to an end." Even *The Times* (June 10) admitted that "public opinion

34. *Parl. Debs., HC,* February 7, 1938, vol. 331, 659.

35. Toynbee, *Survey of International Affairs, 1938,* I, 368–69. Chamberlain told the Commons on June 14 that between mid-April and mid-June, twenty-two British-owned ships were involved in air attacks on Spanish ports, eleven of which were either sunk or seriously damaged. *Parl. Debs., HC,* June 14, 1938, vol. 337, 42.

is much exercised at this growing abuse of airpower." Apparently there were definite limits to appeasement after all, even in the eyes of these Conservative journals, and all the more so when British property, British lives, and British vital interests were directly affected.

In the House of Commons during the same period (June–July) the critics multiplied their attacks and questions and constantly demanded effective reprisals.

The Government was well aware of public sentiment. Alexander Cadogan, the Permanent Under-Secretary for Foreign Affairs, told the American Ambassador, Joseph Kennedy, that he situation had the Cabinet "almost distracted" and frankly "up against it." British shippers were crying for protection; the country was beginning to feel that the Government was "not courageous" and that Britain's great prestige was rapidly diminishing.[36] Nevertheless, the Government came to the conclusion that there was little or nothing it could do to meet the demands of shipowners and the public at large for the protection of British ships from the Spanish Nationalist campaign.

Chamberlain defined the Government's attitude in the Commons on June 14. Faced with a situation "without precedent in previous experience," the Government had given earnest consideration to the question of what action, if any, it could take without reversing its declared policy of non-intervention which would be likely to give protection to British shipping. It had considered "retaliatory action of various kinds," but was "not prepared to embark upon such measures which, apart from their inherent disadvantages," could "not be counted upon to achieve their object." In short, Chamberlain preferred to withstand the charges of cowardice and incompetence than to take a position which he felt might mean war, simply because Britain did not approve of the bombing. The Prime Minister repeated previous warnings to British shipping that, while the Government would continue to afford protection on the high seas, ships entering ports must do so at their own risk.[37]

36. Kennedy to the Secretary of State, London, June 10, 1938. *U.S. For. Rel., 1938,* I, 215.

37. *Parl. Debs., HC,* June 14, 1938, vol. 337, 41–44.

The dissatisfaction felt by the Opposition was evident in the intense questioning to which Chamberlain was subjected. Nor was their uneasiness diminished by his further statement on June 21. Enlarging upon the difficulty of taking action to protect ships while they were in Spanish territorial waters, Chamberlain explained that "while war continues we must expect a succession of these incidents." That was like setting a torch to a powder keg. Sinclair, Josiah Wedgwood, and Lloyd George blasted this spineless attitude, the latter accusing the Government of "behaving like a bevy of maiden aunts who have fallen among buccaneers." They were joined by Duncan Sandys (Conservative), who insisted that the "greatest maritime power in the world" could not afford to abdicate her legitimate right as a neutral in the face of violence. She had a solemn duty to all sea-faring peoples to "resist violence and to uphold the law of nations."[38]

Two days later Attlee resumed the attack. Chamberlain, he charged, had made an alliance with Mussolini in defense of which he was prepared to sacrifice interests and rights for which Britain had stood for years. It was the Government's objective, Chamberlain replied, to avoid the inevitable result of intervention—an extension of the conflict into a general European conflagration. There was no reason, as far as he could see, for altering the Government's course.

Among those who had had all of the Government inaction they could tolerate was Winston Churchill. It was "debasing . . . a currency which we have defended for generations." It was legitimizing methods which not merely insulted the British flag, but which struck at "the very life of our community." No other government which he had seen in his nearly forty years in the House would have cast off these outrages as a mere question of profiteering, as Chamberlain had done. So far from making greater security for peace, the Government's abjection would actually bring nearer "all those dangers which the entire House hoped to withhold from the British people."[39]

In consequence of this mounting criticism, late in June Perth called to Ciano's attention the effect of the bombing attacks upon

38. *Ibid.*, June 21, 1938, vol. 337, 936–1017.
39. *Ibid.*, June 23, 1938, vol. 337, 1343–88.

British public opinion, warning that strong anti-Italian feeling was growing both in Parliament and among the public. While assuring Ciano that Britain intended to abide faithfully by the policy of non-intervention, Perth impressed upon him the urgency of the situation in a most revealing note:

> Public opinion is demanding more energetic action from the Government. The accusation is being openly made against Chamberlain that he is unable to protect the interests of his own country, and what is most serious is that the accusation is not being made by the Opposition alone but also by a section of the Conservative Party. Chamberlain's personal position has suffered thereby. If his policy should be condemned, the consequences would certainly endanger the good progress of Anglo-Italian relations.[40]

Meanwhile the outcry in the British press continued. Its effect was not lost upon Chamberlain. In recounting a conversation with the Prime Minister on July 5, Kennedy recorded: "He feels that while the bombing of British ships has been slowed down he anticipates it may start again any time, and of course if people continue to read in their papers every day that British ships are being bombed his hand may be forced." According to Kennedy, Chamberlain was "inwardly very sore" that he had to take "all this nonsense" from Mussolini, but he repeated again and again: "My job is to try to keep England out of war if I possibly can; therefore I am doing a lot of things that are difficult for me to do."[41]

Under these circumstances it was difficult for the British Government to talk of putting the agreement with Italy into effect. After the Non-Intervention Committee had accepted on July 5 the British plan for making non-intervention "a reality,"[42] Perth repeated to Ciano that simple adhesion to the British plan could not be accepted by the British as a settlement of the Spanish question. Nothing could be done until the evacuation plan was

40. Conversation with the British Ambassador, Rome, June 28, 1938. *Ciano's Diplomatic Papers,* p. 219.

41. Kennedy to the Secretary of State, London, July 6, 1938. *U.S. For. Rel., 1938,* I, 56–57.

42. *Daily Telegraph,* July 6, 1938.

actually put into operation.[43] The extent to which this relative and, as it turned out, momentary show of British firmness was attributable to the public pressure to which the Chamberlain Government was being subjected, is impossible to measure. In view of Chamberlain's earlier reluctance to commit himself to a definition of "a settlement" and his later (after Munich) acceptance of what was by comparison a "soft" settlement, it is reasonable to assume that the pressure of criticism was considerably more than a negligible factor. It apparently influenced, at least for a time, the conditions which the Government would accept, even if it had little bearing on the actual direction of British policy.

Accompanying the clamor for action against the bombing of British ships was the constant demand by the Labor and Liberal press and the Opposition in Parliament that the "farce" of non-intervention in Spain be ended. Italy, it was rightfully argued, paid no attention to non-intervention; why should Britain not at least grant to Republican Spain its right to purchase arms instead of "betraying" the legitimate democratic government there? The hope that a Francoist Spain would not become a strategic lever in the hands of his Fascist helpers, as Liddell Hart pointed out in the *Fortnightly,* rested "on a rather slender possibility, while the graveness of the danger if it does is a certainty."[44]

This critical din continued unabated for some months. Illustrative of the irritation still widely felt on both points when the House of Commons recessed (July 29) were the acid remarks of Morgan Jones (Laborite):

> When a few poor British seamen are bombed, butchered and machinegunned as they battle for their lives in the sea, what happens? The Prime Minister says to the murderers, 'You naughty boys.' That will give great comfort . . . to the widows in Swansea, the Hartlepools and South Shields. It will ease the pain of their hearts to know that the Prime Minister . . . has reprimanded their husbands' assassins very severely. . . .

43. Conversation with the British Ambassador, Rome, July 11, 1938. *Ciano's Diplomatic Papers,* pp. 225–26.

44. Liddell Hart, "Strategy and Commitments," *Fortnightly,* CXLIX (June, 1938), 645.

> We cannot really purchase peace at the price of silence in the sight of these endless iniquities perpetrated in Spain day after day. . . . We are unfaithful to the League in treating the Spanish Government in this shabby way. There has been nothing like it since the days of Pontius Pilate, the first great non-interventionist.[45]

Most of the criticism, while punctuated by the occasional outcry of a dissident Conservative, came from the Labor Party, which the Conservatives neither respected nor trusted—for a variety of reasons, of course, completely apart from their outlook on foreign affairs. It therefore carried little weight with the Government, which looked upon it much like an honorable man might view the testimony of a known liar. Distrust of him is so general that even when he does tell the truth—or as in this instance, have a telling point—there is no inclination to pay much attention to him. Was not the Labor position on Spain similar, after all, to that of Russia, which to every regular Conservative was absolutely suspect?

Opposition criticism was continually met by the same vague and unsatisfying Government argument: any act that could be interpreted as intervention would almost inevitably lead to a general European war. The constant repetition of this response could not help but lead critics to the conclusion (as it eventually did) that the Government's only aim was the avoidance of war at any cost. Whether this was true or not, the Government did little by way of careful exposition of its position to combat the idea, and was itself largely to blame for the gradual emergence of the charge.

There was already in evidence, and it was to develop as time progressed, a Government contempt for any and all critics—to the point where it was hardly deemed necessary or even desirable to meet criticism with cogent explanations of Government policy. Chamberlain, of course, was absolutely convinced of the rightness of his own course, and criticism of it was usually taken as something of a personal affront. But the matter was more complex. Were cogent explanations of the Chamberlain policy possible?

45. *Parl. Debs., HC,* July 26, 1938, vol. 338, 2965–66, 2967–68.

Had a clearly-defined policy been formulated, or was there, as the Opposition charged, more than a little drift? If there is validity in the old adage that "it is the truth that hurts," perhaps this helps to explain the Government's unsatisfying and sometimes irritated responses to the critics' charges.

In this particular instance, the British Government preferred to close its eyes to Italian action in Spain and, succumbing to its mortal fear that war would result from any resolute action on its part, refused to defend its own ships or allow the Republican Government in Spain to purchase arms, all the while hoping that Mussolini's attitude would mellow, and that he would exert some pressure in Spain to bring about a "settlement." In these circumstances, criticism of the Government's policy toward Italy and Spain might well have reached significant proportions by late summer, 1938, had the attention of all Englishmen not been distracted by another and even greater problem, the German threat to Czechoslovakia.

CHAPTER FIVE

The Problem of Czechoslovakia

IN A CONVERSATION with Ribbentrop in London on the very eve of the *Anschluss,* Chamberlain asked the German Foreign Minister to tell Hitler that it was his "sincere wish and firm determination" to clear up Anglo-German relations.[1] Though the events of March 12 put a momentary damper on Chamberlain's resolve, the Czechoslovak crisis which unfolded during the summer of 1938 gave him ample opportunity to apply his appeasement policy to Germany. It also provided the critics of appeasement a corresponding opportunity to give vent to their anxieties and fears.

The origin and development of the Czech crisis of 1938 are so well-known and so thoroughly traced elsewhere as to preclude any need for their repetition here, except in general outline.[2] Hitler had in November, 1937, fixed the subjugation of Czechoslovakia as one of the basic objectives of future German policy.[3] He had available for use toward this end a ready-made tool: the three and one-half million Germans who inhabited the Sudetenland on the outer fringes of Czechoslovakia and among whom dissatisfaction with Czech rule had developed. Through financial subsidization and other pressures, Hitler was able to influence the

1. Memorandum by the Foreign Minister, London, Mar. 13, 1938. *G. D.,* I, 276–77.

2. Especially noteworthy for detailed treatment of the Czech crisis are the following: Wheeler-Bennett, *Munich;* R. G. D. Laffan, *The Crisis Over Czechoslovakia, January to September, 1938* ("Survey of International Affairs," II [for year 1938]), (London, 1951); Keith Eubank, *Munich* (Norman, Oklahoma; 1963); Gilbert and Gott, *The Appeasers;* and A. J. P. Taylor, *The Origins of the Second World War* (New York, 1962).

3. This is suggested in the famous Hossbach Memorandum, Berlin, Nov. 10, 1937. *G.D.,* I, 29–39. The extent to which Hitler had developed fixed plans for achieving this and other foreign policy objectives has become the subject of some controversy among historians, especially since the publi-

growth, in numbers, demands, and truculence, of the Sudeten German Party, and to make it, by March, 1938, little more than a Nazi instrument for use against the Czechoslovak Government.

Despite Germany's peaceful assurances to Czechoslovakia, it became increasingly clear that the German Government intended to force a settlement of the Sudeten question.[4] At the Sudeten German Party Congress in Carlsbad in late April, the pretense that the party sought autonomy was all but discarded in favor of union with Germany. The right to control the Sudetenland "in accordance with the ideology of the German people" was demanded—and that could mean little less than the establishment of Nazi rule. The party program also called for a complete revision of Czechoslovakia's foreign policy, namely, the abandonment of alliances with France and Russia and presumably the gravitation of Czechoslovakia into the German political and economic orbit. Then, in the wake of the Czech Government's refusal to negotiate on these terms, the Germans, both in the Sudetenland and in Germany proper, began a fresh outburst of abuse against Czechoslovakia, the former primarily by demonstrations, the latter by grossly exaggerated press reports.[5]

In the face of these ominous developments, the attitude of the British Government was a vital question. Despite bitter criticism of Chamberlain's declaration in the House of Commons, March 24, that Britain would not give a guarantee to Czechoslovakia, the Prime Minister showed no intention of going beyond the British note to Prague of March 23, which had described Brit-

---

cation of A. J. P. Taylor's *The Origins of the Second World War,* in which the fixed-plan theory is rejected, pp. 69–73, 128–31. For various explanations by former Nazis of Hitler's decisions at this point, see E. Malcolm Carroll, "Recent German Publications and German Foreign Policy, 1933–1945," *The American Political Science Review,* XLVI (June, 1952), 531–32.

4. Note Hitler's speeches to the Reichstag on February 20 and in Leipzig, March 26. Norman Baynes, *The Speeches of Adolf Hitler, April 1922–August 1939* (London, 1942), II, 1404–06; *The Times,* Mar. 28, 1938. Nevile Henderson wrote Halifax from Berlin on April 1 that Germany's next main objective was the settlement of the Sudeten question at all costs, so there should be no delay in attempting to find a peaceful solution. Henderson to Halifax, Berlin, Apr. 1, 1938. *B. D.,* I, 108–12.

5. Laffan, *The Crisis Over Czechoslovakia,* pp. 94–99; Wheeler-Bennett, *Munich,* pp. 46–47.

ain's obligations to Czechoslovakia as those of one member of the League to another.[6] Rather, every possible step should be taken by Britain and France to help remove the causes of friction by encouraging the Czech Government to seek urgently a settlement of questions affecting the position of the German minority.[7]

At the invitation of the British, Daladier and Bonnet, the French Premier and Foreign Minister (who had taken office less than three weeks before) journeyed to London on April 27 to discuss the matter. Halifax made it plain that the British Government looked at the Czech situation from the military angle. Reports from the Chiefs of Staff showed that it would be difficult to defend Czechoslovakia. British and French forces were, in any case, far from ready. Germany could not be prevented from overrunning Czechoslovakia, and the Czech nation would have to wait until the end of the ensuing war before it could be re-established. Therefore, it was essential that the Czechs reach a settlement with the Sudetens, and Britain and France should use all their influence to that end. Daladier agreed on the need to pressure the Czechs to grant reasonable concessions, but believed it should also be made clear that Britain and France would not permit the destruction of Czechoslovakia. Chamberlain concurred in principle, and it was finally decided that there should be simultaneous approaches to Berlin and Prague, the former by the British alone, the latter by the British and French jointly.[8]

Instructions were duly sent to the British representatives in Berlin and Prague to act in accordance with this decision.[9] Newton, the Minister in Prague, was told to urge that negotiations

6. Halifax to Newton, F.O., Mar. 23, 1938. *B. D.*, I, 90–91.

7. Halifax to Phipps, F.O., Mar. 22, Apr. 11, 1938. *Ibid.*, I, 82–86, 140–42.

8. Record of Anglo-French Conversations, held at No. 10 Downing Street, on April 28 and 29, 1938. *B. D.*, I, 198–234; Georges Bonnet, *Défence de la Paix* (Geneva, 1946–1948), I, 112–17. Halifax assured the German Chargé in London that no new commitments had resulted from these talks. For this prompt assurance Berlin was grateful. The German Chargé d'Affaires in Great Britain to the German Foreign Ministry, London, Apr. 29, 1938. *G. D.*, II, 246–47; The German Ambassador in Great Britain to the German Foreign Ministry, London, May 3, 1938. *Ibid.*, II, 255–56.

9. Halifax to Newton, F.O., May 4, 1938. *B. D.*, I, 241–43; Halifax to Henderson, F.O., May 4, 1938. *Ibid.*, I, 243–46.

between the Czech Government and the Sudeten German Party begin immediately. They should be comprehensive and should aim at a lasting settlement on the lines of a "state of nationalities." During the third week in May the Czech Government did in fact undertake to begin direct negotiations with Henlein, the Sudeten party leader.[10] But the German attitude left little room for optimism. Ambassador Henderson was informed in Berlin that the Carlsbad program alone was a just and reasonable basis for negotiation; if the Czechs rejected it and bloodshed resulted, Hitler "would be compelled to take immediate action."[11]

By this time Chamberlain apparently had begun to think that, if war was to be avoided, Czech "concessions" might have to include the cession of the Sudetenland to Germany. The New York *Herald Tribune* (May 15) carried a dispatch from London in which an American journalist, Joseph Driscoll, declared the British convinced that Czechoslovakia could not survive in its present form and that frontier revision might be advisable. That Driscoll's version of British policy was based upon a conversation with Chamberlain emerged from information divulged in the House of Commons some weeks later.[12] This raises the question why, if Chamberlain was already prepared to accept the cession of the Sudetenland to Germany, the British did not advise the Czechs to give way to Hitler and make the best terms they could while there was yet time. The explanation probably lies in the fact that Henlein, visiting London on May 12–14, exhibited a conciliatory attitude. He was perhaps prompted by his early conversation with Robert Vansittart, nominally Chief Diplomatic Advisor to the Government although Chamberlain had long since ceased to listen to his warnings about Germany, who told Henlein bluntly that Britain and France would fight

10. The German Minister in Czechoslovakia to the German Foreign Ministry, Prague, May 17, 1938. *G. D.*, II, 281.

11. Henderson to Halifax, Berlin, May 12, 1938. *B. D.*, I, 284–86.

12. On June 20 Chamberlain evaded a direct answer to Geoffrey Mander as to whether he had supplied Driscoll with material for his article, and on the following day neither admitted nor denied the truth of a rumor that he had given an interview to Driscoll and other journalists. *Parl. Debs., HC,* June 20, 1938, vol. 337, 856–58. On June 27, however, Lady Astor confirmed the report that Chamberlain had met several American journalists at her house on May 10. *Ibid.*, June 27, 1938, vol. 337, 1541.

if need be, and that "war would flatten his Sudetenland."[13] This seemingly revived the hope that Czechoslovakia could be peacefully reconstructed into a federal state.

The problem was soon further complicated by the so-called May crisis.[14] During mid-month the situation in the Sudetenland deteriorated, "incidents" occurred daily, and an exaggerated German press campaign reached such a pitch that another lightning *coup* seemed impending. Rumors spread of German troop movements on the Czech frontier. On the night of May 20, the Czechs decreed a partial mobilization of their army.[15]

The British—or at least Halifax, for the Foreign Secretary apparently acted on his own initiative in this instance[16]—moved with unusual dispatch. Henderson, upon instructions from Halifax, urged the German Government to use its influence with Henlein to promote negotiations with the Czechs. Should a conflict arise, Henderson told Ribbentrop, France had obligations to Czechoslovakia and would be forced to intervene. Britain could not guarantee that she would not become involved also.[17] The British

13. Lord Vansittart, "A Morally Indefensible Agreement," *The Listener,* XL (November 4, 1948), 676.

14. For a more detailed account of this, see Gerhard L. Weinberg, "The May Crisis, 1938," *The Journal of Modern History,* XXIX (September, 1957), 213–25. Its effect was decisive for the future of Europe, for it was at this point that an exasperated Hitler decided to smash Czechoslovakia by military action "in the near future," and issued a directive for the preparation of a plan for the attack. Directive for Operation "Green" From the Führer to the Commanders in Chief, With Covering Letter From the Chief of Supreme Headquarters, the Wehrmacht, Berlin, May 30, 1938. *G. D.*, II, 357–62.

15. Sir Nevile Henderson, *Failure of a Mission: Berlin, 1937–1939* (New York, 1940), p. 136; The German Minister in Czechoslovakia to the German Foreign Ministry, Prague, May 21, 1938. *G. D.*, II, 304–05.

16. See Arthur H. Furnia, *The Diplomacy of Appeasement: Anglo-French Relations and the Prelude to World War II, 1931–1938* (Washington, D.C., 1960), pp. 314–15. Furnia describes Chamberlain as being "furious with Halifax" later.

17. Henderson to Halifax, Berlin, May 21, 1938. *B. D.*, I, 334–35. Hitler's interpreter later recorded that Henderson spoke with great emphasis at this meeting. Paul Schmidt, *Hitler's Interpreter* (New York, 1951), pp. 84–86. A curious coincidence added weight to the British warning to Germany. The British Naval Attaché in Berlin was going on normal leave on May 21. Since several other families of the staff were to accompany him and there was no room on the regular train, an extra coach was requested. Rumors immediately spread that the whole British Embassy staff was

warning was repeated on May 21 in a personal message from Halifax to Ribbentrop: "If resort is had to forcible measures, it is quite impossible . . . to foretell results that may follow, and I would beg [you] not to count upon this country being able to stand aside if from any precipitate action there should start European conflagration."[18] At the same time, however, Halifax reminded the French that Britain was not bound to join them if they went to the aid of Czechoslovakia, and instructed Newton to tell the Czech Government that the best policy for it would be to come forward with a generous offer to Henlein in an attempt to clinch a settlement.[19] In that way the British Government tried to maintain balance and moderation on both sides.

The German Government insisted all along that the reports of troop concentrations in Saxony were "pure nonsense."[20] By May 28, tension had relaxed to the point where Hodza, the Czech Premier, was ready to cancel mobilization measures and resume negotiations with Henlein.[21]

The Government's action during this crisis received widespread approval in the British press. Some newspapers praised the "moderation" it had shown in pressing upon Prague and Berlin alike the urgent need for circumspection, among them the pro-Government *Times* (May 23, 24), the Conservative *Daily Telegraph* (May 23), and the Unionist Cardiff *Western Mail* (May 24). Other journals, including the Liberal Bradford *Yorkshire Observer*

---

evacuating Berlin, and Weizsäcker, the German Secretary of State, telephoned Henderson and begged him not to be an alarmist. The extra coach was then cancelled. Henderson, *Failure of a Mission,* pp. 140–41; Coulondre, *De Staline á Hitler,* pp. 149–50.

18. Halifax to Henderson, F.O., May 22, 1938. *B. D.,* I, 341.

19. Halifax to Phipps, F.O., May 22, 1938; Halifax to Newton, F.O., May 23, 1938. *Ibid.,* I, 356–57, 362.

20. Minute by the State Secretary for the Foreign Minister, Berlin, May 20, 1938; Minute by the Counselor of Legation Kessel in the Foreign Ministry for the State Secretary, Berlin, May 20, 1938. *G.D.,* II, 296. Colonel Jodl of the Supreme Headquarters of the Wehrmacht confirmed this when, on May 21, he informed the Foreign Ministry that no concentrations of troops had taken place apart from "peacetime maneuvers." Minute by an Official of the Foreign Ministry (Heyden-Rynsch) for the State Secretary, Berlin, May 21, 1938. *Ibid.,* II, 307–08.

21. The German Minister in Czechoslovakia to the German Foreign Ministry, Prague, May 28, 1938. *Ibid.,* II, 353.

(May 23) and the Liberal *Liverpool Daily Post* (May 23), commended the firmness shown in Berlin. The independent *Glasgow Herald* (May 24) urged continuation of the "rudimentary and emergency" collective security of the past few days; its success warranted it. The Labor *Daily Herald* (May 24) agreed:

> If this method [firm Anglo-French warning against aggression] succeeds, as one may now begin to hope, then it is an example and a lesson. . . . If every Government knows beforehand that the use of force is too risky to contemplate, if every question that may create acrimonious and dangerous dispute is dealt with before feelings rise high, then peace can be firmly and lastingly established.

Tribute to the Government's "plain words" was paid by the Liberal *News Chronicle* (May 23), which insisted that Britain must seek to induce Germany to negotiate on a more reasonable solution than a partition of Czechoslovakia or acceptance of dictatorship from Berlin.

The spectacle of journals like the *Daily Herald* and the *News Chronicle* not only supporting the Government's action but openly commending it was quite unnatural. It was to be explained, of course, not in terms of a changed position on the part of those newspapers, but in a distinct shift, apparently, in the Government's attitude. Indeed, their approval affords some of the best evidence as to how marked the Government's departure from its usual position was.

Government action had been firmer than usual, and with France and Russia, as well as Czechoslovakia, showing similar firmness, the "rudimentary collective security" of which the *Glasgow Herald* had spoken was in evidence. A suspected potential aggressor was greeted not by appeasement but by a show of willingness to resist on the part of a potential victim and its allies. This, however, was to be short-lived.

Aside from Halifax's initiative, there is little to explain British firmness.[22] And the task is all the more difficult since, regrettably,

22. Fritz Hesse, Press Counsellor of the German Embassy in London, suggests that the British may have learned of "Operation Green," Hitler's plan of action against Czechoslovakia, and determined to oppose it. *Das*

there is so little evidence available on actual decision-making. That the Government was influenced by the warning voices of respected critics is beyond proof, but nevertheless merits consideration. The need for firm action in the face of German threats to Czechoslovakia had been expressed frequently in public speeches and in signed articles in the press. As early as February, 1938, influential writers such as S. Grant Duff had begun to warn that "it is neither honest nor wise to meet German 'claims' about the Sudeten Germans and thereby lose the last ally we have in Central Europe." Besides betraying Czechoslovakia, it would free for action in the West the whole military machine of Germany.[23] Arnold Toynbee, speaking at Chatham House on March 10, argued that "the League system is the first and last line of defence." If Britain failed to make a success of collective security, the world would be unified politically not by peaceful agreement but by force.[24]

Then as the German menace to Czechoslovakia increased, so did the warning voices in Britain. By May, there were numerous expressions of concern from highly-regarded Englishmen. Utilizing the pages of the *Contemporary Review,* G. E. Hobhouse, a former Liberal M. P., wrote that if Britain now held back from stating a bold, firm policy, Hitler, "emboldened by a long-continued impunity, will spring on Prague as he sprang on Vienna."[25] G. E. R. Gedye, a well-known journalist whose dispatches appeared in the *New York Times,* warned that Hitler was broadcasting on two different frequencies: to Vienna he transmitted only the Horst Wessel song; to London "Peace, perfect peace in this dark world of sin" and "You and I together, love, Never mind the weather, love."[26] British opinion must realize, asserted the distinguished historian of Central Europe, R. W. Seton-Wat-

---

Spiel um Deutschland, pp. 118–21. But evidence to support this view is lacking.

23. S. Grant Duff, "Germany and Czechoslovakia," *Contemporary Review,* CLIII (February, 1938), 189.

24. *International Affairs,* XVII (May, 1938), 317–331.

25. C. E. Hobhouse, "The International Situation," *Contemporary Review,* CLIII (May, 1938), 521.

26. G. E. R. Gedye, "Austria—The Curtain Falls," *Ibid.,* CLIII (May, 1938), 543.

son, that what was at stake was not "help for Czechoslovakia" but the question whether all the Danubian and Balkan countries were to preserve their independence or become mere annexes of Germany.[27] Winston Churchill, in an address at the Free Trade Hall in Manchester, May 9, urged once more that Britain gather together all countries prepared to resist acts of violent aggression. He argued:

> If we could rally even ten well-armed states in Europe, all banded together to counter-attack the aggressor upon a combined plan, then we should be so strong that the immediate danger would be warded off, and a breathing space be gained for building later a still broader structure of peace. Is that not far better than being dragged piecemeal into a war when half those who might have been your friends and allies will have already been pulled down one by one?[28]

This was, to be sure, a conglomeration of warnings from a conglomerate constituency, but it provides evidence of a growing appreciation that the threat to Czechoslovakia was real and would at length involve more than the independence of the Czech nation. And although Chamberlain and his colleagues were not convinced of it at the time, their ultimate conversion to this view—which did eventually occur—was probably all the more definite because the view had been so long and effectively expounded.

Yet amid these warning voices Chamberlain soon resumed his efforts to placate Germany. Even before the May crisis had passed, he re-applied the "soft touch" to British policy, explaining to the House of Commons, May 23, that "the German Minister for Foreign Affairs . . . welcomed the efforts being made by His Majesty's Government in promoting a comprehensive and lasting settlement by negotiation in Czechoslovakia and . . . the German Government fully shared their desire to see negotiations

27. R. W. Seton-Watson, "Czechoslovakia After the German Coup," *Ibid.*, CLIII (May, 1938), 532.

28. Winston S. Churchill, *Blood, Sweat, and Tears* (New York, 1941), pp. 23–27.

succeed."[29] In this Chamberlain stretched the truth. What the German Ambassador had actually said to Halifax on Ribbentrop's behalf was that the British should exercise pressure in Prague, "where strong language was needed."[30] In response to Chamberlain's statement, Attlee reiterated that the settlement must not entail any infringement of the "just rights of the Czechoslovak people."[31]

Early in June Czech-Sudeten talks were re-opened. In reality, however, the gulf had widened beyond the possibility of agreement. The Sudeten Germans now demanded virtual independence and an equal voice, along with other racial groups, in the affairs of the central government. An administrative reform bill put forward by the Government in mid-July was unacceptable to the Sudeten German Party.[32] The result was deadlock, and bilateral discussions collapsed, not to be resumed. At that point the Sudeten German question ceased to be a matter of Czech internal politics and became the object of European *haute politique*.[33]

There occurred at that very moment a fleeting contact between the British and German Governments which, in other circumstances, might have been significant for appeasement. Captain Fritz Wiedemann, Hitler's personal adjutant, arrived in London to explore the possibility of a visit by some "important German personage" (probably Göring) to discuss Anglo-German relations and if possible to arrive at a "comprehensive agreement".[34] Noth-

29. *Parl. Debs., HC,* May 23, 1938, vol. 336, 824–25.

30. Halifax to Henderson, F.O., May 22, 1938. *B. D.,* I, 355; The German Ambassador in Great Britain to the German Foreign Ministry, London, May 22, 1938. *G. D.,* II, 322–23.

31. *Parl. Debs., HC,* May 23, 1938, vol. 336, 825–26.

32. According to this bill, the provincial Diets would be wholly elected and would receive control over a proportionate share of the provincial budget for such purposes as education, social welfare, public works, and health. What was not clear was whether they would have any considerable legislative powers. In short, the Government was not prepared to surrender unified state control of what could not be held to be cultural or private affairs of the nationalities.

33. The story of Czech-Sudeten German negotiations from mid-June to mid-July, 1938, is told in detail in Laffan, *The Crisis Over Czechoslovakia,* pp. 177–87.

34. This occurred on German initiative. See Herbert von Dirksen, *Moscow, Tokyo, London: Twenty Years of German Foreign Policy* (Norman, Oklahoma, 1952), p. 200. The probing might have been prompted

ing came of this. Halifax, who received Wiedemann at home with Chamberlain's approval, declared the present moment of tension over Czechoslovakia "not propitious"—though admitting that it would be different if a settlement had been reached there, or even if Germany could give some assurance that she was not contemplating the use of force in the Czech question.[35] A follow-up message from the Foreign Office held that, short of the re-establishment of normal relations between the German and Czech Governments, a reciprocal Anglo-German understanding "to cooperate in promoting . . . a peaceful settlement in Czechoslovakia . . . would offer better prospect of successful issue to any conversations than might otherwise be expected."[36] That was certainly enough to sour Hitler on any "big deal" with Britain, if indeed there had been sincerity behind the Wiedemann mission in the first place.[37]

In view of the general concern about appeasement, it is surprising that this event caused little stir in the British press. The *Daily Herald* (July 19) and the *Glasgow Herald* (July 22) suspected that Wiedemann was in London "more to inquire than to inform." Perhaps Germany wished to remind Britain that in any discussion on Czechoslovakia, she claimed the right to be taken into account, suggested the *News Chronicle* (July 22). The *Liverpool Daily Post* (July 23) hoped that Halifax and Chamberlain had maintained the firm attitude they had adopted when the Czech question had been critical in May. Generally, however, press reaction approached the point of disinterestedness. Did this mean that even those organs which had been so critical of

by a series of reports sent to Berlin by the German Ambassador in London (Dirksen) who, in assessing British opinion, reported that there was still a real desire among responsible statesmen for a comprehensive settlement with Germany, but also a growing determination in all quarters to resist any use of force by Germany for the achievement of her ambitions. The German Ambassador in Great Britain to the German Foreign Ministry, London, June 8, June 10, July 5, 1938. *G. D.*, II, 390–95, 403–09, 469–73.

35. Record of a conversation between Viscount Halifax and Captain Wiedemann on July 18, 1938. *B. D.*, I, 584–89.

36. Letter from Sir A. Cadogan to Captain Wiedemann, F.O., July 18, 1938. *Ibid.*, I, 589–90.

37. Hesse suggests that the British considered Wiedemann himself to be sincere, but recognized the mission as a German attempt to betray Britain. *Das Spiel um Deutschland*, p. 125.

appeasement in the past were not really as concerned as it had appeared? Later evidence does not support this view. Rather, the Wiedemann episode seems to have been taken as too nebulous to be meaningful. Government firmness during the May crisis was remembered reassuringly. And perhaps most important, the whole affair coincided with a much-publicized visit of the King and Queen to Paris, which kept the press preoccupied.

In the House of Lords, July 27, Halifax refused to divulge information about Wiedemann's visit, merely stating that it was a welcome opportunity for exchanging "views on matters of common interest to both our Governments.[38] He was not pressed to say more.

The mid-July deadlock in the Czech-Sudeten negotiations persuaded the British Government to initiate a long-contemplated proposal of mediation. Lord Runciman, Lord President of the Council, agreed to act as mediator,[39] and (with both French and Czech approval[40]) Chamberlain announced and explained his mission in the House of Commons on July 26. He would act in a personal capacity, not as a representative of the British Government. He would be a conciliator, hearing all the facts and arguments from both sides and suggesting expedients and modifications in the demands of both parties.[41]

The care which Chamberlain exercised in making Runciman's position clear beyond doubt is perhaps revealing in itself. Since the May crisis, uneasy skeptics had continued to warn against "surrender" to Germany, and Chamberlain's emphasis on Runciman's "independence" from the British Government seems to reflect the need to allay any fears that he would carry British

38. *Parl. Debs., HL,* July 27, 1938, vol. 110, 1284.

39. Halifax to Newton, F.O., July 16, 1938. *B. D.,* I, 567–68. Runciman was less than enthusiastic about his prospects for success, declaring: "You are setting me adrift in a small boat in mid-Atlantic." Lord Strang, *Home and Abroad* (London, 1956), p. 139.

40. Phipps to F.O., Paris, July 20, 1938; Newton to Halifax, Prague, July 23, 1938. *B.D.,* I, 601–03, 620.

41. *Parl. Debs., HC,* July 26, 1938, vol. 338, 2957. Templewood records: "Perhaps none of us fully realised at the time that the Mission, however much we insisted that its purpose was mediation and not negotiation, inevitably dragged us more deeply into the forefront of the struggle between Germans and Slavs." *Nine Troubled Years,* p. 298.

concessions in his pocket. In that two-month period, for example, Eden had assaulted appeasement on several occasions. In public addresses at Leamington, June 11, and at Stratford-on-Avon a month later, he warned that lasting peace could not be gained by a policy of concession and rebutted quite specifically the charge that those who had wished to see Britain take a firmer stand "in the last six months" on behalf of the principle of good faith in international relations would thereby have plunged the country into war.[42] "Unwise concessions for the sake of an uncertain peace now may involve defeat at a later date," declared the *Statist* (June 25) as it echoed a sentiment which ran through other uneasy journals at that time. From the point of military strategy, no less an authority than Liddell Hart had advised:

> It would be folly to buy momentary relief from the danger of war at the price of ultimate downfall. A settlement in Czechoslovakia that spelt the exclusion of Russia's forces from the balance, while establishing Germany's domination of Czechoslovakia, would be a very bad bargain, strategically, for the ultimate settlement of Europe. . . . History warns us that nothing has proved more upsetting to peace-seeking calculations than the temptation of buying peace.[43]

Skeptical voices had also arisen in response to an address on foreign policy which Chamberlain had delivered at Kettering on July 2. His text was the supreme necessity of avoiding war.[44] The air of generality which pervaded his words left him open to the charge that he had failed to grasp the central issue. He was the object of bitter attack, the *Economist* (July 9) felt compelled to remind him, not because he was trying to keep the peace but because he was pursuing methods which ran a grave risk of failure. Again Chamberlain had failed to distinguish between the goal and the policy to be followed in pursuing the goal, and there was some fear that the aggressors might come to interpret

42. *The Times,* June 13, July 8, 1938.

43. Liddell Hart, "Strategy and Commitments," *Fortnightly,* CXLIX (June, 1938), 649.

44. See Neville Chamberlain, *In Search of Peace* (New York, 1939), pp. 139–45.

his love for peace as a lack of will to fight. "If that conviction once gains acceptance," the *Economist* wrote, "Mr. Chamberlain's own fear of war will have made war inevitable." The *National Review* (July) developed the same point when it charged the Government with repeating the very mistakes it had made before the World War. W. H. Carter, in the *Fortnightly,* deplored that Chamberlain should "exude complacency" and remain oblivious to the effect on Britain's national reputation of his "truckling to the dictators."[45]

The occasion for Chamberlain's announcement of Runciman's mission was the first general debate on foreign policy in the Commons since the end of June. Sir Archibald Sinclair welcomed the appointment of Runciman "in an advisory capacity," but emphasized the importance of supporting Czechoslovakia against excessive demands. Appeasement would certainly result in war or in craven surrender to the aggressor powers. He asked several probing questions. What had Wiedemann come to London to say? Was there any truth in the rumor that the Government was trying to hustle the Czechs in their negotiations? It seemed evident to him that Germany was considering another military *coup*. If she were left in any doubt as to Britain's determination to resist aggression against Czechoslovakia, the British Government would bear a heavy responsibility for the resulting catastrophe. Now was the time, Sinclair concluded at length, for Britain to "stand firm for our principles and for our ideals of peace, freedom, justice, and international good faith."

Chamberlain carefully corrected Sinclair's interpretation of Runciman as an "adviser to the Czechoslovak Government," denied hustling the Czechs, and made no reference to Wiedemann. He was optimistic, feeling the atmosphere "lighter" throughout the continent. If a peaceful solution could be found to the Czech question, "I should myself feel that the way was open again for a further effort for general appeasement."

How adversely this struck some of his listeners! If the Prime Minister considered the destruction of Austria, the obliteration of democracy in Spain, and the daily menacing of Czechoslovakia

45. W. H. Carter, "Reconnaissance on the Home Front," *Fortnightly,* CL (July, 1938), 14–22.

a lightening of the atmosphere, what could a heavy atmosphere possibly be? Morgan Jones (Labor) wanted to know. As for the Runciman mission, it savored "too much of the squeezes which the Government have applied to various other countries in the interest of peace" for Laborite Josiah Wedgwood, who added prophetically:

> What is the excuse for enabling the Nazi rule to be extended all round the frontiers of Czechoslovakia? The excuse is, as ever, that it is to be done in the interests of peace. I tell this House it is in the interests of war, inevitable war, and a war that we shall not be able to win. Every time you sacrifice one of your potential allies to this pathetic desire to appease the tyrants you merely bring nearer and make more inevitable that war which you pretend you are trying to avoid.[46]

These words were almost duplicated by Eleanor Rathbone (independent). How could the Government continue with appeasement? There were no signs that it was succeeding; instead, every fresh concession made the aggressor powers more openly arrogant and insolent. She thought Churchill right in his belief that it was not too late to rally the peace-loving nations within the League. The one "tremendous fear" which she shared with the members of the Labor Party was that during the Parliamentary recess "one pass after another may be sold, and that we shall come back to find that the whole European position has deteriorated."

Collective security was again pressed upon the Government, this time with Geoffrey Mander (Liberal) a primary exponent. "A little bit of it" arose suddenly on May 21, he observed, but the Government should not rest content with that casual alignment of forces. It should be thought out, planned, organized, so that the whole world would know exactly where everybody stood and what would happen to an aggressor. If the extreme demands of the Sudeten Germans were met, a precedent would be set which must inevitably be followed by similar agitation and propaganda by Germans in Switzerland, Denmark, France, Poland,

46. *Parl. Debs., HC,* July 26, 1938, vol. 338, 2993–94.

and even in Brazil. If Mander's last point was too inclusive to be effective, the major plea of Richard Acland (Liberal) was not: the least Britain could do was to stand firm and quit nagging the French to follow a course obviously detrimental to their own safety.

From the Conservative side, A. C. Crossley perhaps came closest to catching the general sentiment of the critics. He approved the idea of sending Runciman to Prague, but saw only disaster resulting from any weakening of the attitude which the Government had assumed during the May crisis.[47]

Generally among the critics there was concern lest the Government slip back into its old ways, lest the Runciman mission reveal a swift abandoning of the move toward collective security which Government action in the May crisis had seemed to presage. There was concern lest there should emerge some sort of "deal" which would only weaken Britain's position and whet the appetites of the aggressor powers, lest appeasement be translated to mean unreasonable concessions to those who had already shown themselves unappeasable anyway. This was the essence of the critics' anxiety, whether they spoke from a Labor, Liberal, dissident Conservative, or independent standpoint. It was not a matter of partisan academicism; it was a matter of British and European peace and security.

This debate was the last on foreign policy until October 3. Parliament recessed early in August. During the Parliamentary session from February to August there had been twenty-four important debates on foreign policy. The Prime Minister and the Under-Secretary of State had to answer fourteen hundred questions on foreign affairs.[48] These unusually high figures indicate not only the interest but the anxiety which Chamberlain's policy had aroused throughout the country.

Runciman's mission received some attention in the House of Lords. Lord Snell was concerned lest Britain fail to build a bridge "on which there is traffic both ways, and not merely a one-way traffic of concession from Czechoslovakia to Berlin."

47. *Ibid.,* July 26, 1938, vol. 338, 2938–3033.

48. Butler, the Under-Secretary of State, gave these figures at the close of the July 26 debate. *Ibid.,* July 26, 1938, vol. 338, 3033.

She had no right to require of the Czechs any concession she herself would not make if in Czechoslovakia's position. Viscount Cecil feared that Runciman's activity would necessarily involve the British Government, which would have to bear the responsibility for whatever happened. He thought the League still the one hope for peace, adding pessimistically: "If we go back to the old system, as I am afraid the reasoning of the Prime Minister indicates, we are going to have another desolating war. . . ." But the Marquess of Crewe welcomed Runciman as a "missionary" to Czechoslovakia, and Lord Ponsonby termed the mission "a wise move, an original move." Halifax assured Viscount Cecil that Runciman's status was one of complete independence from the British Government.[49]

The press reacted favorably to the announcement of Runciman's journey to Prague. Some newspapers doubted that it could accomplish much, but they agreed that the effort should be made. The *Daily Telegraph* (Aug. 2) and the Conservative *Daily Mail* (July 27) were unreserved in their approval. *The Times* (Aug. 4) was especially enthusiastic: since mediation had always been one of the main functions of the League, Runciman would do precisely the sort of work which the League had been expected to do. More cautious was the Bradford *Yorkshire Observer* (July 27) which approved the mission, but simultaneously pointed out that "firmness has paid much better than concessions" and insisted upon a newly-constituted League as essential to the preservation of peace. Runciman's mission was "probably unique in its vagueness," but everyone must wish him success, wrote the *Liverpool Daily Post* (Aug. 3). Of a like opinion was the *Glasgow Herald* (Aug. 2), though it had warned earlier (July 26) that if Germany was unwilling to reach an honest and reasonable settlement, there should be no question of "trying to drive the Czechs to the impossible." The normally anti-Government *Economist* (July 30) and the non-partisan *pectator* (July 29) shared the view that Runciman's mission was "a hopeful development."

The *Daily Herald's* (July 27) response was conditional. If Runciman was to be a genuinely independent adviser, good; but if he went to threaten the Czechs to do as Britain said or take

49. *Parl. Debs., HL,* July 27, 1938, vol. 110, 1252–82.

the consequences, bad. "No settlement which sacrifices future security for a temporary bridging of difficulties can be a good settlement." Runciman would journey to Prague with the "general good will" of everybody concerned, said the *News Chronicle* (July 27). The British had only to stand firm to secure a fair settlement of the Czech controversy. To the *Manchester Guardian* (July 27), the mission was "for better or for worse, the most daring initiative in European affairs taken by the National Government" since the day Hoare "led the sanctions brigade into action at Geneva." However, if the Czechs, on Runciman's advice, made concessions which they otherwise would not have made, "the British Government will be morally responsible for seeing that they do not suffer thereby." The general concensus of the usually critical journals was clear: it was well that Runciman should proceed to Prague, but clearly with a mission of promoting a just and reasonable settlement, not "putting a squeeze" on the Czechs.

The British mediator arrived in Prague on August 3, but by mid-month had achieved nothing. Between the preservation and destruction of Czechoslovakia there was no room for compromise. The Czechs were willing to grant everything short of what would endanger the security and integrity of the republic; Henlein and Hitler appeared unwilling to accept anything short of what Prague could never grant. Four plans for settlement were developed and rejected, until early in September the conversations were broken off.[50]

The crisis deepened. Sudeten German Party members fomented civil disturbances in the Sudetenland. Atrocity stories in German newspapers became sensational. Hitler's speech at the Nazi Party Congress in Nuremberg, September 12, dripped venom, the Führer exclaiming that "if these tortured creatures do not receive justice and help, they can get both from us."[51] Next day rioting in the Sudentenland reached such a pitch of violence that the

50. For more detail on the Runciman mission, see F. T. A. Ashton-Gwatkin, "The Personal Story of the Runciman Mission," *The Listener,* XL (October 21, 1948), 595–97; Wheeler-Bennett, *Munich,* pp. 84–92; Laffan, *The Crisis Over Czechoslovakia,* pp. 211–62.

51. Baynes, *Speeches of Adolf Hitler,* II, 1487–90.

Czech Government declared martial law there. Order was soon restored, but the die had been cast. Runciman, having failed in a last futile attempt to re-open negotiations, returned to England, and Henlein issued a proclamation demanding the union of the Sudetenland with Germany.[52]

Meanwhile in London firm action was urged upon the British Government from various quarters. Duff Cooper, First Lord of the Admiralty, pressed for a semi-mobilization of the fleet as a warning to Germany against aggressive action.[53] Churchill recommended to Halifax a joint note from Britain, France, and Russia stating their deep anxiety at German military preparations, their interest in a peaceful solution of the Czech controversy, and the fact that a German invasion of Czechoslovakia would raise "capital issues" for all three.[54] From the anti-Nazi German Counsellor of Legation in the Hague came the unofficial message: "Stand firm. Do not retreat one step. If you make no concessions, Hitler will be forced to give way."[55] By roundabout means,[56] Litvinov, the Russian Foreign Commissar, advised calling the League Council, staff conversations among Russia, France, and Czechoslovakia, and consultation among the peaceful powers with a view perhaps to a joint declaration including Britain, France, and Russia.[57]

A distinct sentiment against surrender emerged from the sensation caused by the famous *Times* leader of September 7, in which editor Geoffrey Dawson said of the Sudetenland:

52. W. W. Hadley, *Munich: Before and After* (London, 1944), p. 61; Wheeler-Bennett, *Munich,* p. 93; Laffan, *The Crisis Over Czechoslovakia,* pp. 261–62.

53. Duff Cooper, *Old Men Forget,* pp. 225–28.

54. Churchill, *The Gathering Storm,* p. 293. Such a note might also get President Roosevelt's support, Churchill thought.

55. Wolfgang zu Putlitz, *The Putlitz Dossier* (London, 1957), p. 152.

56. This information was given to Churchill by Maisky, the Russian Ambassador in London. Churchill assumed that Maisky had intended his remarks for the Foreign Office, but had approached him because the Russians preferred to channel their advice through a private person rather than make a direct offer to the Foreign Office.

57. Churchill, *The Gathering Storm,* pp. 294–96. Templewood, in his memoirs, denies any possibility of Russian action and feels Maisky was only "fishing in troubled waters." *Nine Troubled Years,* p. 302. Viscount Maugham inclines toward the same view. *At the End of the Day* (London,

> In any case the wishes of the population concerned would seem to be a decisively important element in any solution that can hope to be regarded as permanent, and the advantage to Czechoslovakia of becoming a homogeneous State might conceivably outweigh the obvious disadvantages of losing the Sudeten German districts of the borderland.

This outright suggestion of secession of the Sudeten fringe from Czechoslovakia provoked (in Dawson's own words[58]) "a hubbub" and a "volley of abuse" in Opposition and Conservative newspapers alike. The Liberal Bradford *Yorkshire Observer* (Sept. 8), for example, demanded "No Anschluss!" The integrity and independence of Czechoslovakia was vital to the security of France, "and it cannot be less than Mr. Chamberlain's and Lord Halifax's policy." On the Conservative side, the *Daily Telegraph* (Sept. 8) asserted that "no more sinister blow could have been struck at the chances of settlement. . . . There could be no more dangerous or deplorable misrepresentation of the British view." If Chamberlain had long since decided that secession was the only solution to the Sudeten problem, he had not taken the whole Conservative press along with him in that view. The press generally saw the article as a damaging indiscretion and misrepresentation. And this view was soon fortified by a Foreign Office statement—issued at the prompting of Jan Masaryk, the Czech Minister in London, but apparently without much urging, for Dawson recorded that the Foreign Office had gone "up through the roof"[59]—that *The Times'* suggestion "in no way represents the view of His Majesty's Government."[60]

Chamberlain met with the principal Cabinet ministers and Foreign Office officials on the afternoon of September 9 to consider sending a strongly-worded warning to Hitler. (That the Prime Minister was being urged to do so from "quarters" both

1954), pp. 376–80. Sir William Strang doubts the possibility of Anglo-French-Russian military cooperation in the summer of 1938, but admits that the grounds for attempting it were no less compelling than in 1939, when it was tried. *Home and Abroad,* pp. 152–53.

58. Wrench, *Geoffrey Dawson,* pp. 371–72.

59. *Ibid.,* p. 372.

60. *The History of the Times* (New York, 1952), IV (pt. 2), 933.

in London and Paris was acknowledged by a Foreign Office official.[61]) Late that night a telegram was sent to Henderson instructing him to make it quite plain to Hitler (through Ribbentrop) that Britain would stand by France in the event of war.[62] Henderson implored the Government not to insist upon his carrying out these instructions, for he believed it would have an effect opposite to that desired.[63] The Government gave way.[64]

The American Ambassador in London still gained the impression from Halifax that the British were veering from their determination to keep out of a conflict in Czechoslovakia. While no good could come from war, a short one might mean, in Halifax's words, the end of "this impossible Nazism which, unless destroyed will very likely make it impossible for democracies to live." Chamberlain was outwardly very calm, quipping upon leaving the Cabinet meeting of September 9: "This really is not as much fun as shooting grouse."[65]

The Prime Minister, in fact, was quite unconvinced of the advisability of strong action. He realized, he wrote his sister, that if aggression took place, there would be many, including Churchill, who would say that the British Government must bear the responsibility; and that if they only had had the courage to tell Hitler that if he used force Britain would at once declare war, that would have stopped him. Yet he believed—and he felt fortified in this view by his recent reading about a former British Foreign Secretary, George Canning—that Britain should not let the vital decision as to peace or war pass out of her own hands into those of the ruler of another country, "a lunatic at that."[66]

61. Kennedy to the Secretary of State, London, Sept. 9, 1938. *U.S. For. Rel., 1938,* I, 584.

62. Halifax to Kirkpatrick, F.O., Sept. 9, 1938. *B. D.,* II, 277–78.

63. Ogilvie-Forbes to Halifax, Berlin, Sept. 10, 1938; Henderson to Halifax, Nuremburg, Sept. 10, 1938. *Ibid.,* II, 280, 283–84.

64. Halifax to Henderson, F.O., Sept. 10, 1938. *Ibid.,* II, 285.

65. Kennedy to the Secretary of State, London, Sept. 10, 1938. *U.S. For. Rel., 1938,* I, 585–86.

66. Feiling, *Life of Neville Chamberlain,* p. 360. Chamberlain's reference to Canning is noteworthy. He told his sister about reading a "very interesting book" (Harold Temperley's *Foreign Policy of Canning*). "Over and over again, Canning laid it down that you should never menace unless you

But the other view was constantly before him. At a Cabinet meeting on September 12, Duff Cooper reminded his colleagues that Britain was being advised from all sides to make it plain to Germany she would fight: such advice had come from the press, from Churchill, from the French Government, from the United States Government, even from the Vatican. Yet this advice, supported by an overwhelming weight of opinion, was being rejected upon the counter-advice of one man, "the hysterical Henderson."[67] A group of Liberal leaders, including Viscount Samuel, Lloyd George, and Archibald Sinclair, met on September 13 to formulate a Liberal statement of policy and sent the following message to the Prime Minister:

> Nothing is more likely to lead to war than doubt in the mind of the German rulers as to where Great Britain stands. . . . We are therefore anxious to assure His Majesty's Government that we will whole-heartedly support any further steps they make take to make it clear beyond doubt to the world that an unprovoked attack upon Czechoslovakia cannot be regarded with indifference by Great Britain, and that if France were to be involved in hostilities consequent upon such an attack this country would at once stand firmly in arms by her side.[68]

Something of the same idea, through not so strongly worded, was embodied in a statement issued by the annual Trades Union Congress in Blackpool the week before: "The time has come for a positive and unmistakable lead for collective defense against aggression. . . . It is in the historic assembly of our democratic State that these principles should be reaffirmed with the utmost energy and determination."[69] Whatever Chamberlain's own views, he could not, indeed, he did not, labor under the illusion that

---

are in a position to carry out your threats, and . . . we are certainly not in a position in which our military advisers would feel happy in undertaking to begin hostilities if we were not forced to do so." See *Ibid.*, p. 321; Macleod, *Neville Chamberlain*, p. 228.

67. Duff Cooper, *Old Men Forget*, pp. 226–27.

68. Samuel, *Memoirs*, pp. 276–77.

69. *The Times*, Sept. 5, 6, 1938.

they were largely unquestioned, though frequently his actions seemed to belie this fact.

During the last days of August and early September, there was agitation in some sections of the press for more positive action by the British Government. *The Times* (Aug. 21), the *Daily Mail* (Aug. 31), and the independent *Observer* (Aug. 21) were agreed that only prompt and far-reaching concessions by the Czechs could solve their minority problem. Other journals, however, emphasized that there should be no question of leaving the Czechs to their fate in the face of aggressive German demands. The *Liverpool Daily Post* (Aug. 26) recommended a new and unequivocal declaration regarding Britain's interest in central Europe. The *Glasgow Herald* (Aug. 27) was more specific: "Britain must be just as concerned about Czechoslovakia's independence as she was in May. Hitler's course will be aggressive or non-aggressive according to the amount of opposition there is to him in Europe." In the view of the independent *Financial News* (Sept. 1), it was Britain's duty to announce in the plainest possible language that aggression against Czechoslovakia would not be tolerated. The *Manchester Guardian* (Sept. 5) concurred in different terms: the German Government must be made to realize that however much Britain declares her ultimate liberty of choice, France could scarcely be involved in a war arising out of Czechoslovakia without Britain also being drawn in.

Continuing the firm tone with which it had met *The Times'* suggested secession of the Sudetenland, the *Daily Telegraph* (Sept. 10) declared: "Peace is not to be preserved by indifference to the coercion of a small nation by a powerful neighbor." The Cardiff *Western Mail* (Sept. 10) warned that Britain must not stand idly by and allow Czechoslovakia, like helpless Austria, to become the victim of brutal aggression. Europe simply "cannot do without collective security," alleged the *Glasgow Herald* (Sept. 12). The *Financial News* (Sept. 12) repeated its call for a "stern and outspoken note" to Germany. The independent *Sunday Pictorial* (Sept. 11) demanded: "Mr. Chamberlain, give us a lead." "Hitler does not appreciate weakness; he can only understand strength," exclaimed the *Liverpool Daily Post* (Sept. 13).

From the periodical press came more warning voices, including those of several highly-respected English historians. Outlining a "real policy of peace" in the *Contemporary Review,* S. Grant Duff urged the Government to tell Germany directly that Britain could guarantee the Sudeten Germans no more than was their right as citizens of a democratic country, and that any German attempt "to use them against Czechoslovak independence will lead inevitably to a new world war in which our place will be by the side of our allies."[70] In the same journal, historian G. P. Gooch lamented that "unfortunately, devotion to the League of Nations can hardly be reckoned among the characteristics of the Chamberlain Ministry since the resignation of Mr. Eden."[71] A. L. Rowse, writing in the *Political Quarterly,* described British policy as simply "bankrupt." How could anyone trust Hitler's or Mussolini's word? They were self-declared breakers of agreements. All would have been so much easier, he reflected, if only the Government had "played straight with the collective system since 1931."[72]

In short, as the Czech crisis approached its critical point, there could be no doubt in Chamberlain's mind, if indeed he was the keen political observer his friends claimed him to be, that there existed a sizeable and potent body of opinion which held that firmness was the essence of statesmanship in the impending Czechoslovak situation. That he appreciated this himself is very doubtful, especially since he made no attempt to alert the British people to the sort of hardship and courage which might be expected of them. In sum, the notion that the road to Munich was paved in part by the Prime Minister's understanding of the mentality of his entire people is altogether open to question.

Early in September the British Government was warned of Hitler's true intentions by the Counsellor of the German Embassy in London, Theodor Kordt. Acting upon the initiative of his brother, Erich, Ribbentrop's *chef de cabinet* (who had sent

70. S. Grant Duff, "British Policy and Czechoslovakia," *Contemporary Review,* CLIV (August, 1938), 153.

71. G. P. Gooch, "The Grouping of the Powers," *Ibid.,* CLIV (August, 1938), 138.

72. A. L. Rowse, "Reflections on the European Situation," *Political Quarterly,* IX (July-September, 1938), 334–50.

secret information to London via a cousin), Kordt approached Halifax and urged that, while seeking a peaceful settlement of the Sudeten question, the British should at the same time express in unambiguous language their intention to oppose any attempt to use force. Hitler would hardly dare to launch a war, Kordt told Halifax, if a public British declaration brought it home to the German people that an attack against Czechoslovakia would make war with Britain inevitable. Halifax listened "in a most earnest and attentive manner," Kordt later told his brother. He thanked Kordt for his frankness and promised to inform Chamberlain and several of his colleagues in the Cabinet; the matter would be carefully examined and treated confidentially.[73]

But Kordt's visit was of no consequence. There was little concrete data on which the British Government could make crucial decisions. Kordt's message came from an alleged cabal of undisclosed composition and unknown strength, a group whose capacity to act was unknown and in fact remains uncertain yet.[74] Chamberlain further pursued his policy of appeasement.

When the Runciman mission failed, Neville Chamberlain was a statesman cornered by realities. In diplomacy "the word soon gets passed around," and the ambivalence of the British attempt

73. Erich Kordt, *Nicht aus den Akten, Die Wilhelmstrasse in Frieden und Krieg: Erlebnisse, Begegnungen, und Eindrücke, 1928-1945* (Stuttgart, 1950), pp. 250, 279–81; Ernst von Weizsäcker, *Memoirs of Ernst von Weizsäcker* (Chicago, 1951), pp. 144–45.

74. It is now known that there was in Germany a "heterogeneous group" (as Weizsäcker described it), including generals and high political officials, which had been planning to overthrow the Hitler regime. In September, 1938, they had organized a counter-plan to be put into effect concurrently with Operation Green. Their plan was stifled by the extension of Chamberlain's appeasement efforts; Operation Green was never executed. Sir John Wheeler-Bennett suggests that what this group was really aiming at in approaching the British was an undertaking that they would bring pressure to bear upon Poland to make territorial concessions to a Germany which had eliminated Hitler and expunged the record of the Nazi regime. In other words, the fundamental principles of German foreign policy would remain the same whatever the regime in power. *The Nemesis of Power: The German Army in Politics, 1918–1945* (London, 1953), p. 445. For other estimates and details of the conspiracy, see Walter Goerlitz, *History of the German General Staff, 1657–1945* (New York, 1954), pp. 333–38; Churchill, *The Gathering Storm,* pp. 311–13.

Kordt was not the only German to make an official approach to the

to deter the Germans from armed action by pointing to the probability of British intervention, while discouraging the Czechs from fighting by hinting at its improbability, was not long concealed.[75] The Czech situation remained explosive. It was then that Chamberlain set in motion a plan which he considered "so unconventional and daring that it rather took Halifax's breath away": he offered to go at once to Germany to meet Hitler in a last effort to find a peaceful solution.[76]

Chamberlain revealed his plan to the Cabinet on the morning of September 14 and received unanimous and enthusiastic approval.[77] Thus the Prime Minister, who after the May crisis had described the German Government as "utterly untrustworthy and dishonest,"[78] and the Inner Cabinet (Halifax; Sir Samuel Hoare, Home Secretary; and Sir John Simon, Chancellor of the Exchequer),[79] which frequently referred to Hitler as "the mad-

---

British. In mid-August Ewald von Kleist visited London and conferred with Vansittart and Churchill. He emphasized that the German generals were against war, and that Britain and France must make Hitler understand that their firm attitude in May was not a bluff. Appendix IV, *B. D.*, II, 683–89. Weizsäcker gave the British similar information, once through Carl Burckhardt, League of Nations High Commissioner in Danzig, and again through Sir G. Warner, the British Minister in Berne. *Ibid.*, II, 689–92. Warner to Halifax, Berne, Sept. 5, 1938. *Ibid.*, II, 242. Lieutenant-Colonel Hans Boehm-Tettlebach visited London in early September for General Halder, one of the opposition leaders. Whom he contacted is uncertain. Ribbentrop, *Zwischen London und Moskau*, p. 141 n.

75. Strang, *Home and Abroad*, p. 134.

76. *Halifax to Phipps*, F.O., Sept. 14, 1938. *B. D.*, II, 323–24; Feiling, *Life of Neville Chamberlain*, p. 357.

77. Duff Cooper, *Old Men Forget*, p. 228; Templewood, *Nine Troubled Years*, p. 302. His decision had been made without the knowledge of the full Cabinet. He had discussed the idea with Hoare on September 10—it had been in his mind for some days—but he had kept it to himself in order to ensure its full effect at the final moment. Templewood, *Nine Troubled Years*, p. 300; Amery, *My Political Life*, III, 266; Birkenhead, *Halifax*, pp. 393–94.

78. Feiling, *Life of Neville Chamberlain*, p. 354.

79. The Inner Cabinet gradually took the place of the Foreign Policy Committee in the late summer of 1938. As the critical situation was changing constantly and the frequent summoning of a large committee became difficult, Chamberlain came to rely more and more heavily upon Halifax, Hoare, and Simon. This small committee, with its advisers Cadogan and Wilson, met almost continuously during the last three weeks of September. Templewood, *Nine Troubled Years*, pp. 291–92, 301. Templewood fully

man,"[80] decided to pursue appeasement right into Hitler's lair.

Of more than passing interest is the fact that only a few hours after Chamberlain made his decision to visit Germany the French Government abdicated all initiative in this area of foreign affairs to the British. Shortly after 10 p.m., September 13, a telegram arrived in the Foreign Office from Daladier in effect begging Chamberlain to do something to avoid a situation where France might have to live up to her obligations to Czechoslovakia.[81] This certainly strengthened Chamberlain's hand.

The British press greeted Chamberlain's move on September 15 with universal approval, hailing it as "a courageous departure from diplomatic precedents" or as "a gallant initiative." Commendations were not restricted to the Conservative journals. The *Liverpool Daily Post* spoke of "a flash of light across a darkening sky." The *Glasgow Herald* thought it an act of "very great courage." Chamberlain's journey would be "generally welcome," wrote the *Financial News;* it would have "the cordial and heartfelt approval of the world," declared the Cardiff *Western Mail.* Even the staunchest Opposition papers approved. The *Daily Herald* felt the Prime Minister's decision had the "quality of dramatic intervention which was needed at this moment." To the more reserved *Manchester Guardian,* it was a "bold move." The *News Chronicle* (Sept. 16) felt "the earnest thought of men and women all over the world was to approve the simple sincerity of Mr. Chamberlain's action and to wish him God-speed."

It is important to note, however, that much of the initial support from the press was based on the belief that the visit would provide an opportunity for Chamberlain to impress upon Hitler Britain's determination to stand firm against excessive German demands or any attempt at a violent solution of the Czech crisis. The *Manchester Guardian* made this explicit: "Chamber-

---

discusses the functioning of the Inner Cabinet in chapter XXV, entitled "The Big Four." See also Amery, *My Political Life,* III, 266.

80. Kennedy to the Secretary of State, London, Sept. 13, 1938. *U.S. For. Rel., 1938,* I, 592.

81. Phipps to Halifax, Paris, Sept. 13, 1938. *B. D.,* II, 313–14. The extent to which evasive British replies to earlier French questions concerning the defense of Czechoslovakia contributed to the French attitude is still uncertain and disputed.

lain will have it in his hands to show that Britain remains firm in her intentions, and that his motive is simply a supreme effort to find a way to peace that can be honourably accepted." The *Glasgow Herald* noted that the British and French dare not allow the independence of Czechoslovakia to be endangered. The Czechs should be supported firmly on the limit-line of concession to which they had already gone, wrote the *News Chronicle*: "If the British were willing to sacrifice the Czech democracy to keep themselves out of trouble, the ultimate retribution would be overwhelming—and overwhelmingly deserved." The whole purpose of the visit, the *Daily Herald* postulated, was not, and could not be allowed to be, the striking of a private bargain. Chamberlain went only to present the Anglo-French view, to hear the German view, and then to report back to the Cabinet as the first stage in further discussions in which Czechoslovakia must participate. The *Daily Telegraph* (Sept. 17) agreed, in fact, that if peace were to be forged, it must be not merely peace with honor, but peace with justice, which the conscience of the world could accept as such. Even *The Times* (Sept. 17) insisted that the double purpose of the Government was unmistakable—to find a just solution while throwing its whole weight against a violent attempt at a settlement.

The series of conferences between Chamberlain and Hitler which followed are synonymous with appeasement and need not be reconstructed here except for the purpose of reference. In the course of their three-hour talk at Berchtesgaden on September 15, it became clear that Hitler did not envisage a compromise settlement. Only if he received "then and there" British assurance that she would accept in principle the secession of the Sudetenland was there any use in continuing the conversation. Chamberlain could not give such assurance immediately, but promised to consult the Cabinet if Germany, in the meantime, would refrain from active hostilities. Hitler agreed, provided there was no provocation from the Czech side, and a further meeting was arranged.[82]

82. Notes by Mr. Chamberlain of his conversation with Herr Hitler at Berchtesgaden on September 15, 1938. *B. D.*, II, 338–41. For enlightening

Chamberlain hurried back to London and promptly called the Cabinet together. Although he had found Hitler, at first sight, "the commonest little dog" he had ever seen,[83] he, like Runciman, was convinced that only the cession of the Sudeten areas to Germany would dissuade Hitler from an invasion. A section of the Cabinet, led by Halifax and Duff Cooper, objected. Heated debate ensued, but a final decision was delayed until the following day, September 18, when Daladier and Bonnet were to join the discussion.[84]

Rumblings were heard within the Cabinet later that day (so Cadogan informed Joseph Kennedy). There was displeasure that the Inner Cabinet was being consulted constantly to the exclusion of the full Cabinet, and there were intimations that a row would develop if Chamberlain tried to force the principle of self-determination on the Cabinet.[85] Earl Winterton, Deputy to the Secretary of State for Air, had expressed to Duff Cooper the day before his belief that those who differed from the Government must press their views to the point of resignation. In the Cabinet meeting, Duff Cooper had stated emphatically that there were limits to the humiliation he was prepared to accept; if he were convinced that surrender would bring lasting peace, he would favor it, but it was obviously a British interest to resist Germany.[86] Halifax, too, according to one biographer, at first opposed the transfer to the Reich of Czech minorities as morally indefensible, and was backed by Malcolm MacDonald, the

sidelights on this conference, see Ivone Kirkpatrick, *The Inner Circle* (London, 1959), pp. 94–98.

83. This is what he apparently told the Cabinet. But in a subsequent conference with Labor leaders, Chamberlain gave Dalton the feeling that he was greatly impressed by Hitler. Dalton, *The Fateful Years,* p. 183.

84. Duff Cooper, *Old Men Forget,* pp. 229–30; Churchill, *The Gathering Storm,* pp. 300–01. Other sources do not mention the debate. Templewood, for example, merely records: "The acceptance of the principle of self-determination with its certain implication that it would mean the separation of the Sudetenland from Czechoslovakia, seemed to us to be inevitable if war was to be prevented." *Nine Troubled Years,* p. 303. Hore-Belisha's papers, however, reveal that he had certain significant reservations. R. J. Minney, *The Private Papers of Hore-Belisha* (New York, 1961), pp 140–42.

85. Kennedy to the Secretary of State, London, Sept. 17, 1938. *U.S. For. Rel., 1938,* I, 607–08.

86. Duff Cooper, *Old Men Forget,* p. 230.

Colonial Secretary.[87] The impact of these arguments upon Chamberlain and the rest of the Cabinet was apparently undermined, however, by other influences, among them Runciman's advice and Mussolini's open commitment to Hitler's cause. Despite the postponement of a formal decision, Sir Samuel Hoare that evening told Barrington-Ward, deputy editor of *The Times,* that it had been agreed that Czechoslovakia was already disintegrating and it was not worth a war to stop the process.[88]

Whatever occurred at that Cabinet meeting—the memoirs of British ministers are disappointingly silent in this regard[89]—Chamberlain ultimately determined to pursue his own policy. On Sunday, the 18th, the Inner Cabinet and the two French ministers held several long sessions at which agreement was reached upon proposals to be submitted to the Czech Government.[90] The Anglo-French plan involved the immediate cession to Germany of all areas in Czechoslovakia containing over 50 percent Germans. In return the British and French were prepared to join in an international guarantee of the new Czech frontiers against unprovoked aggression.[91]

There was objection in the Cabinet to this proposal. Duff Cooper, Earl Winterton, Oliver Stanley (President of the Board of Trade), Walter Elliot (Minister of Health), and Leslie Hore-Belisha (Secretary of State for War) were reported to be extremely lukewarm toward it. "Most of us disliked the idea," the

87. Campbell-Johnson, *Viscount Halifax,* p. 479. The Czech Minister in London had told Joseph Kennedy back on May 14 that he had found Halifax more in favor of a determined stand than Chamberlain. Kennedy to the Secretary of State, London, May 14, 1938. *U.S. For. Rel. 1938,* I, 498–500.

88. *History of the Times,* IV (pt. 2), 938.

89. Except for Duff Cooper's revelations (in *Old Men Forget*), little evidence of what transpired in various Cabinet meetings is available. Apparently all the other ministers who have published memoirs subscribed to Winterton's view that "it would be a breach of honor, the Privy Councillor's oath, and the official Secrets Act to give the slightest indication of the form or content of the prolonged discussions in a series of Cabinet meetings concerned with the crisis." The Rt. Hon. Earl Winterton, *Orders of the Day* (London, 1953), p. 239.

90. Record of Anglo-French Conversations Held at No. 10 Downing Street on September 18, 1938. *B. D.,* II, 373–400; Bonnet, *Défense de la Paix,* I, 238–42; Templewood, *Nine Troubled Years,* pp. 305–06.

91. Halifax to Newton, F.O., Sept. 19, 1938. *B. D.,* II, 404–06.

latter's diary later revealed, "but in the end there didn't seem to be any alternative. . . ."[92] Chamberlain himself realized (as he told Kennedy) that he would be charged with the rape of Czechoslovakia. But the only alternative was war, and "I can see no rhyme or reason in fighting for a cause which, if I went to war for it, I would have to settle after it was over in about the same way I suggest settling it now."[93]

Resistance also appeared elsewhere: the Czech Government found the Anglo-French proposals unacceptable.[94] As a result, the British and French Ambassadors in Prague were instructed to call upon President Benes (they did so at 2 a.m., September 21) and urgently suggest that the Czechs reconsider. In the British view, the Anglo-French plan afforded the only chance of avoiding immediate attack. Newton and his French counterpart warned: "If on reconsideration [the] Czech Government feel bound to reject our advice, they must of course be free to take any action they think appropriate to meet the situation that may thereafter develop."[95] Though couched in decent phrases of diplomacy, the meaning was clear. Great Britain would not fight. And France was repudiating her treaty obligations so often publicly declared to be sacrosanct. Benes immediately summoned the Czech Cabinet, which decided at length to accept the Anglo-French proposals.[96]

The Anglo-French plan had meanwhile been accorded a varied reception in the British press. Most newspapers recognized that it involved great sacrifice for the Czechs. A few, including the *Daily Mail* (Sept. 20) and the Cardiff *Western Mail* (Sept. 20) then took refuge in the hope that the new Czech state would be stronger because it would be more homogeneous. A far greater number of journals, however, revealed various degrees of disapproval. The Bradford *Yorkshire Observer* (Sept. 20) complained that Anglo-French policy was on a "slippery slope. . . . There is to be dismemberment where integrity was understood to be

92. Minney, *Private Papers of Hore-Belisha,* p. 142.
93. Kennedy to the Secretary of State, London, Sept. 19, 1938. *U.S. For. Rel., 1938,* I, 621–22.
94. Newton to Halifax, Prague, Sept. 21, 1938. *B. D.,* II, 431–34.
95. Newton to Halifax, Prague, Sept. 21, 1938. *Ibid.,* II, 449–50.
96. Newton to Halifax, Prague, Sept. 21, 1938. *Ibid.,* II, 444–45.

promised." Most people, the *Liverpool Daily Post* (Sept. 20) contended, would feel that Britain was paying a very distasteful price for peace. For the *Glasgow Herald* (Sept. 21) a readiness to meet potential peacebreakers on their own ground seemed no longer to exist outside Czechoslovakia, and without that it was questionable whether the slide towards war in Europe could be checked. The *Manchester Guardian* (Sept. 21) called the plan "a sacrifice of Czechoslovakia and a surrender to Herr Hitler." The slight palliatives it contained made no difference to its essence; Britain had accepted a moral defeat which would have consequences beyond her present range of vision. The *News Chronicle* (Sept. 20) shared that sentiment, and the *Daily Herald* (Sept. 20) spoke of "shameful betrayal." There could be no defense for frontier revision accepted under the manifest threat of force. It might avert the present danger, "but Europe will have to find some better foundation for peace than policies devised as this one has been." In summary, those journals which earlier had encouraged British firmness to assure a just and honest solution to the Czech problem now saw their gravest fears being realized.

Looking at the plan solely from the British point of view, the *Daily Telegraph* (Sept. 21) considered a British guarantee to Czechslovakia a concession which could be justified only by the certainty that the sabre-rattling diplomacy of Germany would end once and for all. The Bradford *Yorkshire Observer* (Sept. 21) thought the advisability of Britain's becoming entangled with two totalitarian states in a precarious frontier guarantee—a guarantee of a small, weak state robbed of its natural mountain frontier—very doubtful.

An attempt had been made by the Government on September 17 to influence certain Opposition journals to come out strongly on the side of peace. Sir Samuel Hoare visited the editors of the *Daily Herald* and the *News Chronicle* (and perhaps others) to urge moderation.[97] He in fact continued to meet regularly with the leaders of the press during the last days of September.[98]

97. Kennedy to the Secretary of State, London, Sept. 17, 1938. *U.S. For. Rel., 1938,* I, 609–611.

98. Templewood, *Nine Troubled Years,* p. 318.

Possibly as a result, jingoism was competely absent from the British press—but that might well have been the case even without Hoare's efforts.

Churchill expressed his view of the Anglo-French plan in a statement to the press on September 21:

> The partition of Czechoslovakia under pressure from England and France amounts to the complete surrender of the Western Democracies to the Nazi threat of force. Such a collapse will bring peace or security neither to England nor to France. On the contrary, it will place these two nations in an ever weaker and more dangerous situation.[99]

At the same time the three executive bodies of the Labor movement (the General Council of the Trades Union Congress, the national committee of the Labor Party, and the committee of the Parliamentary Labor Party) issued a statement which termed the Anglo-French proposals a "shameful surrender" to the threats of Hitler. The long-established British traditions of democracy and justice had been dishonored. That would not bring peace. With every surrender to violence peace receded. If war were to be averted and civilization saved, "the peace-loving nations must make immediate and concerted effort to restore the rule of law." Afterwards, Labor leaders personally protested the Government's course, Attlee and Greenwood in an interview with Chamberlain, Dalton and others in a conference with Halifax.[100]

British public opinion was "probably a shade" against the plan, Kennedy reported to Washington. There was definite opposition in the Cabinet, and unless Chamberlain could bring back from Godesberg, where he was soon to meet Hitler again, some commitment from the Führer such as demobilization, or some idea of his future steps, a break in the Cabinet was probable.[101]

99. Churchill, *The Gathering Storm*, pp 303–04.

100. *The Times,* Sept. 22, 1938; Dalton, *The Fateful Years,* pp. 188–89. According to Dalton's report, "nothing was wanting in emphasis in the statements which the deputation made on behalf of the Labor movement."

101. Kennedy to the Secretary of State, London, Sept. 21, 1938. *U.S. For. Rel., 1938,* I, 631. Duff Cooper and Oliver Stanley were the two

September 22 found Chamberlain in Godesberg conferring with Hitler again. The mere transfer of the Sudetenland from Czechoslovakia to Germany was no longer sufficient, Hitler said; instead, Czech troops must evacuate all areas having a population over 50 percent German by September 28, plebiscites must be held to determine the status of questionable areas, and a new frontier be drawn by a German-Czech or international commission. Surprised and indignant, Chamberlain engaged the Führer in acrimonious and desultory debate, but three hours of talk yielded nothing and the conference adjourned in deadlock.[102]

After an exchange of letters next day, they met at 10:30 that night. At Chamberlain's request, Hitler produced a map and memorandum of German proposals. They provided for Czech evacuation of the Sudeten frontier districts within forty-eight hours. Chamberlain argued vigorously over the time limit, and Hitler agreed to extend it to October 1. This amended version Chamberlain consented to submit to the Czechs, although he could neither accept it personally nor recommend it to Prague.[103]

While at Godesberg, Chamberlain was aware of the pressure of British public opinion. In his letter to Hitler, he chided the Führer for failing to realize the impossibility of his agreeing to any plan unless he had reason to believe that it would be considered by public opinion in Britain, in France, and in fact in the world generally, as carrying out the principles already agreed upon in an orderly fashion and free from the threat of force. This was no concocted argument. It was corroborated by Halifax, who telegraphed Chamberlain that the "great mass of public opinion seems to be hardening in sense of feeling that we have

---

ministers who felt Chamberlain must insist upon some minimum concession such as German demobilization. Duff Cooper, in fact, hoped Chamberlain would tell Hitler that he had done more than everything that he had so far undertaken. Further he could not go, and would prefer, if necessary, to go to war. Duff Cooper, *Old Men Forget,* pp. 231–32.

102. Notes of a Conversation between Mr. Chamberlain and Herr Hitler at Godesberg on September 22, 1938. *B. D.,* II, 463–73.

103. Notes of a Conversation Between the Prime Minister and Herr Hitler at Godesberg, September 23–4, 1938. *Ibid.,* II, 499–508. For enlightening sidelights of the Godesberg talks, see Strang, *Home and Abroad,* pp. 139–40; Kirkpatrick, *The Inner Circle,* pp. 112–21; Vernon Bartlett, *And Now, Tomorrow* (London, 1960), pp. 28–33.

gone to the limit of concession and that it is up to the Chancellor to make some contribution."[104] The extent to which the Prime Minister's response to Hitler rested on his assessment of public opinion is moot, but the reference seems to testify to a real awareness of its limiting effect.

There was great anxiety in Britain about the Godesberg conversations. Duff Cooper warned Halifax on September 22 that he could never consent to an occupation of Czechoslovakia by German troops. Halifax agreed. He had no intention of allowing German troops to enter Czechoslovakia except with the consent of the Czech Government. Churchill, too, was concerned; in a private conversation he violently denounced the Prime Minister. A section of the London public was also agitated. That evening a crowd estimated at 10,000 gathered in Whitehall in support of a protest against the Anglo-French plan, crying "Stand by the Czechs!" and "Recall Parliament!"[105] On the afternoon of September 23, Halifax wired Chamberlain requesting authority to get on with "precautionary steps," including mobilization.[106] Simultaneously, Duff Cooper authorized the recalling of men from leave to the fleet, the bringing up of all crews to full complement, and the dispatch of 1900 men to the Mediterranean to bring that fleet up to establishment and to man the Suez Canal defenses.[107]

Chamberlain returned to London on the afternoon of September 24, and the Cabinet met that evening. Exactly what Chamberlain recommended and what then transpired is uncertain—and disputed[108]—but in any event, there was spirited debate as to what Britain's course of action should be. Both Duff Cooper

104. British Delegation to Halifax, Godesberg, Sept. 23, 1938; Halifax to British Delegation, F. O., Sept. 23, 1938. *B. D.,* II, 482–83, 490.

105. Duff Cooper, *Old Men Forget,* p. 232; *The Times,* Sept. 23, 1938.

106. Halifax to Henderson, F.O., Sept. 23, 1938. *B. D.,* II, 483–84.

107. Duff Cooper, *Old Men Forget,* p. 234.

108. Duff Cooper holds that the Prime Minister recommended that the German terms be accepted. *Ibid.,* p. 234. L. S. Amery supports that view. *My Political Life,* III, 268. But Templewood insists that at an immediate meeting of the Inner Cabinet, it was decided that Hitler's terms were unacceptable, a view then strongly confirmed by the full Cabinet. *Nine Troubled Years,* p. 312. Chamberlain's own papers are silent on the point. Macleod, *Neville Chamberlain,* p. 247.

and Hore-Belisha advised immediate mobilization, since this was the only language which Hitler understood. And Duff Cooper, according to his own account, vigorously protested any acquiescence in the German terms.[109]

Next day the discussion continued. In a startling reversal of opinion—which followed a night of torturous reflection and came as a "horrible blow" to Chamberlain—Halifax now (in his own words) "plumped for refusal of Hitler's terms."[110] Duff Cooper and Hore-Belisha both believed Britain obligated to support the Czechs. Others disagreed, and five hours of debate produced no decision. At length Duff Cooper suggested that he resign, his continued presence in the Cabinet serving only to delay and annoy those who thought differently. Though not surprised, Chamberlain asked him not to take precipitate action.[111] Later, at least four, and perhaps six, other Cabinet members were reported to be contemplating resignation if Hitler's ultimatum was accepted: Stanley, Winterton, De La Warr (President of the Board of Education), probably Hore-Belisha, and possibly Elliot and W. S. Morrison (Minister of Agriculture).[112]

Daladier and Bonnet flew to London again on the evening of September 25 and met with the Inner Cabinet at 10 Downing Street. The French Government had found Hitler's Godesberg memorandum unacceptable and proposed a return to the Anglo-French plan. When Chamberlain asked what should be done if Hitler refused, Daladier replied that "in that case each of us would have to do his duty." There followed a rather exasperated exchange of views as Chamberlain tried to learn exactly what France would do militarily, and Daladier, irritated by British doubts concerning French military potential, asked whether Chamberlain was ready to accept Hitler's demands passively. This "grim bout of fencing" (Strang's words) continued without con-

109. Duff Cooper, *Old Men Forget,* pp. 234–35; Minney, *Private Papers of Hore-Belisha,* p. 145.

110. Sir Alexander Cadogan played a key role in Halifax's change of mind. For a full explanation, see Birkenhead, *Halifax,* pp. 399–400.

111. Duff Cooper, *Old Men Forget,* pp. 235–36; Minney, *Private Papers of Hore-Belisha,* pp. 146-47.

112. Kennedy to the Secretary of State, London, Sept. 25, 1938. *U.S. For. Rel., 1938,* I, 652. See also Amery, *My Political Life,* III, 269.

crete conclusions, Chamberlain eventually requesting that General Gamelin, the French Chief of Staff, fly to London on the next day.[113]

Chamberlain next met with his Cabinet for the third time in twenty-four hours. The opposition there and the French rejection of Hitler's demands apparently had moved him. As Halifax had urged him to do, he proposed one final effort to reach agreement with Hitler. Next day he would send Sir Horace Wilson to Hitler with a personal letter appealing to him to allow the details of the transfer of territory to be settled by an international body of Germans, Czechs, and British. If Hitler refused, Wilson would tell him that France would fight for Czechoslovakia and Britain would join France. This constituted a startling reversal of Chamberlain's earlier position, yet none of his supporters (according to Duff Cooper's account[114]) uttered a word of criticism at the reversal—an enlightening commentary on the strength of conviction of Chamberlain's closest Cabinet colleagues and the extent to which they were willing to submit to his leadership.

On the morning of September 26 General Gamelin conferred with Chamberlain and Sir Thomas Inskip, Minister for the Coordination of Defense, discussing the military potential of France, Germany, Italy, and Czechoslovakia; the possibility of war was frankly considered.[115] Immediately thereafter Chamberlain reassured Daladier that Britain "could not afford to see France overrun or defeated by Germany," and that she "would come to her assistance if France were in danger." But so long as there

113. Record of an Anglo-French Conversation held at No. 10 Downing Street on September 25, 1938. *B. D.*, II, 520–35; Strang, *Home and Abroad,* pp. 140–43; Bonnet, *Défense de la Paix,* I, 268–69. See also Templewood, *Nine Troubled Years,* pp. 312–15. Strang describes this meeting as "one of the most painful which it has ever been my misfortune to attend."

114. *Old Men Forget,* p. 237. Duff Cooper records that Chamberlain made this announcement almost casually, and he could hardly believe his ears. He asked Chamberlain to repeat it, for he thought he had misunderstood.

115. General Gamelin, *Servir: Le Prologue du Drame (1930– Aout 1939)* (April, 1946), pp. 351–52. No record of this conversation has been traced in the British Foreign Office archives, but a short verbal report to the Cabinet indicated that the resistance potential of Czechoslovakia was a major topic of discussion. (footnote), *B. D.*, II, 575.

remained a slender chance of peace, no opportunity for securing it should be neglected. In this context, Chamberlain reported his intention to send Wilson to Berlin and received French support.[116]

Chamberlain then informed his Cabinet that he had definitely assured the French of British support if they went to war. That assurance was given just in time to prevent a break in the Cabinet, for Duff Cooper and Stanley had agreed before the Cabinet meeting that they would resign unless the French received such assurance before leaving London.[117]

That same day Churchill, whose contacts with the Government had become more frequent and intimate with the mounting crisis, met with Chamberlain and Halifax to urge upon them the proposal he had set forth in his letter to Halifax on August 31: a declaration showing the unity of sentiment and purpose among Britain, France, and Russia[118] against German aggression. They discussed in detail a communiqué to that effect. That evening Halifax issued a statement the gist of which ran: "If, in spite of the efforts made by the British Prime Minister, a German attack is made upon Czechoslovakia, the immediate result must be that France will be bound to come to her assistance, and Great Britain and Russia will certainly stand by France."[119]

When Churchill returned to his apartment, he found about fifteen Conservatives, including Lord Cecil, Lord Lloyd, Sir Edward Grigg, Sir Robert Horne, R. J. Boothby, Brendan Bracken, L. S. Amery, and Richard Law, assembled there. By this time, Amery wrote later, "those of us who were perturbed by the Government's apparent weakness began getting together." The dissident Tories had in fact been meeting since Eden's resignation in February. They were divided into two groups: the

116. Record of an Anglo-French Conversation held at No. 10 Downing Street on September 26, 1938, at 11:20 a.m. *B. D.,* II, 536–41; Bonnet, *Défense de la Paix,* I, 271.

117. Duff Cooper, *Old Men Forget,* pp. 237–38.

118. Litvinov had declared on September 23 that if France honored her obligations to Czechoslovakia, the Soviet Government would also fight. United Kingdom Delegation to Halifax, Geneva, Sept. 24, 1938. *B. D.,* II, 497.

119. Churchill, *The Gathering Storm,* p. 309; Birkenhead, *Halifax,* pp. 402–03.

followers of Churchill, including Bracken and Boothby, and the followers of Eden, comprising about twenty members including Cranborne, Law, and Harold Macmillan. Duncan Sandys acted as liaison between the two groups, attending the meetings of both.[120]) The talk at Churchill's apartment turned largely on the importance of bringing Russia into the picture—and the intensity of feeling concerning the Soviet Union in Tory circles indicates the pitch their anxiety had reached. All were greatly reassured when Churchill described to them the character of the communiqué.[121]

Duff Cooper again urged the immediate mobilization of the fleet on September 27, and learned from the First Sea Lord, Sir Roger Backhouse, that Chamberlain would make an announcement to that effect in a broadcast speech to the nation that evening.[122] The decision had been made, according to Templewood, in "one of the meetings" of the Inner Cabinet after it had learned that Sir Horace Wilson had been received by Hitler with hostility. Chamberlain gave the order to the First Sea Lord, and Duff Cooper was "subsequently informed."[123]

The Prime Minister's address, however, was a depressing utterance for those who had hoped for some sign of firmness. It contained no word about the mobilization of the fleet, no mention of France, and little apparent concern for Czechoslovakia. Though he promised to resist any nation which he believed determined to dominate the world by force, he warned that Britain must be very clear before embarking upon war that "the really great issues" were at stake:

> However much we may sympathize with a small nation confronted by a big and powerful neighbour, we cannot in all circumstances undertake to involve the whole British Empire in war simply on her account. If we have to fight, it must be on larger issues than that.[124]

120. Wheeler-Bennett, *King George VI,* p. 356 n.

121. Churchill, *The Gathering Storm,* p. 309; Amery, *My Political Life,* III, 277–78.

122. Duff Cooper, *Old Men Forget,* pp. 238–39.

123. *Nine Troubled Years,* p. 317.

124. *The Times,* Sept. 28, 1938.

Duff Cooper was furious. So were many others who, like Churchill, felt sure Britain was "preparing to scuttle."[125]

When the Cabinet met at 9:30 p.m. immediately after Chamberlain's speech, Wilson reported on his mission to Germany. He had not delivered the important part of his message, namely, that Britain and France would fight, before Hitler's Sportspalast speech;[126] when he did deliver it on the following day, September 27, it was tied in with additional clauses and misinterpreted by Hitler.[127] In Wilson's opinion the only thing to do was to advise the Czechs to evacuate the Sudetenland. Duff Cooper could take no more. If Britain advised the Czechs to surrender, he told his Cabinet colleagues, she would be guilty of one of the basest betrayals in history. If the Prime Minister gave way, it would probably be the end of his Government—at least it would be the end of Duff Cooper's connection with it.[128]

After the meeting, Duff Cooper questioned Chamberlain about his failure to announce the mobilization of the fleet. He had meant to originally, the Prime Minister replied, but had later decided against it; now he supposed there was no use keeping it a secret. Thereupon, Duff Cooper telephoned the press section of the Admiralty to release the news to the morning newspapers.[129] Mobilization orders were issued from the Admiralty late the next morning.

In Chamberlain's words and actions at this juncture it is not difficult to sense a conflict between two sets of arguments—which may well help to explain both the actual fluctuations in the Prime Minister's outlook and the differences of opinion over

125. Duff Cooper, *Old Men Forget,* pp. 238–39. Churchill does not record his personal reaction, although he does refer to the Prime Minister's "balancing broadcast." *The Gathering Storm,* p. 315.

126. In this speech Hitler bellowed that if the Sudetenland was not yielded by October 1, Germany would occupy it. Baynes, *Speeches of Adolf Hitler,* II, 1487–99.

127. Notes of a Conversation between Sir Horace Wilson and Herr Hitler at Berlin on September 26, 1938; Notes of a Conversation between Herr Hitler and Sir Horace Wilson at Berlin on September 27, 1938. *B. D.,* II, 554–57, 564–67. The German version in *G. D.,* II, 934–35, 963–65, is essentially the same. See also Kirkpatrick, *The Inner Circle,* pp. 123–26.

128. Duff Cooper, *Old Men Forget,* pp. 239–40.

129. *Ibid.,* p. 240.

his attitude toward the developing crisis. On the one hand were the practical arguments for avoiding war. On the other hand was the pressure of public sentiment, which had distinctly hardened against further appeasement.[130]

The British press had come out firmly against the Godesberg memorandum, and its tone had remained firm during the following days. The *Liverpool Daily Post* (Sept. 23) termed the German threats to trample Czechoslovakia "repellently mean and sadistic," and demanded that Chamberlain must now insist upon concessions from the German side. The Conservative *Financial Times* (Sept. 27) and the *Financial News* (Sept. 26) agreed with that view. If Hitler were allowed to end the Czech crisis in his own high-handed and imperious manner, there could be no more peace or security in Europe. For the *Glasgow Herald* (Sept. 26), Hitler, in the Godesberg demands, was plainly challenging a European war. If the Führer resorts to force, the Cardiff *Western Mail* (Sept. 28) exclaimed, he will find Britain, France, and Russia in the field against him. The Bradford *Yorkshire Observer* (Sept. 22) lamented that "recent British policy has been sadly lacking in firmness." No one in Britain wanted war, the *Sunday Pictorial* (Sept. 25) asserted, but if it came the whole country would be united and could trust in the justice of Britain's cause. The *Daily Telegraph* (Sept. 29) presumed that Britain would not tolerate further concessions to Germany; the German system of perpetually raising the price of peace had exhausted the patience of the Western powers. The world had been deceived in the hope it had experienced when Chamberlain went to Berchtesgaden, the *Manchester Guardian* (Sept. 22) contended. Did Chamberlain's action mean that he was ruling out the only solution—a stand by the peace-loving states against the tide of aggression? The *Daily Herald* (Sept. 28) warned that it was not Czechoslovakia alone that was threatened, but every principle of international mediation, justice, and equity.

There were a few dissenting voices. The Edinburgh *Weekly Scotsman* (Sept. 24) believed a partition of Czechoslovakia inevitable, the only alternative to a "sanguinary struggle in which

130. See Charles Madge and Thomas Harrison, *Britain by Mass-Observation* (Harmondsworth, Middlesex, 1939), pp. 65, 74–75, 101.

final extinction is all too probable." *The Times* (Sept. 22) admitted that Chamberlain had made a surrender, but insisted that it was not to Hitler but to justice. This was not dishonorable. Yet even *The Times* declared (Sept. 24) that if Germany was hungering for aggression, every British citizen knew where he stood. No one would welcome the alternative to yielding, but no one would flinch from it.

Signed articles and editorials demanding support for the Czechs and the strengthening of collective resistance to aggression appeared intermittently in sections of the periodical press throughout September, 1938. In the vanguard were the *Economist,* the *Statist,* the independent *Fortnightly,* the Liberal *Contemporary Review,* the *Spectator,* and the radical *New Statesman and Nation.* Of particular note was a poem which appeared in the latter journal (Sept. 24), heaping abuse upon the Chamberlain policy in a number of couplets such as:

> Meine Herren and Signori,
> Clients of the British Tory,
> Kindly note that Number 10
> Requests your patronage again.
>
> Frontiers promptly liquidated,
> Coup d'etats consolidated,
> Pledges taken and exchanged,
> Acquisitions rearranged,
>
> European intervention
> Given personal attention.
> Have you problems of Partition?
> Let us send a British Mission.
> Breaking with Geneva's firms,
> We offer Nazis favoured terms.

Labor continued to air its position in unequivocal terms. Following the declaration of September 21 denouncing the Anglo-French plan, Labor Members of Parliament sustained the attack in public addresses. D. N. Pritt at Bridgend, A. V. Alexander at

Wellington, P. J. Noel-Baker at Huddersfield, and Emanuel Shinwell at Seaham, delivered speeches strongly supporting the Czechs, denouncing capitulation to Hitler, and urging the policy of collective security behind international law.[131]

Then came the break in the apparent deadlock. Chamberlain, in writing to Hitler on September 26 as part of the message Wilson carried to Berlin, had once more urged settlement by negotiation upon the Führer.[132] The next evening a rather conciliatory reply arrived at the Foreign Office.[133] Encouraged, Chamberlain responded with a personal message expressing his readiness to go to Berlin at once to discuss arrangements for the transfer of the Sudeten territories with Hitler and representatives of the Czech Government, together with representatives of France and Italy if the Führer so desired.[134] (Just a few hours before, Halifax had wired to Henderson for immediate delivery to Hitler British proposals for the orderly transfer of territory which the Czech Government had earlier agreed to cede.[135])

On the afternoon of September 28, Parliament met to receive Chamberlain's account of his negotiations with Hitler and the subsequent developments. The Prime Minister had been speaking for some eighty minutes when he was interrupted by Sir John Simon, who handed him a note. Chamberlain smilingly reported the substance: Hitler had invited him, as well as Mussolini and

131. *The Times,* Sept. 26, 1938.

132. Letter from Chamberlain to Hitler, Sept. 26, 1938. *B. D.,* II, 541–42.

133. Henderson to Halifax, Berlin, Sept. 27, 1938. *Ibid.,* II, 576–78. British resolution, as expressed in the message conveyed by Wilson, may well have had an effect on Hitler. In addition, a propaganda march of German troops through Berlin on September 27 was received with an uneasy and sinister silence by the German public, and a gravely disappointed Hitler is reported to have cried to Goebbels that with people like that you could never carry on a war. Goerlitz, *The German General Staff,* pp. 337–38. Still another influence on Hitler may have been President Roosevelt's appeal of September 26 to find "a peaceful, fair, and constructive settlement" of the dispute. Shephard S. Jones and Denys P. Myers, *Documents on American Foreign Relations: January 1938–June 1939* (Boston, 1939), p. 287.

134. Halifax to Henderson, F.O., Sept. 28, 1938. *B. D.,* II, 587.

135. Halifax to Henderson, F.O., Sept. 27, 1938. *Ibid.,* II, 572–73.

Daladier, to Munich for a conference.[136] The announcement touched off an intense emotional outburst—about which considerable controversy arose later when the "mass hysteria" of the Commons was used in defense of the Munich settlement which followed.[137] Then Attlee, Sinclair, James Maxton, and George Lansbury rose to wish the Prime Minister good luck and Godspeed.[138]

For the most part the British press greeted Chamberlain's announcement with relief and hope, just as it had greeted his trip to Berchtesgaden two weeks before. The Bradford *Yorkshire Observer* (Sept. 29) paid tribute to the Prime Minister for making possible one more chance for peace. The pivotal point, it suggested, had been his firmness in telling Hitler that the Godesberg memorandum was unreasonable, a firmness most assuredly strengthened by the "fierce public opinion against further concessions" which was "flowing in this country." For the *Financial Times* (Sept. 29), Chamberlain's efforts to preserve peace had assumed "heroic proportions." The Cardiff *Western Mail* (Sept. 29) called it "splendid personal initiative." Both *The Times* (Sept. 29) and the *Manchester Guardian* (Sept. 29) saw reason for hope, while recognizing that it might mean no more than a respite. The *News Chronicle* (Sept. 28) contented itself with warning that there must be no concessions from the side of the democracies, but the *Daily Herald* (Sept. 29) took that idea one step

136. Hitler was probably influenced in part by Mussolini's active support for Chamberlain's proposal. Urged by the British to do so, the Duce had requested on the morning of September 28 both a twenty-four hour delay in German mobilization and Hitler's acceptance of Chamberlain's proposal. See Laffan, *The Crisis Over Czechoslovakia,* pp. 430–33.

137. It is often stated that the whole House took part, but that has been specifically denied by some, including Geoffrey Mander, who claims: "Those in my immediate neighborhood . . . remained seated." *We Were Not All Wrong* (London, 1944), p. 18. Duff Cooper's explanation seems cogent: the Government supporters cheered Chamberlain while the Opposition sat glum and silent. Then when Attlee gave his blessing to the plan, the Conservatives cheered him, cheers in which the Opposition had to join, though looking a little foolish. *Old Men Forget,* p. 240. In any event, Harold Nicolson argued later, the members were not cheering Munich; they were cheering release from war, a very different thing. "The Commons and the 1938 Crisis," *The Listener,* XL (November 25, 1948), 796.

138. *Parl. Debs., HC,* September 28, 1938, vol. 339, 26–29.

further: if Britain now stood fast for justice and equity, she might yet secure a great victory for the forces of peace and reason. The *Glasgow Herald* (Sept. 29) welcomed the Munich meeting for it embodied a return to the idea of collective security; Britain would now undertake for the first time a real commitment in central Europe, a guarantee of Czechoslovakia's frontiers. And if the Munich effort should unhappily fail, "we shall now quite certainly see very real collective action to restrain a wanton aggressor."

What might have happened had Hitler not resorted to another conference is tempting, though of course futile, to contemplate. British opposition to appeasement had most definitely hardened, and this had had a corresponding influence on the Government. As it was, the respite brought relief throughout the nation, and on the morning of September 29, Chamberlain, riding on air in every sense of the word, flew off to Munich.

CHAPTER SIX

The Meaning of Munich

THE STATESMEN OF Great Britain, France, Germany, and Italy met in Munich on the afternoon of September 29. The Czech delegates were allowed to sit outside in the hall, but not to enter the conference room. After thirteen hours of discussion, during which Chamberlain apparently negotiated with some obstinacy, the Munich Agreement was signed.[1]

In reality the conference was but a ceremony. Its very existence meant that in all essentials Hitler had won his demands. What the conference did was to extort from the Führer the modification of the most offensive and provocative of the new conditions which he had insisted upon at Godesberg. For the purposes of evacuation, the Sudeten German territory was divided into four zones, occupation of which was to begin on October 1 and continue progressively until October 7. The conditions of evacuation were to be laid down by an International Commission in Berlin consisting of the Secretary of State of the German Foreign Office, the British, French, and Italian Ambassadors in Berlin, and a representative of Czechoslovakia. This commission was also charged with ascertaining the remaining territory of predominantly German character to be occupied by German troops by October 10, with determining the territories in which plebiscites were to be held and fixing the conditions of the plebiscites, and with the final delimitation of the frontier. A joint German-Czech commission was to be entrusted with working out the details of the right of option into and out of the transferred territories, which was to be exercised

1. For enlightening accounts of the conference by two men who were present, one a British official, the other a newspaperman, see Kirkpatrick, *The Inner Circle,* pp. 127–34 and Bartlett, *And Now, Tomorrow,* pp. 33–36.

within six months. Britain and France undertook to guarantee the new frontiers of Czechoslovakia, and Germany and Italy agreed to join the guarantee as soon as the question of Polish and Hungarian minorities in Czechoslovakia had been settled.[2]

Later in the morning of September 30, Chamberlain and Hitler signed—upon the initiative of the former, who acted entirely alone and for uncertain but variously interpreted reasons[3]—a declaration whereby they resolved that in the future the method of consultation should be adopted to deal with any questions that might concern the two countries; they further declared their determination to continue efforts to remove possible sources of difference, thereby contributing to the peace of Europe.[4]

In effect Hitler had gained everything. By October 1 his troops would enter the Sudetenland, not fighting their way in, but completing the occupation in ten days without resistance. He had paved the way for the total destruction of Czechoslovakia. He had shattered the French security system, driven Russia out of the European alignment, and isolated Poland. He had inflicted a defeat upon Great Britain and France without firing a shot. But Munich had averted war, and for Neville Chamberlain that result outweighed all others.

If Chamberlain had any misgivings about Munich, they must have been eased by the reception given him by both the German and British people on September 30. Despite the rain which was falling when he departed from Munich, a great throng gathered outside his hotel to see him leave. According to an American

2. Memorandum, Berlin, Sept. 29, 1938. *G. D.*, II, 1014–16.

3. Ivone Kirkpatrick, who assisted Chamberlain in all three of his meetings with Hitler, testifies that he was never able to discover what passed through the Prime Minister's mind on this occasion, but submits the following as the most likely hypothesis: Chamberlain thought the best chance with Hitler was to try to bind him by a public declaration and then to proclaim the belief that Hitler would keep his word. *The Inner Circle,* p. 130. Chamberlain's recent biographer, Iain Macleod, suggests a quite different motive, quoting the Prime Minister as follows: "If he [Hitler] . . . sticks to it . . . fine, but if he breaks it that will convince the Americans of the kind of man he is." *Neville Chamberlain,* p. 256. But according to Hitler, Chamberlain said the declaration was essential for his Parliamentary position. *Ciano's Hidden Diary, 1937–1938* (New York, 1953), p. 172.

4. Note of a Conversation between the Prime Minister and Herr Hitler, Sept. 30, 1938, at the latter's Flat in Munich. *B. D.*, II, 635–40.

newspaperman, they crowded about his car. Women wept, children threw flowers, men grew hoarse from cheering.[5] Upon his arrival in England the scene recurred. To the cheering crowds at Heston, Chamberlain read the text of his agreement with Hitler and described the Czech solution as the prelude to a larger settlement that would bring peace to all Europe. In London he accompanied the King and Queen to the balcony of Buckingham Palace amid a delirious uproar and the singing of "For they are jolly good fellows." When he arrived in Downing Street, the crowds outside clamored to see him. Chamberlain realized (so Halifax testifies) that this popular enthusiasm was only momentary; yet he needed to acknowledge the greeting accorded him. "What can I say?" Chamberlain asked. "Say that you have come back with peace with honor, and go on to the balcony where Dizzy said it before," answered one of his staff. With these words running through his tired mind, Chamberlain stepped to the balcony and spoke those ill-fated words: "This is the second time in our history that there has come back from Germany to Downing Street peace with honor. I believe it is peace in our time."[6]

For one brief moment Chamberlain filled the imaginations of men in all countries as the savior of peace. Perhaps no more than ten percent of the British public, immediately after the event, understood the full implications or realized what would be the ultimate consequences of Munich.[7] But the time was soon to come, and swiftly—after men had been able to recover their poise and to think calmly—when doubts arose and a sense of shame appeared, and when Chamberlain's critics renewed with ever-increasing vigor their charge that the appeasement policy was selling the pass of European civilization. For Duff Cooper, Munich did not eliminate the principle of invasion of Czechoslovakia, and when the Cabinet met on the evening of September 30, he offered his resignation. Chamberlain seemed, he later recalled, "as glad to be rid of me as I was determined to go."[8]

5. Birchall, *The Storm Breaks,* p. 317.
6. *The Times,* Oct. 1, 1938; Templewood, *Nine Troubled Years,* pp. 320–21; Halifax, *Fullness of Days,* p. 202.
7. This is the estimate of Sir Robert Bruce Lockhart, "September Crisis —and After," *The Listener,* XL (October 28, 1948), 636.
8. Duff Cooper, *Old Men Forget,* pp. 242–43.

Though Churchill records that the Cabinet was "shaken to its foundations,"[9] Duff Cooper notes that in the meeting of September 30, there was no criticism of Munich by other Cabinet members.[10] What had happened to those who had sided with Duff Cooper throughout September? Perhaps they were converted to the Prime Minister's point of view by the cheering London crowds. Perhaps they simply shared in the vast relief that war had been averted. In any event, they chose to subvert their earlier anxieties to the apparent victory of the moment, and in the process failed to call proper attention to the dangerous defeat which Munich indeed was. The effect of this on the Prime Minister and the British people generally is difficult to calculate, but it undoubtedly helped to cover up the earlier division within the Cabinet and to convey a sense of security following Munich which was in no way compatible with the reservations and fears of a few short days before. That this reaction might be explained as "only human" does not lessen its importance; it contributed significantly to the continued slumber of the nation.

The immediate reaction of the British press to Munich was one of profound relief, the expressions of which ranged as far as *The Times*' (Oct. 1) joyous proclamation that "no conqueror returning from a victory on the battlefield has come home adorned with nobler laurels than Mr. Chamberlain from Munich yesterday" and columnist Beverly Baxter's optimistic pronouncement in the Conservative *Sunday Graphic* (Oct. 2) that "because of Neville Chamberlain the world my son will live in will be a vastly different place. . . . In our time we shall not see again the armed forces of Europe gathering to strike at each other like savage beasts."

But significantly, most journals, while applauding the Prime Minister's work in preserving peace, also voiced deep concern for the future. The Conservative *Daily Telegraph* (Oct. 1) tempered its joy with the clear warning that experience had shown that Hitler's assurances could not always be taken at face value. Britain must not think that she had not paid a very high price for peace, the Liberal *Manchester Guardian* (Oct. 1) ad-

9. *The Gathering Storm,* p. 324.
10. Duff Cooper, *The Second World War* (New York, 1939), p. 15.

monished. Czechoslovakia had been rendered helpless, with the result that Hitler would now be able to advance again whenever he chose, and with greatly increased force. The Liberal *News Chronicle* (Oct. 1) warned that Munich had drastically weakened Czechoslovakia's chances for survival and the prospects of democracy throughout Europe, while the Liberal *Liverpool Daily Post* (Sept. 30) saw the powers now under an inescapable obligation to protect the independence of the new Czech state. Chamberlain had destroyed what had remained of collective security, exhorted the pro-Labor *Reynolds News* (Oct. 2); peace had been sacrificed for a semblance of peace.

Representative of the tone of the press as a whole was the independent *Glasgow Herald* (Oct. 1), which cautioned that although Britain was naturally happy for peace, she must not be blind to bare facts. Munich was a "diktat" which aroused a feeling of uneasiness for the future; everything now depended upon Hitler. The moral of Munich was that Britain must become stronger militarily than she had ever been before. She must redouble her defense efforts and pursue rearmament with renewed energy.

While the press fluctuated between thankfulness for peace and anxiety for the future, the House of Commons reconvened on October 3. According to Parliamentary custom, Duff Cooper, since he had resigned, opened the debate with a personal explanation of his action. The great defect in British policy in recent weeks, as he saw it, had been the failure to make it plain exactly where Britain stood and what she would do in various circumstances. This was the major difference between him and the Prime Minister. While Chamberlain believed in addressing Hitler in the "language of sweet reasonableness," Duff Cooper believed him more open to the "language of the mailed fist." In Duff Cooper's mind Hitler had agreed to the conference at Munich not because of any communication addressed to him from Britain, but because of the mobilization of the British fleet and the subsequent realization that Britain would fight. He reasoned:

> It was not for Serbia that we fought in 1914. It was not even for Belgium, although it occasionally suited some

> people to say so. We were fighting then, as we should have been fighting last week, in order that one Great Power should not be allowed, in disregard of treaty obligations, of the laws of nations and the decrees of morality, to dominate by brutal force the continent of Europe. . . . For that principle we must ever be prepared to fight, for on the day when we are not prepared to fight for it we forfeit our Empire, our liberties and our independence.[11]

In essence, Duff Cooper did not believe it possible to come to a reasonable settlement of outstanding questions with Germany; therefore, it was better for him to go.[12]

Chamberlain did not reply directly, but described the path which leads to appeasement as long and bristled with obstacles. Now that a settlement had been reached in Czechoslovakia, "it may be possible to make further progress along the road to sanity." He saw "sincerity and good will" on both sides of the

11. *Parl. Debs., HC,* October 3, 1938, vol. 339, 32. In his speech Duff Cooper combatted the belief that the policy which culminated in Munich was dictated by British unpreparedness for war. This is still highly controversial, though it is now known that in the Spring of 1938, the Chiefs of Staff advised Chamberlain that war with Germany over Czechoslovakia must be avoided, no matter what the cost, until the British rearmament program began to bear "substantial fruit." P. K. Kemp, *Key to Victory: The Triumph of British Sea Power in World War II* (Boston, 1957), p. 26. For views tending to support Duff Cooper, see Selby, *Diplomatic Twilight,* p. 100; General Lord Ismay, *The Memoirs of General Lord Ismay* (New York, 1960), pp. 92–93; and Cyril Falls, "Should the Democracies Have Fought in 1938?" *The Listener,* XL (November 11, 1948), 718. On the other side, see Kemp, *Key to Victory* and Sir John Slessor, *The Central Blue: The Autobiography of Sir John Slessor, Marshal of the RAF* (New York, 1957), pp. 146–50. A more recent account by Robin Higham sees both sides: while Chamberlain was uncomfortably aware of Britain's vulnerability to air attack, "his pessimism was . . . too extreme." *Armed Forces in Peacetime: Britain, 1918–1940: A Case History* (Hamden, 1962), pp. 185–86.

12. Duff Cooper's speech was apparently most effective. No sooner had he resumed his seat than he received a note from Churchill calling it "one of the finest Parliamentary performances I have ever heard." Harold Macmillan (Conservative) wrote him that same day: "It was the finest thing I've heard since I've been in the House." Josiah Wedgwood (Labor) commended him in writing for standing against the race of "clucking old hens and damned cowards." And Malcolm MacDonald, the Colonial Secretary, wrote him that he had done "the right and honourable thing in resigning." Duff Cooper, *Old Men Forget,* pp. 248–49.

Anglo-German declaration,[13] though he simultaneously noted that Britain could not afford to relax her rearmament program.

A seething Clement Attlee preferred to characterize Munich as only an armistice in a state of war. Brute force had won the victory, not reason and moderation. Labor had long urged a firm Anglo-French-Russian declaration against aggression, but the Government had consistently ignored it. The day Britain left the path of collective security, she took a step towards war. Attlee called for a "real peace conference" to deal with the causes of war which were troubling the world. Sinclair followed with a similarly scorching censure. What and whose foreign policy was it that had brought Britain to the edge of war he asked. Not that of Labor, which had constantly opposed it. Not that of the Liberals—they had always advocated another. Not Eden's—he had resigned office rather than be responsible for it. Not Churchill's—he had consistently condemned it. "That policy . . . of successive retreats in the face of aggressive dictatorships . . . was the policy of the Prime Minister." To claim that Munich was a victory for negotiation over force was flagrantly untrue. Peace could be firmly established only by offering convincing proof to Germany that the nations which wanted international relationships regulated by reason and negotiation were prepared to work together to resist force.

The Opposition leaders seated, Anthony Eden warned in calm but determined language that foreign affairs could not be continued on the basis of "stand and deliver." Successive surrenders brought only successive humiliation, and in turn, more humiliating demands. There must be a determined effort to conduct a foreign policy upon which the nation could unite, and an effort in the sphere of defense far greater than anything hitherto attempted. Richard Law (Conservative) complemented Eden's views. Could anyone really believe that self-determination had anything to do with the transfer of the Sudetenland to Germany or with the entire policy of Hitler he asked. The claim of "peace in our time" was absolutely incredible. How could anyone believe that

13. Sir John Simon believes that Chamberlain did not anticipate Hitler's subsequent breach of the Munich Agreement; he apparently was convinced of Hitler's good faith. *Retrospect,* p. 254.

those men who had risen to power, maintained themselves in power, and achieved their greatest triumphs all by violence and treachery had suddenly been convinced by the magnetic eye of the Prime Minister that violence and treachery did not pay? Britain had much to lose by war, but her greatness was not based upon calculations of that kind.

To Laborite Hugh Dalton, Chamberlain had brought back a "scrap of paper torn from 'Mein Kampf'." He was particularly disturbed about the cold-shouldering of Russia, fearing that most of Chamberlain's supporters would rather lose the British Empire with Russia neutral than to hold it with Russia as an ally.[14] If Chamberlain's policy continued, more friends, more allies would be sacrificed until Britain would be left to face the military might of Germany alone. For Dalton, too, the only answer was a league of states which would accept as their premise common resistance to aggression and the peaceful settlement of all disputes. The British Government's "ambition to be eaten last" was futile, for left alone Britain would be eaten all the same, and would not be consulted about the date of the banquet.

Though bitterly attacked during the debate, Chamberlain was not without supporters. Laborite George Lansbury and four Conservatives defended the Prime Minister, Sir Samuel Hoare contending that the course Chamberlain had taken was the only one open to a responsible government. Any other would have plunged Europe into world war.[15]

Halifax's explanation of Munich to the House of Lords contained some significant variations in emphasis. He spoke of the "unusual lengths" to which Britain had gone in pressuring the Czechs to accept the Anglo-French proposals, a point which Chamberlain did not mention. With regard to a guarantee to Czechoslovakia, he felt Britain bound to make "a counter-con-

14. On October 4 it was the unpleasant duty of Coulondre, the French Ambassador in Moscow, to inform Potemkin, the Russian Vice-Commissar for Foreign Affairs, officially of the content of the Munich Agreement. When he had finished, Potemkin replied: "I simply wish to state that the Western powers have deliberately kept the USSR out of the negotiations." And after a long silence, he exclaimed: "My poor fellow, what have you done? For us, I see no other consequence but a fourth partition of Poland." Coulondre, *De Staline á Hitler,* p. 165.

15. *Parl. Debs., HC,* October 3, 1938, vol. 339, 31–156.

tribution to balance the reduction of Czechoslovakia's defensive strength. In no other circumstances . . . should we have felt morally justified in pressing her Government to go so far." Chamberlain's statement contained no such sentiment. Halifax referred to "the assurance of a joint guarantee by the United Kingdom and France" of the new Czech boundary being "reinforced and buttressed" by Germany and Italy "when the other minority questions have been settled," which suggests that he did not envisage it as wholly conditional upon Axis acquiescence.[16] Thus in his estimate of Munich, Halifax gave a more forcible impression than any of his Government colleagues that Britain was under obligation to the Czechs and that only a departure in the accustomed British noncommittal attitude toward central Europe would be adequate repayment. He thus was in line with his pre-Munich reservations about the Anglo-French plan. This is not to deny Halifax's share in the Munich decisions; rather it is to say that for him Munich was not "peace with honor."[17]

The acrid attack upon the Government in the Commons continued for three more days. Though Labor led the charge, Conservative criticism was conspicuous. On October 4, after Laborite Herbert Morrison spoke at length on the necessity of collective security and chided that a call for steady rearmament was hardly a fitting plea for a man who was satisfied that he had brought about peace, L. S. Amery (Conservative) represented Munich as "the triumph of sheer, naked force, exercised in the most blatant and brutal fashion." He could see no substantial difference between Hitler's Godesberg demands, which Britain had refused, and the Munich terms.[18] Britain could no longer afford

16. *Parl. Debs., HL,* October 3, 1938, vol. 110, 1303–07.

17. In his memoirs Halifax declares the only possible defense—the "genuine defence"—of Munich to be that it was "a horrible and wretched business, but the lesser of two evils." *Fullness of Days,* p. 201. See also Birkenhead, *Halifax,* pp. 405–09. This attitude perhaps helps to explain why Halifax was exempt from the opprobrium directed at Chamberlain by those who were critical of Munich.

18. This opinion was endorsed some years later by Sir William Strang, who wrote in his memoirs that the differences between the Godesberg memorandum and the Munich Agreement proved to be worthless in substance and in fact, although on paper they made a sizeable list. *Home and Abroad,* p. 148.

to be a "go-as-you-please" nation; she must seek mutual cooperation with "any other freedom-loving nation which cares to work with us." With an eye to history, Colonel Wedgwood (Laborite) quoted Patrick Henry: "Is life so sweet and peace so dear as to be purchased at the price of chains and slavery?" Liberal Geoffrey Mander avowed that Chamberlain's policy would inevitably lead to war. Hitler was interested in grievances only insofar as they enabled him to pursue his aim of European domination. To Laborite Robert Gibson, Britain at Munich was like a Samaritan who "took the clothes off the wayfarer and handed them over to the robbers." Chamberlain had "miscalculated his logarithms"; he certainly was not directing the ship of state into any haven of peace. Viscount Cranborne, who had resigned with Eden, derided Chamberlain's "peace with honor." Where was the honor? Giving away territory that belonged to somebody else in order to avoid embarrassment to yourself was not an auspicious way of beginning a new era of peace and justice. If the Government had not yet learned that appeasement was no alternative to rearmament and conciliation no alternative to firmness, it would only pave the way to richly deserved disaster.[19]

On the third day of debate, Sir John Simon moved that the House approve the policy of the Government by which war had been averted and support its efforts to secure a lasting peace. One argument which he used for justifying Munich was that Czechoslovakia, as it had emerged from the Treaty of Versailles, was not a "viable entity." No sooner had he resumed his seat than Arthur Greenwood moved that Simon's motion be amended to read that the House could not approve the Government's policy. The net result of Munich, as he saw it, was that Hitler was now in complete command of central Europe, and a tottering Mussolini had been replaced on his pedestal. There was absolutely no other way to peace than by the road of collective security.

Churchill spoke to that, viewing Munich as "total and unmitigated defeat." Czechoslovakia would be engulfed by the Nazi regime within a matter of months. The past five years of British

19. *Parl. Debs., HC,* October 4, 1938, vol. 339, 172–236.

foreign policy had been "five years of futile good intention, five years of eager search for the line of least resistance, five years of uninterrupted retreat of British power, five years of neglect of our air defenses." While the Prime Minister still hoped for cordial relations with Germany, in Churchill's view:

> There can never be friendship between the British democracy and the Nazi Power, that Power which spurns Christian ethics, which cheers its onward course by a barbarous paganism, which vaunts the spirit of aggression and conquest, which derives strength and perverted pleasure from persecution, and uses, as we have seen, with pitiless brutality the threat of murderous force. That Power cannot ever be the trusted friend of the British democracy.[20]

He had long urged the creation of a superior air force, the organizing of the collective strength of the peace-loving nations, and the making of alliances within the Covenant to restrain Germany, but all in vain. The Western democracies had been "weighed in the balance and found wanting." And Munich was not the end; it was only the beginning—"the first sip, the first foretaste of a bitter cup which will be proffered to us year by year unless by a supreme recovery of moral health and martial vigour, we arise again and take our stand for freedom as in the olden time."

Following a vigorous renewal of the Labor demand for collective security by Sir Stafford Cripps, Harold Nicolson (National Laborite) charged the Government with giving away the key to Europe. For two hundred and fifty years the foundation of British foreign policy had been to prevent the domination of Europe by any single power or group of powers. An essential corollary of that policy had been that Britain should always support the small powers against the strong. But Chamberlain at Munich had abandoned that policy. Rebutting an insinuation that those who stood for moral standards and a settled pattern of international relations were afflicted by a Foreign Office mentality, Nicolson emphatically declared: "I thank God that I possess the Foreign Office mind."[21]

20. *Ibid.*, October 5, 1938, vol. 339, 370.
21. Ibid., October 5, 1938, vol. 339, 337–434.

The final day's debate was largely anti-climax. There was less incisive criticism of past policy, more emphasis on the need for the rule of law and collective security, especially in the remarks of Laborites Noel-Baker, Ellen Wilkinson, and Attlee. Everyone wanted to see the Government's efforts for peace succeed, Attlee noted, but there was nothing in the record of its policy to suggest success. The Government must not drift; it must assume power over events. The world awaited a lead.

Undeterred by the strictures of his critics or by the gloom of their forebodings, Chamberlain closed the debate by contending that Britain must seek to avoid war by analyzing its possible causes and trying to remove them by discussion in a spirit of collaboration and good will. Indirectly replying to Churchill, he suggested that if British policy were based on the view that any sort of friendly relations with totalitarian states were impossible, that the assurances given him personally were worthless, and that those states were bent upon the domination of Europe, then war was inevitable. The familiar catchword "collective security," which had been so popular with the Opposition, was to him only a return to entangling alliances and power politics—"a policy of utter despair." There was no use calling a conference, as Labor suggested, until it was certain that the totalitarian powers would attend, and attend with the intention of aiding Britain in the policy on which she had set her heart.[22] The latter point was a curious contradiction of his earlier statement of faith in the peaceful assurances given him by the dictators.

It is rather remarkable that in a debate on a policy based on "peace in our time" the only issue on which there was agreement was the vital need for the rapid completion of Britain's rearmament. Churchill and Duff Cooper urged it for the dissident Conservatives, Attlee grudgingly concurred, and Chamberlain and his lieutenants pledged it on behalf of the Government. But while the Prime Minister paid lip service to rearmament, it was patent that his enthusiasm was centered upon the development of that new era, the foundations of which he believed had been laid at Munich.

When the House divided, Greenwood's motion was defeated,

22. *Ibid.*, October 6, 1938, vol. 339, 539–58.

150 to 369; Simon's motion was victorious, 366 to 144.[23] Again the mere statistics of the division do not tell the whole story of the debate. The Munich issue had cut across party lines (a fact which the Government spokesman, R. A. Butler, openly acknowledged in closing the debate on October 5), and speaker after speaker, from all parties, had risen to denounce the Munich Agreement; to blame the Government for having allowed the League to die; to chastise it for having cold-shouldered Russia; to denounce it for having betrayed the Czechs; and to pour scorn upon the famous guarantee.

In one sense the critics of appeasement seemed to cry out with one voice. In another sense, however, it was during the debate on Munich that the differences of approach and emphasis, long present among the critics, individuals and groups alike, emerged with some clarity. Labor's demand for and confidence in "collective security" was once again obvious, though on this occasion no real attempt was made to re-define the term, apparently on the assumption that since the time of Eden's resignation its reference to a gathering together of peace-loving nations for some kind of collective action in defense of peace and mutual security was apparent to all. That its precise meaning was somewhat unclear would probably have been generally acknowledged, but it was the differing interpretations of the lack of precision which was important. The Government saw what it interpreted as a vague and nebulous suggestion as no alternative to its own policy at all, indeed as nothing more than a futile whip with which periodically to flail those in positions of responsibility. On the other hand, the Labor-Liberal Opposition saw a vital principle (crudely, though in essence, "hang together or hang separately") involved, and interpreted the open-endedness of the idea as an advantage inasmuch as it would permit a working out of details deemed necessary with the passing of time. Besides, the details could not be spelled out in full, for they were to be arrived at in collaboration with other countries. This was the essential meaning of Attlee's call for "a real peace conference," to include a great number of nations, which from this point on was another general article of faith in the Labor creed.

23. *Ibid.*, October 6, 1938, vol. 339, 554, 557–58.

From the dissident Conservative side came a strong appeal for "a great national effort," which, although also somewhat ill-defined, involved at least a conscious attempt to alert the British people to the fact that all was not well in Europe and that sacrifices of one kind or another might soon be demanded of them. This was coupled with the call for a new kind of national government, which meant not necessarily the resignation of Chamberlain but certainly the inclusion of men like Churchill and Eden in the Cabinet, as well, possibly, as able and vigorous members of the Labor Party. (Labor did not share this notion, for it had already passed the point where cooperation in a Chamberlain Cabinet was even a vague possibility. Whenever Labor critics referred to the constitution of the Government—which was infrequent in the period immediately following Munich—it was always in terms of a new Labor cabinet.) There was greater emphasis in dissident Conservative ranks on the necessity of a great increase in armaments, which Labor was still reluctant to push, and less hesitation to think in terms of what might be described as frank and open power politics. Churchill had spoken of the need for a superior air force, and had even dared to propose the conclusion of alliances—albeit within the framework of the Covenant—a thought which was anathema to Chamberlain and his colleagues.

Appeals for a return to the principles of the League—evidencing once more concern for the rule of law in international affairs, even if only from the selfish, yet nonetheless appealing point of view of self-preservation—were powerfully voiced by Conservatives (some of whom had not previously been associated with the dissident element of the Party), Laborites, and Liberals alike. The one thing which, above all else, seems to have brought these critics together again was their common fear that the Chamberlain Government simply did not understand the implications of what was going on in central Europe, and was, therefore, disinclined to take measures, whatever they might be, necessary for the maintenance of European peace and security.

The fears of the critics were not without foundation. How could Chamberlain insist on continuing discussions in "the spirit of collaboration and good will" after his experiences at Godesberg and Munich? How could he be content to speak about "not affording to relax" British rearmament, when what was needed was a program far more vigorous, far more imaginative, than anything the Chamberlain Government had as yet envisaged? What conclusion was to be drawn from the Government's primary defense of Munich, not on the merits of the settlement, not even on the grounds of military unpreparedness—of which so much was made later—but on the grounds that Czechoslovakia was not, in Simon's words, "a viable entity"? Did that not miss the point altogether? What the critics were concerned about was the manner and method whereby the Nazis had attained their end, and what this necessarily implied for all of Europe. Of this the Government showed no awareness whatsoever. The critics were not opposed to the Government's efforts for peace; they simply did not see how the Government's methods could succeed in obtaining the ends desired. The distinction was apparently one too subtle for the Government to grasp—or if it did, it still persisted in tarnishing its opponents as warmongers and irresponsible troublemakers. This was an inducement more than sufficiently powerful to pull Winston Churchill and Hugh Dalton, Duff Cooper and Stafford Cripps, Leo Amery and Harold Nicolson seemingly together, at least in Parliamentary debates, on behalf of a common cause. They may have been members of different parties; they may have espoused different solutions for the various problems of national existence, but they were all Englishmen deeply concerned about the preservation of British and European security and convinced that something far different from what the Chamberlain Government apparently envisaged was essential for the maintenance of that security. To be sure, their positions inevitably involved political implications of a partisan variety, but to suggest that this was the primary motive of their actions was to do a hurtful injustice to the concern which they shared for their nation and Europe. Finally, when the Government replied to its critics, it made little or no attempt to distinguish among them, which had the effect of throwing them together, whether they wished it that way or not.

Those speeches made in the Commons in favor of the Munich settlement somehow lacked force and did not seem to reflect the feeling or the conscience of the House as a whole. Chamberlain had begun the debate on a note which irritated many members. "Today we all meet in joy and thankfulness," he had said on October 3. But, Harold Nicolson attests, "we were not in fact feeling either glad or grateful; we were feeling ashamed."[24] The Commons was not in a mood to be impressed by Chamberlain's exposition on how the terms of Munich were an improvement over Godesberg. The members were more inclined to agree with Attlee: "We have felt that we are in the midst of tragedy. We have felt humiliation. We have seen the cause of democracy, which is, in our view, the cause of civilisation and humanity, suffer a terrible defeat."

So it was that, though the Government majority was unimpaired its victory was a hollow one. (As cartoonist David Low later saw it, Chamberlain's supporters, "having committed themselves to a fairy tale," could not bring themselves to face cold reality and were determined to wish appeasement into a success both as a matter of loyalty to Chamberlain and to protect their own political investment.[25]) This was especially so in view of the later testimony of the British historian, L. B. Namier: "The more there was of doubt lurking deeper down, the greater was at first the annoyance and irritation with anyone who dared to give expression to it."[26] Government supporters could search the division lists in vain for the names of most of the prominent Conservatives who were not members of the Government. Churchill, Amery, Macmillan, Duff Cooper, Eden, Cranborne, and at least a score of others registered their disapproval by abstention. In fact, during the Munich debate and in the days immediately following, the dissident Conservatives sought grounds for active cooperation with Labor—Amery-Attlee and Macmillan-Dalton conversations looking toward that end. Nothing concrete came of them.[27]

24. "The Commons and the 1938 Crisis," *The Listener,* XL (November 25, 1948), 796.

25. David Low, *Low's Autobiography* (New York, 1957), pp. 309–10.

26. "Munich Survey: A Summing Up," *The Listener,* XL (December 2, 1948), 836.

27. *Ibid.,* III, 298–99; Dalton, *The Fateful Years,* pp. 199–207. Amery explains the failure to reach any agreement by declaring that Labor

The Labor Party, of course, was handicapped in presenting its case by the fact that it had consistently opposed an increase in armaments. Condemnation of the Government for weakness came ill from those who had resisted its efforts to make itself stronger. This had bedeviled Labor not only during the Munich debate but from the beginning of its open opposition to appeasement. Although the majority of the party had, in 1931, after no little intra-party strife, approved a British contribution to the armed forces of the League, it had continued to oppose purely national armaments. This position, taken largely on theoretical grounds, had for Laborites an element of doctrinal consistency in it, and indeed made their constant insistence on collective security meaningful in terms of where for them real military strength lay. But the mass of Englishmen outside the ranks of Labor continued, especially in view of the declining vitality of the League, to think of military strength in national rather than international terms.

While this made the Conservative opposition even more significant, it also placed the dissident Conservatives in a difficult position. They had lost faith in the policy of the Government without gaining any in the Opposition. This certainly helps to account for their abstaining from the vote rather than voting against Chamberlain, as Churchill had at first urged. Moreover, Chamberlain's transparent honesty of purpose was everyhere recognized; perhaps he could yet be made to see the necessity of collective action instead of dangerous bargaining with aggressors. As Amery later explained: abstention was "enough to mark our disapproval of the Government's policy on the particular issue without indicating general hostility" and would keep the dissident Conservatives from "separating . . . from the main body whom events would presently bring around to our point of view."[28]

Labor leaders did not try to make much party capital out of the Munich settlement. It was too popular, at least momentarily,

---

was dead set against Chamberlain and would do nothing as long as he was Prime Minister. Dalton suggests the failure was due to a division among the dissident Conservatives on tactics and lengths to which they should go, and their reluctance to vote against the Government.

28. *My Political Life,* III, 287.

in the country. When people have been close to war and are presented, at the eleventh hour, with peace, they are usually too happy to inquire what the blessing may have cost. This appeared to be the case in Britain immediately after Munich, and Labor's recognition of the fact seemed to have made them somewhat more politically realistic than the Government was inclined to admit.

To let the matter rest there, however, is to miss an essential point. The debate in the Commons seemed to have a calming effect. Herein lay its real significance. It took away the excitement and hysteria of Chamberlain's return from Munich, and, as it proceeded from day to day, tended to leave the more passionate and partisan aspects on one side and to approach a more serious and thoughtful review of the resulting situation. The threat of personal danger had receded, and it began to dawn on many Englishmen how curious it was that Munich should be received with far greater enthusiasm by the "losers" in London and Paris than by the "winners" in Berlin and Rome. They came gradually to recognize that the very deliverance which they had celebrated with such rejoicing had been purchased with the sacrifice of Czechoslovakia. There was now room for guilt, humiliation, and even shame along with the sense of relief. This four-day debate in the Commons, October 3-6, led more Englishmen to thinking and talking hard common sense. The debate was instrumental in giving the country the enlightenment, and therefore the courage, which it required for the eventual revitalization of its moral and martial vigor, of which Churchill had spoken.[29] The impact of this was not immediately evident, but the apparently sudden show of British resolve in March, 1939 is far more understandable when viewed in the light of the debate.

The foregoing suggests that the immediate post-Munich period might have been an opportune time for the Chamberlain Government to have undertaken some new initiative, some more positive action, to meet the growing totalitarian threat to European peace and security. That it remained unconvinced that any such thing

29. See Nicolson, "The Commons and the 1938 Crisis," *The Listener*, XL (November 25, 1948), 796.

was necessary is well known. The essential point is that a significant segment of the British people was alarmed by the events of late September, deeply concerned about the future, and in this sense ready for a more vigorous foreign policy in a new direction. And all the disclaimers of later years notwithstanding, who can say that the British people would not have followed had a lead been given? In short, the traditional argument that the policy of the Chamberlain Government was only an accurate reflection of British public feeling, and that its freedom of action was greatly limited by public complacency, breaks down still further. This is not to deny that the dominant feeling among Englishmen was relief that war had been averted. Rather it is to suggest that there was a powerful undercurrent of anxiety and concern on which more astute statesmen might well have capitalized. To say that the British people were still somehow unable to sense the danger posed by Nazi Germany, and thus unwilling to support any policy other than Chamberlain's approach of appeasement—this in the face of their September experiences in digging slit trenches and trying on gas masks—certainly seems to underestimate the political sensibilities of most Englishmen. And if, as the effects of Munich slowly wore off, there was a gradual return to false confidence and complacency, this was at least as much the result of Government actions in promoting such an atmosphere as it was a natural development.

The recovery from the weekend debauch of emotion was reflected in the press, though there was still a wide divergence of reaction. Uncertainty characterized the views of many journals. The *Glasgow Herald* (Oct. 4) saw no means of determining whether Duff Cooper was right or wrong in his belief that a stronger stand would have helped British dealings with Germany —"we may hope for the best but . . . still prepare for the worst." In the future, however, it later declared (Oct. 12), Britain must make no concessions unless she obtained a suitable return in security. The Liberal Bradford *Yorkshire Observer* (Oct. 3, 4) insisted upon a "complete review and revision" of British foreign policy; after all, Duff Cooper was the second Cabinet member who could not approve Chamberlain's course. Britain required more of her leaders than that they should buy a respite at the cost of a small nation or the mere postponement of the evil day. But on October 7, the same newspaper declared that while Chamberlain's direct approach to the dictators was a great risk, it was also a great opportunity, which he must be given the chance to explore. Less pointedly than usual, the independent *Economist* (Oct. 8) observed a need for taking "whatever measures were possible" to deflect the dictators' whims into peaceful channels by increasing the risks of engaging in war. The longer the independent *Financial News* (Oct. 5) pondered Munich, the more uncertain the danger of war appeared. Continuing peace rested upon a number of assumptions the validity of which remained to be proved. It did suggest that a broadening of the Government might be a wise move, a view also held by the *Liverpool Daily Post* (Oct. 7).

Unreserved condemnation of the Government's policy emanated daily from the Labor *Daily Herald* (Oct. 3-7) and the Liberal *News Chronicle* (Oct. 3-8), accompanied by a vigorous demand for collective resistance to aggression on the grounds that peace was possible only where international law and order were respected. Britain's association with Russia, in particular, should be strengthened. For the *News Chronicle* (Oct. 8), events of recent weeks indicated that good intentions in statesmen were not enough. A thorough understanding of international problems and clear vision were essential to give vital leadership to a nation. Lord Lloyd also expressed that opinion in a letter published in the *Daily Telegraph* (Oct. 4). While recognizing Chamberlain's sincerity of purpose, he aptly pointed out that sincerity was no safeguard against error and misjudgment.[30] As for Munich: "It was Mr. Disraeli who said that England's two great assets in the world were her fleet and her good name. Today we must console ourselves that we still have our fleet." Britain had made "another sickening surrender to blackmail," lamented the independent *Fortnightly* (Oct.). There must be some pooling of power in a peace-keeping organization, for German expansion must be checked "here and now." "How much longer will Mr.

30. David Low emphasizes this point in his memoirs, writing of Chamberlain: "No one impugned his motives, but only his judgment." *Autobiography,* p. 309.

Chamberlain turn a blind eye to this persistent twisting of the lion's tail?" it asked.

The conference proposed by Attlee received support in the radical *New Statesman and Nation* (Oct. 8). The alternative was to make ready for war—or helplessly watch the growth of a universal Fascist tyranny in which there would be no war because there would be nothing left for which to fight. The *Reynolds News* (Oct. 9) called for a "firm alliance against aggression between Britain, France, and Russia, to which America, China, Spain and many other of the smaller states of Europe would gladly adhere." That was the only way to salvage what remained of collective security from the "ruin Mr. Chamberlain's policy had made in Europe." Chamberlain must "stick to British principles" and strengthen Britain's association with Russia and the United States, the *Manchester Guardian* warned (Oct. 3). Duff Cooper's resignation seemed to indicate that the Prime Minister had no constructive program, but merely hoped to "save British skins" by keeping in with the dictators no matter what the price. "An entire change in our foreign policy" was demanded (Oct. 7). Britain must assert her leadership among the states which would resist aggression; her policy must no longer be "weak and truckling." Challenging the levity which assumed that to have averted war was to have averted all serious cause for apprehension, the non-partisan *Spectator* (Oct. 7) agreed that "the whole of British foreign policy must be reconsidered, and may have to be reshaped radically."

A few journals were unreservedly enthusiastic about the results of Munich. The Edinburgh *Weekly Scotsman* (Oct. 8) saw in the Anglo-German declaration full justification of Chamberlain's policy. Britain must take the risk of trusting Germany, argued the Cardiff *Western Mail* (Oct. 3), whose attitude before Munich had been somewhat firmer. The claim that peace had been achieved for only six months was "a foolish and quite inexcusable disparagement of the Prime Minister's work for which there is no plausible much less convincing evidence." *The Times* (Oct. 3) declared that "the policy of international appeasement must of course be pressed forward" (though it did advise equal attention for the policy of preparation); suggested (Oct. 4) that the Government's case in the Commons was "almost impregnable"; and asserted (Oct. 5) that "the feeblest of all attitudes is that which ingerminates distrust of every German action or profession and calls for 'a stand against the dictators'," all the while complaining that Chamberlain's policy necessitates the continuance of British rearmament.

These lines in *The Times,* however, did not express the apprehension felt by some of the members of its staff about Munich. Some junior members were so unhappy about the paper's policy that they resigned; some senior members were also dissatisfied, but did not sever their relations with the paper.[31] Anthony Winn, the young lobby correspondent in the Commons, resigned when his report of Duff Cooper's speech, which did not accord with the policy of the paper, was suppressed by the editor, who then inserted a column of his own describing the speech as "a damp squib," while still heading the column "from our Lobby Correspondent."[32]

In reviewing the press in the period immediately following Munich, it is evident that few journals had clearly changed positions on the question of British foreign policy. Most of the open criticism still came from those organs which had been critical of Government policy before Munich; most of the warnings emanated from the previously skeptical. Very significant was the absence of any sense of confidence among those journals most favorable to appeasement, and the increased emphasis on "reviewing" and "re-thinking" British policy in the light of recent events. Munich was indeed a stunning experience, and even those papers unwilling to abandon the Government and its general policy could not help but be sobered by all that had happened. Again this was of no direct consequence for a few months, but its long-range impact was great. The dam of appeasement had not yet broken, but the pressure was building.

Throughout October the Chamberlain policy remained the object of attack in public speeches and signed articles in the periodical press. A few examples, chosen so as to indicate the variety of criticism and the diversity of the critics, illustrate

31. *History of The Times,* IV (pt. 2), 944–45.
32. Duff Cooper, *Old Men Forget,* pp. 249–50.

this point. Speaking in Manchester on October 1, Harold Nicolson predicted that peace had been achieved for only six months. Chamberlain had missed one of the greatest opportunities that ever fell to the lot of a British statesman. Had he taken a firm stand at Munich, he would have established, "perhaps forever, the superiority of democratic faith over Fascist conceptions." Instead, ill-advised by the Inner Cabinet and Sir Horace Wilson, he had surrendered.[33] Sir Percy Harris, Liberal Chief Whip, contended at Bethnal Green, October 13, that Eden should be reinstated in the Government and that, since the League provided the only alternative to power politics, "we must, therefore, reconstruct it in the light of recent events."[34] At Fraserburgh, October 15, Robert Boothby, Conservative M. P., termed Munich Britain's greatest diplomatic defeat since the Treaty of Utrecht, and soundly denounced the policy which had led up to it. The future, he asserted, required a great national effort like the one in 1918.[35] Herbert Morrison, attacking appeasement at North Shields on October 23, was "sick of this Chamberlain myth." The Prime Minister's friends were saying he got Britain out of war—"he nearly got us into war."[36]

In an address of October 16 (aimed primarily at the American people but certainly meant for broader consumption), Churchill once again called for a stronger foreign policy. Holding that no benefit or progress had ever been achieved by submission to organized and calculated violence, he saw the glory of nations founded upon the spirit of resistance to tyranny and injustice. Alexander the Great, he recalled, once remarked that the people of Asia were slaves because they had not learned to pronounce the word "No." "Let that not be the epitaph of the English-speaking peoples or of Parliamentary democracy, or of France, or of the many surviving Liberal states of Europe." The means of resistance remained to the forces of freedom; they must be quickly gathered together.[37] Lloyd George scathingly censured

33. *The Times,* Oct. 3, 1938.
34. *Ibid.,* Oct. 14, 1938.
35. *Ibid.,* Oct. 17, 1938.
36. *Ibid.,* Oct. 24, 1938.
37. Churchill, *Blood, Sweat, and Tears,* pp. 69–74.

Chamberlain's policy at a meeting of the London Free Church Federation Ministers' Club on October 26, contending: "We have a transient peace which disregards conscience, which trampled on good faith and honour, and we have turned a deaf ear to the cry of the oppressed." During the last few years Britain had descended the ladder of dishonor rung by rung. Was she going, could she go, any lower?[38]

The *Contemporary Review* carried the noted Liberal journalist J. A. Spender's assertion that Britain must return to the League of Nations and bring Russia back into European diplomatic circles.[39] Robert Parker contended in the *Fortnightly* that the maintenance of Czechoslovakia was one of Britain's "most important necessities," politically, militarily, and economically. It was the last barrier separating Hitler from his dream of "the ninety million Empire." How could Czechoslovakia be saved if threatened? Only by war —never by concessions.[40] Strong censure came from the eminent historian R. W. Seton-Watson, who challenged the Prime Minister to produce from the history of British foreign policy any document so humiliating and so contrary to the spirit of Britain as the Anglo-French plan which had been forced upon Czechoslovakia. He referred to Chamberlain's "pathetic" belief in Hitler and his "naivety" in claiming "peace in our time." He denounced his neglect of Russia, declaring: "Where the jungle law rules, as it does today, one seeks help where one can find it." The Prime Minister's exclusive control of foreign policy he found abominable. And the crowning blow was that Chamberlain had taken advantage of the "vertiginous course of events" to present Parliament and public opinion with *faits accomplis* amounting to a total reversal of the foreign policy on which the Government had won its majority.[41]

While the critics were for the most part the same individuals, nothing had occurred to lessen their anxiety or calm their fears;

38. *The Times,* Oct. 27, 1938.
39. J. A. Spender, "Munich—Before and After," *Contemporary Review,* CLIV (November, 1938), 521.
40. Robert Parker, "The Czech Crisis: The Background," *Fortnightly,* CL (October, 1938), 400, 406.
41. R. W. Seton-Watson, "Munich and After," *Ibid.,* CL (November, 1938), 532–39.

and that they now bespoke the concern of a far larger segment of the British populace than before is altogether likely. While the arguments were hardly new, if they were pertinent before Munich, they were the more so now. And that public criticism still came from the "traditional" opponents of Chamberlain and appeasement should not obscure the fact that what might be called private criticism had certainly broadened and deepened. Indeed, the passions which raged in Britain over the Munich Agreement were of the bitterest sort. Throughout the country families were split into optimists and pessimists, into pro-Chamberlainites and anti-Chamberlainites—the latter of whom, Sir Bruce Lockhart reflected ten years later, seemed "more serious and less violent."[42] Men and women long bound together by party ties, social amenities, and family connections glared at one another in anger and scorn. Churchill records that among Conservatives, families and friends were divided to a degree which he had never seen before, and Duff Cooper reports that among his own acquaintances he could count at least twelve married couples who were divided upon the issue.[43]

Within a week after his resignation Duff Cooper must have been strengthened in his conviction that he had taken the proper course. He received over four thousand communications by mail and telegraph, and had to engage a special staff of secretaries to deal with them. A few were abusive, but ninety percent were congratulatory. In the latter group were letters from Lord Cork, Commander-in-Chief at Portsmouth, and Captain Lord Louis Mountbatten, both expressing complete agreement with him.[44]

Chamberlain, too, received a number of grateful messages. Some were from Germans, including Franz von Papen, former Chancellor, who described the "unrestrained joy of the ordinary people in Germany."[45] Noel Buxton transmitted to Chamberlain the sentiment of a German ex-naval officer, who felt like one having been condemned to death and set free in the last minute.

42. Lockhart, "September Crisis—and After," *The Listener,* XL (October 28, 1948), 635.

43. Churchill, *The Gathering Storm,* p. 324; Duff Cooper, *Old Men Forget,* p. 251.

44. Duff Cooper, *Old Men Forget,* p. 245.

45. Franz von Papen, *Memoirs* (New York, 1953), p. 442.

"The man who gave the world this last chance . . . is your Prime Minister. . . . We will thank him and bless him all our life long."[46]

Hitler's feeling was another matter. Shortly after Munich it began to appear that Chamberlain, in pursuing appeasement, would not have cooperation from him. The Führer delivered a speech at Saarbrücken, October 9, which might normally have aroused the resentment and anger of any British Prime Minister. Though he complimented in patronizing phrases "the two other statesmen who exerted themselves to find a way to peace," he warned that "it only needs that in England instead of Chamberlain, Mr. Duff Cooper or Mr. Eden or Mr. Churchill should come to power, and then we know quite well that it would be the aim of these men immediately to begin a new World War."[47] Still more pointed, though probably unknown in Britain, was his private tribute to Chamberlain (as reported to Kirkpatrick by an informant in Hitler's entourage): "If ever that silly old man comes interfering here again with his umbrella, I'll kick him downstairs and jump on his stomach in front of photographers."[48]

Immediately after his resignation, Duff Cooper undertook to write a weekly column in the *Evening Standard*. Hitler's speech provided a suitable subject for his first article (Oct. 11), in which he wrote:

> In politics the desire to avert war no more justifies the adoption of a policy that is foolish than the desire to avoid death from thirst proves the wisdom of a stranded mariner who

46. Mosa Anderson, *Noel Buxton: A Life* (London, 1952), p. 141. To Noel Buxton Chamberlain replied: "I agree . . . that the German desire for peace must have its effect on Hitler, and I hope too that the personal contact I have established with him will help. The trouble with the German rulers is that even when they have a good case they treat it in such a way as to alienate sympathy. But I think that is partly due to their conviction that 'Nobody loves them'."

47. Baynes, *Speeches of Adolf Hitler*, II, 1534–35.

48. Kirkpatrick, *The Inner Circle*, p. 135. Hitler's attitude toward Munich boded ill for the hope that it had assured peace for any length of time. The Führer was resentful; he had closed a compromise instead of carrying through German "rights." Chamberlain had "spoiled everything." In short, since Hitler had made peace against his will, Munich had not removed the danger of war. See Kordt, *Nicht aus den Akten*, p. 278; Otto Meissner, *Staatssekretär unter Ebert-Hindenburg-Hitler, Der Schicksalsweg des deutschen Volkes von 1918–1945, wie ich ihn erlebte* (Hamburg, 1950),

> drinks salt water. Wrong-doing is sometimes punished in this world, and folly nearly always. . . . I would, therefore, suggest that the time has come when, instead of waiting for fresh demands to be made of us, we should state firmly where we stand.[49]

Despite Hitler's diatribe and the warning voices of the critics, the leading Cabinet ministers were loath to break the link with Germany. In various speeches Chamberlain, Simon, and Hoare, among others, directly or indirectly suggested that Germany make her demands known in order that negotiations might be started.[50] According to Joseph Kennedy, the British had no great objection even to returning Germany's colonies—although the basis on which that could be done was a disturbing question.[51]

The critics of appeasement continued to warn the Government of the danger of its policy. Sir Robert Vansittart, Chamberlain's Chief Diplomatic Adviser from the Foreign Office (whom the Prime Minister saw three times in three years, and never once alone) cautioned the Government of "the bitter sneers" in Germany after Munich. The members of the Government were disbelieving; they were "not prone to suspect really evil intentions."[52] As Feiling wrote of Chamberlain: "Simple he was . . . and obstinately sanguine in that he was bent on finding decency even in dictators."[53] As far as the Government was concerned, appeasement still soared in the heights it had reached at Munich.

---

p. 470; Kurt Assmann, *Deutsche Schicksalsjahre, Historische Bilder aus dem zwieten Weltkrieg und seiner Vorgeschichte* (Wiesbaden, 1950), pp. 61–62.

49. Quoted in Duff Cooper, *The Second World War,* p. 38.

50. Dirksen's Survey of his Ambassadorship to London, *Documents and Materials Relating to the Eve of the Second World War* (New York, 1948), II, 160–61. (Hereinafter cited as Dirksen Papers.)

51. Kennedy to the Secretary of State, London, Oct. 28, 1938. *U.S. For. Rel., 1938,* I, 95–96.

52. Lord Vansittart, *Lessons of My Life* (New York, 1943), p. 13; Lord Vansittart, "The Decline of Diplomacy," *Foreign Affairs,* XXVIII (January, 1950), 186.

53. *Life of Neville Chamberlain,* p. 365.

CHAPTER SEVEN

Munich Winter

DURING THE TWILIGHT that followed Munich the international outlook was obscure. On the surface the forces of peace seemed to be gaining ground. This was the "golden age" of appeasement. Although Halifax and others had urged immediately after Munich a re-constitution of the Cabinet which would have brought in Churchill, Eden, and even the Laborites, if they would join,[1] no important changes occurred, and Chamberlain and his advisers pursued their policy with unruffled complacency. Yet warnings of disaster continued to emanate from every side.

When Parliament reassembled on November 1, the emotional sense of relief which had prevailed in October was almost gone. There was a marked tendency to avoid extolling the Munich Agreement as a great achievement of statecraft and an increasing inclination on the part of many Government supporters to take the view that the less said about it the better. The chill of reaction had grown as the International Commission established in Berlin to settle all questions arising out of the transfer of the Sudetenland to Germany accepted with monotonous regularity terms dictated by Germany.[2] The shock of that realization inevitably gave rise

1. See Halifax, *Fullness of Days,* pp. 202–03; Birkenhead, *Halifax,* p. 407. Chamberlain's only attempt to broaden the Government was a late October invitation to Lord Samuel (Liberal) to become Lord Privy Seal. He declined. Wheeler-Bennett, *King George VI,* p. 358 n.

2. The "fifth zone" which the German Army had occupied had been determined on the basis of the population status of 1918, which in essence meant the census of 1910, and the "preponderance" figure of 51 percent. Protocol Signed by the German Foreign Minister and the Ambassadors of Great Britain, France, and Italy, Berlin, Oct. 5, 1938. *G. D.,* IV, 32–33. That was the German demand, the Czech request for the census of 1930 and the "preponderance" figure of 75 percent having been overruled by the Commission. Contrary to the Munich accord, the project for plebiscites

to angry talk of "cowardly betrayal" as eight members (from all parties) revived, on November 1, many of the criticisms leveled at the Government during the Munich debate a month before. The Opposition deplored the functioning of the International Commission as "a body to register the demands of Herr Hitler" (Attlee's words), and Brigadier-General Edward Spears (Conservative) denounced its "puppet" character, chiding caustically that if the British representative had put up any protest, "no rumor of that has reached the outside world."[3]

But with the situation in central Europe momentarily calm, Chamberlain once again turned his attention to Italy, announcing on November 2 that "the time was ripe to take a further step forward in the policy of appeasement" by bringing into force the Anglo-Italian Agreement concluded in April. Ten thousand Italian infantrymen had been withdrawn from Spain, he declared. Furthermore, he had "definite assurances" from Mussolini that the remaining Italian forces would be withdrawn when the non-intervention plan came into operation, that no further troops would be sent, and that Italy did not plan to order compensatory air forces to Spain in lieu of the infantry which had been withdrawn. In Chamberlain's view, the Spanish question was no longer a menace to the peace of Europe—the criterion he had adopted for a "settlement" of the Spanish problem—so there was no valid reason for delaying longer enforcement of the agreement. He moved that the Commons "welcome the intention" of the Government to bring the agreement into force.

Chamberlain's motion reopened the whole question of Anglo-Italian relations which had been so bitterly debated during the spring and summer of 1938. It was soon evident that in the intervening period the viewpoints, as well as the composition, of neither side had changed. Labor, led by Arthur Greenwood, resumed its vitriolic attack upon the Government's Spanish policy.

---

in areas to be determined by the Commission was abandoned altogether and the frontier settlement left to a German-Czech commission, in which, of course, the Germans could dictate their own terms. Minutes of the Eighth Meeting of the International Commission Held in Berlin on October 13, 1938. *Ibid.*, IV, 63–66.

3. *Parl. Debs., HC,* November 1, 1938, vol. 340, 65–67, 136–37.

It had long assumed that a "settlement" in Spain would mean the end of the conflict there, but Chamberlain evidently envisaged no such thing. Concerned only with retaining the friendship of the "tottering dictator," he might well be described as "the boneless wonder of the age." The withdrawal of the 10,000 troops Greenwood saw as only a token withdrawal of men who were tired of war or who through illness or disease had become ineffective soldiers. That was hardly a sincere contribution toward the fundamental British objective of ending foreign intervention in Spain; it was only an Italian trick to play for time and to prolong the war. Greenwood concluded:

> The Government are engaged in a crazy policy, whittling away the freedom of the people. They have already sacrificed Abyssinia; they have already sacrificed Austria; and within recent days they have sacrificed Czechoslovakia. To-day they are in effect throwing Spain to the wolves . . . regardless of the consequences to Spain, regardless of the possible consequences to ourselves, to democracy and to the Empire in particular.[4]

Seven more Laborites rose to support Greenwood's charge. Among them was Colonel Wedgwood, who was wholly exasperated with the policy of "perpetual surrender." "Only a month ago," he lamented, "we saved our skins for a time by the sacrifice of Czechoslovakia. Now we are going to save our skins at the expense of the Spanish people—for a time. . . . What is coming next?" Dr. Edith Summerskill put the same sentiment in other words: "The Prime Minister went to Munich in the role of European obstetrician . . . and produced a monstrosity of which we were asked to be the godparents. Now, we are told there is another case, this time an Italian one, ready for delivery, but we on these benches say that the time is premature." Referring to the wording of Chamberlain's motion, Lieutenant-Commander Fletcher remarked acidly that the Commons was getting so "strong on welcoming" that he would not be surprised "if the House meets one of these days and passes a resolution welcom-

4. *Ibid.*, November 2, 1938, vol. 340, 217.

ing Herr Hitler on his arrival in this country to take over the Government."

Speaking for the Liberals, Wilfred Roberts opposed Chamberlain's motion because it represented "a further stage in the renunciation of that policy" on which the Government had been elected. Conservatives Anthony Eden and Viscount Wolmer lent weight to the Labor view. Graphically retracing Italian violations of non-intervention, Eden denied that the essential condition which Britain had laid down as a prerequisite to the enforcement of the agreement had been satisfied; rather, it had been waived. To bring the agreement into force on such conditions was not in the real interest of Britain. Wolmer spoke to the same point. The Government had made a bargain and must insist that it be carried out. Where was this "line of continually giving way" going to stop? Throughout the debate there were bitter denunciations of the general policy of appeasement, but, true to the pattern of foreign policy debates throughout 1938, when the Opposition had had its say, the Government supporters gave Chamberlain a substantial majority, in this instance, 345 to 138.[5]

It is impossible to determine whether Chamberlain's undiminished support was more attributable to English party discipline, a genuine conviction among his followers that appeasement was still worthy of their support, or sheer ignorance or indifference concerning the implications of the policy. But it is a striking fact that, although Chamberlain's description of what constituted a "settlement" in Spain—a definition which he had carefully avoided earlier—left much to be desired, no apparent concern about this was to be found among his supporters. At least it did not reflect in the Commons debate or the vote on Chamberlain's motion. The historian is left frankly puzzled about the extent to which Chamberlain had a *carte blanche* to do essentially anything he liked. If the explanation lies in English party discipline, this would seem to raise questions about that phenomenon, and especially the way it operates in times of crisis, worthy of further examination by statesmen and political scientists alike. If the explanation lies in ignorance or indifference among Government supporters, this

5. *Ibid.*, November 2, 1938, vol. 340, 207–332.

would seem a damning indictment which needs little elaboration. If the explanation lies in a still-lingering conviction that appeasement was every bit as "worthy" as it had been, the question remains how this confidence could have survived the events of September.

It must be acknowledged, of course, that the appeasement of Italy and the appeasement of Germany were two different things, and that the notion still lingered that to detach Italy from Germany would be a significant gain for the forces of peace in Europe —a gain worth a considerable price. After all, it was Germany which had caused the crisis of September, and Mussolini had, or so it appeared, actually played the role of peacemaker. But what of Spain? Was British friendship with Italy to be built on the provision that Italy could do whatever she wanted there provided her activity did not, in British eyes, constitute a threat to the peace of Europe (a provision which, of course, completely defied definition)? And what of Mussolini's assurances? Was there any reason for believing them? These were questions which might have been expected to stir, at least mildly, members of any party charged with their nation's welfare. But they did not, and it is little wonder that this was perturbing to the critics.

In the House of Lords, Halifax argued that there was no intrinsic connection between the Anglo-Italian Agreement and the civil war in Spain except that which arose from the fear that the war might lead to international complications. Repeating Chamberlain's contention that Mussolini's withdrawal of troops evidenced his good intentions and represented a major contribution toward eliminating the Spanish question as a source of international friction, he too proclaimed that the time was right to bring the agreement into force. This view was contested by Lord Snell, the Marquess of Crewe, Lord Marley, Viscount Cecil, and the Earl of Listowel, but the final vote (55 to 6) favored the Government even more overwhelmingly than in the Commons.[6]

Having expended much energy and space on the issue of an agreement with Italy in April, some newspapers were rather uninterested in the question of bringing the already-signed agree-

6. *Parl Debs., HL,* November 3, 1938, vol. 110, 1621–78.

ment into force. Not that the Government's action did not receive attention, but the excitement engendered was not intense. The agreement was actually implemented on November 16, and many journals withheld comment until then. Some Conservative journals, including the *Daily Mail* (Nov. 3, 16), the *Financial Times* (Nov. 9), and the *Daily Telegraph* (Nov. 3) approved the action as "a contribution to peace." The pro-Government *Times* (Nov. 17) merely hoped the pact would mark the beginning of better Anglo-Italian relations, though it saw no use to pretend "that public opinion could be altogether pleased with the circumstances in which the treaty was finally approved." This was also the view of the Unionist Cardiff *Western Mail* (Nov. 17). Nor was the Liberal *Liverpool Daily Post* (Nov. 3) enthusiastic; in the absence of any change in Italy's attitude, how could the agreement "make for general appeasement?"

The Liberal *Manchester Guardian* (Oct. 31; Nov. 3) saw nothing to justify the assumption that a "settlement" had been reached in Spain. Chamberlain had only persuaded himself that there had been a change because he was determined to complete the "working agreement" with Mussolini. Spain had been betrayed, blared the pro-Labor *Reynolds News* (Nov. 6). How could the agreement with Italy be welcomed when it was "shorn of the very condition" (a "settlement" in Spain) which Chamberlain himself had earlier declared to be essential? In a more general vein, the Labor *Daily Herald* (Nov. 4) warned that the need for conciliation must not be allowed to destroy the existence of right and wrong in international affairs. Indeed, conciliation is "a meaningless word unless . . . dictated . . . by justice," and there was little concern for justice in this whole affair. The independent *Economist* (Nov. 5) felt that "international morality can only look the other way while we condone the swallowing of one League member and armed assault upon another." It was very doubtful whether the agreement with Italy could even be defended on the grounds of expediency; Britain was "paying cash" in a gamble where the odds seemed strongly against her success. And the *New Statesman and Nation* (Nov. 12) saw Chamberlain laboring under a "nineteenth century illusion" that he could purchase good relations from the totalitarian states. He was flattered by the friendly overtures of the dictators, whose good will he hoped to win by prompt compliance.

Though many of the critical journals spoke from a partisan point of view, the differences of approach which might have been expected were not in evidence. It was their primary and almost exclusive concern that, even though the enforcement of the Anglo-Italian Agreement might bring a temporary relaxation of tension, the acceptance of an agreement which in effect condoned Italy's activity in Spain (which they saw as entirely unjust and lawless) would hardly provide a foundation for genuine Anglo-Italian friendship and mutual respect. In short, no particular alternative to the Government's policy was propounded, except a clear and simple refusal to make any kind of agreement with Italy in the circumstances which prevailed. It was largely a question of faith. There were some who still believed, or at least acted as if they did, that Italy could be trusted to keep her word; but there were also some who saw no reason whatsoever to rely on Italy's word. And there were those who felt that, even if Italy did keep her word in this instance, that would be no substantial contribution to the peace and security of Europe, for the dangerous Spanish situation would still remain.

Foreign policy was the subject of a lively controversy in the Commons during the second week in November. Taking the opportunity presented by the opening of a new session of Parliament, the Opposition once more lashed out at appeasement. On this occasion Attlee began with a ringing attack on the Government's lack of a constructive program in foreign affairs and its disregard of the League of Nations. As usual, Sinclair seconded his arguments on behalf of the Liberals. R. J. Boothby demanded that British foreign policy be based "upon the principle of collective security and the establishment of law in international affairs, as against the reign of brute force." Britain could not come to terms with the dictators if it involved any further sacrifice of principles or of other people.[7]

Keynoting the second day's debate, Sir Stafford Cripps pictured nothing more disastrous than British foreign policy "based upon that spirit which shown at Munich, a spirit of giving in to armed

7. *Parl. Debs., HC,* November 8, 1938, vol. 341, 19–43.

force and its demands and of putting aside all . . . standards of international justice and morality." Chamberlain still held the "simple faith" that if Germany and Italy were allowed to overwhelm the smaller powers, they would be kind enough to stop immediately upon coming up against the vital interests of the British Empire. Such a notion was neither morally defensible nor realistic.

Cripps' argument was pursued by subsequent speakers of various shades of political affiliation. One after another Ernest Evans (Liberal), Arthur Henderson, Lloyd George, Campbell Stephen (Independent Laborite), and Viscount Cranborne advanced essentially the same points. Their criticism was couched largely in general terms and presented in such a general context that its effect was considerably blunted. But it affords further illustration of the constant existence of a body of opinion, and a vocal one, which saw appeasement as altogether invalid and dangerous. The Government, of course, was hardly moved by this. D. J. Colville, Secretary of State for Scotland, ineffectually retaliated: "The Government refuse to accept the doctrine that war is inevitable. . . . The evils of disease can be coped with, and we believe that the evils of war can be coped with too."[8]

Meanwhile, events in Germany did not enhance the Reich's reputation in Britain. During the second week in November, the German Government conducted a nation-wide anti-Semitic pogrom, during which Jewish property was systematically destroyed and thousands of Jews arrested and sent to concentration camps.[9] This outburst of savagery deeply shocked and aroused opinion in Britain. The British press universally condemned it, and in several instances its effect on British policy toward Germany was specifically cited. The Conservative *Sunday Times* (Nov. 20), for example, declared that "it would be blindness not to recognize that it [the 'international sky,' and by implication, Anglo-German relations] has been blackened . . . by the terrible events in Germany." But there was another view, like that of the independent

8. *Ibid.*, November 9, 1938, vol. 341, 132–259.

9. R. G. D. Laffan et al., *Survey of International Affairs, 1938* (London, 1953), III, 153–54; Wheeler-Bennett, *Munich*, pp. 297–99. The pretext for this pogrom was the fatal shooting of Baron vom Rath, a young Third Secretary of the German Embassy in Paris, by a young Polish Jew, apparently incensed by sufferings inflicted on his parents in Germany.

Observer (Nov. 27), which held that while "a dangerous emotion has been stirred by the spectacle of atrocity as a method of government . . . logically the German maltreatment of the Jews has no bearing upon the policy of appeasement."

The effect of the pogrom on British efforts to promote a rapprochement with Germany was deemed significant by Herbert von Dirksen. The German Ambassador reported to Berlin that while there were other reasons for the delay of an approach he had been expecting from the British Government,[10] these factors would not in themselves have caused "indefinite postponement" had it not been for the anti-Semitic outburst in Germany. That had been grist to the mill of the Opposition. Pessimism had overtaken those sections of the British public which had actively supported Anglo-German friendship, and in consequence, Chamberlain's prestige had deteriorated. It remained to be seen, in fact, whether Chamberlain himself was of the same mind as he had been before November 10.[11]

On November 23 Chamberlain and Halifax journeyed to Paris for discussions with Daladier and Bonnet on questions of foreign policy and defense.[12] It may be noteworthy in the history of appeasement that this visit was the first occasion on which Halifax accompanied Chamberlain on his diplomatic travels. Admittedly, this was an unhurried flight to an allied republic, not to an unfriendly, uncooperative dictatorship in time of crisis.[13] But the

10. He specifically mentioned the Chamberlain-Halifax visit to Paris scheduled for the last week in November, and the growing feeling in Government circles that Britain was entitled to expect a response from the German side to its already-expressed desire for better relations.

11. The Ambassador in Great Britain to the Foreign Ministry, London, Nov. 17, 1938. *G. D.*, IV, 332–34. When surveying his ambassadorship in London in September, 1939, Dirksen wrote of "an extremely strong reaction in England" against the anti-Jewish demonstrations in Germany. *Dirksen Papers,* p. 161.

12. It was then that Chamberlain learned of, and gave his approval to, the text of a Franco-German Declaration, corresponding to the Anglo-German Declaration signed at Munich, which was subsequently signed by Bonnet and Ribbentrop at Paris on December 6. Record of Anglo-French Conversations Held at the Quai d'Orsay on November 24, 1938. *B. D.*, III, 286–87.

13. Templewood claims that Chamberlain did not take Halifax with him to Berchtesgaden because he did not want to embroil him in what he thought would be an unpopular adventure. *Nine Troubled Years,* p. 379.

presence of both Halifax and Cadogan in Paris brought to an end the Berchtesgaden-Godesberg-Munich procedure. In fact, after the first enthusiasm for Munich had faded away, the entire Cabinet appeared much less willing to allow its powers over foreign policy to be put into commission again. Halifax had not objected to his exclusion from Chamberlain's trips to Germany during the September crisis, but his earlier nebulous outlook on Europe had been brutally clarified by reality and his thinking about policies and procedures had undergone considerable revision.[14]

The Paris visit was followed by an announcement that Chamberlain and Halifax would fly to Rome early in January for discussions with Mussolini and Ciano. This was variously received by the press. *The Times* (Nov. 29) considered such a trip "welcome for many reasons"; the *Daily Telegraph* (Nov. 29) thought it "of happy augury"; the independent *Glasgow Herald* (Nov. 29) termed it a "natural development" in Chamberlain's pursuit of a wide and enduring settlement. Realizing that the prospect of such a trip might cause anxiety among the British public, the Cardiff *Western Mail* (Dec. 20) at length assured its readers that Chamberlain was going to Rome not to make concessions but only to further Anglo-Italian amity.

Other journals could not share that optimism. The *Manchester Guardian* (Dec. 2) feared lest Chamberlain, "so adept at appeasement," encourage the growing Italian demand for Tunisia.[15] The *Daily Herald* (Nov. 29) opposed any gesture toward Italy as long as she still waged war in Spain, and demanded (Dec. 10): "Stop this visit!" Mussolini would surely try to use it to play off Britain against France with the object of getting another installment of appeasement on the Munich model. The Liberal *News Chronicle* (Dec. 3) agreed. Chamberlain had just returned from a visit to

14. See Campbell-Johnson, *Viscount Halifax,* p. 509; Birkenhead, *Halifax,* pp. 394, 420–21, 425.

15. When Ciano spoke in the National Assembly on November 30 of Italy's desire to consolidate, the assembly rose to its feet with cries of "Tunis, Djibuti, Corsica!" *Ciano's Diplomatic Papers,* p. 251. In fact, two weeks earlier Ciano had instructed Grandi in London to "predispose English opinion—if it is impossible actually to prepare it" to Italian claims against France, which might be advanced at any moment. Letter to the Ambassador in London, Grandi. Rome, Nov. 14, 1938. *Ibid.*

Paris which had resulted in "a complete identity of views" between the Western democracies. If he could establish cordial relations with the country which now openly threatened France, he would prove himself "not so much a diplomat as an acrobat."

The press was generally unmoved by the signing of the Franco-German Declaration in Paris on December 6,[16] a fact which in itself may evidence increasing doubt as to the value of appeasement.[17] *The Times* (Dec. 7) typified the mood of the pro-Government journals when it expressed "general satisfaction." The *Daily Herald* (Dec. 7) exemplified the reaction of the Opposition journals: taken at face value the agreement was fine, but the world had learned by experience that such notes no longer had their face value. Indeed, they were worthless, so there was no point whatsoever in attaching any significance to this agreement.

Throughout early December the Opposition in the Commons continued to show anxiety over where Chamberlain's foreign policy was leading Britain—and this, coupled with domestic and party difficulties, led the Prime Minister to wonder whether he could ever "shake down with this 'uneasy and disgruntled House' without an election."[18] The unrest culminated in another Labor motion of no-confidence on December 19, this one directed against Chamberlain personally. Hugh Dalton, the mover, charged the Prime Minister with a succession of "grave misjudgments" which had brought Britain into dire peril. Caustically denouncing every facet of Chamberlain's policy, including the proposed trip to Rome, and following Labor's long-established line of argument, he asserted that Britain's only hope lay in welding together into an effective combination all those nations in eastern Europe which

16. See footnote 12.

17. Dirksen reported that although Ribbentrop's purpose in going to Paris had been known in Britain for some time, "strangely enough the press has so far refrained from any editorial comment." But he felt that Chamberlain's position would probably be strengthened because the Franco-German Declaration would calm those Conservative critics who had reproached him for signing the Anglo-German Declaration at Munich without previously consulting the French. The Ambassador in Great Britain to the Foreign Ministry, London, Dec. 6, 1938. *G. D.*, IV, 347–48.

18. Feiling, *Life of Neville Chamberlain,* p. 386.

were threatened by Germany—Russia, Poland, Rumania, Yugoslavia, Turkey, and Greece.

Dalton's arguments had little effect upon Chamberlain, who chided the Opposition for offering no sensible alternative policy. Of his own course, the Prime Minister declared:

> If that policy, having had a full chance of success, were nevertheless to fail, I myself would be the first to agree that something else must be put in its place. But I have been getting a great number of letters which convince me that the country does not want the policy to fail, and, whatever views may be expressed in this House, I am satisfied that the general public desire is to continue the efforts we have made.[19]

The statement clearly reveals the essence of Chamberlain's post-Munich thinking. Appeasement must be pursued, if for no other reason, because the British people did not want it to fail. Of course the British people did not want to see the policy fail. Success probably would have meant peace. But the crucial question was not whether the people wanted appeasement to succeed, but whether it could succeed. Chamberlain apparently did not see beyond the general hope for success, and it was this kind of naive outlook which ultimately leads toward the conclusion that he did not really comprehend the danger of the German menace to Europe and especially to Great Britain. A significant component of Chamberlain's mind was hope, and the line between his hope and belief was ill-defined if indeed existent. On the other hand, the critics gravely doubted—in fact many flatly denied—that appeasement had any chance of success and based their denunciations on that ground. It was not that they, like the rest of the British people, did not want appeasement (in terms of its pre-Munich definition) to succeed; it was simply that they were already convinced, with considerable evidence to support their view, that the policy had no chance of success, and must therefore be abandoned.

The Prime Minister resented Dalton's reference to the coming Rome visit. Not only was his inference that he might "betray the cause" personally insulting, but it was highly discourteous to his

19. *Parl. Debs., HC,* December 19, 1938, vol. 342, 2517–18.

hosts in suggesting that they would invite Chamberlain and Halifax to do any such thing. In regard to Germany, Chamberlain still awaited a sign that she shared the desire of removing the menace of war and was prepared to make a contribution to peace. Stubbornly he insisted that his policy "has been right all along."

His insistence rated a challenge by Sinclair. Labor, Liberals, and all those Conservatives most experienced and instructed in foreign affairs had not only condemned the Government's policy but had advocated a constructive alternative. Britain must "grapple her friends to her," including the United States, Holland, Belgium, Switzerland, France, and Russia. "Then instead of running after dictators from Berchtesgaden to Munich . . . to Rome, begging them to name their price for a few more months of peace, we should take the moral initiative in laying down the principles of international order based on justice and fair play."

Whenever the Government was under attack, Lloyd George was usually in the thick of it. This debate was no exception. He could not understand Chamberlain's "extraordinary complacency." German and Italian promises had been broken repeatedly; their assurances were worthless. Peace with aggressive nations could be secured only by showing firmness. Sarcastically censuring Munich, he continued:

> They [Chamberlain and Daladier] both ran away as hard as they could from their obligations, but the Prime Minister, in spite of his more advanced years, kept well ahead; and M. Daladier said: 'See him, the British Prime Minister, running faster and farther than even I. What a magnificent old sprinter.'

Lloyd George was troubled about "sending a man in that frame of mind to Rome"; he was "no match for the astute, crafty, ruthless, unscrupulous dictators."[20]

This general argument was sustained by a new voice, Vernon Bartlett (independent), a newspaperman who just one month earlier had won his seat by defeating the Conservative candidate in Bridgewater. He, too, feared Chamberlain's trip to Rome. It

20. *Ibid.*, December 19, 1938, vol. 342, 2551–52.

was Italy which had demands to make, not Britain, and it was doubtful whether the best way of keeping those demands within the bounds of moderation was for Chamberlain to go to Mussolini instead of Mussolini coming to Chamberlain. Laborite F. Seymour Cocks renewed the call for collective security. By seeking friendships, building up alliances, and sending military missions to Russia and Turkey, for example, Britain could do much more to stave off danger than by "umbrella-carrying visits to Munich or to Rome." In fact, Seymour Cocks warned, "unless the policy of the Government is reversed . . . we are doomed."

Several Conservatives, while refusing to support Dalton's motion, also berated Chamberlain's policy. Viscount Cranborne believed the Government should make it clear just where it stood before Chamberlain ever left for Rome. With reference to appeasement in general, Sir Derrick Gunston suggested that although Britain hated war, "it likes justice even more, and will make all sacrifices asked of it to carry out a firm, strong, and just policy." Sir John Simon's defense of the Government was based on the assertion that since Munich nothing had happened to justify a reversal of the approval accorded Government policy then. The House divided, and Dalton's motion was defeated, 143 ayes to 340 noes.[21]

Chamberlain's continuing insistence on the "rightness" of his policy and Simon's closing statement are especially noteworthy in view of the fact that just three days before, the Cabinet had learned of extensive plans which the Germans were developing for a surprise air attack on London. That they took the report seriously is evident in their decision to bring into London from Lichfield an anti-aircraft regiment, which, when stationed in Wellington Barracks, could readily be seen from the German Embassy.[22] But this was insufficient cause to admit even the slightest fallacy in appeasement.

Opposition to and anxiety over appeasement continued to appear in prominent periodicals. Charles E. Hobhouse wrote in the *Contemporary Review* that whatever history's verdict on Chamberlain might be, it would justly condemn the British peo-

21. *Ibid.*, December 19, 1938, vol. 342, 2503–626.
22. Kirkpatrick, *The Inner Circle*, pp. 138–39.

ple, for whom and to whom he was responsible, if they did not take warning and prevent any recurrence of his action at Munich.[23] P. V. Emrys-Evans, Conservative M.P., asserted in the *Fortnightly* that appeasement was "sadly out of touch with realities." It broke down in every crisis because its authors had not yet realized that those whom they wished to appease had no desire to be appeased.[24] Similarly, C. Delisle Burns wrote: "We are beginning to see the disastrous consequences of the amateur diplomacy of top dogs who know nothing of history and cannot see further than next week."[25] Utilizing the columns of the *Nineteenth Century,* Charles Tower rebelled against the "business as usual" attitude, against "comfortable illusions." Nazi ambitions and methods would have to be met "by a much sterner, completer, and more unified effort than has yet been generally appreciated in this country."[26]

The Conservative *National Review* (Dec.) cautioned that Hitler, having obtained his Godesberg objective at Munich, was no longer in need of Chamberlain's good offices in central Europe, and now believed that all he had to do was give orders to Britain. "For the last 18 years," it lamented, "Conservatives have heard nothing but the language of defeatism from their leaders, and have been taught nothing but how to retreat from strong positions to weak ones." The non-partisan *Spectator* (Dec. 16) decried complacent Government references to Munich; to "look back upon that agreement with satisfaction is to provoke nothing but apprehension and despair regarding the results of a further application of such a policy." The complaint of the radical *New Statesman and Nation* (Dec. 24) was that when he saw the dictators Chamberlain appeared to have nothing to say on behalf of the causes for which Britain stood. Never for a moment did he display any realization of the avowed aims of Germany and Italy. The alternative to appeasement, in the view of the *Economist*

23. Charles E. Hobhouse, "The New Deal in Europe," *Contemporary Review,* CLIV (December, 1938), 652, 657.
24. P. V. Emrys-Evans, "Facing the Issues," *Fortnightly,* CL (December, 1938), 681–83.
25. C. Delisle Burns, "Top Dog Diplomacy," *Fortnightly,* CL (December, 1938), 695.
26. Charles Tower, "Business As Usual," *Nineteenth Century,* CXXIV (December, 1938), 657.

(Dec. 24) was the "technique of firmness." It would involve onerous commitments and painful decisions, yet if the line were once resolutely drawn, there was reason to hope that no one would dare overstep it. The danger lay not in drawing the line, but in obscuring it for the sake of appeasement.

These views may indeed seem a grab-bag of adverse reactions to appeasement, a hodge-podge of opinions bereft of any unifying element. Nevertheless they illustrate one essential fact: as 1938 drew to a close, the validity of appeasement was widely questioned and denied, and while the Government was still nowhere near the point of considering these denials as anything but the outcries of "jitterbugs" and narrow-minded partisans, the notion that appeasement was still a largely unchallenged and altogether popular policy is without foundation.

Chamberlain's speech of December 13 to the Foreign Press Association revealed that perhaps even he was beginning to have doubts. He deplored the attitude of the German press, "which in few cases has shown much desire to understand our point of view."[27] Any disillusionment he may have felt, however, was not in evidence a week later when he and Mrs. Chamberlain sent out Christmas cards showing a picture of his plane flying over a cloud bank on the way to Munich.[28]

A most disturbing aspect of the Munich crisis for most Englishmen was the revelation of deficiencies in Britain's defenses. If the Munich debate disclosed anything it was a nearly unanimous demand that rearmament be pushed forward with all celerity and force. Almost all Englishmen were agreed on the necessity of continuing naval rearmament, developing the air force, and training the civilian population in precautions against aerial attack. To this Chamberlain had pledged himself, and such action was pressed upon him by a constant din in both Parliament and press.

After Munich, every Commons debate on foreign policy involved the question of defense and rearmament, and every section

27. Chamberlain, *In Search of Peace,* p. 242.
28. *Glasgow Herald,* Dec. 23, 1938.

of the press demanded the strengthening of British arms. That demand in itself did not necessarily express opposition to appeasement. But it represented a growing realization on the part of the Government and people alike that in any further negotiations Britain must be able to negotiate from strength, not from weakness, and, if the worst occurred and Britain was drawn into war, she would not be totally unprepared.

Though Chamberlain had set his heart on peace, he had, since his assumption of the premiership, been aware of the growing demand for defense measures and rearmament. After the Austrian *Anschluss* rearmament was to be given preference over peace-time habits and requirements, and the needs of the air force were to have precedence over the needs of the army and navy. Chamberlain had told the Commons on March 24, 1938:

> We have now come to the conclusion that in the present circumstances acceleration of existing plans has become essential, and moreover, that there must be an increase in some parts of the programme, especially in that of the Royal Air Force and the anti-aircraft defences. In order to bring about the progress that we feel to be necessary, men and materials will be required and rearmament work must have priority in the nation's effort. . . . This priority will enable us to expedite the programme of air-raid precautions.[29]

By the time of Munich there had been little substantial progress. What happened in the interval had been an extension of the plans, with the result that Britain's first-line strength was left much as it had been, though it was given a power of expansion that could gradually gather volume.[30] The absence of further progress was probably accountable to several factors, among them Chamberlain's concentration on and hopes for appeasement, Labor's traditional opposition to rearmament, and the peace-time psychology which still seemed to linger among a sizeable segment of the British people.

After Munich, all the service departments recognized the alarm-

29. *Parl. Debs., HC,* March 24, 1938, vol. 333, 1410–11.
30. Templewood, *Nine Troubled Years,* p. 334.

ing shortages which the crisis had exposed and forwarded new claims. There was division in the Cabinet over the urgency of rearmament, but an agreeable compromise eventually was reached on the basis of making all possible preparations without disturbing British trade or irritating the Germans and Italians by large-scale measures.[31] Halifax was among those who supported increased armaments, describing as "the greatest lesson of the crisis [Munich] . . . the unwisdom of basing a foreign policy on insufficient armed strength."[32] But, as cartoonist David Low later explained, it was a tough job to get things moving against "the mass of indecision, reluctance and plain damned stupidity."[33]

Emphasis was placed on the acceleration of aircraft production. In the event of war, Britain relied upon the French Army to hold the line in Europe until she had mobilized and trained her manpower. Rearmament on this basis was not questioned by military experts either in London or Paris. Then, too, reliance on the French affected British naval policy. The British depended upon the French fleet to hold the Mediterranean, thus giving their own fleet freedom of action. Since Hitler, in the autumn of 1938, had not, with the exception of pocket battleships, built up to the strengths to which he was entitled in the Anglo-German Naval Agreement of 1935, British naval construction was not great enough to detract from the emphasis on air power.[34]

When Chamberlain spoke of rearmament in the Commons on November 1, he explained that air-raid precautions had assumed such proportions that a separate Ministry of Civilian Defense, headed by Sir John Anderson, had been established. But he rejected the proposal of the Liberal Party to set up a Ministry of

31. Churchill, *The Gathering Storm,* pp. 329–30. See Minney, *The Private Papers of Hore-Belisha, passim.*

32. Letter from Halifax to Sir E. Phipps, F.O., Nov. 1, 1938. *B. D.,* III, 252.

33. Low, *Autobiography,* p. 310. Irked by the lack of urgency in defense preparations after Munich, Low once suggested that the slogan "Business As Usual" be painted on British factory roofs in foreign languages so that enemy airmen would know the British were keeping calm. *Ibid.*

34. Templewood, *Nine Troubled Years,* p. 335. For documentary material on Anglo-German naval negotiations after Munich see *G. D.,* IV, chap. II.

Supply. Such a ministry would need compulsory powers, he argued, and was unnecessary because Britain did not contemplate "the equipment of an army on a Continental scale." Britain had no aggressive designs; the purpose of her rearmament was to defend herself and her communications, and to enable her to enter upon diplomatic discussions with other powers on an equal footing.[35]

In mid-November the Minister for Air, Sir Kingsley Wood, announced that the Air Estimates for the following year would be about £ 200 million, and that the program for expanding the first-line strength of the Royal Air Force was being accelerated[36] When in February, 1939, the Defense Estimates were submitted to Parliament, they showed an increase of £135 million over those for the previous year.[37] Sir John Simon informed the Commons that the personnel of all three services had greatly increased during 1938, and that, in the case of the Royal Air Force, there had been an addition of "large numbers of up-to-date aircraft," production of which was increasing month by month. He gave assurance that Wood's promise of an increased and accelerated air program would be continued.[38]

The financial requirements of the armed services were approved by the Commons with little opposition. What dissent existed was expressed by the Labor Party, a fact which undoubtedly compromised the effectiveness of its opposition to appeasement in the eyes of many. In his memoirs, Attlee concedes that support for the League of Nations necessarily entailed a British contribution toward the armed forces of the League, and declares that the majority of the Party supported that. Yet it had always been the custom of the Labor Party to vote against the Service Estimates —a custom always understood, by the party, to be a vote either against the proposed level of armaments or against the policy

35. *Parl. Debs., HC,* November 1, 1938, vol. 340, 73–89.

36. *Ibid.,* November 10, 1938, vol. 341, 349, 351.

37. Great Britain. *Statement Relating to Defence, Presented by the Prime Minister to Parliament by Command of His Majesty, February, 1939.* Command Paper 5944, London, 1939.

38. *Parl. Debs., HC,* vol. 344, 54–55. Detailed treatment of the course of British rearmament may be found in M. M. Postan, *British War Production* (London, 1952), *passim,* and Higham, *Armed Forces in Peacetime,* pp. 191–242.

of the government of the day, but not as a vote against all armaments. In view of what he calls the "misrepresentation" of Labor's position, Attlee admits that it was "perhaps unwise and pedantic" to continue "this old-fashioned practice."[39] Perhaps the core of the matter was this: Labor's policy of resisting rearmament probably owed its adoption mainly to the fact that it offered a convenient transition stage from deep-seated pacifism to resistance to fascism, a change not easy to effect suddenly.[40]

In the months following Munich, British hopes for a political agreement with Germany melted away.[41] The Government still considered it worthwhile to pursue the possibility that economic relations might be improved to the extent that they would have a favorable effect on political relations. Within three weeks after Munich, the British took the initiative in this regard. On October 18 Sir Frederick Leith-Ross, Chief Economic Adviser to the British Government, conferred with Rüter, a former Commercial Counselor at the German Embassy in London, and von Süsskind, an official in the Economic Policy Department of the German Foreign Ministry, both of whom were members of a delegation on the way to Eire for commercial negotiations.[42] While in London, Rüter and von Süsskind also talked unofficially

39. Attlee, *As It Happened,* pp. 138–39. Hugh Dalton supports this view. *The Fateful Years,* p. 175.

40. See Roy Jenkins, *Mr. Attlee: An Interim Biography* (London, 1948), p. 185. Josiah Wedgwood explains in his memoirs that Labor men always find it exceedingly difficult to change their minds, for that involves explanations to "less well-informed men and women who have committed themselves publicly and repeatedly to the obsolete policy." To Dalton, Citrine, and Bevin he gives all the credit for finally persuading Labor to vote for armaments—for swinging Labor onto "the right side, 1935–1939." *Memoirs of A Fighting Life,* p. 231.

41. Fritz Hesse, apparently on orders from Berlin, maintained a loose contact between Sir Horace Wilson and Ribbentrop during the last days of 1938 and early 1939. The subject of an Anglo-German rapprochement was raised in very general terms, but nothing had developed by mid-March, when events on the continent drastically altered the whole picture. See Hesse, *Das Spiel um Deutschland,* pp. 156–57; Dirksen's Survey of His Ambassadorship in London, *Dirksen Papers,* pp. 165–66.

42. The Ambassador in Great Britain to the Foreign Ministry, London, Oct. 19, 1938. *G. D.,* IV, 315–17.

and confidentially at the Board of Trade on the question of increasing German exports to British colonies.[43]

When the German delegation revisited London on its return from Eire, it was agreed in principle that conversations should begin in the near future between representatives of the Federation of British Industries and the Reich Federation of Industry.[44] (Negotiations between the British and German coal industries for the establishment of a coal cartel designed to avoid a "price cutting war" had already begun, culminating at the end of January, 1939, in an agreement which in effect divided coal export markets.[45]) After numerous proposal exchanges, the first meeting of these industrial groups was set for mid-March, and the British also arranged for Oliver Stanley, President of the Board of Trade, to visit Berlin at approximately the same time.[46] In order to lay the groundwork for Stanley's visit, Ashton-Gwatkin, Counselor in the British Foreign Office, spent the week of February 19-26 in Germany. He was cordially received and got the impression that the Germans had in mind a number of definite economic proposals.[47] By March 15, discussions between the Federation of British Industries and the Reich Federation of Industry were underway in Düsseldorf.[48]

The efforts which the British Government made after Munich to improve economic relations with Germany thus appeared to meet with some success. Negotiations were about to be carried on to the ministerial level when the events of March 15, 1939, put an abrupt end, for the time being at least, to attempts to create a détente.[49] Following the pattern set in the first Leith-

43. Counselor of Legation Rüter to Counselor of Legation Clodius, Dublin, Oct. 20, 1938. *Ibid.,* IV, 318.

44. The German Economic Mission in Great Britain to the Foreign Ministry, London, Nov. 9, 1938. *Ibid.,* IV, 329–30.

45. The Ambassador in Great Britain to the Foreign Ministry, Jan. 28, 1939. *Ibid.,* IV, 394–95.

46. *Ibid.,* IV, 399 (fn.). It was later arranged that Hudson, the Secretary of the Department of Overseas Trade, would accompany Stanley.

47. Report by Ashton-Gwatkin on his visit to Germany and interviews with German Statesmen, February 19 to February 26, 1939. *B. D.,* IV, 597–608.

48. Memorandum by an Official of the Economic Policy Department, Berlin, Mar. 15, 1939. *G. D.,* IV, 430.

49. Only an outline of these negotiations has been given here. For a

Ross-Rüter conversation, these efforts were kept secret throughout.

The first important event in European diplomacy in 1939 was the Chamberlain-Halifax journey to Rome. The uneasiness which had appeared in sections of the press at the time the impending visit was first announced did not diminish. In the days preceding their departure, expression of this anxiety took many forms. The *Spectator* (Dec. 16), the *Statist* (Dec. 31), and the *Economist* (Jan. 7) stated simply and openly their hope that Chamberlain would resist the temptation to buy Italian friendship by further unilateral concessions. The *Manchester Guardian* (Dec. 29) saw the future of Europe turning largely on the question of whether Chamberlain was going to Rome to make more concessions or to convince Mussolini that nothing more was to be gained by force. The absence of an agenda for the talks concerned the *National Review* (Jan.), but perhaps the accompanying Foreign Office officials could prevent any great mischief being done by "loose conversation pieces." "Call it off!" the *News Chronicle* (Dec. 29) at first demanded of the visit; "even a novice must by now have begun to realize that the more you concede to the bullies of Europe the more they demand, and that where Spain is concerned, the Duce is not giving Britain a square deal." Then, adjusting to the idea of the visit, it sarcastically suggested (Jan. 3) that if the Prime Minister insisted on going to Rome, he should first read, "since he seems to be fond of nursery rhymes," the one beginning "Will you walk into my parlor? said the spider to the fly." Even the *Daily Telegraph* (Dec. 28) reminded Chamberlain that in visiting Mussolini he was treading on "delicate ground." But it was the *Liverpool Daily Post* (Jan. 9) which probably expressed most accurately the general feeling among

fuller discussion, utilizing many of the pertinent documents available in *G. D.*, IV, see Laffan et al., *Survey of International Affairs, 1938,* III, 194–201. Since these negotiations involved the Board of Trade, not the Foreign Office, they are not covered by the published British documents; hence, the British side is undocumented. See also Gilbert and Gott's treatment of economic appeasement in *The Appeasers,* pp. 189–206.

Englishmen: "Fears and hopes go with them, and it would be difficult to say which at the moment predominate."

Motivated in part by the hope of dividing Italy and Germany,[50] Chamberlain and Halifax proceeded to Rome on January 10. The conversations there wandered over the entire scope of Anglo-Italian relations. At the end of the first day, Ciano recorded in his diary that the talks were "in a tired tone." The subjects discussed were not highly important, and both sides betrayed mental reservations. In fact, he wrote, "the visit was kept on a minor tone, since both the Duce and myself are scarcely convinced of its utility."[51] Later talks brought no change, and Ciano telephoned Ribbentrop that the whole visit was a "big lemonade," absolutely harmless, "a game ending in no score."[52]

Despite the absence of concrete results Chamberlain was satisfied with the Italian trip. (One Halifax biographer cites an intangible result, feeling that a Halifax audience with Pope Pius XI must have quickened the Foreign Secretary's sense of danger in the moral neutrality implied by appeasement.[53]) The Prime Minister had constantly maintained that it was only a friendly visit and thus explained to his sister on January 15:

> I may say at once that I consider I have achieved all I expected to get, and more, and that I am satisfied that the journey has definitely strengthened the chances of peace. To give my first impressions of Mussolini, I found him straight-

50. Churchill suggests that Chamberlain was "more than ever" alive to the need for that. *The Gathering Storm,* p. 334.

51. *The Ciano Diaries: The Complete Unabridged Diaries of Count Galeazzo Ciano, Italian Minister for Foreign Affairs, 1939–1943,* edited by Hugh Gibson (New York, 1946), pp. 9–10. Birchall claims in *The Storm Breaks* (p. 345) that Mussolini was so uninterested that on the last day of Chamberlain's stay he went skiing instead of attending the farewell banquet.

52. *The Ciano Diaries,* pp. 10–11. The German Ambassador in Rome thought differently, however, reporting to Berlin that the visit was "certainly not without importance for future developments" for it had promoted mutual understanding on both sides. The Ambassador in Italy to the Foreign Ministry, Rome, Jan. 18, 1939. *G. D.,* IV, 560–61. For Halifax's general impressions of the conversations, see *Fullness of Days,* pp. 204–06.

53. Campbell-Johnson, *Viscount Halifax,* p. 502.

> forward and considerate in his behaviour to us, and moreover he has a sense of humour which is quite attractive. . . . He was emphatic in his assurances that he intended to stand by his agreement with us, and that he wanted peace, and was ready to use his influence to get it.[54]

Suspicion of Mussolini's professed good will toward Britain was apparently still far from Chamberlain's mind, a situation the more alarming in view of the fact that, coincidental with Chamberlain's visit to Rome, Italian newspapers were openly boasting that four Italian divisions were leading a new Franco offensive in Spain and that one of them was the Littorio Division, composed of the very "veterans" whose alleged withdrawal had been considered by the British Government as good ground for bringing the Anglo-Italian Agreement into effect.

The outcome of the visit received diverse interpretations in the British press. Some newspapers felt the journey had proved thoroughly worthwhile. *The Times* (Jan. 16) admitted that "neither side scored," but neither side had tried to score, and this was the best possible beginning for further, comprehensive negotiations. In the view of the *Daily Telegraph* (Jan. 14), the visit had helped "mutual understanding," and the Edinburgh *Weekly Scotsman* (Jan. 21) agreed that the trip was "not to be regretted" for that reason. The *Liverpool Daily Post* (Jan. 14) noted that Chamberlain had been well-received in Italy, "and that may be of far-reaching importance."[55]

Other journals were much less satisfied. The *News Chronicle* (Jan. 16) could not understand how Chamberlain could express belief in Italian good faith and good will when Italian troops, guns, and airplanes were at that moment engaged in a supreme

54. Feiling, *Life of Neville Chamberlain,* p. 393.

55. Ciano noted in his diary on January 11: "The welcome of the crowd was good, particularly in the middle-class section of the city, where the old man with the umbrella is quite popular." *The Ciano Diaries,* pp. 9–10. Chamberlain apparently made some impression in Taranto, Italy, too. The Taranto police were astonished on January 22 to see a man strolling down the street bereft of all apparel except for an umbrella. When they hustled him off to jail, he explained: "I'm Mr. Chamberlain." He was thereupon sent to a hospital for mental observation. *Liverpool Daily Post,* Jan. 23, 1939.

effort to annihilate democracy in Spain. While this "cynical disregard for facts and morality" continued to guide British foreign policy, restoration of unity and strength in Britain was impossible. The same sentiment appeared in the *Manchester Guardian* (Jan. 20), which later declared (Jan. 23) that only "simpletons" could believe that Mussolini had spent two and one-half years in Spain just to enjoy ideological success over "Bolshevism." The *Glasgow Herald* (Jan. 16) claimed that "after Rome" political realism implied that Britain must be prepared to speak and act as firmly as any possible opponent. Of the many journals which had opposed the Rome visit, only the *Economist* (Jan. 21) openly expressed relief, which must have been felt by others as well, that "Mr. Chamberlain did not give anything away." The *National Review* (Feb.) caught that sentiment later when it explained: "A sigh of thankfulness went up to Heaven from both England and France when he [Chamberlain] emerged on January 15 without having visibly compromised either country."

According to Frederick Birchall, the *New York Times* correspondent who was in London during Chamberlain's visit to Rome, the British were quite insistent upon the point that whatever Mussolini wanted, he was not going to have British help in obtaining it. In fact, he claims the British were quite nervous about this. Every day the British press attaché took pains to emphasize: "Please make it clear that he [Chamberlain] didn't give him [Mussolini] anything and didn't promise him anything." That, Birchall suggests, meant that there must never be another Munich. The people had "taken hold" and were pressing the statesman.[56]

Lloyd George publicly attacked the Government's foreign policy in general, and the Rome visit in particular, in a speech at Llandudno on January 19. Chamberlain had shaken the hand that was giving orders to sink British ships and kill British sailors, he charged. The Government had shown "gross stupidity" in letting the dictators place Britain in a most dangerous strategical position. He was still looking forward to "an awaken-

56. Birchall, *The Storm Breaks,* pp. 344–45. Birchall also claims that in London the feeling that if war was coming, Britain might as well get on with it, was "pretty unainmous."

ing in the national spirit of Britain . . . which will rouse and inspire democracy throughout the world to a great combined effort to save liberty from utter overthrow in our generation."[57] But Chamberlain's position remained steady. Standing firmly by his dual policy of appeasement and rearmament in a speech to the Birmingham Jewelers' Association on January 28, he enjoined his listeners: "Let us then continue to pursue the path of peace and conciliation, but until we can agree on a general limitation of arms let us continue to make this country strong."[58]

While the pressure on Chamberlain was not reflected in this speech, it was shown, at least in the view of Herbert von Dirksen, in an address which Sir Samuel Hoare, the Home Secretary, made in Swansea on January 26. When Hoare spoke at length on the strength of Britain and the Empire to withstand an emergency and the value of that strength as a safeguard to peace,[59] Dirksen interpreted this as "a concession to growing undercurrents of opinion among some members of the Conservative Party, who demand that the Government should have more backbone and adopt a more determined attitude towards the totalitarian states, since the milder tone used in the past has met with no success." He knew "from a reliable source" that Chamberlain was being subjected to increasing pressure by this group.[60]

Chamberlain reported his Rome conversations to the Commons on January 31 in a message which, according to Ciano, had earlier been submitted to Mussolini for approval.[61] His satisfaction was obvious; though neither side was able to accept all the views of the other, "we did achieve our purpose since when the conversations were over, each side had a clearer insight than before regarding the other's standpoint."

57. *The Times,* Jan. 20, 1939.

58. Chamberlain, *In Search of Peace,* p. 257.

59. *The Times,* Jan. 27, 1939.

60. The German Ambassador in London to the Foreign Office, London, Jan. 27, 1939. *Documents on the Events Preceding the Outbreak of the War* (Berlin, 1939 and New York, 1940), p. 254. (Hereinafter cited as *German White Book.*)

61. *The Ciano Diaries,* p. 17. Ciano recorded: "The Duce approved it and commented, 'I believe this is the first time that the head of the British Government submits to a foreign government the outline of one of his speeches. It's a bad sign for them'."

The debate which followed was concerned almost exclusively with the question of Spain.[62] The charge against the Government's policy was carried by Labor members and the Liberal spokesman, Sir Archibald Sinclair. In essence, Labor was amazed at Chamberlain's faith in Mussolini's asurances and his indifference to the fate of Spain. The Republican forces there had been battling for democracy and freedom while Britain, by refusing to sell them arms, was holding their hands behind their backs and preventing them from defending themselves. Labor's demand was, in Attlee's words, "that this country should cease the hypocritical farce of non-intervention and restore to the Spanish Government that right which is theirs inherently as the Government of a sovereign State."

Chamberlain, ignoring the reality of Italian intervention, found it "impossible to agree" with Attlee. He denied the charge that appeasement had failed, countering: "On the contrary, I maintain that it is steadily succeeding." As evidence he cited Hitler's speech to the Reichstag on the previous day,[63] from which he "very definitely" got the impression that it was not the speech of a man preparing to throw Europe into another crisis.

Sinclair's "deepest regret" was that the Government, in the face of the threatening Italian attitude towards France, had given no assurance of its determination to stand by France in protecting her vital interests. Even the German people were asking whether the British had any ideals or principles. In Spain, Britain was "conniving at a conspiracy" among the German, Italian, and Spanish dictators to crush the liberties of the Spanish people. "It is high time we said to Herr Hitler and Signor Mussolini, 'What you do in Germany and Italy is your own affair, but the British people will not stand your meddling with the liberties of Europe.' "

62. Attlee had been demanding a discussion of Spain for some days. He had written to Chamberlain on January 19 urging the desirability of calling Parliament to discuss the situation. *The Times,* Jan. 20, 1939.

63. Hitler's reference to Britain in this speech was much less hostile than any other of his recent utterances. In addition to denying any territorial claims on Britain and France except the return of German colonies, he stated that Germany had no intention of causing the British Empire any trouble. Baynes, *Speeches of Adolf Hitler,* II, 1575.

In closing the debate, R. A. Butler spoke at length on what the British Government was doing to help Spanish refugees. The Government's case was simply that, if it scrapped non-intervention, it would run the risk of turning the Spanish problem into a world conflict.[64] This statement, in view of the fact that the Government's chief argument for bringing the Anglo-Italian Agreement into operation two and one-half months earlier had been that the Spanish problem had ceased to be a menace to the peace of Europe, suggests rather forcefully that the Government had determined to close its eyes to German and Italian intervention and to follow unilateral non-intervention at almost any cost.

Though the Labor attack on the Government's foreign policy continued with unabated vigor in the early months of 1939, the party was torn by internal dissension. Sir Stafford Cripps, convinced that the Chamberlain Government must be overthrown and replaced by a popular front government, sent a memorandum to the National Secretary of the Labor Party on January 9 recommending that the party invite the cooperation of "every genuine anti-Government Party, or group of individuals" who would be prepared to give support to, among other things, "a positive policy of peace by collective action with France, Russia, the United States of America and other democratic countries for the strengthening of democracy against aggression and a world economic reconstruction based upon justice to the people of all classes and nations."[65] It will be seen at once that there was more involved in the Cripps memorandum than foreign policy, yet it did include a frontal attack upon appeasement.

The Executive of the Labor Party rejected the memorandum and accused Cripps of having "publicly indicated his view that the Labor Party is incapable of returning a Government by itself." When Cripps refused to withdraw the memorandum, he was promptly expelled from the party. Undeterred, he launched a petition calling for a government which would, in regard to foreign affairs, "secure our Britain, organize a Peace Alliance

64. *Parl. Debs., HC,* January 31, 1939, vol. 343, 37–173.

65. Eric Estorick, *Stafford Cripps: Master Statesman* (New York, 1949), pp. 142–43.

with France and Russia, that will rally the support of the United States and every other peace-loving nation and end the shameful policy which made us accomplices in the betrayal of the Spanish and Chinese people to Fascist aggression."[66] He then toured the country, making speeches to promote his campaign. He received some support from secretaries of local Labor Party organizations and unknown "small people" within the Labor movement. In addition, he was supported by some persons of note outside Labor: Victor Gallancz, J. M. Keynes, Bernard Shaw, J. B. Priestley, David Low, Liberal Members of Parliament Sir Richard Acland and Wilfred Roberts, and even Sir Archibald Sinclair and David Lloyd George. Aneurin Bevan and G. R. Strauss (who were expelled from the Labor Party along with Cripps), Gollancz, and several others joined Cripps in addressing "revivalistic" meetings.[67]

Though the whirlwind campaign continued for four months, it was doomed to failure from the beginning. The two groups absolutely essential to its success, the Labor Party and the dissident Conservatives, refused to have anything to do with it. The dissident Conservatives were by no means willing to associate themselves with the socialist implications of Cripps' program—they were already under attack in their own constituencies by the Conservative Party machine[68]; Labor (including the trade unions) undoubtedly feared that an electoral alliance, far from strengthening the opposition to the Chamberlain Government, might create disunity and bewilderment among the rank and file of the Labor Party.[69] Though Cripps apparently gained considerable support for a time, the change in British foreign policy after March 15, 1939, undoubtedly slowed down the petition

66. *Ibid.*, p. 145.

67. Patricia Strauss, *Cripps: Advocate Extraordinary* (New York, 1942), pp. 198–200. See also Colin Cooke, *The Life of Richard Stafford Cripps* (London, 1957), pp. 230–39.

68. See Churchill, *The Gathering Storm*, pp. 330–31; Duff Cooper, *Old Men Forget*, pp. 252–53; Rowse, *Appeasement*, p. 86. For Churchill matters had come to such a pass that he had made it clear that if a resolution of censure were carried against him, he would resign his seat and fight a by-election.

69. Labor's view is fully developed in Dalton, *The Fateful Years*, pp. 208–22; Jenkins, *Mr. Attlee*, p. 203; and Francis Williams, *Ernest Bevin: Portrait of a Great Englishman* (London, 1952), pp. 210–11.

campaign. When the Labor Party Conference held at Southport in late May approved his expulsion by an overwhelming majority,[70] Cripps's Popular Front was condemned to futility. But it is significant as one more expression of disgust with appeasement, and a vigorous attempt to do something positive about it.

Meanwhile, during February and early March, the ministers identified with Munich attempted to sponsor—over the protests of Halifax and without participation by the Foreign Office—a wave of optimism in Britain. They gave no evidence of waning faith in their policy; rather they seemed to be consciously competing in issuing optimistic statements to the country. One of them applied to those who still sounded notes of warning the name "jitterbugs."[71] Chamberlain, in a speech at Blackburn on February 22, quoted Shakespeare: "Come the three corners of the world in arms, and we shall shock them."[72] Hoare, addressing his constituents in Chelsea on March 10, spoke of a possible "golden age."[73]

Though attempts at psychological analysis in this situation are risky, one interpretation might be that the Government's concern for promoting optimism bears direct testimony to the fact that there was no natural reason for it and betrays the misgivings of the ministers themselves as to the faltering effectiveness of their policy. Perhaps this effort even reflects growing misgivings on the part of the British people at large, for Churchill observed at this moment—so he told an American businessman—a readiness in the British people to resist further demands, even at the cost of war. Chamberlain was being pushed, Churchill observed, toward the adoption of the "Churchillian recipe,"[74] whether he

70. Strauss, *Cripps,* p. 229.

71. Duff Cooper, *Old Men Forget,* p. 252; Duff Cooper, *The Second World War,* p. 148.

72. *German White Book,* p. 259.

73. *The Times,* Mar. 11, 1939. Hoare claims that Chamberlain had advised him to discourage the view that war was inevitable, and to insist upon the great possibilities of peace. It was a later misinterpretation of his words which led to their being considered an unconditional prophecy. Templewood, *Nine Troubled Years,* p. 328.

74. Langer and Gleason, *The Challenge to Isolation,* p. 57. Churchill wrote in his diary on February 9 that the attitude of the Government was stiffening and there was a sense of gathering strength. The navy was ready; the steady flow of aircraft and munitions had at last begun. "The day may

liked it or not. In any event, the pronouncements of Government ministers during these weeks seemed to evidence one of two things: no real appreciation of the danger of the totalitarian threat to Europe, or a deep appreciation which they steadfastly refused to acknowledge. Though the former appears more likely, and at first glance more alarming, the latter is equally alarming if it is a democratic government's responsibility to inform its people of impending dangers both within and without.

The Government's optimism, whether real or contrived, was periodically shattered by the outcries of the Opposition against appeasement. Critics of the Government's policy still decried the situation in Spain, where the Franco forces were about to emerge victorious. When on February 27 Chamberlain announced in the Commons that, after "very careful consideration," the Government had that day taken formal action recognizing the Franco regime as the government of Spain,[75] Labor retaliated on the following day with a motion of censure. In a scorching condemnation of Chamberlain, Attlee asserted that the Prime Minister had done more than any other man "to show his contempt for . . . and to break down the rules of international law." He felt it a "disgraceful allegation" to claim, as Chamberlain had done, that there was no effective government in Republican Spain. What assurance did he have that Franco would not join the Axis? Labor saw in this action of the Government

> a gross betrayal of a friendly Government, a gross betrayal of democracy, the consummation of two and one half years of the hypocritical pretence of non-intervention, and a connivance all the time at aggression, and this is only one step further in the downward march of His Majesty's Government in which at every stage they do not sell but give away the permanent interests of this country. They do not do anything to build up peace or stop war, but merely announce

---

yet come when the peaceful, law-respecting British nation may once again be able to pursue its journey without having to wait and listen on the wireless from week to week to the dictatorial orations from countries it defeated or succored in the past." Churchill, *Step by Step,* pp. 291–92.

75. *Parl. Debs., HC,* February 27, 1939, vol. 344, 873.

> to the whole world that anyone who is out to use force can always be sure that he will have a friend in the British Prime Minister.[76]

Chamberlain denied Attlee's "breach of international law" charge and expressed the hope that this debate would not degenerate into a "personal squabble." Britain had received assurances from Franco that there would be no general reprisals for what could be described as strictly political offences. In the Prime Minister's view, "recognition is really only a formal act which brings the relations between this country and General Franco's Government into relationship with reality."

An exasperated Sinclair reiterated Attlee's arguments, concluding a long censure by charging: "The Government's policy has strengthened the dictatorships, weakened the democracies, and betrayed one after another those countries that trusted us, and their epitaph will be, 'We have eaten dirt in vain.'" Before the debate closed, Laborites Ellen Wilkinson, Colonel Wedgwood, G. F. Strauss, Frederick Seymour Cocks, and Herbert Morrison, as well as Wilfred Roberts (Liberal) and William Gallacher (Communist), all denounced Chamberlain's policy in terms similar to Attlee's. Eden spoke briefly, but deserted the Opposition forces on this occasion. Refusing to discuss the policy which had led up to this point, he believed that, under existing circumstances, it was expedient to recognize Franco. To refuse recognition would be "to encourage the conflict to go on after it has passed a period when nobody thinks that the result could be changed." In the end, Attlee's motion met with defeat, 137 ayes to 344 noes.[77]

The press generally accepted the recognition of Franco as a foregone conclusion. *The Times* (Feb. 28) considered the Government was on "impregnable ground"; recognition of the successful party was the "logical culmination of thirty months' consistent policy." The *Financial Times* (Feb. 28) favored recognition because in it lay the prospect of closer relations with Spain, a country with which Britain normally did a substantial amount of

76. *Ibid.,* February 28, 1939, vol. 344, 1108.
77. *Ibid.,* February 28, 1939, vol. 344, 1099–218.

trade. The Edinburgh *Weekly Scotsman* (Mar. 4) approved for the same reason. "We may be disappointed," the Cardiff *Western Mail* (Feb. 25) observed, "but conditions of recognition cannot be dictated to the victor." The *Glasgow Herald* (Feb. 28) thought recognition "inevitable." It was useless to argue that "international morality" should forbid recognition of the regime which would soon dominate all of Spain. It was better for Britain to place herself in a position where she could make her influence felt in Burgos.

The *Liverpool Daily Post* (Feb. 28) tersely suggested that since the Republican Government had been dispersed, "the act of recognition can hardly be challenged." So said the *Manchester Guardian* (Mar. 1), after having lamented (Feb. 28) that Franco had gotten everything by yielding nothing. The *News Chronicle* (Feb. 28), which along with the *Daily Herald* had waged a long campaign for the abandonment of non-intervention and the sale of arms to Republican Spain, believed recognition "the shameful culmination of one of the blackest chapters in this country's history." Nevertheless, it was a fact and had to be faced. With that, the *Economist* (Mar. 4) agreed.

The House of Lords did not consider the Government's Spanish policy until March 9, but the ardor of the critics there had not cooled in the meantime. Lord Snell felt the Government had no constructive contribution to make to the need for better international relations, chiding:

> The world cries aloud for peace through comprehension and reorganisation. His Majesty's Government offer 'appeasement'— and the very word which they have chosen to describe their motives and their policy is in itself revealing. Appeasement! It indicates that they have no plan of their own, no sense of direction, and nothing in the way of reconstruction to offer. It appeases by the method of retreat.[78]

Viscount Cecil, the Earl of Listowel, and Lord Strabolgi all made one final thrust at the policy of non-intervention, inducing Halifax at length to admit that there had been "breaches of the

78. *Parl. Debs., HL,* March 9, 1939, vol. 112, 81.

Non-Intervention Agreement." It had been a "leaky dam." But, he argued, "there is all the difference in the world between a leaky dam and no dam at all, and the fact does remain that by that dam, leaky or not, a general conflagration in Europe has been prevented."[79]

By March, 1939, the misery that Munich had imposed upon Czechoslovakia had been brought home very painfully to the British Government. The loss of the Sudetenland had made the Czechs economically dependent upon Germany. Politically, they had been forced to pursue a policy of close cooperation with the Reich.[80] The application of the Munich accord had increased the severity of its original terms.[81] And the one provision of that agreement which had been designed to compensate Czechoslovakia for her great sacrifices—the guarantee of her frontiers—had never come into effect.

What had happened to the promised guarantee? Sir Thomas Inskip, the British Minister for the Co-ordination of Defense, had told the House of Commons on October 4 that the Government felt "under a moral obligation to Czechoslovakia to treat the guarantee as now being in force."[82] Two days later, however, Chamberlain noted that since there were "several important considerations" which had not yet been decided, it was useless to discuss the matter at that stage.[83] When Parliament reconvened on November 1, it was evident that much of the Government's fervor for the guarantee had already cooled. Chamberlain explained on that occasion:

> The position [concerning the guarantee] remains exactly

79. *Ibid.*, March 9, 1939, vol. 112, 78–126.
80. See the Chargé d'Affaires in Czechoslovakia to the Foreign Ministry, Prague, Oct. 10, 1938. *G. D.*, IV, 51–52.
81. In addition to the International Commission's acceptance of virtually all the terms demanded by Germany and the abandonment of plebiscites, the Hungarian claims on Czechoslovakia were settled not by bilateral agreement between the two countries but by an arbitral award handed down by representatives of Germany and Italy, in which Czechoslovakia fared none too well. Documents on the Vienna Award, *G. D.*, IV, 118–27. See also R. W. Seton-Watson, *A History of the Czechs and Slovaks* (London, 1943), p. 375; Arthur B. Keith, *The Causes of the War* (London, 1940), p. 368.
82. *Parl. Debs., HC,* October 4, 1938, vol. 339, 303.
83. *Ibid.,* October 6, 1938, vol. 339, 477.

> the same and it cannot be cleared up until the whole question of minorities in Czechoslovakia has been settled. . . . Our original offer was to enter into an international guarantee, but what the terms of that guarantee will be, and who will be the partakers in that guarantee, is not a question on which I can give the House any further information today.

> We never guaranteed the frontiers [of Czechoslovakia] as they existed. What we did was to guarantee against unprovoked aggression—quite a different thing. That did not mean that we gave our seal to the existence of frontiers as they were then or at any other time. Our guarantee was against unprovoked aggression and not the crystallization of frontiers.[84]

It eventually emerged from the conversations in Paris in late November that the British wished to give a joint guarantee which would include Germany and Italy and would come into force only as a result of a decision by three of the four powers. France favored a joint and individual guarantee, whereby the refusal of one guarantor to fulfill his obligations would not liberate the others from fulfilling theirs. A compromise formula was at length adopted: Prague was to be consulted, and London and Paris would consider that opinion in making their decision.[85]

The British and French were to have no German or Italian cooperation on the matter of the guarantee. Soon after Munich, Hitler revealed in private conversation that he regretted having bound himself, indeed conditionally, to the promise of a guarantee.[86] And Ribbentrop, in Paris in early December, sidetracked the issue by asserting that the "best and most effective" guarantee of Czechoslovakia would consist solely in the establishment of friendly relations between that country and Germany.[87] In late December Coulondre, the new French Ambassador in

84. *Ibid.*, November 1, 1938, vol. 340, 79–80.

85. Record of Anglo-French Conversations Held at the Quai d'Orsay on November 24, 1938. *B. D.*, III, 300–06; Bonnet, *Défense de la Paix,* II, 56–57.

86. Meissner, *Staatssekretär unter Ebert-Hindenburg-Hitler,* p. 470.

87. Memorandum by an Official of the Foreign Minister's Secretariat, Dec. 6, 1938. *G. D.*, IV, 474.

Berlin, got no more satisfaction from Weizsäcker: "Could not this matter be forgotten? Since Germany's predominance in that area is a fact, would not the guarantee of the Reich be sufficient?. . . . In any case we are in no hurry to settle this question."[88]

When Chamberlain raised the question with Mussolini in Rome in mid-January, the Duce replied that he had no objection in principle to a guarantee of Czechoslovakia, but he would consider any decision at that moment premature. Czechoslovakia must first put her affairs in order at home by means of a new constitution, make a declaration of neutrality, and establish in reality the new frontiers which were then only marked on the map.[89]

On February 8 the British and French made a joint approach to Germany on the matter of the guarantee.[90] The reply, which was not received until March 2, claimed that the conditions of guarantee posed by the Munich Agreement had not been realized and the territorial adjustments with neighboring states had not, in actuality, been completed. General development in this European zone fell within the sphere of the most important interests of the Reich, and it was necessary to await a clarification of the internal development of Czechoslovakia and the improvement resulting therefrom in her relations with the surrounding states before undertaking a further statement of policy.[91] In short, Germany did not intend to join in any guarantee of Czechoslovakia.

Unfortunately for the Czechs, discussions never progressed

88. Coulondre to Bonnet, Berlin, Dec. 22, 1938. *The French Yellow Book: Diplomatic Documents, 1938–1939* (New York, 1940), p. 46; Coulondre, *De Staline á Hitler,* p. 249.

89. Conversation Between the Duce and Chamberlain, Rome, Jan. 12, 1939. *Ciano's Diplomatic Papers,* pp. 265–66.

90. Note Verbale from the British Embassy, Berlin, Feb. 8, 1939. *G. D.,* IV, 207–08; Note Verbale from Coulondre to the Reich Foreign Office, Feb. 8, 1939. *French Yellow Book,* pp. 59–60.

91. Note Verbale to the French Embassy, Berlin, Feb. 28, 1939. *G. D.,* IV, 218–20; Note Verbale from the Foreign Office to the British Embassy, Berlin, Feb. 28, 1939. *Trials of War Criminals Before the Nuernberg Military Tribunals under Control Council Law No. 10* (Washington, D.C., 1950–1952), XII, 849–50.

beyond that stage. Within two weeks' time, Czechoslovakia had ceased to exist as a sovereign state, and the British policy of appeasement rocked on its foundations.

Though there may be truth in the assertion of the editor of the *Economist* (Nov. 12, 1938) that "the interpretation of isolated election results is an art akin to astrology," it is necessary to account briefly for the by-elections held in Britain between April, 1938, and March, 1939, and to suggest their meaning in terms of popular sentiment with regard to the Government's policy. Obviously, more was involved in each by-election than the issue of foreign policy, but since the European scene was fraught with so much tension it is not unreasonable to suppose that foreign policy was a major issue in many of the by-elections.

After Labor turned a Conservative majority into a Labor majority in West Fulham in early April, 1938, and duplicated that feat in the Lichfield Division of Staffordshire on May 5, it seemed as if a general trend against the Government might be underway. But in the Aylesbury Division of Buckinghamshire (May), West Derbyshire (June), and the Stafford Division of Staffordshire (June), the Government retained the seats it had won in previous elections, though in each case the Labor vote showed a substantial increase. Labor held its seat in Barnsley (June), increasing its majority by 3,000 votes. The Conservatives had more reason to be disturbed about the East Willesden by-election in late July, where their vote declined by 10,000. Yet, combined with a large majority in the previous election and a decline of 3,000 in the Labor vote, the Government held the seat.

Munich was followed by a series of by-elections more discomforting to the Government. After the Government retained its seat in Oxford city (Oct.) by a reduced majority, Labor reversed a Conservative majority in Dartford (Nov.) and increased its majority in Doncaster (Nov.). The most serious shock to the Government's electoral prestige was delivered in the Bridgwater Division of Somerset, where the well-known journalist Vernon Bartlett, standing as an anti-Munich, Independent Progressive candidate in a straight fight with a supporter of Chamberlain, secured a 2,000 vote majority; the general election of 1935 had given the Conservative candidate a majority of 10,000 votes over his nearest opponent. Foreign policy played an important role in the campaign. "Outside" speakers whose anti-appeasement sentiments were generally well-known—they included Megan Lloyd George, Wickham Steed, and J. B. S. Haldane—appeared on Bartlett's behalf, and Bartlett later testified that, despite the rural character of the constituency, the questions after every public meeting dealt as much with foreign policy as with domestic matters.[92]

Meanwhile, however, the Government had retained its seat in Walsall (Nov.), and in late November did the same in West Lewisham and in the Fylde Division of Lancashire, though in each instance with reduced majorities. And the Government was undoubtedly encouraged by the results of the Kinross and West Perthshire by-election in late December. The Duchess of Atholl, who had recently resigned as a protest against Chamberlain's foreign policy, had held the seat for the Conservatives since 1923. She stood at the by-election as an independent, and lost to the Conservative candidate by more than 1,000 votes.

In the early months of 1939, the Government retained seats in East Norfolk (Jan.), in the Ripon Division of Yorkshire (Feb.), and in the Holderness Division of East Yorkshire (Feb.), though again, in each instance, with a considerably reduced majority. Labor retained its hold upon Batley and Morley (Mar.) by a slightly increased majority.[93]

Thus it appears from the by-elections that there was a trend opposing Chamberlain. Though the Government lost only a few seats, its victories were accompanied in most instances by reduced majorities. In many places the Labor vote rose sharply, while the Liberal vote declined, the correlation of which is impossible

92. *The Times,* Nov. 19, 1938. *The Times* termed Bartlett's victory a "remarkable personal triumph." On this occasion 84 per cent of the electorate went to the polls, an unusually high figure for a by-election. Bartlett's memoirs contain an interesting account of the campaign. *And Now, Tomorrow,* pp. 39–44.

93. All the election data herein presented are from *The Times,* April 7, 1938–March 10, 1939.

to determine. Lending support to the supposition that discontent with the Government's foreign policy played a considerable part in the rising Labor vote in the Parliamentary by-elections is the fact that in municipal elections held throughout England and Wales on November 1, 1938, Labor showed no corresponding gains. The Labor Party gained 62 places and lost 79, while the Conservatives gained 57 places and lost only 37.[94] In summary, the by-elections held between Eden's resignation and March 15, 1939, do not give evidence of such a swing against Chamberlain's administration as would have brought about a Labor victory had a general election been held. But neither did they encourage the Government to believe it had an enthusiastic country supporting it.

94. *Ibid.*, Nov. 3, 1938.

CHAPTER EIGHT

The Great Awakening

ON THE EVE OF MARCH 15, 1939, the British people were bitterly divided over questions of foreign policy. The schism had been widening over a period of months and even years. One major faction had imputed to the other a political ineptitude and moral baseness, and the party on whom these aspersions had been cast had sullenly resented it without being able to feel quite certain that the odious charges were altogether undeserved. Down to the night of March 14, 1939, the truth about Hitler's policy was still open to conjecture. But that was dramatically changed when the Führer's legions swept over Czechoslovakia on March 15.[1] To those who expected peace on the basis of the Munich Agreement, it came as hideous disillusionment. To the critics of the Government's policy it came as confirmation of their worst fears; to almost all Englishmen it came as the final awakening to the menace of Nazi methods to European freedom and security.

When, however, Chamberlain addressed the House of Commons on the afternoon of March 15, he appeared quite unperturbed. He quickly dismissed the "moral guarantee" to Czechoslovakia envisaged by Inskip after Munich; the Slovak Diet's declaration of independence (March 14) had

> put an end by internal disruption to the State whose frontiers we had proposed to guarantee, and, accordingly, the condition of affairs described by the Secretary of State for the Dominions, which was always regarded by us as being

1. The immediate background of the destruction of Czechoslovakia has been fully developed elsewhere. See especially Laffan et al., *Survey of International Affairs, 1938,* III, 247–69.

> only of a transitory nature has now ceased to exist, and His Majesty's Government cannot accordingly hold themselves any longer bound by this obligation.[2]

Chamberlain admitted regret that the method by which the changes in Czechoslovakia had been brought about were not in accord with the spirit of Munich: But, he continued:

> Do not let us on that account be deflected from our course. Let us remember that the desire of all peoples of the world still remains concentrated on the hopes of peace. . . . Though we may have to suffer checks and disappointments from time to time, the object that we have in mind is of too great significance to the happiness of mankind for us lightly to give it up or set it on one side.[3]

Chamberlain's language was the dialect of appeasement, but it appeared that day an alien tongue in the House of Commons. Beginning with David Grenfell's vehement denunciation of Chamberlain's "remarkable state of detachment," eleven Labor members challenged the Prime Minister to acknowledge the demise of appeasement and to seek through common action with other nations to arrest this "black death of totalitarian aggression." "We have been told that the Government are trying to find appeasement," Grenfell observed. "All that we witness day after day is a steady and violent disintegration of the European system, and appeasement, instead of modifying or retarding that disintegration, only gives an added impetus to it." That Chamberlain could still believe that the Munich settlement was reached in good faith was "incredible." Britain must let it be known that she would stand by all nations who would defend liberty and freedom. Hugh Dalton delivered a particularly telling thrust. Damning the Prime Minister's use of Slovakia's declaration of independence as merely "a door through which we could run out," he moved on to ask whether these events in Czechoslovakia

2. As Halifax reportedly wrote the French Ambassador, "the one compensating advantage" of Hitler's action was that it "brought to an end the somewhat embarrassing commitment of a guarantee." Amery, *My Political Life*, III, 286 n.

3. *Parl. Debs., HC,* March 15, 1939, vol. 345, 435–40.

had come as a surprise to the Government. If so, it reflected sadly on the efficiency of British diplomatic representatives and the secret service. If not, it was a grave reflection on the Government that it had taken no action to meet the impending crisis. What Dalton wanted to know was "on which horn of that dilemma the Government prefer to be impaled." Or as Sydney Silverman put it: any man who, seeing what had happened since Munich, could still say that that policy was right either "deliberately means to mislead this House and mislead the country or else he is completely and intellectually incapable of understanding what is going on in the world around him."

For the Liberals, Sir Archibald Sinclair begged the House to take a "fresh, clear, and objective view" of the situation. The Government had been misleading public opinion by saying that international tension was declining, but the time for truth had come. Instead of following Chamberlain's "disastrously misconceived" policy, Britain must gather her friends to her and convince the world that she would resist aggression by all the means in her power.

The most remarkable thing about the debate was the fact that seven Conservatives rose to condemn the Prime Minister's policy. Eden was convinced that

> if the present methods in Europe are to be allowed to continue unchecked, we are heading straight for anarchy, for a universal tragedy which is going to involve us all. . . . Britain must make a great national effort at unity and strength. Then our duty would be to examine . . . the new military and strategic position that confronts us in Europe, to consult all those nations who are likeminded with us . . . to discuss with those nations what our policy is to be and where we will make our stand, and, having determined that, to make with them at once the military plans to give effect to our decisions.[4]

Commander R. T. Bower, who had not hitherto spoken against Chamberlain's policy in the Commons, flatly declared: "This

4. *Ibid.*, March 15, 1939, vol. 345, 461–62.

plan of appeasement has failed." Richard Law made the same point and just as abruptly. Bower agreed with Eden that Britain must contact at once all countries who were prepared to stand with her in defense of democratic ideals. So did Duncan Sandys, who not only proposed an immediate conference to that end but warned that British leadership was vital if this were to be done.

As the debate wore on, Sir John Simon undertook to defend the Government. He was certain there was "no alternative which can be recommended for the approval of the country other than the policy which the Prime Minister followed at Munich." Britain must be very careful, he noted, not to enter into "any extensive general and undefined commitment with the result that, to a large extent, our foreign policy would depend, not on this country, this Parliament and its electors, but on a lot of foreign governments." The effect of his statement is one of the most eloquent proofs of the change of sentiment in the House of Commons. In October, 1938, though there would have been dissenting voices, Simon's view would have received the support of a vast majority. But in March, 1939, it provoked savage criticism and roused the House to a pitch of anger rarely seen. Communist W. Gallacher at once stormed that "never has a Minister . . . given such an exhibition of complete and hopeless political bankruptcy." Conservative Vyvyan Adams, fearing that Hitler might next say that if Britain did not give Germany a colony he would bomb London, or Leeds, or Liverpool, proclaimed: "In God's name—I say this in all seriousness—let us not give way to that kind of threat." Laborite J. J. Davidson raged: "I want to say plainly to the Government that when the time does come to make some defence of their own interests, I will advise the workers to see the Government in hell before they undertake the job which should have been dealt with long ago."[5]

Chamberlain had defended appeasement, but to most of those who spoke in the Commons on March 15, the policy was visibly in ruins. It is true that much of the violent criticism came from

5. *Ibid.*, March 15, 1939, vol. 345, 441–564. Churchill did not speak in this debate. He apparently was anxious to join the Government after Prague (see Templewood, *Nine Troubled Years,* p. 385), and did not want to deepen his differences with Chamberlain.

those who had attacked Munich in the first place, but there was a perceptible change of temper in the House at large, a clear indication that many supporters of the Government were deeply disturbed and genuinely unhappy about the views and tactics of their leaders.

There followed throughout the country an underground explosion of public opinion, impossible for the historian to trace precisely, but reflected with force in the volume of acute criticism which spurted from the British press. The mildest term that could be applied to Germany's action, wrote the Conservative *Daily Telegraph* (Mar. 16) was "a monstrous outrage." Munich had been reduced to "complete and utter mockery," and its spirit was dead and buried, for "who can appease a boa-constrictor?" The Unionist Cardiff *Western Mail* (Mar. 16) demanded that Britain's policy be changed at once; further talk of appeasement to Hitler would be "greater folly than reading a tract to a Bengal tiger." Even the pro-Government *Times* (Mar. 17) saw Nazism revealed in all its cunning and ruthlessness, and thought it a "wholly natural impulse" that would urge the other nations of Europe "to confer forthwith on the best means of defending together all that they are agreed on holding sacred." *The Times*' statement was a notable one, for this was the first occasion on which it admitted that Germany was following a policy of threats against non-Germanic neighbors and of acquisition of their territories in defiance of all promises. It was no longer possible even for Printing House Square to believe that Germany could be restrained by evoking the "moral factor." And this shock and disillusionment with appeasement was characteristic of the sentiment which prevailed in many Conservative newspapers.

The Liberal and independent newspapers were almost unanimous and universally vigorous in their demand for a new approach to foreign affairs. To the Liberal Bradford *Yorkshire Observer* (Mar. 16) Munich had become "another scrap of paper." Britain must gather about her all the available forces interested in the maintenance of peace, wherever they could be found. Peace could not be advanced by attempting to placate the dictators. The Liberal *Liverpool Daily Post* (Mar. 16) expressed the same view: "Collective security must be organised, and that without delay, on the broad firm base of democratic principles. It seems, in fact, as if only by a combination of the liberal peoples can the world be saved from disaster." Current events showed the "utter futility" of Chamberlain's policy, the Liberal *News Chronicle* (Mar. 16) declared. It must be changed at once or the Prime Minister himself must be changed. Next day (Mar. 17) the *News Chronicle* reiterated: "Mr. Chamberlain's policy is impossible. Some visible and outward sign that . . . appeasement has been dropped is urgently needed; and it is difficult to see anything which will satisfy this need short of Mr. Chamberlain's retirement." An editorial entitled "A Policy in Ruins" left no doubt as to the Liberal *Manchester Guardian's* (Mar. 16) opinion of appeasement. Chamberlain's "dream fantasy" had been shattered. The most serious charge that could be brought against the Government, the paper stated (Mar. 17), was that it had made no attempt for solidarity in the Western world. British policy was as uncertain as ever.

The independent *Financial News* (Mar. 16) considered the German invasion of Czechoslovakia "its own commentary on the whole flimsy facade erected at Munich to disguise the failure to deter Germany from an act of open aggression last September." The independent *Glasgow Herald* (Mar. 17) asserted that "Munich ended with Czechoslovakia and . . . the conclusions that must be drawn from this are reinforced in the mind of every civilised man by the devastating force with which he [Hitler] has enslaved the Czech people." These and other independent journals were especially forceful in pointing out the obvious "lesson" of Munich. The non-partisan *Spectator* (Mar. 17) added still another point: nothing would create more confidence than the entry of Churchill or Eden into the Cabinet—provided, of course, its policy was one they could support.

The Labor press, long critical of appeasement, naturally joined in the growing din. For the Labor *Daily Herald* (Mar. 16), the occupation of Prague was Hitler's "postscript to Munich," and the threat could be met only by "an intensification of our own measures of security and by a determined policy of cooperation with France, Russia, and with the United States against a common danger." Likewise, the Labor *Leeds Weekly Citizen* (Mar. 17) was convinced of the worthlessness of appeasement. Nobody in the world trusted British policy any longer. Getting in a final partisan punch, it added: "We have been brought to this pass by a Government which was formed to defend democracy and collective security and which has spent its energies destroying both."

A few newspapers failed to urge vigorous action upon the Government, the Conservative *Daily Mail* (Mar. 16) for example, gullibly holding that the final destruction of Czechoslovakia was caused by internal disruption and asserting (Mar. 17) that Britain's safety depended entirely upon her own armed might. But such remarks constituted a very small minority.

The overwhelming sentiment of the press on March 16-17 was obviously that appeasement was totally discredited and must, therefore, be abandoned at once. Most of those newspapers which, at the time of Munich, had been inclined to give the policy a "fair trial" now recognized its utter futility; those which had warned the previous September that this outcome was to be expected were in a stronger position, from the vantage point of telling criticism, than ever before. Everywhere in the press it was agreed that appeasement must be replaced with some sort of vigorous, and quite probably collective, action. Here and there (especially in Opposition journals, of course), it was openly noted that the alternative to this was the departure of the Prime Minister himself. The forcefulness and virtual unanimity of this judgment, coming as it did in a time of sudden crisis, could not help but weigh heavily on a Prime Minister who was himself disillusioned and vexed.

The demand for collective action among the peace-loving states of Europe also received strong support in statements issued by several "peace organizations." Lord Cecil, president of the International Peace Campaign, warned on March 15 that nothing could save Europe from a collapse into international anarchy or world domination by the Rome-Berlin Axis except a "resolute effort by the peace-loving Powers to restore effective international control through the League of Nations." Next day, the Executive Committee of the League of Nations Union urged that Britain initiate, in conjunction with other states, some kind of measure to halt aggression. The cooperation of France was assured; that of Russia should be sought.[6]

March 16 brought no apparent change in Chamberlain's outlook. His replies in the House of Commons to questions about the Czechoslovak situation were still distressingly noncommittal. One brief exchange illustrates this graphically:

Sinclair: Have the British Government lodged any protest with the German Government . . . ?
The P.M.: No, Sir, we have not done so.
Sinclair: Is it proposed to lodge a protest?
The P.M.: I could not answer that question without notice.
. . . .
Maclean: Has the Prime Minister or the Government any intention of withdrawing the Diplomatic Corps from Berlin?
The P.M.: The question . . . is now under consideration.
Viscountess Astor: Will the Prime Minister lose no time in letting the German Government know with what horror the whole of this country regards Germany's action?
(no reply)[7]

Chamberlain's failure to gauge the changed temper of the nation precipitated a severe crisis within the Conservative Party. Throughout March 16 the volume of criticism, among Conservative Members of Parliament and in the country at large, of his apparently stubborn refusal to be deflected from appeasement continued to grow until it became apparent that, if Chamberlain insisted upon blind adherence to his past policy and did not make a stronger statement of Britain's future policy toward Germany, his personal position as Prime Minister and leader of the party would be endangered.[8] In addition to the spreading conviction that something more than appeasement was vitally necessary if the dictators' surge of aggression were to be halted, most Conservatives undoubtedly realized the political implications of insist-

6. *The Times,* Mar. 16, 17, 1939.
7. *Parl. Debs., HC,* March 16, 1939, vol. 345, 612–15.
8. This is especially reflected in the press on March 16.

ing upon a policy which had been discredited in the eyes of an increasing number of the electorate.[9]

Chamberlain was scheduled to speak at Birmingham on March 17. To have accepted what had happened with the best grace possible would have been in harmony with his earlier statement to the House. But the Birmingham speech struck a new note. Chamberlain now recognized that his "restrained and cautious exposition" in the Commons had given rise to "misapprehension." When he had made that speech, he explained, the Government's information on what had occurred in Czechoslovakia was only partial and unofficial, making a considered opinion impossible. Now his error could be corrected. He still believed that Hitler had been justified in his pre-Munich policy, but the invasion of Czechoslovakia fell "into a different category." It caused Britain to ask: "Is this the last attack upon a small state, or is it to be followed by others? Is this, in fact, a step in the direction of an attempt to dominate the world by force?" There was hardly anything he would not sacrifice for peace, Chamberlain asserted, but one thing he must except, and that was "the liberty that we have enjoyed for hundreds of years, and which we will never surrender." Therefore, he "felt bound to repeat" that

> while I am not prepared to engage this country by new unspecified commitments operating under conditions which cannot be foreseen, yet no greater mistake could be made than to suppose that, because it believes war to be a senseless and cruel thing, this nation has so lost its fibre that it will not take part to the utmost of its power in resisting such a challenge if it ever were made.[10]

While Chamberlain's speech did not light a fiery cross, it was a definite contradiction to the mood and policy of his statement in the Commons. He had come to see that he must respond more vigorously to Germany's cynical occupation of Czechoslo-

9. Dirksen felt this factor was of "decisive importance." *Dirksen Papers*, p. 170.

10. *The British War Blue Book: Documents Concerning German-Polish Relations and the Outbreak of Hostilities Between Great Britain and Germany on September 3, 1939* (New York, 1939), pp. 6–13.

vakia. Feiling attributes his changed tone to the fact that he was "informed by fuller knowledge, and by strong representations as to the opinion in the House, the public, and the Dominions."[11] Chamberlain undoubtedly had been through a period of intense stress, and the pressure exerted upon him by Parliament and press had made a deep imprint. In addition, Henderson's report from Berlin on March 16 certainly must have helped to undermine any notion that appeasement could be carried further. The British Ambassador, who had long gone far beyond the line of duty in sympathizing with the German point of view, reported that

> the utter cynicism and immorality of the whole performance defies description. . . . His Majesty's Government will doubtless consider what attitude to adopt towards a Government which has shown itself incapable of observing an agreement not six months old and which is apparently set on domination by force of the whole of the Danube basin.[12]

Then, too, the influence of Halifax and the Foreign Office weighed upon the Prime Minister. The Foreign Secretary had never displayed such fanatical devotion to Munich as had some of his colleagues. He had differentiated between belief and hope, and had been increasingly inclined to share the view long held by some of his senior advisers that trust in Hitler's good faith was both futile and dangerous. He had gone along with Chamberlain's attitude, at least as long as loyalty demanded, but he was not prepared to see the Conservative Party torn asunder because of the Prime Minister's personal obstinacy. Halifax was by nature a quiet, docile man. He was also an experienced politician, and he recognized the signs of disobedience to party authority. In the moment of crisis he had put the issue squarely before Chamberlain: Parliament, the Conservative Party, and the country were demanding a clear and unequivocal statement of Britain's attitude toward German aggression; if it were not

11. *Life of Neville Chamberlain,* p. 400.
12. Henderson to Halifax, Berlin, Mar. 16, 1939. *B. D.,* IV, 278–79. Henderson later wrote that the occupation of Prague destroyed the "entire arguable validity" of the German case. *Failure of a Mission,* pp. 218–19.

forthcoming, he must expect insurrection both in the party and the House of Commons.[13]

Finally, of course, Chamberlain did not like being cheated. As a signatory of the Munich Agreement, he was certainly entitled to the consultation provided for in the Anglo-German Declaration if Hitler thought Munich ought to be undone. Then too, it was impossible—and Chamberlain realized it—to reconcile the incorporation of seven million Czechs and Slovaks into the Reich with Hitler's oft-stated aim of including only Germans. When the long-professed principle of self-determination, having served its purpose, was abandoned in favor of the policy of unlimited *Lebensraum,* even Chamberlain could not fail to see the implications. That his disillusionment was complete is evidenced by a private speech he made to his supporters in Parliament near the end of March, in which he openly admitted that his trust had been misplaced.[14]

Those who had warned against Hitler must now be heard. Their voices had suddenly broken through the crust of incredulity. They seemed to have been proven right. Embarrassing to the Government though it might be, that fact would have to be recognized quickly and openly. Some action more satisfying to the distraught and fearful conscience of the nation would have to follow at once.

The press received Chamberlain's Birmingham speech warmly, but the really notable aspect of its reaction was the sense of

13. In his speech to the Lords on March 15, Halifax showed a grasp of the implications of Germany's action when he pointed out distinctly: "Now for the first time they are effecting a military occupation of territory inhabited by people with whom they have no racial connection." *Parl. Debs., HL,* March 15, 1939, vol. 112, 217–18. "The difference of opinion between Chamberlain and Halifax, which has already shown itself occasionally, is becoming more and more evident, the latter advocating a stronger attitude." So the German Embassy reported on March 17. *German White Book,* p. 281. Next day, this message followed: "The more extreme group within the Cabinet, represented especially by Lord Halifax, who is entirely under the influence of the Foreign Office, gained the upper hand." *Ibid.,* p. 282. See Stuart Hodgson, *Lord Halifax* (London, 1941), pp. 181–85; Campbell-Johnson, *Viscount Halifax,* pp. 510–13; Wheeler-Bennett, *Munich,* pp. 354–55; Birkenhead, *Halifax,* p. 432.

14. Jones, *A Diary with Letters,* p. 430. See also Amery, *My Political Life,* III, 308.

urgency that, far from permitting the matter to rest where the Prime Minister had left it, Britain must push vigorously ahead in the new direction. This was apparent in journals of all political hues. The *Daily Telegraph* (Mar. 18) again pronounced appeasement dead. It had received a fair trial with an outcome which all must deplore. Britain must apply herself "now and henceforth" to the "new orientation." That was the sentiment of the Conservative *Financial Times* (Mar. 18), too. *The Times* (Mar. 18), so long a supporter of appeasement, openly proclaimed that "this is clearly a moment for consultation between like-minded nations," while the Cardiff *Western Mail* (Mar. 18) declared that no British statesman would ever repeat the mistake of placing reliance on Hitler's pledges. "He is a gangster who must be arrested at the first opportunity, unless the German people are capable of removing him."

Appeasement had reached its tragic end, the *Daily Herald* (Mar. 18) asserted; it lay in pieces at Chamberlain's feet "along with the dust of the body of what was once free Czechoslovakia." The Prime Minister's Birmingham denunciation would be welcomed everywhere, but more than denunciation was needed if the threat of Germany to dominate Europe by force were to be answered. Britain must build a peace front with France, Russia, and the United States. Faith in Chamberlain's judgment in international affairs was no longer possible; it inspired no confidence anywhere. His resignation was essential. Not unnaturally, this view found expression throughout the Labor-oriented press.

From the Liberal vantage-point, the *Manchester Guardian* (Mar. 18) observed with satisfaction that Birmingham marked a decisive change in Britain's national policy. Chamberlain would now be judged by the speed and completeness with which he carried out the new policy. If he went back on it, he, and perhaps the British nation, were doomed. The *News Chronicle* (Mar. 18) expressed "intense relief" that Chamberlain had at last recognized the futility of his policy, but with the *Daily Herald,* doubted whether he was the man to lead Britain with energy and determination along an entirely new path. He would be judged now not by words but by deeds, for "the policy enunciated at Birmingham . . . must be translated, and without delay, into action." For the Bradford *Yorkshire Observer* (Mar. 18), Chamberlain had spoken "the mind of the nation" in summoning the peoples of the world to join in a grand alliance for peace.

The necessity for immediate action was also obvious to independent journals. Most representative, perhaps, was the *Sunday Pictorial* (Mar. 19) which urged: "Mr. Chamberlain has given us brave words; now we want brave action," including the introduction of compulsory national service, close cooperation with America, immediate steps to form a mutual defensive alliance with Russia, France, Holland, Poland, and Belgium, and national unity in the Government.

Especially noteworthy was the position of the influential independent *Observer,* whose editor, J. L. Garvin, had long had intimate connections with the Chamberlain Government, and earlier (especially in the pre-Munich period) had viewed the Chamberlain approach to foreign policy with a sort of gay optimism. Now (Mar. 19), while allowing that Chamberlain had repaired his shaken position at Birmingham, that paper insisted that the nation waited for something more. Strong words were impotent by themselves in comparison with the size, daring, and ruthlessness of German deeds. There must be a deep change in the temper of the British Government, and above all, Britain and France must seek a working understanding with Russia. This apparently independent desertion of "the cause" by long-time editorial compatriots, especially when linked with the accumulating demands for action pouring forth from other editors, forcefully illustrated the extent to which the events of recent days had altered the Prime Minister's position. The realization of this must have been all the more painful when punctuated by caustic reflections like those of "Sagittarius" in the *New Statesman and Nation* (Mar. 18):

> Through Munich, Prague, and yet beyond
> Appeasement's path must be pursued;
> Democracy need not despond
> While Britain's word is still as good
> As Hitler's bond.

As the demand for vigorous action surged through Britain,

the Government protested Germany's action in Czechoslovakia. On the afternoon of March 15 Halifax spoke to Dirksen with cutting candor, and two days later instructed Henderson to make it plain to Germany that Britain regarded the events in Czechoslovakia as a "complete repudiation" of the Munich Agreement and "devoid of any basis of legality."[15] But Germany registered no deep alarm in the face of the British protest (which was accompanied by a simultaneous representation from France). Weizsäcker, in fact, at first refused to accept the notes, then eventually regarded them as if they had been sent by mail.[16] Next day an official German communiqué stated that the Reich was not in a position to accept protests for such action was devoid of political, legal, or moral foundation. By that time Henderson was on his way back to London, having been recalled—apparently on Halifax's initiative—"to report."[17]

The Birmingham speech seemed to indicate that Britain was finished with appeasement, but that alone was definite. There was no clear decision as to the degree of support to be offered other potential victims of aggression, cooperation to be sought with other great powers, or sacrifice to be demanded from the British people. The problem of delineating the policy which was to replace appeasement was brought to a head by the immediate German threat to Rumania. Even before Chamberlain had delivered his address at Birmingham, the Rumanian Minister in London reported that Germany had demanded of Rumania a monopoly of exports (chiefly oil and wheat) and the acceptance of industrial restriction in return for a German guarantee of Rumania's frontiers. The Rumanian Government regarded these demands "as in the nature of an ultimatum." Consequently, Halifax sought to obtain, through the British representatives in Paris, Moscow, Warsaw, Angora, Athens, and Belgrade, an im-

15. Halifax to Henderson, F.O., Mar. 15, 1939; Halifax to Henderson, F.O., Mar. 17, 1939. *B. D.,* IV, 270–72, 291; Birkenhead, *Halifax,* p. 434.

16. Weizsäcker, *Memoirs,* pp. 176–77; Bonnet, *Défense de la Paix,* II, 153. Weizsäcker claims that he was acting on orders from higher up.

17. Official German Communiqué, Mar. 18, 1939. *German White Book,* p. 282; *B. D.,* IV, 291 n. Henderson's recall seems to have been pressed upon a hesitant Chamberlain by Halifax, whose first thought was to withdraw the British Ambassador from Berlin altogether. See Wheeler-Bennett, *Munich,* pp. 360–61; Campbell-Johnson, *Viscount Halifax,* p. 514.

mediate "expression of opinion" from the Foreign Ministers in those capitals.[18]

The replies which Halifax received during the next several days covered the whole gamut of evasion. Poland questioned the report of a German ultimatum and wished to consult with Bucharest. Greece, Turkey, and Yugoslavia were reluctant to express opinions, desiring to wait and see what Britain would do. The Rumanians themselves were interested only in knowing whether they could count on British and French support in the event of German aggression.[19] In fact, the Rumanian Minister for Foreign Affairs denied that there was any threat to Rumania's political or economic independence and suggested that the Rumanian Minister in London had misrepresented the situation "in an excess of zeal." So Halifax ordered the suspension of further questioning of the smaller governments.[20]

There remained the question of the French and Russian attitudes. The French reply, not forthcoming until March 20, indicated a readiness to assist Rumania if she became the object of German aggression, but recommended that Britain and France decide on a common attitude.[21] Of more immediate importance was the Soviet response. It held that no good purpose would be

18. Halifax to Phipps, F.O., Mar. 17, 1939; Halifax to Seeds, F.O., Mar. 17, 1939; Halifax to Kennard, Knatchbull-Hugessen, Waterlow, Campbell, F.O., Mar. 17, 1939. *B. D.*, IV, 360, 361.

19. Kennard to Halifax, Warsaw, Mar. 18, 1939; Waterlow to Halifax, Athens, Mar. 19, 1939; Knatchbull-Hugessen to Halifax, Angora, Mar. 18, 1939; Campbell to Halifax, Belgrade, Mar. 19, 1939; Phipps to Halifax, Paris, Mar. 18, 1939. *Ibid.*, IV, 370–71, 387, 374–75, 384–85.

20. Hoare to Halifax, Bucharest, Mar. 18, 1939; Halifax to Knatchbull-Hugessen, Waterlow, Campbell, and Kennard, F.O., Mar. 19, 1939. *Ibid.*, IV, 369–70, 386. Germany's reaction to the claim that an ultimatum had been sent to Rumania was to inquire of the small powers of eastern Europe whether they felt themselves threatened by the Reich, a question to which negative answers were a foregone conclusion. The Rumanian-German question was settled on March 23 by the conclusion of a commercial treaty between the two governments. Sir Hughe Knatchbull-Hugessen, the British Ambassador in Angora, inclines to the view that, in spite of the Rumanian denials, the German ultimatum was, in fact, presented in Bucharest. As support for that view, he suggests "the rapidity with which Rumania handed herself over to German exploitation." *Diplomat: In Peace and War* (London, 1949), p. 155.

21. Campbell to Halifax, Paris, Mar. 20, 1939. *B. D.*, IV, 396–97.

served by various governments inquiring of each other what action others would take before making up their own minds. Rather, repeating the maneuver of the previous year after the Austrian *Anschluss,* Moscow proposed that delegates of the British, Soviet, French, Polish, Rumanian, and Turkish Governments meet at once, possibly in Bucharest, to discuss the possibilities of common action.[22]

Halifax is said to have looked with favor upon a plan outlined by King Carol of Rumania whereby he believed he could rally Poland, Bulgaria, and the Balkan Entente in resistance to German aggression if Britain, France, and Russia would guarantee their support. The Soviet proposal thus seemed to indicate to Halifax Russia's willingness to participate in drawing a line against further Nazi aggression from Poland to Rumania, Greece, and Turkey. But there was another school of thought in the British Cabinet. Led by Sir John Simon, the "moderates" apparently felt it useless to try to stop Hitler short of the Near East. Moreover, these former proponents of appeasement still advocated limited liabilities on the Continent, and it is likely that they felt any conference such as Russia proposed might involve Britain in those "unspecified commitments operating under circumstances which cannot be foreseen" which Chamberlain had deprecated at Birmingham.[23] At any rate, the Soviets were informed on the afternoon of March 19 that while the idea of a conference should not be ruled out, the British Government hoped to make "further progress . . . before attempting to decide whether or not the conference procedure would be appropriate at a later stage." As reasons for Britain's decision, it was asserted that in present circumstances the Government could hardly send a responsible minister to take part in a conference, that it was dangerous to hold such a conference without the certainty of success, and that Britain was considering a proposal, not altogether dissimilar to

22. Seeds to Halifax, Moscow, Mar. 19, 1939. *Ibid.,* IV, 385. Maisky, the Russian Ambassador in London, told Hugh Dalton a short time later that this proposal was designed to test British and French intentions, of which the Russians were suspicious. Dalton, *The Fateful Years,* p. 233. If so, the Russians were hardly reassured by Britain's response.

23. See Wheeler-Bennett, *Munich,* pp. 364, 367–68; Campbell-Johnson, *Viscount Halifax,* pp. 515–17; Birkenhead, *Halifax,* p. 435.

Russia's, which might be expected to yield results more rapidly.[24]

Feiling holds that Chamberlain's hesitation in negotiating with Russia was derived not from ideological prejudices, but from "facts presented to him by military and intelligence reports, and by other States."[25] Other factors undoubtedly entered the decision. The situation was confused and the final replies of several small governments were being awaited. The denial of the German ultimatum to Rumania seemed to make the situation less pressing, and in consideration of the aversion of nations like Poland and Rumania to dealings with Russia, London may well have felt that the Soviet proposal was too pretentious and dangerous. The influence of the "limited liability" group in the Cabinet was still strong. Finally, despite Feiling's contention, it is quite likely that Chamberlain and a number of his colleagues, long distrustful of Russia both ideologically and militarily,[26] were by no means ready to submit to Russian leadership in a coalition against aggression.

Britain's counter-proposal was apparently conceived in Chamberlain's own mind. He wrote his sister on March 19:

> As soon as I had time to think I saw that it was impossible to deal with Hitler after he had thrown all his assurances to the winds. . . . I have worked out a plan which a few ministers have accepted today, and which I shall put to the Cabinet tomorrow. It is pretty bold and startling, but I feel that something of the kind is needed, and though I can't predict the reactions in Berlin, I have an idea that it won't bring us to an acute crisis, at any rate at once. . . . As

24. Halifax to Seeds, F.O., Mar. 19, 1939. *B. D.,* IV, 392–93.
25. Feiling, *Life of Neville Chamberlain,* p. 403.
26. Chamberlain wrote his sister on March 26, 1939: "I must confess to the most profound distrust of Russia. I have no belief whatever in her ability to maintain an effective offensive, even if she wanted to. And I distrust her motives, which seem to me to have little connection with our ideas of liberty, and to be concerned only with getting every one else by the ears." *Ibid.,* p. 403. The low British estimate of Russia's military effectiveness stemmed in large part from the belief that the great purge of the Russian Army had left it in a gravely weakened condition. Templewood declares that "after the great purge" Stalin was in no position to join in coercive action against Hitler even if he wished to do so. *Nine Troubled Years,* p. 302.

always, I want to gain time, for I never accept the view that war is inevitable.[27]

This "bold and startling" plan became known on March 20, when the British Government proposed that France, Russia, and Poland join with Britain in signing and publishing a formal declaration to the effect that, in the event of a threat to the independence of any European state, the four signatory powers would consult at once on measures to be taken in order to organize common resistance.[28]

Late on the evening of March 22, the French gave their "entire assent" to the British proposal. That same evening the British Ambassador in Moscow learned from Litvinov that Russia was willing to give her signature as soon as both France and Poland had done so.[29] It remained for the Poles to give the project a fatal blow. Joseph Beck, the Polish Foreign Minister, replied that his Government might be willing to join in a declaration with Britain and France, but the association with Russia was dangerous; it might provoke Hitler and lead to war.[30] As an alternative to the British proposal, Beck favored a secret bilateral agreement along the lines of the suggested declaration, which would not prejudice any final decision regarding the projected four-power declaration.[31] His object in suggesting such an arrangement was obvious: the association of Poland with the Soviet Union in a public declaration could be avoided. Chamberlain's four-power declaration was doomed to failure.

Chamberlain and Halifax may have anticipated the Polish re-

27. Feiling, *Life of Neville Chamberlain,* p. 401.
28. Halifax to Phipps, Seeds, and Kennard, F.O., Mar. 20, 1939. *B. D.,* IV, 400–01.
29. Phipps to Halifax, Paris, Mar. 22, 1939; Seeds to Halifax, Moscow, Mar. 22, 1939. *Ibid.,* IV, 467.
30. Kennard to Halifax, Warsaw, Mar. 22, 1939. *Ibid.,* IV, 453–54.
31. Kennard to Halifax, Warsaw, Mar. 22, 1939; Halifax to Kennard, F.O., Mar. 24, 1939. *Ibid.,* IV, 463–64, 500–03. Herein lay the key to Beck's foreign policy. While he desired an entente with Britain, he refused to be caught in any system of general security. Against the Reich he would put a British alliance, but without provoking Hitler by an alliance with Russia, in whom he had no confidence anyway. Thus perhaps he could be both resistant and flexible at the same time. See Colonel Jozef Beck, *Final Report* (New York, 1957), pp. 177–78; Grigore Gafencu, *Last Days of Europe: A Diplomatic Journey in 1939* (New Haven, 1948), pp. 48–49.

sponse. At any rate, in a conversation with Bonnet in London on March 22, they considered what the next Anglo-French step would be if the Polish reply were evasive or negative. On the assumption that Rumania would be the next potential victim of German aggression, the conversation tended toward the following conclusions: Rumania must resist and Poland must support her. In order to persuade Poland to commit herself to Rumania, Britain and France would have to give Poland a private undertaking that they would join in resistance also. Thereafter, it might be suggested to both Poland and Rumania that they should not raise any objection to an Anglo-French attempt to secure Soviet participation.[32] The implication of this discussion was clear. It seemed best, under the circumstances, to make sure of Poland, apparently regarded by the Cabinet as a more formidable military power than Russia,[33] and to enlist her aid for Rumania, so that a line might be established in eastern Europe beyond which Hitler could not advance except at the risk of war. An attempt to secure Russian aid could be made later.

While the British Government wrestled with the problem of organizing resistance to further German aggression, Hitler was again in action. Under the threat of immediate occupation by German troops, Memel was ceded by Lithuania to the Reich on March 22. Next day Germany assumed responsibility for "the protection of the political independence of the State of Slovakia." Poland, recognizing definite danger signals, sent urgent instructions to the Polish Ambassador in London to request the signing of the bilateral agreement Beck had proposed and on March 25 ordered a partial mobilization. Simultaneously a flood of rumors and reports concerning the Polish mobilization and German troop concentrations on the Pomeranian border reached London. It became known that Germany had re-submitted to Warsaw "generous and modest" proposals for a settlement of the Danzig and Corridor

32. Record of an Anglo-French Conversation held in the Prime Minister's Room at the House of Commons, on March 22, 1939. *B. D.,* IV, 457–63; Bonnet, *Défense de la Paix,* II, 161–64.

33. It has since been verified that British military opinion in 1939 considered Poland a more valuable ally than Russia. See Halifax, *Fullness of Days,* p. 210; Templewood, *Nine Troubled Years,* pp. 342–45; Strang, *Home and Abroad,* p. 167; Amery, *My Political Life,* III, 309.

problems and that those proposals had been rejected by the Polish Government.[34] As Chamberlain admitted in the House of Commons much later, Britain "did not know that Poland might not be invaded within a term which could be measured by hours and not by days."[35]

Nor was the pressure of events in central Europe the only thing which bore down heavily upon the British Government during this period. Agitation in the press for more vigorous action to meet the emergency drew renewed vitality daily from the failure of the new trend in British policy to produce concrete results. A veritable campaign for an anti-aggression front in Europe—impossible for the Government to ignore—resulted. The *Daily Mail* (Mar. 23) exemplified the prevailing anxiety. Long a most ardent advocate of isolation, it had completely changed its tune and was now desperate for action—any action. "What are they doing?" it demanded to know of the Government. Britain must have "backbone"; she must pursue any new policy with vigor. Less frantic, but just as anxious, the *Daily Telegraph* (Mar. 20) caught the prevailing mood in asserting:

> Clearly what the situation demands is a policy which is at once closely concerted between the Powers, which formulates exactly the course to be followed in given circumstances, and which is capable of instant application. In default of such a policy Europe will crumble piecemeal before the spreading Nazi attack.

Germany's own policy and methods were making her encirclement "a natural and even an inevitable process," *The Times* (Mar. 20) hastened to admit, while the Cardiff *Western Mail* (Mar. 24) proclaimed "no safe alternative to an alliance of all Powers, regardless of their ideologies, who are resolved to make a stand against the Nazi domination of Europe." The aggressors must be confronted, the latter journal reiterated (Mar. 29), "with a file on which they will break their teeth. All the forces of civilisation

34. See Memorandum by the Foreign Minister, Berlin, Mar. 21, 26, 1939; Memorandum by an Official of the Foreign Minister's Secretariat, Berlin, Mar. 27, 1939. *G. D.*, VI, 72, 121, 136.

35. *Parl. Debs., HC,* October 3, 1939, vol. 351, 1876–77.

must be rallied in a solid phalanx against the greatest menace that ever threatened it with destruction." In short, a new departure not only had support in Conservative newspapers; it was absolutely demanded.

The voice of Labor, the *Daily Herald,* pressed daily for the organization of an effective front against aggression. There was only one policy, it declared (Mar. 20): immediate collaboration embracing a military alliance with France and Russia and the closest possible cooperation with the United States. It protested delay (Mar. 24) and insisted that a decision be taken immediately, whether it was for a three-power declaration followed by a conference with Poland, or a four-power conference. On March 28 it asked: "Is the Government prepared to face up to the implications of German aggression and act accordingly, or is it not? It is time we had a definite answer." Meanwhile, the pro-Labor *Reynolds News* (Mar. 19) had joined in warning that nothing less than complete, open collaboration among Britain, France, Russia, and America would now suffice to halt aggression's march. And by March 26, that newspaper was convinced, as was the *New Statesman and Nation* (Mar. 25), that Chamberlain was not the man for the job; the fate of the British people must no longer be left to a Prime Minister whose lack of courage and principle was a menace to the nation.

A variation on the latter theme found expression in Liberal journals. "Bring back Mr. Eden!" demanded the Bradford *Yorkshire Observer* (Mar. 23); events were moving with great rapidity, and the country and the world anxiously awaited a statement. The *Liverpool Daily Post* warned (March 20) against any hesitation or trepidation in the new circumstances, seeking the achievement at once of a united front of the free peoples of the world; then (Mar. 30) urged the broadening of the Government as a sign of Britain's resolution to resist aggression. Likewise, the *Manchester Guardian* first suggested (Mar. 24) that the other countries of Europe would feel less despair if Britain and France showed "a firmer resolve to maintain the liberties of Europe than they have done to the present." On March 29 it evidenced both anxiety and disgust: "That the Government of this country must energetically build a peace front is not to be denied. But whether it can be done by this Government and under the present leadership is another question altogether."

Like the Labor *Daily Herald,* the Liberal *News Chronicle* daily waged a campaign for the peace front. It urged (Mar. 21) that Britain assume greater leadership; it was her duty as "the fountainhead of European democracy." A declaration of consultation was certainly not sufficient, it argued (Mar. 23); "what Poland needs is an assurance that if she is attacked, Britain and France will attack in the West." During the following days, a categorical assurance of aid for Poland and Rumania in the event of aggression was urged with increasing vehemence—a proposal especially interesting in the light of what eventually occurred.

Any doubt as to the breadth of the demand for vigorous action in a new direction—and it is difficult to see how there could have been any—was surely eliminated by the positions taken in independent journals. The *Economist* early (Mar. 18) complained that the Government was not willing to do to save the peace what it would certainly do to win a war, namely, seek allies and make alliances. For the *Glasgow Herald* (Mar. 20), all chances of checking aggression and of banishing the dread of war depended wholly upon the willingness of Britain and France to act "with drastic decision and rapidity." After Memel, it openly stated (Mar. 23) that Britain might have to give "very specific pledges of assistance" against German aggression. The *Financial News* (Mar. 24) impatiently asked: "Is the elucidation of our policy towards the aggressor always to await the next succeeding act of aggression?" "Hitler acts, we speak," lamented *Time and Tide* (Mar. 25). "Action, not drift!" cried the *Spectator* (Mar. 31). The *Observer* (Mar. 26), pursuing further its change of heart indicated earlier, acidly remarked with reference to the Government's proposal for a four-power declaration of consultation: "Consultation never stopped anything. Action is the only thing that will stop Germany."

If anyone in the Government had harbored the notion that the outcry for action which had dominated the press immediately after March 15 was a temporary phenomenon which would quickly recede, he was grossly mistaken. Rather, it persisted in proportion to the Government's failure to come up with anything definite. The psychological impact of this failure upon Ministers, who seem themselves to have been badly shaken and converted to the view that "something" must be done, certainly contributes substantially to an explanation of the startling action which was indeed taken a few days later.

Meanwhile, Halifax, in a speech to the House of Lords on March 20, had made it evident that his old inhibitions were gone. Under his searching moral scrutiny the whole sordid fabrication of Czech oppression was laid bare. "If I could sum up my own thought in these various explanations," he declared, "I could wish that instead of the communications and explanations which have been issued and which carry scant conviction, German superior force had been frankly acknowledged as the supreme arbiter that in fact it was." The position in Europe was entirely changed with the arbitrary suppression of an independent sovereign state by force. The free peoples must re-think their attitude toward Germany. For Halifax, the process obviously involved a new readiness to acknowledge the urgency of collective security.[36] He was apparently ready to take up without quibble or mental reservation the supreme challenge of Nazism to European peace and security.

In this, the first foreign policy debate in the Lords since before March 15, the expiring "Munich policy" received still more body-blows, and the strengthening of ties binding the peaceful nations was pushed with authority. The Archbishop of Canterbury caught the prevailing sentiment of the Lords in one concise statement:

> While we must admit that it is hateful indeed at the present time, after the lessons of twenty years ago of the folly and futility of war, that we should contemplate massing more force which may ultimately be used for an indescribably odious purpose, yet we are driven to this because we are convinced that there are some things that are more sacred even than peace, and that these things must be defended.[37]

The tremendous change which had occurred in the sentiment of the British people is evident in one of the fortnightly letters which Churchill composed for his own records. On March 24 he wrote:

36. *Parl. Debs., HL,* March 20, 1939, vol. 112, 311–19.
37. *Ibid.,* March 20, 1939, vol. 112, 321.

> A veritable revolution in feeling and opinion has occurred in Britain. . . . This mass conversion of those who had hitherto been hopeful took place within a single week, but not within a single day. It was not an explosion, but the kindling of a fire which rose steadily, hour by hour, to an intense furnace heat of inward conviction.[38]

The change was even more graphically expressed by Beverly Baxter, a Conservative M.P. who had constantly supported appeasement and who had been so optimistic after Munich. Writing "an open letter to Hitler" in the *Sunday Graphic* (Mar. 26), a staunch Conservative journal, he asserted:

> I doubt if any member of the Embassy staff, no matter how capable, is in a position to explain to your Excellency the reaction of the British public today. It is something entirely different and quite new. No foreigner could possibly sense it. . . . The entire British nation woke up [after Prague] to one realisation. . . . The truth is, your Excellency, we are bored to death with you. Oh, God, how bored we are! . . . May I put it bluntly? There is not a man in these islands who would not rather die in battle than live in a world that accepts your standards.

Georges Bonnet, the French Foreign Minister—who is not remembered for his own resolution—also testifies to the transformation of opinion in Britain. During a three-day visit to London, he was struck by the frequency with which he heard remarks like that of the wife of an important British official (unidentified), who told him "with passion" at Buckingham Palace (March 21): "I have several sons whom I love, but I would prefer to see them die than to accept a Europe under the domination of Hitler." In fact, in his view, the pressure of public opinion was so violent that the British Cabinet would have been swept away if Chamberlain had not publicly stated at Birmingham his will to oppose all future German "enterprises."[39]

This violent change in British opinion toward Germany was

38. Churchill, *Step by Step,* pp. 302–03.
39. Bonnet, *Défense de la Paix,* II, 164.

brought to bear directly upon the Government by the Members of Parliament who had traveled to their constituencies over the weekend of March 17–19 in order to test the feeling there. They returned, as Dirksen viewed it, under the influence of the "rabid attitude" which prevailed in the country and exercised a corresponding influence upon the Government.[40] The Commons did not debate foreign policy during this critical interval (the last two weeks of March, 1939), but during the question periods in the House, Chamberlain was pressed with unrelenting regularity to say what action the Government proposed to take. And there were, of course, other and even more effective ways by which members, especially those of the Prime Minister's own party, could impress their observations and feelings upon the country's leaders.

Chamberlain also felt the pressure of dissatisfaction from within his own Cabinet. Shortly after Prague, Halifax, with unaccustomed boldness, advocated the formation of an entirely new National Government, which would include Churchill and Eden and comprise the leaders of all parties. He apparently was supported in this by Hoare, the Home Secretary, who felt (so his memoirs claim) that Churchill's inclusion in the Government would impress Hitler with Britain's firm resolution to resist further aggression.[41] There is little reason to doubt Halifax's position—indeed, he had taken the same view immediately after Munich. But it is perhaps permissible to wonder, in view of his previous outlook, just how far the Home Secretary was prepared to press the "big changes" to which his memoirs refer. Yet, even a modest move in this direction, coming from one so intimately associated with the Prime Minister and in the trying circumstances of late March, 1939, would constitute a departure sufficiently sharp to command Chamberlain's attention.

The demand for immediate, vigorous action continued to pour forth from a number of public speakers. Greenwood at Wolverhampton, Arthur Henderson at Towley Regis, Attlee, Eden,

40. Dirksen's Survey of his Ambassadorship in London, September, 1939. *Dirksen Papers,* p. 171.

41. Campbell-Johnson, *Viscount Halifax,* p. 511; Templewood, *Nine Troubled Years,* p. 386.

Viscount Cecil, and Vernon Bartlett in London all insisted that the peace-loving nations of Europe must unite immediately in defense against aggression. On March 23 a deputation of the three national committees of the Labor movement visited Chamberlain to urge upon him a peace pact to secure united action by Britain, France, Russia, and others. They came away, so it was reported, convinced that Chamberlain had a deep sense of the shattering of confidence by Germany's destruction of Czechoslovakia and that there were no difficulties in the way of Russia's joining in a declaration against aggression.[42]

The Cabinet met daily at this time of crisis. It must have been painfully obvious that some immediate, definite action was absolutely essential. The Parliament and public were clamoring for a vigorous lead, the reports of German threats to Poland continued to pour into London, the small nations of Europe (as shown in their replies to British inquiries) awaited British initiative in resisting aggression. What could be done? A conference had been ruled out by the British rejection of the Russian proposal; the suggestion of a four-power declaration for consultation had proved futile. There was general agreement in the Cabinet that a line should be laid down and Berlin told that to cross it would mean war; the question of where the line should be drawn remained unsolved.[43] The difficult decision apparently was made on the evening of March 27, hastened by a sudden Nazi press offensive against Warsaw, identical in its violence with those which had preceded the seizure of Prague and Memel, and reports of German troop movements on the Polish frontier.[44] That decision far outstripped the expectations of even the most ardent critics of appeasement.

Late on the evening of March 29 (two days having been con-

42. *The Times,* Mar. 20–29, 1939. See also Dalton, *The Fateful Years,* pp. 230–33.

43. So Kennedy reported to Washington. Kennedy to the Secretary of State, London, Mar. 24, 1939. *U.S. For. Rel., 1939,* I, 99.

44. See Feiling, *Life of Neville Chamberlain,* pp. 403–04; Langer and Gleason, *The Challenge to Isolation,* p. 73; Campbell-Johnson, *Viscount Halifax,* p. 521. As Halifax saw it, if the alternatives were those of remaining inactive or embarking on war, his choice would be war. Birkenhead, *Halifax,* p. 434.

sumed by consultation with the French, who on the afternoon of March 29 agreed to act in conjunction with Britain[45]) the British envoys in Warsaw and Bucharest were instructed to propose that if Poland and Rumania were to fight to defend their independence, Britain and France would aid them, provided Poland helped Rumania if necessary. In return, Poland was to promise to support Britain and France in case of attack by Germany or in case they went to war to resist German aggression anywhere in western Europe or in Yugoslavia. Britain and France, it was added, would maintain friendly contact with Russia to prevent her from lapsing into isolation and to assure her benevolent neutrality and possible support.[46] Poland, having already urgently requested a bilateral agreement with Britain, immediately approved the British proposal.[47] Consequently, on March 31 Chamberlain made in the House of Commons what was described as "one of the most remarkable public declarations in the history of British foreign policy."[48]

The Prime Minister calmly explained that in the Government's opinion there should be no international question incapable of solution by peaceful means, and thus no justification existed for the substitution of force or the threat of force for the method of negotiation. But, he continued:

> . . . . In the event of any action which clearly threatened Polish independence, and which the Polish Government accordingly considered it vital to resist with their national forces, His Majesty's Government would feel themselves

45. Phipps to Halifax, Paris, Mar. 29, 1939. *B. D.*, IV, 540.

46. Halifax to Kennard and Hoare, F.O., Mar. 29, 1939; Halifax to Kennard and Hoare, F.O., Mar. 27, 1939. *Ibid.*, IV, 541, 515–17.

47. Kennard to Halifax, Warsaw, Mar. 30, 1939. *Ibid.*, IV, 548.

48. Wheeler-Bennett, *Munich*, p. 374. Rumania's reply, received in London on March 31, was guarded. The Minister for Foreign Affairs felt no great confidence in Poland and would have to consult the Balkan allies before contemplating a pact of mutual assistance with Poland. Furthermore, the essential thing had already been accomplished in that Britain's determination to call a halt to German aggression had now been clearly established. He expressed gratitude for Britain's communication and promised to consult the Cabinet further. Hoare to Halifax, Bucharest, Mar. 31, 1939. *B. D.*, IV, 555. Despite Rumania's reply, the British went ahead with the part of the proposal concerning Poland.

> bound at once to lend the Polish Government all support in their power. They have given the Polish Government an assurance to this effect.[49]

And so had the French.

Considering Chamberlain's record, it must have been difficult for the members of the House of Commons to believe that he had beaten his unfurled umbrella into a flashing sword, but that was in fact what the Prime Minister had done. When questioned on the meaning of his statement, he answered clearly and unequivocally. Perhaps the stunned reaction of the Commons is best indicated by the unchallenged remark of Lord Cranborne, long-time opponent of appeasement, that Chamberlain's statement "has been received with great satisfaction in all parts of the House."[50]

Chamberlain's announcement of the guarantee to Poland completely reversed his Birmingham stand against "new unspecified commitments operating under conditions which cannot be foreseen," and moved dangerously close to placing in the hands of the Polish Government the ultimate decision whether Britain should be involved in war. Even at the time it was recognized as an important turning point in European international relations. Chamberlain told the Commons on April 3 that it would "have a chapter to itself when the history books come to be written."[51] Churchill later summarized its essence in another way:

> History . . . can be scoured and ransacked to find a parallel to this sudden and complete reversal of five or six years' policy of easy-going, placatory appeasement, and its transformation overnight into a readiness to accept an obviously imminent war on far worse conditions and on the greatest scale.[52]

49. *Parl. Debs., HC,* March 31, 1939, vol. 345, 2415.

50. *Ibid.,* March 31, 1939, vol. 345, 2417. Churchill confirms that the guarantee was supported by "the leaders of all parties and groups" in the Commons. *The Gathering Storm,* p. 346.

51. *Ibid.,* April 3, 1939, vol. 345, 2482.

52. Churchill, *The Gathering Storm,* p. 347. Templewood maintains that the decision whether or not Britain should take part in a war was retained in British hands and defends that position by asserting: "The two conditions under which we undertook to intervene were, firstly, a clear threat to Polish independence that we should ourselves define, and secondly,

To assign a single explanation to Chamberlain's extraordinary turn would be folly. The Prime Minister apparently sensed the full implications of the pledge to Poland and was somewhat reluctant to give it.[53] But he felt compelled to act by the popular protest against any continuance of appeasement and the urgent public demand for an effective peace front. (Sir William Strang records that the guarantee "was designed, no doubt, among other things, to meet what was recognized to be an imperative demand by public opinion that Poland should not be allowed to go the same way as Czechoslovakia.[54]) This circumstance, coupled with the constant pressure in Parliament, with the fact that Halifax and most of the Cabinet had come to favor a positive policy designed to deter Hitler from further aggression, with Chamberlain's personal indignation at having been double-crossed by Hitler, and with an increasing realization of the menace of Nazi brutality to European freedom and security—all this could hardly have failed to move any Prime Minister, especially one of whom it had been said that if his policy did not change, he himself must be changed.

The circumstances surrounding the actual drafting of Chamberlain's declaration remain vague, but it was (in the words of Strang) "an improvisation" which "seems to have sprung fully grown from the Ministerial mind," with no canvassing of military or political advisers.[55] Apparently drafted on the afternoon of March 30 by Chamberlain, Halifax, and Cadogan,[56] it was simply an attempt to make it "unmistakably clear" to Hitler "that the particular acts of aggression which he was believed to have in mind would result in general war" (Halifax's words).[57]

Chamberlain's declaration was received almost joyfully by much of the British press. The *Daily Telegraph* (Apr. 1) was relieved

---

Polish armed resistance to the aggression." *Nine Troubled Years,* p. 349.

53. See Langer and Gleason, *The Challenge to Isolation,* p. 75.

54. Strang, *Home and Abroad,* p. 161.

55. *Ibid.,* p. 161. Amery agrees that the guarantee "had no conceivable military justification." *My Political Life,* III, 310. And Halifax explains that Poland and Rumania had no illusions as to the concrete help Britain could give them. *Fullness of Days,* p. 209.

56. Strang, *Home and Abroad,* p. 161. The drafting must not have been without difficulty, Halifax thereafter remarking that more such tasks would incline him to commit suicide. Dalton, *The Fateful Years,* p. 241.

57. Halifax, *Fullness of Days,* p. 209.

that Britain had at last broken the era of "splendid isolation." She now had a definite commitment she could stand by and know exactly where she stood. The *Financial Times* (Apr. 1) looked upon the guarantee as insurance against a *fait accompli* before consultations with Poland and other countries were completed, and "it was impossible to say how urgently needed such an insurance was." For the Bradford *Yorkshire Observer* (Apr. 1), Chamberlain had erected a stop sign which would have continuing validity. The whole country would approve his statement and would not be slow to accept its implications. "Firm, plain, straightforward and entirely free from provocation, the pledge is precisely what not only Poland but all Europe needed," rejoiced the Cardiff *Western Mail* (Apr. 1). Britain was returning to collective security, which was likely to be all the more effective "since it has a precise and unequivocal objective," exulted the *Liverpool Daily Post* (Apr. 1). The guarantee was a "new and historic" development in British foreign policy said the *Glasgow Herald* (Apr. 1); it constituted "a new realism" in Britain. The *Financial News* (Apr. 1), though skeptical of the exact terminology of the guarantee, welcomed it as "an end to blackmail," and the *Observer* (Apr. 2) greeted it as the only logical alternative inasmuch as conciliation, reason, and understanding were impossible with Germany.

Some journals, while heartily welcoming the guarantee to Poland as the first step in a vitally-needed European anti-aggression front, concentrated immediately upon the need for something more. The *Manchester Guardian* (Apr. 1) believed the Government must lose no time in passing from its "interim policy" to the final scheme. Rumania was in danger, and there was scarcely a state with a Mediterranean coastline that did not have reason to fear either Hitler or Mussolini. It was necessary, too, that Russia be brought into the plan. In complete agreement were the *Daily Herald* (Apr. 1) and the *News Chronicle* (Apr. 1). "The first barricade" was the description of the guarantee in the independent *Sunday Pictorial* (Apr. 2); "the language of an armed anti-Nazi European alliance will alone win respect from the desperate disciples of brute force." The Labor *Leeds Weekly Citizen* (Apr. 7) expressed the same idea in still another way: Chamberlain's momentous declaration "contains rich seed which, if fostered and cultivated, may bear rich fruit." The three-power agreement was only a nucleus which must become a "world-wide federation of peoples" pledged to stand against aggression and work for peace.

A few newspapers were skeptical of the guarantee, though each admitted that there were great gains in the new policy. The *Daily Mail* (Apr. 1) considered the "whole situation and policy" needed greater clarification, and the *Reynolds News* (Apr. 2) branded the manner in which the guarantee had been formulated and announced as "the bad old policy of secret diplomacy." Reluctant to abandon its old policy of no commitments on the Continent, *The Times* (Apr. 1) mischievously suggested that the key phrase in the declaration was not "integrity" but "independence." Carried to its logical conclusion, this implied that Britain was not pledged to stand by Poland in defense of Danzig and the Corridor. The phrase was immediately denounced by Churchill as "sinister" and by others as "similar to that which foreshadowed the ruin of Czechoslovakia." And the Foreign Office issued an inspired disclaimer in no uncertain terms expressing surprise "that attempts should have been made in London to minimize the Prime Minister's statement in the House of Commons. The statement is regarded as of outstanding importance, the meaning of which is perfectly clear and logical." As a result *The Times* was brought into conformity and on April 4 rejected all "watering down."[58]

The House of Commons met to discuss Britain's diplomatic revolution on April 3. It became evident immediately that, while political leaders of all hues welcomed the guarantee to Poland, in the view of both the Opposition and many Government supporters it was not enough. It was only a first step in organizing the forces of Europe against aggression.[59] Opening the debate for Labor, Arthur Greenwood firmly proclaimed: "The chapter entitled 'Appeasement' has been closed and the first words of a

58. *The Times,* Apr. 3, 4, 1939; *History of The Times,* IV (pt. 2), 962. It had been suspected "quite wrongly" in the first place, editor Dawson wrote in his diary. Wrench, *Geoffrey Dawson,* p. 390.

59. Dalton records that some Laborites at first opposed the guarantee to Poland unless Russia were included, but the majority view of support for the declaration as it stood prevailed. *The Fateful Years,* pp. 242–43.

new chapter, which I entitle 'Mutual Aid,' have been recorded." The guarantee to Poland must be the nucleus of a "world-wide federation of peoples determined to end aggression." Whoever was threatened was Britain's neighbor. All obligations among this group must be clearly defined, but it must be known to the world that an attack upon one was an attack upon all. The wider scheme must be pushed forward without delay. If the Government halted, it would betray the will of the people; if it succeeded, Chamberlain would "wear the laurels of victory on his brow."

Chamberlain's response indicated how complete his change of position and opinion apparently was. He felt that the guarantee

> does really constitute a new point—I would say a new epoch —in the course of our foreign policy. . . . The assurances of the German Government . . . have now been thrown to the winds. . . . That is the new fact which has completely destroyed confidence and which has forced the British Government to make this new departure. . . . It is no exaggeration to say that public opinion throughout the whole world has been profoundly shocked and alarmed. This country has been united from end to end by the conviction that we must now make our position clear and unmistakable whatever may be the result. . . . The right honourable Gentleman [Greenwood] rightfully said that the matter could not end where it stands today. If that policy [to dominate the world by force] were the policy of the German Government, it is quite clear that Poland would not be the only country which would be endangered, and the policy which has led us to give this assurance to Poland, of course, could not be satisfied or carried out if we were to confine ourselves to a single case which after all, might not be the case in point.[60]

Recognizing that there were ideological differences between Britain and Russia, Chamberlain nevertheless welcomed "the cooperation of any country, whatever may be its internal system of government . . . in resistance to aggression." It was his hope that Britain's action, "begun but not concluded," would prove to be the turning point towards a more wholesome era.

60. *Parl. Debs., HC,* April 3, 1939, vol. 345, 2481–86.

As if not yet certain of the Prime Minister's conversion, Sinclair emphasized again that peace would depend upon the ability of the Government to convince Hitler that this time it really meant to be firm. Britain should try to rally Rumania, Turkey, other Balkan powers, and the key nation of Russia to the cause of resistance. In his view, the question of collective security was now clearly a military one, and he urged that Britain enter immediately into staff conversations with France, Poland, and other countries so that every nation in Europe would know that Britain was ready for action with all her forces should the need arise. With the Prime Minister momentarily set aside as the object of attack, Sinclair denounced Sir John Simon as "the evil genius of British foreign policy" and urged that he and Hoare be replaced by men like Eden and Churchill, who had consistently advocated collective security.

After several years of opposition and criticism, Churchill was now able to declare himself "in complete agreement with the Prime Minister." But he warned that all guarantees were useless unless supported by combinations of strongly-armed states fully prepared, in will and in fact, to make war in defense of the common purpose. To the view that the new policy must be pressed forward Churchill gave strong support:

> Having begun this new policy there can be no turning back. There is no halting-place. . . . To stop here with a guarantee to Poland would be to halt in a No-Man's Land under the fire of both trench lines and without the shelter of either. . . . We must go forward now until a conclusion is reached. Having begun to create a Grand Alliance against aggression, we cannot afford to fail. We shall be marked down and isolated if we fail. It has become a matter of life and death. The policy now proclaimed must be carried to success—to lasting success—if war is to be averted, and if British safety is to be secured.[61]

Lloyd George joined those who congratulated the Government on the initiation of the new policy. Then he, too, turned quickly to the need for strengthening Britain militarily and seeking the

61. *Ibid.,* April 3, 1939, vol. 345, 2500–01.

adhesion of Russia to the new policy. With Russia, the anti-aggression front would have overwhelming forces which Germany could not stand up against; without her, Britain had undertaken a frightful gamble. Eden seconded Lloyd George's emphasis on rearmament and observed that the new policy had at last united the nation in support of the Government in foreign affairs. Ensuing speakers reiterated the need for greater military might and for mobilizing the peaceful powers of Europe (Russian in particular) for the common defense of all. Hugh Dalton put it quite succinctly: "The Government must go much further and faster. . . . All guarantees of mutual aid should be reciprocal; and other states should be brought into the arrangement." In closing the debate, Sir John Simon agreed that the guarantee to Poland presaged commitments in other quarters. The Government was well aware that what was now required was more than an interim declaration, and would throw its whole strength into the essential work of making the country stronger and more united. As for this debate in the Commons, he concluded: "We may mark this day as a date in our history when there has been accepted and approved in every part of the House this immensely significant statement."[62]

After several days of exultation over the guarantee to Poland, the press, perhaps taking a lead from the debate in the Commons, focused attention increasingly upon the need for extending the anti-aggression front to include all countries willing to cooperate. The Cardiff *Western Mail* (Apr. 4) rejoiced that the world was fast learning that the much abused League of Nations "still enshrines the only effective principle and method of dealing with a wanton aggressor." It must therefore be Britain's aim to enlarge, as soon as possible, the group of powers who would share the risks and pool their resources for the purpose of common defense. "So what if Germany is complaining of encirclement," wrote the *Glasgow Herald* (Apr. 3); that is what it was—forced encirclement. The new "League of Security" should include all countries that had reason to fear undue political or economic pressure from the Reich. The *Financial News* (Apr. 4) hoped that negotiations with the eastern European countries would be pressed forward

62. *Ibid.*, April 3, 1939, vol. 345, 2475–588.

with the greatest possible speed. *The Times* (Apr. 3) thought the agreement with Poland should be extended by the inclusion of "any other countries which, feeling their position similarly threatened, may wish to enter into similar commitments." Joining in this view were the *Liverpool Daily Post* (Apr. 5) and the Bradford *Yorkshire Observer* (Apr. 4).

The *Manchester Guardian,* the *Daily Herald,* and the *News Chronicle* repeatedly renewed the call they had made on April 1 for a rapid extension of the anti-aggression front, the *Daily Herald* (Apr. 3) holding that a really effective scheme of defense would include reciprocal defensive pacts among Britain, France, Poland, Rumania, Yugoslavia, Greece, Turkey, and above all, Russia. In following up the initiative already assumed, the "logical first step" would be to give Rumania a guarantee identical to that given Poland, the *News Chronicle* (Apr. 4) said. It was the opinion of these journals, as well as the *Liverpool Daily Post* (Apr. 4) and the *Glasgow Herald* (Apr. 4), that cooperation with Russia was absolutely essential if the peace front were to rest upon solid ground.

In sum, while sections of the Conservative press—perhaps suffering from shock accompanying the realization of just how far Chamberlain had departed from the idea of appeasement—appeared to await a lead from the Prime Minister, the Labor, Liberal, and independent organs were practically unanimous in their urgent demand for further action, and quickly. And there was considerable emphasis on the need to seek the aid of Russia, ideological differences and traditional suspicion of Russia's aims and motives notwithstanding.

The British obligation to Poland was at first a purely unilateral one, undertaken in a moment of crisis, but with the idea that it would be completed by further arrangements to be made with Colonel Beck during his scheduled visit to London early in April. In addition to putting the agreement on a basis of mutual aid, the larger British aim was to link up Poland with Rumania and, if possible, enlist her support in the eventuality of Britain's supporting the Low Countries or Switzerland in resistance to Germany. When Beck conferred with Halifax (April 4–6), he readily agreed to transform the unilateral British guarantee into a reciprocal bilateral agreement. (Pending the completion of the permanent agreement, he assured the British of immediate reciprocity.) But he refused to commit his Government to the support of Britain in defense of the Low Countries and Switzerland, evaded the proposal that Poland conclude a military alliance with Rumania for mutual support in case of attack by Germany or Hungary, and was equally deaf to any suggestion that Russia be associated with the budding peace front.[63] On the latter issue Chamberlain sympathized with Beck's viewpoint. In a private letter he wrote: "I confess I very much agree with him, for I regard Russia as a very unreliable friend . . . with an enormous irritative power on others."[64] The events of March 15 had moved the Prime Minister, but apparently not yet to the point of perceiving a real Nazi threat to Britain which only Russia could counteract. He still insisted on considering the question of Russian association with the peace front as a matter largely academic.

Hardly had the Polish Foreign Minister left London when Mussolini, imitating the technique of Hitler, took his turn at jolting Europe. On April 7 (Good Friday), without a word of warning or shadow of excuse, he invaded Albania and added that crown to those of the Kingdom of Italy and the Empire of Ethiopia already worn somewhat precariously by Victor Emmanuel.[65] In view of recent Italian assurances that they had no wish whatsoever to change the status quo in Albania,[66] the British Government, if it still harbored any belief in Italian good faith, must have been gravely disillusioned. In fact, as Italian troops entered Albania, Ciano assured Perth that Italy intended to respect Albanian independence and integrity and the status quo in the Mediterranean area. Italian action originated in a plea by the "most important chiefs" in Albania that Mussolini end King Zog's misrule, Ciano explained, and in response to that request, Italy had sent troops

63. Visit of the Polish Foreign Minister, April 4–6, 1939; Record of Conversations. *B. D.*, V, 1–9, 9–19, 30–36, 47–49.

64. Feiling, *Life of Neville Chamberlain,* p. 408.

65. Italian plans for the seizure of Albania had been underway since at least the beginning of February. Later, on March 15, having just learned of Hitler's action in Czechoslovakia, Ciano recorded in his diary: "It is necessary to give them [the Italian people] a satisfaction and compensation: Albania." *The Ciano Diaries,* pp. 23, 42–43.

66. Halifax to Perth, F. O., Apr. 6, 1939. *B. D.*, V, 125.

to "restore peace, order, and justice."[67] But Britain demanded the "frankest and fullest" explanation, for those proffered by Ciano had caused "profound misgivings" and would not satisfy—and the specific reference here is worthy of note—British public opinion.[68]

Though the British protest was couched in the usual reserved terms, British indignation was doubtless sharp. Even Chamberlain, who for so long had been confident of his personal influence with the dictators and especially Mussolini, was beginning to learn his lesson. Two weeks before, he had addressed a personal letter to the Duce asking his help in re-establishing mutual trust and assuring the continuation of peace[69]; the invasion of Albania was Mussolini's answer. Subsequently, with his freezing gift of understatement, Chamberlain wrote his sister: "I am afraid that such faith as I ever had in the assurances of dictators is rapidly being whittled away." And yet, in the face of the German danger, or in relation to the role he had cast for Italy, he decided to minimize the Italian threat.[70] Was this his "soft" reaction of March 15 all over again? It certainly appeared so, and this raised a serious question whether Chamberlain really had been converted to the stronger position which his speeches and actions of March 17–31 seemed to suggest.

The British press, however, had no such reservations about denouncing Italy's action. A storm of protest arose much like that which had followed the crushing of Czechoslovakia. In one brief statement the *Financial Times* (Apr. 8) presented the feeling which gained widespread expression: "The Albanian incident makes still more evident the urgent need for the construction of a wider system of mutual security." Mussolini's conduct was just as "cynically contemptuous" as Hitler's, the Cardiff *Western Mail* (Apr. 8) observed. There must be a concentration of diplomacy on the task of erecting a barrier against further aggression before it was too late, it insisted (Apr. 11). The *Daily Telegraph* (Apr. 10) urged the Government to decide quickly what action it would take in regard to the situation created by Italy, asserting:

67. Perth to Halifax, Rome, Apr. 7, 1939. *Ibid.,* V, 128.
68. Halifax to Perth, F.O., Apr., 8, 1939. *Ibid.,* V, 135–36.
69. *The Ciano Diaries,* p. 51.
70. Feiling, *Life of Neville Chamberlain,* p. 404.

> Ministers can be under no misapprehension as to the depth to which public opinion in this country has been stirred. Temper may be a bad counsellor; but how is it possible to suppress the indignation provoked by this latest manifestation of 'the policy of mingled truculence and treachery'?

The same newspaper (Apr. 11) proclaimed the implications of the Albanian invasion obvious: if the non-aggression front were to be feasible, it was absolutely essential that the British guarantee to Poland be extended to Greece without qualification or delay; "civilisation stands at the crossroads." The *Glasgow Herald* (Apr. 10) also urged a British guarantee to Greece, and the *Liverpool Daily Post* (Apr. 12) argued for a guarantee "which covers the whole range of possible aggression."

The seizure of Albania by Italy provided a bridgehead to the Balkans, the *Financial News* (Apr. 11) aptly observed. "With so grave a menace, the need for speedy and decisive action by the democracies was never more urgent." The strategic importance of Albania was also recognized by *The Times* (Apr. 10), which considered that Britain, having already made one momentous departure in foreign policy, "has no choice but to pursue it with speed and decision." Duff Cooper, in his weekly column in the *Evening Standard* (Apr. 11), proclaimed that "the time for limited commitments has passed. Poland possesses no special claim on our good offices. Holland, Denmark, Switzerland, Greece, Yugoslavia and Rumania should receive similar assurances."[71]

Just as they had been doing since the announcement of the guarantee to Poland, the *Manchester Guardian*, the *Daily Herald* and the *News Chronicle* pressed daily, and with increasing vigor, for an extension of Britain's anti-aggression commitments. By April 12 the *Manchester Guardian* found it "intolerable" that only a few days after the British agreement with Poland there was no evidence that the Government was sincerely determined to press on with the policy of collective resistance to aggression. "Where do we stand?" it demanded to know. Realistic appreciation of dangers was not enough, the *Daily Herald* (Apr. 10) warned. "There must be speed, and still more speed, in meeting

71. Quoted in Duff Cooper, *The Second World War,* p. 210.

them." As Britain acted with regard to Poland, so must she act in the Balkans. The *News Chronicle* (Apr. 8) decried Britain's "dilatoriness," and like the *Manchester Guardian,* found the Government's slowness in meeting Italy's challenge "incredible." While Whitehall dithered, Hitler and Mussolini acted. Something further must be done speedily, for "last year's maps are now hopelessly out of date. Weeks, days, even hours, are precious."

Propelled by the wrath of the British people over Italy's brutal action, wrath which had vastly increased since Germany crushed Czechoslovakia three weeks earlier, the British Government could hardly fail to see that the hopes to which it had clung so long—hopes of improved relations with Italy—had now turned to ashes and dust. How painful the truth was: Chamberlain's visit to Rome had been only a waste of time; Eden had been right.

Even if that realization did not move the Government to further action, other pressures played upon it. Churchill, who according to his own account had become much closer to Chamberlain since the Birmingham speech, admonished the Prime Minister on April 9: "I am hoping that Parliament will be recalled at the latest on Tuesday [April 11], and I write to say how much I hope the statements which you will be able to make will enable the same united front to be presented as in the case of the Polish Agreement." It seemed to Churchill that hours counted; it was imperative that Britain recover the initiative in European diplomacy. He warned Chamberlain:

> What is now at stake is nothing less than the whole of the Balkan Peninsula. If these states remain exposed to German and Italian pressure while we appear, as they may deem it, incapable of action, they will be forced to make the best terms possible with Berlin and Rome. How forlorn then will our position become. We shall be committed to Poland, and thus involved in the East of Europe, while at the same time cutting off from ourselves all hope of that large alliance which once effected might spell salvation.[72]

72. Churchill, *The Gathering Storm,* pp. 350–51. Churchill recommended the immediate naval occupation of Corfu, with Greek assent. If Britain was there first, an attack upon even a few British ships would confront Mussolini with beginning a war of aggression upon England. That direct issue

Reports reaching London from British envoys in the Balkans certainly did not reassure the Government. Greece expected an Italian attack upon Corfu and hoped for an immediate indication of Britain's intentions. Turkey openly expressed disappointment at the failure of the British "to give a more definite lead."[73] Nor was Daladier reassuring; he felt there was good reason to believe that the Albanian coup was merely the prelude to a big Italo-German offensive "from the North Sea to Egypt."[74]

Though the Italians were generous with assurances that they contemplated no action against Greece, the British, and Halifax in particular, no longer put much stock in Italian assurances. Halifax thought the "right answer" might be a tightening of mutual obligations of support between Britain and France on the one hand and Greece and Turkey on the other,[75] and the Government eventually decided—precisely how and at what moment is uncertain, but clearly under strong public pressure and prodding—to extend to Greece a guarantee similar to that given Poland. The British hoped to secure Turkey's concurrence in the pledge to Greece, but were ready to proceed without it if France was willing to cooperate.[76]

There followed a brief period of diplomatic "pork-barrelling." The French were still convinced that Hitler would move next against Rumania, if only because the Rumanian oil supply was indispensable to the Nazi military machine; the French also contemplated some public declaration about assistance to Rumania.[77] The British, however, were reluctant to give a guarantee to Rumania at that moment. She was not in immediate danger, they argued, and an immediate assurance to Rumania would destroy the lever Britain possessed for inducing Poland and Turkey to give similar guarantees. Daladier was entirely unconvinced, believing that silence with regard to Rumania would be interpreted

---

would give the best chance to all the forces in Italy which were opposed to a major war with England.

73. Waterlow to Halifax, Athens, Apr. 9, 1939; Knatchbull-Hugessen to Halifax, Angora, Apr. 10, 1939. *B. D.*, V, 145, 164–65.

74. Phipps to Halifax, Paris, Apr. 9, 1939. *Ibid.*, V, 151–52.

75. Halifax to Phipps, F.O., Apr. 8, 1939. *Ibid.*, V, 136–37.

76. Halifax to Phipps, F.O., Apr. 11, 1939. *Ibid.*, V, 166.

77. Phipps to Halifax, Paris, Apr. 12, 1939. *Ibid.*, V, 178.

as disinterestedness in Germany. He reminded the British that he had readily agreed to join in a guarantee to Greece though he was under no treaty obligations to do so, refuted the British arguments for postponing a guarantee to Rumania, and let it be known that France intended to extend the guarantee regardless of British action.[78]

Daladier apparently convinced the British, for when the guarantee to Greece was announced in the House of Commons on the afternoon of April 13, it was accompanied by an identical pledge to Rumania. The British undoubtedly recognized the acute need for common Anglo-French action, and they were probably influenced by the fact that Rumania, after further consideration of the British offer of March 29, had let it be known in London that she would now welcome an Anglo-French guarantee. In fact, on the morning of April 13, according to the British Minister in Bucharest, the Rumanian Foreign Minister "begged me most earnestly" to support the Rumanian request for mention in the Prime Minister's statement. Then, too, word had been received in London early on April 13 that Turkey preferred not to commit herself at the present.[79] That eliminated one of Britain's objections to guaranteeing Rumania.

Chamberlain's announcement of the guarantees in the House of Commons was worded much like the guarantee to Poland:

> In the event of any action being taken which clearly threatened the independence of Greece or Rumania, and which the Greek or Rumanian Government respectively considered it vital to resist with their national forces, His Majesty's Government would feel themselves bound at once to lend the Greek or Rumanian Government, as the case might be, all the support in their power.[80]

Chamberlain expressed "deep disappointment" at the action of the Italian Government, but he by no means took the view that

78. Phipps to Halifax, Paris, Apr. 13, 1939; Halifax to Phipps, F.O., Apr. 13, 1939. *Ibid.,* V, 105, 113–15.

79. Halifax to Hoare, F.O., Apr. 10, 1939; Hoare to Halifax, Bucharest, Apr. 13, 1939; Knatchbull-Hugessen to Halifax, Angora, Apr. 13, 1939. *Ibid.,* V, 74–77, 105–06, 187.

80. *Parl. Debs., HC,* April 13, 1939, vol. 346, 13–15.

the Anglo-Italian Agreement must be considered at an end. He was "unwilling to believe" that his efforts to remove suspicions, promote good will, and keep the peace "will not even yet bear fruit," however discouraging the outlook might seem at the moment.

In the debate which followed, Attlee chided the Prime Minister for his refusal to denounce the Anglo-Italian Agreement, which Chamberlain had supported on the grounds that there would be a "widespread desire"—on whose part he did not say—to see the fulfillment of the remaining provisions. He insisted that Russia must be brought into the anti-aggression scheme immediately and charged that the Government was not bestirring itself sufficiently in the attempt to develop real collective security. "Individual pacts . . . only plug leaks momentarily. We . . . look for something more than a policy that covers us for a week or a fortnight. We want a policy that is going to build up a collective security for the world . . . for years." Sinclair then took up the argument: there was no use sprinkling guarantees around Europe unless they could be translated into ships, airplanes, and troops. That could be done only with the cooperation of Russia. In his view, the Cabinet must be reconstituted with Churchill and Eden replacing Chamberlain and Simon.

Churchill agreed that the Prime Minister's statement of policy simply did not go far enough. The first major step which must be taken—and taken with "utmost speed and vigor"—was the full inclusion of Russia in the defensive bloc; the second was the promotion of Balkan unity. In addition, Britain must marshal all her power at home if she were to lead Europe "back from the verge of the abyss." In support of Churchill, Eden warned that, having embarked upon the new policy, it would be suicidal to stop halfway.

Eleven speakers who followed reiterated in different ways the points made by Attlee, Sinclair, Churchill, and Eden. It was clearly the prevailing sentiment of the House that collective security must be pushed ahead with dispatch. The method of selecting one country here and one there and offering them guarantees was far too slow and gave Britain insufficient security in return. There must be specific arrangements for cooperation and combined action among the larger nations as well as the smaller ones. Russia was absolutely essential to the success of the new policy, and the United States should be brought in if possible. The remarkable fact about this debate was that half the speakers who most ardently supported collective security, and used those exact words, were Conservatives. Not that the Laborites permitted the Conservatives to steal their thunder. Colonel Wedgwood, Hugh Dalton, and others vigorously presented the Labor case, mingling personal jibes at the Prime Minister with broader statements of policy. (Dalton hoped the Prime Minister was not suffering from too much indigestion, inasmuch as he had announced at Birmingham just one year before, with reference to the Anglo-Italian Agreement, that "if it is the Prime Minister who has been fooled," not "the Socialists and Liberals who have fooled themselves, I will be prepared to eat my hat.") It was now apparent that all parties had essentially the same end in view. The new policy, having been initiated at last, must be pushed forward relentlessly.[81]

Press reaction to the guarantees to Greece and Rumania was much like that of the House of Commons. The *Glasgow Herald* (Apr. 14) trusted that "these undertakings will become the foundation of a new and general organisation for mutual aid and security." The *Daily Herald* (Apr. 14) saw it as absolutely essential that these emergency measures be followed at once by a conference of all the nations concerned, including Russia, for only by such a conference could real collaboration be secured. The opinions of almost all the other journals fell somewhere in between those two views. The guarantees were a welcome step in the right direction, the peace front must be further developed, Russia must be included: these were the points most frequently expressed.

By mid-April, 1939, Britain found that, whereas a month before she had stood pledged solely, in Europe, to the defense of France and Belgium, her obligations now stretched to the Black Sea and the Aegean. The same Government which on March 15 had repudiated the possibility of entering commitments with foreign countries had been pushed to commit Britain to take action

81. *Ibid.,* April 13, 1939, vol. 346, 13–94. The debate in the House of Lords on April 13 followed much the same pattern. *Parl. Debs., HL,* April 13, 1939, vol. 112, 611–64.

in almost every quarter of Europe to an extent that she had never before even contemplated. After the seizure of Czechoslovakia by Germany and Albania by Italy, Parliament and public could no longer tolerate the policy of paying compliments to the dictators, assuring them of British good will, and ignoring steps to protect any of their neighbors. Indeed, no government accepting responsibility for British safety could any longer disregard the significance of German and Italian policy.

Chamberlain had been constant in one thing—the determination to avoid a division of Europe on ideological principles. But if one purpose of British national policy was to promote peace and security, there had to be a division between those nations which openly glorified war and those which regarded resort to war, or to the threat of war, as a calamity. After Hitler had occupied Czechoslovakia, the world was left in no doubt about his attitude on that matter. The result was a violent revulsion of feeling in Britain toward the Nazi regime. The Italian seizure of Albania revealed with shocking clarity—to those who had not already seen—Mussolini's true colors, and, coming as it did on the heels of German brutality in Prague, served to reinforce and solidify the revulsion of the British. Chamberlain and his closest colleagues still hoped—with Chamberlain hope was indeed eternal—that Anglo-German relations would improve and that better times would come. In one sense, the act of guaranteeing Poland can be viewed as the placing of a significant barrier in Hitler's way with the primary purpose of inclining him more readily to the hoped-for agreement. But under the pressure of these events and especially the pressure which generated from Parliament and the public because of them, the British Government was forced, irrespective of its hopes and aspirations, to pursue a new line more likely to retard the spread of totalitarian aggression.

Until March, 1939, the British Government had envisaged the employment of an expeditionary force to defend only France and the Empire. After it had pledged its support to Poland, Rumania, and Greece, it became evident that if these smaller eastern countries were to have a chance of survival in war, a British force on the western front sufficient to immobilize a large section of the German Army was an immediate necessity. Coupled with the increasing danger of war, this fact forced the Government to reconsider the needs of its military forces. Shortly after Prague, a more definite program for an expeditionary force to the Continent was agreed upon: within thirty days after the outbreak of war, two corps of two divisions each and an air component must be in France. What had hitherto been desultory and inconclusive staff talks with the French must begin on a methodical plan. The Territorial Army must be doubled. One important change took place in the air program. The threat to Prague had made the danger of German raids on British cities more formidable, so upon the advice of Air Marshal Dowding, priority in the air program was transferred from bombers to fighter squadrons. Finally, the Naval Staff was instructed to plan for operations in the Mediterranean and Atlantic, as well as in the Pacific.[82] In short, the British began to think more realistically about possible involvement in a European war.

As the international outlook blackened, it became essential for Britain to show her determination to resist further aggression. Though Chamberlain was apparently still reluctant to sanction (in the words of L. S. Amery[83]) "the obvious measures of preparation," the latter half of April witnessed two decisions of great importance. On April 20 Chamberlain announced to the House of Commons the decision to establish a Ministry of Supply, a step which he had constantly opposed during the preceding three years though it had been frequently proposed by the Liberal Party with some support from Labor and dissident Conservatives, and pushed by his own Secretary of State for War, Leslie Hore-Belisha. (Leslie Burgin, Minister of Transport, was duly nominated to fill this post, thus causing, according to Hore-Belisha,

82. Templewood, *Nine Troubled Years,* pp. 335–36. See also Minney, *Private Papers of Hore-Belisha,* pp. 185–214.

83. *My Political Life,* III, 310. Amery explains Chamberlain's reluctance in this way: perhaps he did not realize how irrevocably he had committed Britain to war the moment Hitler struck Poland; perhaps because of his inability to realize the scale of Hitler's preparations, he was content that Britain was doing all that could be expected.

"some dismay and disappointment" inasmuch as Churchill had been considered by many to be the favorite.)[84]

One week later, the Prime Minister announced the Government's intention to introduce a bill for limited and temporary military training for young men of 20 and 21 years of age.[85] Conscription had been pressed on Chamberlain from many quarters. The dissident Conservatives had strongly urged it since Prague. France had long appealed to Britain to take such action as a sign of her earnestness.[86] But much of the credit for forcing the belated awakening belongs to Hore-Belisha, who, backed by the growing strength of Parliamentary feeling, took his political life in his hands by persistently demanding in a number of heated conferences with Chamberlain the adoption of compulsory military service.[87]

In the debates which followed the introduction of the conscription bill, the Labor and Liberal Parties gave an exhibition of blind prejudice comparable to that displayed by the more myopic supporters of appeasement in the post-Munich period. They had long denounced the Government for lack of resolution and fortitude. Now, when it was within their power to demonstrate Britain's unity in resistance to aggression, when it could have been shown that Britain was united in her readiness to make definite sacrifices in the cause of peace and to take practical steps to make good her pledges and protests, the two parties adopted an attitude of doctrinal pacifism and party prejudice.

The Opposition adduced a wealth of reasons for opposing the bill. They argued that conscription would weaken and divide the country at a time when it needed to be strong and united, and

84. *Parl. Debs., HC,* April 20, 1939, vol. 346, 496; Minney, *Private Papers of Hore-Belisha,* pp. 155–60, 199–200.

85. *Parl. Debs., HC,* April 27, 1939, vol. 346, 1343.

86. Bonnet records several instances when he personally urged conscription upon the British. *Défense de la Paix,* II, 110–11, 161–62. General Gamelin did likewise at a dinner attended by many members of all parties in the House of Commons in April. Gamelin, *Servir: Le Prologue Du Drame,* p. 440.

87. See Minney, *Private Papers of Hore-Belisha,* pp. 185–200; Churchill, *The Gathering Storm,* p. 355; Duff Cooper, *Old Men Forget,* p. 255; Amery, *My Political Life,* III, 311–12.

that in the background of military conscription lay the danger of industrial conscription. Furthermore, in Attlee's words, Britain "has a rapidly growing Air Force. It has to provide munitions . . . for its Allies, and it cannot, in addition to that, provide a great Continental Army." When Sinclair, following Attlee in the debate of April 27, claimed that the bill would split the country and create a "deep, dangerous, and unnecessary cleavage in public opinion," he invoked the wrath of Churchill, who reminded the House:

> No one has been a more strenuous advocate of the enlargement of our responsibilities and of the vigorous championship of our rights and interests than my right honourable friend [Sinclair], and it is somewhat discouraging to find that, at the first really awkward fence . . . with which he has been confronted, he has found it necessary to take such a very strong attitude of opposition.[88]

But Greenwood, in concluding the debate for Labor, still regarded a break in the voluntary system "criminal" and predicted public revolt against it.[89]

Churchill later recorded that both Attlee and Sinclair were, at the time, "distressed at the course they felt bound on party lines to take."[90] And Attlee admits in his memoirs: "Looking back, I think our attitude was a mistake."[91] Indeed, it is likely that the Opposition's hostile attitude sprang not so much from vehement objection to the fact of conscription as from deference to a long-standing principle, distrust of Chamberlain's general policy, and irritation at not having been consulted about the impending vote on conscription beforehand. The General Council of the Trades Union Congress, from which violent protest might normally have been expected on this issue, had already come around to the view that, however much they disliked peacetime conscription, there was no other course open to the Government.[92] Yet the Parliamentary Laborites took a course

88. *Parl. Debs., HC,* April 27, 1939, vol. 346, 1370.
89. *Ibid.,* April 27, 1939, vol. 346, 1353–70, 1437–45.
90. *The Gathering Storm,* p. 356.
91. *As It Happened,* p. 146. Dalton agrees. *The Fateful Years,* p. 250.
92. Lord Citrine, *Men and Work,* p. 372.

which not only reduced the effectiveness of their earlier criticism of appeasement but deprived them of a certain force of argument in the months thereafter. They most certainly recognized, but could not bring themselves to accept, the fact that such a position helped to undermine the logic of their earlier declarations on collective action and defense.

In later discussions on the bill, several Laborites gave vent to extreme views. David Kirkwood promised to do all he could to get "not only the engineers on the Clyde but the engineers throughout Britain to down tools against conscription." Neil Maclean proclaimed: "I shall advise mothers not to allow their boys to go, and I shall advise the boys not to be conscripted."[93] This attitude was characteristic of certain elements within various labor unions; it was not, however, widely accepted by union executives. When the final division occurred on May 18, it followed party lines and the Government triumphed, 337 to 130.[94] Britain adopted peacetime conscription for the first time in her history.

Unfortunately, the Government's recognition of the need for the new measures of military preparedness was unaccompanied by irrepressible dispatch in their implementation. The Earl of Woolton, who was assigned considerable responsibility for clothing the British Army (in what he described as an "ill-defined position" between the War Office and the new Ministry of Supply) later wrote: "I found nowhere any sense of urgency and I foresaw war breaking out with our army completely unprepared."[95] And when he conveyed his misgivings to Sir Horace Wilson, he was told simply that he was "up against the machine of the civil service" which had beaten Wilson himself on many occasions—a response probably all too true, but not reassuring in the circumstances.

93. *Parl. Debs., HC,* May 4, 1939, vol. 346, 2190; May 8, 1939, vol. 347, 128.
94. *Ibid.,* May 18, 1939, vol. 347, 1778.
95. Woolton, *Memoirs,* pp. 150–51.

CHAPTER NINE

Three Months of Tension

AFTER BRITAIN HAD EXTENDED guarantees to Poland, Rumania, and Greece, the question remained how she could lend effective assistance to those countries, particularly Poland and Rumania, in the event of German aggression. Immediate support, if they were to have any, had to come from the East, from the association of Soviet Russia and Turkey with the peace bloc. Even before the Turks had declined (April 13) to join in the guarantee to Greece, the British envoy in Angora was instructed to propose a treaty of mutual assistance in the event of an Italian attack upon either. Turkey was receptive to the British initiative and returned to London a full set of proposals for collaboration.[1] Further exchanges between the two governments eventually led to a definite agreement in mid-May.

The gaining of Russian support for the expanding peace front presented the British with a more tedious and complicated problem. Chamberlain had already expressed his profound distrust of Russia, both ideological and military, and his opinions were undoubtedly shared by a number of his Conservative colleagues. Within the Cabinet, Halifax apparently was prepared to go to some length to reach an agreement with the Soviet Union—although willingness must not necessarily be equated with determination here. He was supported by Lord Chatfield, Minister for the Coordination of Defense, who suggested both the importance of Russia as a deterrent to Hitler, even though her military strength might be at a low ebb, and the danger of pushing the

1. Halifax to Knatchbull-Hugessen, F.O., Apr. 12, 1939; Knatchbull-Hugessen to Halifax, Angora, Apr. 16, 1939; Knatchbull-Hugessen to Halifax, Angora, Apr. 17, 1939. *B. D.*, V, 179–80, 220, 225–27.

Soviet into the Axis if no approach were made to her. According to his memoirs, Sir Samuel Hoare, the Home Secretary, also shared Chatfield's view, but it is nowhere apparent that he enunciated it with any vigor.[2]

More important, certainly, was the growing public demand in Britain for the inclusion of Russia in the peace bloc. In the House of Commons, April 3, political leaders of all hues regarded the guarantee to Poland as only a first step in organizing the forces of Europe against aggression. The peril of Britain's new situation and the urgency of enlarging the Anglo-Polish combination to embrace Russia and other powers were poignantly stated by Greenwood, Sinclair, Churchill, Lloyd George, Eden, Morgan Price, and Hugh Dalton.[3] The remarks of Churchill and Lloyd George were particularly impressive, Churchill declaring:

> Russia is a ponderous counterpoise in the scale of world peace. We cannot measure the weight of support which may be forthcoming from Soviet Russia. . . . No one can say that there is not a solid identity of interest between the Western democracies and Russia, and we must do nothing to obstruct the natural play of that identity of interest. . . . The worst folly . . . would be to chill and drive away any natural cooperation which Soviet Russia in her own deep interests feels it necessary to afford.[4]

Lloyd George pointed out the military implications of the new situation:

> You have the Polish Army. . . . Well led, they have always fought valiantly. . . . But . . . no valour, no training can

2. Templewood, *Nine Troubled Years,* p. 352. Some of the material presented here appeared first in the author's article "Grand Alliance or Daisy Chain: British Opinion and Policy Toward Russia, April–August, 1939" in *Power, Public Opinion, and Diplomacy,* edited by Lillian P. Wallace and William C. Askew (Durham, N.C., 1959).

3. A Labor deputation had met with Chamberlain on the night of March 30 to emphasize the party's view of the tremendous importance of Russia and, if possible, to get "something about Russia" put in the declaration of the guarantee to Poland. Dalton, *The Fateful Years,* p. 238. But nothing had come of this.

4. *Parl. Debs., HC,* April 3, 1939, vol. 345, 2501–02.

> stand against an overwhelming artillery supported by a tremendous air bombardment. . . . If we are going in without the help of Russia we are walking into a trap. It is the only country whose armies can get there. . . . I ask the Government to take immediate steps to secure the adhesion of Russia in a fraternity, an alliance, an agreement, a pact, it does not matter what it is called so long as it is an understanding to stand together against the aggressor. Apart from that we have undertaken a frightful gamble. . . . If Russia has not been brought into this matter because of certain feelings the Poles have that they do not want the Russians there, it is for us to declare the conditions, and unless the Poles are prepared to accept the only conditions with which we can successfully help them, the responsibility must be theirs.[5]

The demand for the inclusion of Russia in the peace bloc was intensified in the Commons debate of April 13. Chamberlain, speaking with great forbearance toward Italy despite her invasion of Albania, was interrupted by cries of "What about Russia?" Momentarily deserting his prepared typescript, the Prime Minister assured the House that the absence of any reference to Russia in his speech did not mean that Britain was not "keeping in the closest touch with the representatives of that country." The Government's task was difficult. It had to consider not only what Britain wished, but what "other people are willing to do." "I ask the House to believe," he concluded, "that without any prejudice, without any preconceived ideological notions, we are endeavoring to the utmost of our ability so to marshal the forces that are still in favor of peace and which are willing to resist aggression that our efforts may be successful."

In the ensuing debate Sinclair, Wedgwood, and Dalton chided that Chamberlain would have neglected completely to mention the Soviet Union had the reference, in Dalton's words, not been "dragged out of him by interruptions from this side of the House, almost as a dentist would extract a tooth." Attlee pressed for an alliance with Russia as the indispensable basis for build-

5. *Ibid.*, April 3, 1939, vol. 345, 2507–10.

ing up a new system of collective security. Churchill, Eden, Haden Guest, Vernon Bartlett, and Ben Riley forcefully concurred. Sinclair made it clear that only Russian cooperation could translate into ships, airplanes, and troops the guarantees that Britain was "sprinkling around Europe," while Eden re-emphasized Churchill's point of April 3: "It would clearly be suicidal to stop half-way." Dalton acknowledged the problem created by Polish and Rumanian fears of Russia and suggested solving it within the framework of an Anglo-Franco-Russian alliance. He asked Sir John Simon, Chancellor of the Exchequer, who was to conclude the debate, whether the Government had any objection in principle to a triple alliance, adding: "If not, why are they letting time slip by without making a proposal; or will they tell us that they have made the proposal and that it has been turned down by the Russians?" When Simon spoke, he neglected the question until Dalton interrupted him by asking it again, then replied almost casually: "Though I cannot say that that particular proposition has been made, the hon. Gentleman and the House may take it that the Government is raising no objection in principle to any such proposition."[6]

Although the Government's task was undeniably difficult, especially for that particular Government, Simon's casual air could hardly have been expected to reassure the House that the Government was seriously investigating the possibility of an arrangement with Russia. And it was all the more unsatisfying inasmuch as this kind of alliance had received support from Laborites, Liberals, independents, dissident Conservatives, and, outside the halls of Parliament, even some regular Conservatives. Nor could it be said, as the Government had done on so many previous occasions, that the critics had offered no really definite and constructive alternative. It was this kind of Government response, though its vagueness might have been buoyed by tradition, which led the critics to believe then, and others to suspect since, that the Government's apparent change of heart—or policy—in late March, 1939, was not a change in direction at all, but at best a change in emphasis.

6. *Ibid.,* April 13, 1939, vol. 346, 15–140.

The intense concern in Parliament for an immediate extension of the peace front to all countries willing to cooperate, and to Russia in particular, also pervaded the British press. When the Liberal *Manchester Guardian* (Apr. 1) implored the Government to lose no time in passing from its "interim policy" to the "final scheme," it expressly meant that "Russia must be brought into the plan." Later (Apr. 15) it asserted: "An arrangement with Russia, whatever its precise form, has become the keystone of the peace front." In complete agreement were the Labor *Daily Herald* (Apr. 1) and the Liberal *News Chronicle* (Apr. 1), two newspapers which, among others, conducted a tireless campaign toward that end. The *Daily Herald* (Apr. 10) warned that without Russia no policy of mutual defense would be complete, while the *News Chronicle* (Apr. 10) held that a "steel-strong" alliance with Russia was the only hope for peace. Without Russia "the Grand Alliance is indeed a desperately dangerous and improbable affair," declared the radical *New Statesman and Nation* (Apr. 1); the exclusion of Russia was "so mad as to be incredible," exclaimed the independent *Time and Tide* (Apr. 1). For the independent *Economist* (Apr. 8), Russia was the "cement" that would give the peace front strength; thus there was no more urgent and vital diplomatic task than reaching a firm understanding with the Soviet Union, it declared (Apr. 15). Both the independent *Financial News* (Apr. 14) and the Conservative *Financial Times* (Apr. 14) feared lest the Government was blind to the absolute necessity of Russian cooperation, without which, the pro-Labor *Reynolds News* (Apr. 2) warned, the whole system of guarantees would be a "hopeless failure." The independent *Glasgow Herald* (Apr. 4), the non-partisan *Spectator* (Apr. 14), the Unionist Cardiff *Western Mail* (Apr. 13), the independent *Statist* (Apr. 15), the Labor *Leeds Weekly Citizen* (Apr. 7), and the Liberal *Liverpool Daily Post* (Apr. 4) all used other words, but the sentiment was in every case the same.

Many journals pressed for the widening of the peace front without specific, though sometimes with implied, reference to Russia. The agreement with Poland must be followed "with parallel agreements on a wider scale," declared the Conservative *Daily Telegraph* (Apr. 10). "No power is excluded" from the developing peace bloc, claimed the pro-Government *Times* (Apr. 4). "There should be no mental reservations" in securing support for the anti-aggression front, asserted the Liberal Bradford *Yorkshire Observer* (Apr. 4), in what appeared to be a direct reference to Chamberlain's well-known antipathy for Russia.

There was, for rather obvious reasons, a greater reluctance in the Conservative press to mention Russia by name than there was in the Labor, Liberal, and independent press. But phrases like the *Daily Telegraph's* "parallel agreements on a wider scale" and *The Times'* "no power is excluded," certainly implied at least a willingness, if not a determination, in view of the gravity of the situation, to go far beyond the limits earlier envisaged by Conservative opinion in seeking aid for the maintenance of peace and security. As for the British people generally, the Government could be under no misapprehension, the *Daily Telegraph* (Apr. 10) and other newspapers pointed out, about "the depth to which public opinion in this country has been stirred"—a stirring substantiated by a Gallup Poll in Britain during the month of April which resulted in 92 per cent of those canvassed declaring in favor of a British alliance with Russia.[7]

All these factors, combined with the common-sense logic that without Russian cooperation there could be no effective implementation of the guarantees to Poland and Rumania, pressed upon Chamberlain in mid-April, when he and the Cabinet decided to make an approach to Russia. To be sure, the Russians had been annoyed by the British rejection of their March 18 proposal for a conference, and Stalin had warned the Eighteenth Party Congress (March 18) that Russia must be careful not to be "drawn into conflicts by warmongers who are accustomed to have others pull the chestnuts out of the fire." Yet there was reason to believe that Soviet annoyance was only temporary and that the Russians might still be willing to cooperate with the British and French in an anti-aggression front. Sir William Seeds reported from Moscow on April 6 that the press had given no indication that Russia had a grievance against Britain, and in fact, the *Journal de Moscou,* the mouthpiece of Foreign Secretary Litvinov, had recently advocated "participation by all European

7. *Herald Tribune* (New York), May 4, 1939.

peace-loving states in a collective agreement destined to strengthen the security of all such states whether small or great."[8]

Britain made her first concrete approach to Russia on April 15,[9] when Seeds proposed to Litvinov that if any neighbor of Russia should be attacked, "the assistance of the Soviet Government would be available, if desired, and would be afforded in such manner as would be found most convenient."[10] The Soviet reply of April 17 went far beyond the scope of the British request, demanding a full-scale alliance with Britain and France for mutual assistance against aggression, as well as coverage for all the border states between the Baltic and Black Seas and immediate military conversations.[11] Starkly realistic, the Russian reply placed Britain in a quandary as to whether, in her opposition to aggression, she was willing to become full partners in an alliance with Russia. The Government hesitated in consternation. Several weeks of discussion followed among the Cabinet, the Foreign Office, and the various governments concerned, as to the possibility of some compromise between the Russian and British proposals.[12]

The Government feared that a straight pact of mutual assistance would provoke Germany and divide opinion at home. It was not ready to undertake obligations to any of Russia's neighbors other than Poland, Rumania, and Turkey; nor did it like the idea of Russian aid for Poland and Rumania whether they wanted it or not.[13] Perhaps the sharpest thorn in Britain's side was the attitude of Poland, which found the Soviet proposals most objectionable. The Poles feared that their interests would

8. Seeds to Halifax, Moscow, Apr. 1, 1939; Seeds to Halifax, Moscow, Apr. 6, 1939. *B. D.*, IV, 574–75; V, 45–46.

9. The vacillating course and eventual result of the British negotiations with Russia in the summer of 1939 are generally known and have been treated fully elsewhere. For a more detailed account, chronicling events from the published *B. D.*, see Arnold J. and Veronica Toynbee, eds., *The Eve of War, 1939* ("Survey of International Affairs," 1939–1946, X; London, 1958). Ivan Maisky, the Russian Ambassador in London (1932–1943) presents a very biased but nonetheless trenchant account of the negotiations in *Who Helped Hitler?* (London, 1964), pp. 99ff.

10. Seeds to Halifax, Moscow, Apr. 15, 1939. *B. D.*, V, 215.

11. Seeds to Halifax, Moscow, Apr. 18, 1939. *Ibid.*, V, 228–29.

12. Templewood, *Nine Troubled Years*, p. 354.

13. Strang, *Home and Abroad*, p. 164.

be subordinated to those of Russia and that the Soviet Government would treat Poland as a mere pawn.[14] Rumania shared this fear of Russia, and the Rumanian Foreign Minister lent weight to the Polish argument during a visit to London in late April.[15] Thus the British Government consumed time in a desperate attempt to reconcile the following objectives: not to forego the chance of receiving help from Russia in case of war; not to jeopardize the common front by disregarding the susceptibilities of Poland and Rumania; not to forfeit the sympathy of the world at large by giving a handle to Germany's anti-Comintern propaganda; not to jeopardize the cause of peace by provoking violent action by Germany.[16]

While the Government tried to resolve the dilemma, the press ventilated the issue. The *Financial News* (Apr. 29) considered it "incumbent upon the British Government . . . to conclude a firm agreement with Russia." For the *Reynolds News* (Apr. 16), the new approach to Russia must bring concrete results or the last four weeks of feverish diplomatic activity would have yielded nothing. While guarantees strewn all over Europe might make a "pleasant-looking daisy chain," without Russian assistance they would not form a barrier to Nazi aggression which any military expert could trust. The independent *Sunday Pictorial* (Apr. 16) declared that Britain had not yet "grasped the shield of impregnable defence"; the contacts with Russia were not sanctioned by the British people for "an idle tête-a-tête." In the view of the *Manchester Guardian* (May 3), any coalition which did not include Russia would not impress Germany, would not satisfy British public opinion, and would give no reasonable security for peace. The Government must make "every effort to appreciate the Russian point of view" and to convince the Russians of Britain's determination and sincerity. "A close understanding with Russia is imperative," said the *Liverpool Daily Post* (May 8), "and failure to reach one would have a serious effect on public feeling in this country."

14. Kennard to Halifax, Warsaw, Apr. 19, 1939. *B. D.*, V, 244.
15. Visit of the Rumanian Foreign Minister, April 23–26, 1939. *Ibid.*, V, 312–13.
16. Halifax to Kennard and Hoare, F.O., Apr. 28, 1939. *Ibid.*, V, 357.

The negotiations were going at a "snail's pace" lamented the *Daily Herald* (May 3). Of Russia's willingness to accept full responsibilities in the peace front there could be absolutely no doubt. Every section of public opinion desired a rapid conclusion of the negotiations, yet they dragged on. Why not try a direct meeting between Litvinov and Halifax? The *News Chronicle* (May 1) fully agreed with the *Daily Herald* and urged that both political and military staff talks be initiated with Russia at once. The *Glasgow Herald* (Apr. 19) emphasized the necessity of a close understanding with the Soviet Union by reiterating that material aid could reach Poland and Rumania only through Russia.

A few newspapers took a less vigorous point of view. *The Times* (May 4) was willing to agree to "reciprocal undertakings for common action" with Russia, but feared that "a hard and fast alliance might hamper other negotiations and approaches." The Cardiff *Western Mail* (May 2) assured its readers that the Government fully understood the importance of gaining Russian support; it must be given time to complete the negotiations.

During the first days of May, Chamberlain was questioned repeatedly in the House of Commons on the course of the negotiations with Russia. He usually gave vague, placid replies, such as that on May 2: "We are carrying on discussions of a perfectly friendly character. There must necessarily be a great many details which have to be considered, and there are other Governments to be considered. . . . There is no want of goodwill on the part of His Majesty's Government."[17] Such responses did nothing to alleviate the anxiety of those who questioned the sincerity of the Government in approaching Russia and who suspected it was only wasting precious time. Churchill in particular was concerned about the delay. He felt it must be "vividly impressed" upon the Polish Government that the accession of Russia to the peace bloc might be decisive in preventing war, and that the British people, who had recently sacrificed an honored, ingrained custom in accepting compulsory military service, had a right to call upon Poland not to place obstacles in the way of the common cause.

17. *Parl. Debs., HC,* May 2, 1939, vol. 346, 1698.

The Baltic states should be brought into the peace front, and, above all, time should not be lost.[18]

While Britain continued to ponder her reply to the Soviet, a major change occurred in the Russian Foreign Office. Molotov replaced Litvinov as Commissar for Foreign Affairs. The British press reacted to the change with surprising calm. *The Times* (May 4) thought it a "remarkable thing" that Litvinov had not gone sooner and considered it "imprudent to assume" that any change in Russian foreign policy would follow. The *Manchester Guardian* (May 4) could not "altogether avoid the suspicion that if the British Government had been whole-hearted in its efforts we should by now have secured Russian aid against aggression and Mr. Litvinov would still be Commissar for Foreign Affairs," but ventured no opinion beyond that. In an editorial entitled "Litvinov," the *News Chronicle* (May 4) suggested only that Britain's hesitation was in large part responsible for the delay in the negotiations. Lack of comment in the press makes it reasonable to suppose that there was little appreciation of the possibility that Molotov's appointment might herald a reorientation in Soviet foreign policy.[19]

The change in Moscow provoked a fresh crop of questions about Russia in the House of Commons on May 5. Chamberlain, apparently rattled, vented a peevish displeasure on the Opposition. To Attlee's charge that the delays were causing uncertainty, he retorted: "I do realize that uncertainty is being created by a number of people who are all the time suggesting that if there is any fault it must be the fault of the British Government." This "purely partisan attitude" is not "conducive to the interests of this country, but I cannot be held responsible for that." When Gallacher suggested that Chamberlain make "personal contact in order to get Stalin's own view," Chamberlain snapped back: "Perhaps the hon. Member would suggest with whom I should make personal contact, because personalities change rather rapidly."[20] That Chamberlain was at best only lukewarm toward

18. Churchill, *Step by Step, 1936–1939,* pp. 318–19.

19. Russia assured Britain that no change of policy was to be assumed from Litvinov's departure. Halifax to Seeds, F.O., May 6, 1939. *B. D.,* V, 453.

20. *Parl. Debs., HC,* May 5, 1939, vol. 346, 2220–22.

the negotiations with Russia was already becoming obvious.

Chamberlain's Parliamentary behavior did not go unnoticed by the press. The Bradford *Yorkshire Observer* (May 9) in particular was annoyed, declaring that his curt dismissal of questions about the Russian negotiations "hardly does justice to the wide anxiety which exists in the nation over many branches of home and international policy." The Government could not be blamed for negotiating carefully with Russia, but "in this country of all others, public opinion has many free outlets, and the Prime Minister seems sometimes to be too abrupt about the Parliamentary expression of it."

While the British Government was preoccupied with the exchange of proposals with Russia, it was still much concerned with the situation in Germany. Anxious lest the announcement of conscription in Britain should cause excessive alarm in the Reich, it ordered Sir Nevile Henderson back to his post in Berlin (he arrived on April 24) with the express purpose of explaining the measure to the German Government before the actual statement was made in the House of Commons.[21]

Henderson's return to Germany received almost no support in the British press, but it did evoke some unfavorable comment. The *Manchester Guardian* (Apr. 26) feared that his return in the "normal" way would be greeted with much suspicion abroad. The *News Chronicle* (Apr. 24) entitled a lead editorial "Why?" For Henderson's return there would have to be a very good reason indeed; otherwise (Apr. 25), it was a "diplomatic blunder of the first magnitude" which could not fail to revive distrust of British policy in Washington, Moscow, and the Balkan capitals. If the move betokened a readiness to woo Hitler with soft words, the *Economist* (Apr. 29) warned, it was a grave error. In fact, it was unwise in any case, "because it spelled weakness in the reading of the Germans and Italians themselves, and weakening in the eyes of America." *Time and Tide* (Apr. 29) charged Chamberlain with trying to make the British people think appeasement was dead while attempting to convince Hitler that it was only asleep. The general public, it asserted, aroused and apprehensive, was in no mood for a return to appeasement.

21. Henderson, *Failure of a Mission,* p. 230.

Hitler's first public act after Henderson's return to Berlin was not friendly toward Britain. Speaking to the Reichstag on April 28, he denounced the Anglo-German Naval Agreement of 1935, which had been so marked a gain to him at a critical moment in his policy, representing it as a favor to Britain which was now being withdrawn as a mark of German displeasure. He also denounced the German-Polish Non-Aggression Pact, giving as his reason the Anglo-Polish guarantee, "which would in certain circumstances compel Poland to take military action against Germany."[22] The result of this was that Chamberlain's faith was shaken anew. He wrote his sister: "He finds it so easy to tear up treaties and throw overboard assurances, that no one can feel any confidence in new ones."[23] This was hardly a startlingly novel deduction in view of the events of the previous month, and its repetition here suggests that Chamberlain was still having difficulty bringing himself to believe what was so obviously true.

By this time, however, few Englishmen any longer harbored illusions about the good intentions of Germany. Visiting London during the last week of April, 1939, Grigore Gafencu, the Rumanian Foreign Minister, found a "firm, unshakable resolution" in all the ministers, all the Members of Parliament, and all the journalists whom he met. It was universally recognized, he records, that peace was no longer a matter of confidence, but of force. Gafencu was particularly impressed with Churchill, whose "incomparably clear vision was unequaled in Europe," and Halifax, of whom he wrote that no minister "ever showed a greater sense of responsibility." Halifax considered the securing of Russian participation in the defense of Continental security the "most delicate and difficult" problem he had yet to solve.[24]

The British Government eventually reached the conclusion that something on the lines of its original proposal to Russia

22. Baynes, *Speeches of Adolf Hitler,* II, 1632–33. Hitler's speech was in part a reaction to President Roosevelt's personal request of April 15 that he give a guarantee to some thirty countries not to undertake further aggression for ten or even twenty-five years. Langer and Gleason, *The Challenge to Isolation,* p. 91; Wheeler-Bennett, *Munich,* p. 384.

23. Feiling, *Life of Neville Chamberlain,* p. 407.

24. Gafencu, *Last Days of Europe,* pp. 97, 108, 112–17, 124.

was still the best solution. Despite French warning to the contrary,[25] the British reply handed to Russia on May 8 was merely a recast formula of the first proposal reiterating the British suggestion that, in view of the British guarantees to Poland and Rumania, "the Soviet Government would undertake that in the event of Great Britain and France being involved in hostilities in fulfillment of these obligations the assistance of the Soviet Government would be immediately available, if desired, and would be afforded in such a manner and on such terms as might be agreed." Britain's major criticism of the Russian proposal was that, "though logically complete," it took too little account of practical difficulties and would require too long a time for its negotiation. Automatic Soviet assistance to Poland and Rumania, as proposed by Russia, presented those Governments with "difficulties" and placed them in a position which they found "embarrassing." While the hesitation of Poland and Rumania to be closely associated with Russia might be considered unjustified, it existed and had to be taken into account. For that reason, the better plan was to start from what was "immediately practicable" and to build upon this.[26]

Before Russia replied, the British Government was able to announce that it had successfully negotiated a pact of mutual assistance with Turkey.[27] This announcement met with universal approval in the press, and some newspapers made it an occasion

25. The French, in effect, favored a pact of mutual assistance, and Bonnet had so informed the Russian Ambassador in Paris. Phipps to Halifax, Paris, May 3, 1939. *B. D.,* V, 404–06. Convinced of the urgency of a triple alliance, the French generally took a middle ground between the British and Soviet positions, trying to reconcile the lack of precision in the English formulas with the manifest wish of Russia for minutely detailed provisions. See Coulondre, *De Staline á Hitler,* p. 265; Gafencu, *Last Days of Europe,* p. 148.

26. Halifax to Seeds, F.O., May 6, 1939; Seeds to Halifax, Moscow, May 9, 1939. *B. D.,* V, 448–50, 483–87.

27. *Parl. Debs., HC,* May 12, 1939, vol. 347, 953. It was originally intended that this declaration would be tripartite (including France), but when the time earlier agreed upon for the announcement arrived, France and Turkey were still debating the French cession of Hatay to Turkey. Agreement on making the interim declaration and the final treaty tripartite was reached on July 14, 1939.

for re-emphasizing the need for an agreement with Russia. In an editorial entitled "The Whole Hog," the *Daily Herald* (May 13) proclaimed: "Now Russia must be brought in!" The *Glasgow Herald* (May 13) and the independent *Statist* (May 20) hoped that Turkey would prove to be "a point of contact" for the Anglo-Russian negotiations.

Russia's reply to Britain on May 15 maintained the original Soviet position and demanded "reciprocity": a pact of mutual assistance, a guarantee of the "States of Central and Eastern Europe threatened by aggression including Latvia, Estonia, and Finland," and "the conclusion of a concrete agreement . . . as to forms and extent of assistance."[28]

A complete impasse had therefore been reached, and the British Government was faced with the choice of breaking off the negotiations or extending its limited guarantees to a comprehensive alliance with Russia. Several factors, including the constant pressure in Parliament and the press and the course of events in central Europe, influenced it in the latter direction.

The House of Commons, which had not debated foreign policy for a month while the Government pursued negotiations with Russia, aired the question of Anglo-Russian relations again on May 19. "We have procrastinated seriously and dangerously," declared Lloyd George on that occasion:

> I cannot imagine a government taking the risk which the present Government has taken . . . in failing to come to terms with Powers whose assistance to us will not only be useful but . . . essential. . . . Russia offered to come in months ago. For months we have been staring this powerful gift horse in the mouth. . . . What is the good of this political snobbery . . .? The issues are too tremendous for that. . . . Why do we not make up our mind, and make it up without any loss of time, that we should come to the same terms with Russia as we do with France?[29]

Attlee described the line taken by the Soviet Government as the only "realist one." The vast majority of the British people, he

28. Seeds to Halifax, Moscow, May 15, 1939. *B. D.*, V, 558–59.
29. *Parl. Debs., HC,* May 19, 1939, vol. 347, 1812–15, 1820.

believed, felt that the best hope of preventing further aggression was a firm union among Britain, France, and Russia. Yet week by week questions about those negotiations were answered by: "You must not interfere in these delicate negotiations while they are going on." What was the Government waiting for?

A completely different note was struck by Chamberlain. Lloyd George seemed to him "almost to go out of his way to find . . . evidence of the imminence of some frightful catastrophe." The pledges to Poland, Rumania, and Greece were "first aid treatment." It still remained to get support for those assurances from any quarters able and willing to help, but the Government was trying to avoid "opposing blocs." It was endeavoring to build up a peace front against aggression, not an alliance between Britain and other countries, and "we should not be succeeding in that policy if, by ensuring the cooperation of one country, we rendered another country uneasy and unwilling to collaborate with us." Chamberlain explained that there was "a sort of veil, a sort of wall, between the two Governments [Britain and Russia] which it is extremely difficult to penetrate."

When Sinclair, like Attlee, tried to elicit the Government's objections to the Russian proposals, the Prime Minister reacted with obstinacy and embarrassment: "I am not going any further than I have gone already. . . . I must walk warily. . . . We are not concerned merely with the Russian Government. We have other governments to reconsider. . . . I am not going any further. . . . Refrain from pressing us unduly to disclose the exact point where the difficulties arise."

Churchill cut through the Prime Minister's remarks with a statement of hard fact: after many weeks of negotiation, there was a complete deadlock. The differences had not been stated, nor the objection to making an agreement "in the broad and simple form proposed by the Russian Soviet Government." What was wrong with the Russian proposal of a triple alliance? Churchill went on:

> I do not know whether I can commend it to my right hon. Friend by adopting a simile selected as a special compliment to him. It is like setting up an armoured umbrella, under which other countries would be invited to take shelter. . . .

> If you are ready to be an ally of Russia in time of war . . . why should you shrink from becoming the ally of Russia now, when you may by that very fact prevent the breaking out of war? I cannot understand all these refinements of diplomacy and delay. . . . You will not extend your responsibilities, or your burdens, by extending your guarantees to cover all those countries [Latvia, Estonia, and Finland] . . . You are in it up to the neck already, and the question is how to make your system effective, and effective in time.[30]

It was Eden's firm conviction, too, that an understanding with Russia would be "a definite gain to peace," and "the sooner, the more complete, the more far-reaching that agreement, the better." If Britain were going to build a deterrent to aggression, it would be folly not to build the most powerful deterrent possible. How could a tripartite alliance based on complete reciprocity be thought to run counter to the peace front? "After all, France has already her own arrangements with Soviet Russia. No one thinks that they run counter to the peace front." There were difficulties in any course Britain might pursue. Having embarked on one, it was wise to pursue it with vigor and conviction.

When Sinclair eventually gained the floor, he tried to convey to the Government "the impression of blank astonishment and deep disappointment . . . felt abroad by men of all parties, by all friends of peace and justice, at the attitude of His Majesty's Government towards Russia." The Government's pretexts for not accepting Russia's offer were "feeble and ridiculous." "What you require for keeping a door shut when somebody is trying to get through it," he admonished, "is merely bulk and weight. That is why Russia would be so useful to the cause of peace at the present time." Without her, Britain could not preserve peace.[31]

Agitation in the press for the conclusion of a pact with Russia gained momentum. The *Daily Telegraph* (May 20), believing that "the Government would . . . be interpreting the general desire of the country . . . by coming to an arrangement with Russia with as little further delay as possible," asserted (May 22)

30. *Ibid.,* May 19, 1939, vol. 347, 1843–44.
31. *Ibid.,* May 19, 1939, vol. 347, 1812–86.

that the future could not be risked for the sake of a formula. When Britain had already gone far beyond her traditional policy, "the nicely calculated less or more becomes otiose and irrelevant." To the *Liverpool Daily Post* (May 17), Russia's demand for reciprocity seemed a considerable commitment, but "small compared to the British guarantees to Poland and Rumania." Britain could not feel secure without a Russian agreement, it declared (May 25), and if that implied a defensive alliance, then a defensive alliance there must be! The *Daily Herald* (May 8) was very emphatic: "The country is determined to have a Russian alliance. The country must have its Russian alliance!" The Government could continue "to refine formulas or elaborate compromises" only at the cost of betraying national interests, it stormed (May 24). The *Glasgow Herald* (May 11) considered an alliance with Russia "the most obvious means of checkmating aggression" and doubted (May 20) whether the suspicions of Poland and Rumania were so deep that they could not be convinced that to accept help from Russia was better than the prospect of having to withstand a German onslaught while Russia stood aloof. In the view of the Bradford *Yorkshire Observer* (May 20), "British diplomacy should be less belated and more decisive." A substantial system of security could not be built without Russia, it claimed (May 24), and "Conservative opinion has begun to accept that condition, despite Chamberlain's recent refusal to recognize how national opinion feels on the point."

The *Manchester Guardian* (May 20) thought it "absurd" to rebuff Russia because the Government did not want "an alliance." The argument for an alliance with Russia, as the *Observer* (May 21) saw it, led "irresistibly to a consummation which shall put the final seal on a convincing, businesslike, decisive 'encirclement for defence' against Germany." "What is Chamberlain up to now?" asked the *Sunday Pictorial* (May 14). Russia was ready to sign a three-power alliance, but Chamberlain feared such an alliance might "embarrass" him. "Is he still dreaming of turning our friends into enemies, and our enemies into friends? Let us have action this week!" The *News Chronicle* (May 24) affirmed that "public opinion has long been convinced that a firm military understanding with Russia is essential if the peace front is to be made really effective." The *Spectator* (May 19) and the *New Statesman and Nation* (May 20) considered an agreement with Russia "the prime condition of peace." If Chamberlain's hesitations were based on the idea that a Russian alliance would lend support to the Nazi legend of encirclement, the *Spectator* warned, "Britain might as well go into isolation, for a government that resolves to make no move that Dr. Goebbels is capable of distorting can manifestly make no move at all." It would be a "great pity," reasoned the *Economist* (May 20), if insistence on a purely tactical point should cause Britain to lose her last chance of building a decisively strong Eastern front. The Government would have much more reason on its side "if it makes a minor concession to attain its major aim." The *Statist* (May 13) considered the failure of negotiations with Russia "unthinkable," as did the *Time and Tide* (May 20), whose caustic editorial aimed at Chamberlain was entitled, "He Cannot Say. . . ." As for the Prime Minister's apparent fear that an alliance with Russia would frighten off the smaller countries, *Time and Tide* declared, there is "a law in physics established by Newton which he appears to have overlooked: the greater body attracts the lesser."

Other newspapers, such as the Unionist Edinburgh *Weekly Scotsman* (May 20), were less vehement, simply finding it "gratifying" that the negotiations were being pushed ahead. And a few journals were satisfied that the Government was acting wisely. *The Times* (May 9) reminded its readers that the negotiations were neither simple nor purely bilateral, so a speedy conclusion could not be expected. So did the Cardiff *Western Mail* (May 11), although it later (May 25) expressed disappointment that no agreement had yet been reached. The Government's reluctance to form a hard-and-fast triple alliance pleased the *Daily Mail* (May 11): "it might involve us in areas beyond Europe." But this was distinctly a minority view.

The course of events in central Europe in mid-May did not diminish the pressure bearing upon the British Government to continue the negotiations with Russia. In Berlin, May 22, Germany and Italy signed the "Pact of Steel," a military alliance "without mental or other reservations." It was also becoming increasingly evident that a crisis—of what proportion none could tell—was developing around the militarization of the Free City of Danzig.[32]

In the case of Danzig, British public opinion had, by this time, come to regard it "no longer a place but a principle" (so the memoirs of General Lord Ismay, Secretary of the Committee of Imperial Defense, attest[33]). This is evident in the press comments of early May, when the German advances toward that city were particularly menacing. The Bradford *Yorkshire Observer* (May 6) emphatically stated that there must be no "lukewarm attitude" toward Danzig, no attempt to make out that it was a side issue and not a danger point in the European balance of democratic security. Poland should not be allowed to succumb to unreasonable demands, the *Glasgow Herald* (May 2) proclaimed. The *Daily Telegraph* (May 3) and the *Manchester Guardian* (May 6) held that Poland must receive the unqualified support of her guarantors in her resistance to the surrender of any of her rights, and the Conservative *Sunday Graphic* (May 7) warned that Britain was "committed as a nation to give every assistance to Poland in withstanding naked aggression." "Danzig and the Vistula are to Poland what London and the Thames are to England," the *Observer* (May 7) contended. And Duff Cooper, in the *Evening Standard* (May 9), warned that the good faith of Britain was bound up with the frontiers of Poland.[34]

Indicative of British opinion toward Germany at the time are the observations of German Ambassador Herbert von Dirksen upon his return to London in early May. He found the political scene entirely changed. In contrast with the feeling that had prevailed in the summer of 1938, when the "broad masses" did not want to fight and remained passive, "they had now taken over the initiative from the government and drove the Cabinet on. British public opinion did not aim at starting a war, but only at a resolute attitude towards Germany and on armed intervention in the event of aggression by Hitler."[35]

32. See Wheeler-Bennett, *Munich,* p. 402; Schmidt, *Hitler's Interpreter,* p. 130.
33. *The Memoirs of General Lord Ismay* (New York, 1960), pp. 96–97.
34. Quoted in Cooper, *The Second World War,* p. 260.
35. Dirksen, *Moscow, Tokyo, London,* p. 218.

After Britain's receipt of the Russian reply of May 15, there followed more discussions with France, Rumania, Poland, and now with the Baltic states. Halifax attended a meeting of the Council of the League of Nations in Geneva, apparently learned of the budding Nazi-Soviet conversations for the first time, and returned to London convinced that any agreement that Britain might make with Russia would have to be along Soviet lines.[36] He secured support in the Cabinet, and the Government decided "after many meetings and searchings of heart" (Sir Samuel Hoare records) to continue the negotiations on the Soviet basis. To save face, however, the British decided to cloak the whole project under the Covenant of the League of Nations[37]—a curious and revealing maneuver in view of Chamberlain's earlier estimate of the League.

Accordingly, the new proposal dispatched on May 25 accepted the principle of mutual assistance and provided that the contracting powers—acting in accordance with the principles of the League—"would concert together as to the methods by which such mutual support and assistance could, in the case of need, be made most effective." This support and assistance was to be given "without prejudice to the rights and position of other Powers."[38]

Molotov rejected this proposal. It was "cumbrous," "vaguely-worded," made effective cooperation dependent upon the "interminable delays" of League procedure and was, therefore, "no serious contribution." Typical of British reserve, it was calculated to insure the "maximum of talk and the minimum of results." Russia wanted effective guarantee of action, he declared, not words and conversations.[39]

36. Campbell-Johnson records that Halifax received "abundant information that Germany was working with accustomed thoroughness for agreement with Russia" and the Foreign Minister—if indeed he had condoned the Cabinet's refusal to consider the Soviet plea for a tripartite pact in the beginning—"certainly revised his opinions at Geneva." *Viscount Halifax,* pp. 529–30. Halifax says nothing of this in his memoirs.

37. Kennedy to the Secretary of State, London, May 24, 1939. *U.S. For. Rel., 1939,* I, 259–60; Templewood, *Nine Troubled Years,* p. 354; Strang, *Home and Abroad,* p. 167.

38. Halifax to Seeds, F.O., May 25, 1939. *B. D.,* V, 679–80.

39. Seeds to Halifax, Moscow, May 27, 28, 1939. *Ibid.,* V, 701–02, 710–12.

On June 2 Russia again proposed a pact of mutual assistance, insisting in effect on the deletion of all reference to the League and the inclusion of direct guarantees to Belgium, Greece, Turkey, Rumania, Poland, Latvia, Estonia, and Finland. In addition, the Soviets now demanded that the political pact become effective only after the conclusion of a military convention.[40]

The issue was clear. Russia would not join in the peace front unless Britain and France guaranteed the Baltic states, but the British Government was not inclined to force upon those states arrangements which they did not want[41]—especially since it feared possible involvement in a purely Nazi-Soviet quarrel in the Baltic area.[42] British disappointment at Russia's reply was summarized in one terse statement in *The Times* (June 5): "The result is a completely new draft . . . or as it should be called, the Three-Power pact, eleventh edition, revised and enlarged, private circulation only."

Disheartened though the Government was,[43] it continued to seek a solution, impelled partly by the growing conviction of the Soviet's importance and partly by the persistent agitation in Parliament and the press. Chamberlain announced in the Commons on June 7 that a representative of the Foreign Office would go to Moscow to convey to Seeds full information about the British attitude on all outstanding points.[44] The choice fell upon William Strang, head of the Central European Division of the Foreign Office and a former Counsellor in the Moscow Embassy.

The British press generally approved the decision to send Strang to Moscow, although the prospects for his success engendered little enthusiasm. For example, the *Manchester Guardian*

40. Seeds to Halifax, Moscow, June 2, 1939. *Ibid.*, V, 753–54.

41. The Baltic states and Finland, apparently fearing Russian assistance as much as German aggression, had made it clear in London that they strongly opposed any proposal of automatic assistance. See Foreign Office Memorandum, June 12, 1939. *Ibid.*, VI, 35; Strang, *Home and Abroad,* p. 170.

42. See Templewood, *Nine Troubled Years,* pp. 355–56.

43. Chamberlain told Joseph Kennedy that he was "not at all sure he would not call the whole thing off." Kennedy to the Secretary of State, London, June 9, 1939. *U.S. For. Rel., 1939,* I, 272.

44. *Parl. Debs., HC,* June 7, 1939, vol. 348, 400–01. The Government's first idea was to recall Seeds for consultation, but he was ill at the time and unable to travel.

(June 8) and the *Daily Mail* (June 8) called it "a wise move"; the *Liverpool Daily Post* (June 13) passively wished him well; and the *Glasgow Herald* (June 8) declared that it would be a sign of Britain's "seriousness in this matter." The opinion was expressed in some quarters that a higher official should have been chosen to make the trip. The *New Statesman and Nation* (June 10) believed that Strang's appointment would strengthen the suspicion that more delays were intended; "it is so obvious . . . that one of the principal Cabinet Ministers ought to go." The *Economist* (June 10) opined: "That Lord Halifax himself or Sir Robert Vansittart has not been chosen to visit Moscow . . . may not be a pity according to whether the choice was directed by motives of prestige . . . or by a conviction that agreement is so close that Mr. Strang's help will be sufficient to obtain it." Even the *Daily Mail* (June 8) admitted, albeit derisively, that "to have sent a bigger man would no doubt have satisfied the dramatic instincts of the Russians." "Send Lord Halifax," demanded the *News Chronicle* (June 8).

Despite the dispassionate reception of the Strang mission by the press, it had by no means lost interest in the Russian negotiations. The demand for their conclusion continued, although the comments of most newspapers came to be tempered more by calm anxiety than the earlier violent impatience. The Bradford *Yorkshire Observer* (June 1) and the *Glasgow Herald* (June 7) asserted that the Government must realize that what Russia asked was not unreasonable. The Labor *Leeds Weekly Citizen* (June 2) agreed: "Russia sees the European situation through clearer eyes than does our Prime Minister, and her remedy for the disease is sound and logical." If just a "fraction of the soothing qualities" which the Government had used on Germany were applied to Russia, the *Manchester Guardian* (June 10) maintained, "Britain would be much better off today." The conduct of the negotiations was "too reminiscent of the old diplomacy" for the *Financial News* (June 9). Seemingly representative of majority opinion was the considered view of the *Liverpool Daily Post* (June 1):

> There has been far too much niggling on our part. We ought to have tried at the outset to understand the Russian stand-

> point and make prompter efforts to meet it. Instead we have hesitated so long that a situation has been created which may cause irritation in some quarters. It is deplorable that that should be the case, and it is to be hoped that steps will at once be taken to put an end to the difficulties over the pact with Russia, which is so necessary for resistance to aggression.

British "jumpiness" at this juncture is illustrated by the reaction to a speech Halifax made in the House of Lords on June 8. The Foreign Secretary observed that "the really dangerous" element in the European situation was that the German people should drift to the conclusion that Britain had abandoned all desire to reach an understanding with Germany and that any further attempt at such a thing must be written off as hopeless.[45] This was interpreted in some quarters as presaging a return to appeasement—a none-too-welcome implication. The *News Chronicle* (June 9), for example, pointedly advised that Halifax would do better to push on with rearmament and the completion of the peace front. Some journals, such as the *Daily Telegraph* (June 12) and the *Manchester Guardian* (June 12), recognized an "innocent motive" in rebutting Germany's encirclement charge, but the first reaction was so strong that Halifax had to make an explanatory statement in the Lords four days later. He then declared it "a sign of some confused thinking" to suggest that his speech implied any change whatever in British policy.[46]

If Halifax lost ground with the British public by his June 8 speech in the Lords, he more than made up for it at Chatham House on June 29. His address there ruled out completely the possibility of further British retreat. It indicated that henceforward appeasement was no longer an openly avowed aspiration but a furtive intrigue. The whole fantastic fraud of German *Lebensraum* was exposed with ruthless cogency. Germany was encircling herself, Halifax declared, and it was entirely up to her whether the encirclement continued. "It is well that this should be stated plainly so that there may be no misunderstand-

45. *Parl. Debs., HL,* June 8, 1939, vol. 113, 358.
46. *Ibid.,* June 12, 1939, vol. 113, 435.

ing here or elsewhere." In the past Britain had always stood out against the attempt of any single power to dominate Europe at the expense of the liberties of other nations. British policy was therefore "only following the inevitable line of its own history, if such an attempt were to be made again." The Foreign Secretary concluded:

> The threat of military force is holding the world to ransom, and our immediate task is . . . to resist aggression. . . . If we are ever to succeed in removing misunderstanding and reaching a settlement which the world can trust, it must be upon some basis more substantial than verbal undertakings. . . . There can be no firm bargains on the basis of giving something concrete in return for mere assurances. . . . Let us . . . be very sure that whether or not we are to preserve for ourselves and for others the things we hold dear depends in the last resort upon ourselves, upon the strength of the personal faith of each one of us, and upon our resolution to maintain it.[47]

One Halifax biographer claims that this address roused the politically representative and diverse audience at Chatham House "to a pitch of vocal enthusiasm which in itself conveyed a tonic inspiration to the listening millions in their homes."[48] Judging from the press reception of the speech, that is no exaggeration. The Bradford *Yorkshire Observer* (June 30) reported that "no finer expression of current British aims in world affairs has been uttered." Behind such a policy the whole nation could stand united. The Cardiff *Western Mail* (June 30) called it the "most impressive" warning given Germany in a long time. "It is difficult to imagine a more cogent or admirable statement of British policy," declared the *Liverpool Daily Post* (June 30), while the *Daily Herald* (June 30) rejoiced that Halifax had "spoken the mind of the people" in a way which the Government had rarely done. In the view of the *News Chronicle* (June 30), it was a "finely balanced speech." Halifax had said not only the things that needed

47. *Speeches on Foreign Policy by Viscount Halifax,* edited by H. H. E. Craster (London, 1940), pp. 287–97.
48. Campbell-Johnson, *Viscount Halifax,* p. 526.

saying, but he had said them "in the right order." *The Times* (June 30) and the *Glasgow Herald* (June 30) also approved, and the *Manchester Guardian* (June 30) believed the address

> without question the finest speech on foreign policy made by a Minister of the National Government since it came to power. Unshakably firm, irrefutably just, it expressed the ideas of those who look forward to a happier future with no less clarity than it reflected the present temper of the British people.

Meanwhile, on June 15, Britain proposed a compromise to Russia, providing for immediate action by the contracting parties if one of them went to the assistance of another state which had consented to receive aid. There would be consultation only if one of them considered its security "menaced by a threat to the independence or neutrality of any other European power."[49] Russia immediately rejected this, replying that, since she had been asked to join in guaranteeing Poland, Rumania, Greece, and Turkey, a British refusal to guarantee the Baltic states would put Russia in a "position of inequality, humiliating to the Soviet Union." Perhaps the only solution, therefore, was to return to a simple defensive pact covering only direct attack on one of the signatory powers.[50] This was unacceptable to the British, for it would be of no benefit in protecting Poland and the other states already guaranteed by Britain.[51]

The British tried again on June 22, suggesting that the alliance should operate in case of aggression "which, being directed against another European state, thereby constituted a menace to the security of one of these three countries" (the contracting parties). But when the Soviets asked who would decide whether the aggression constituted a menace to the security of one of the contracting parties, the British negotiators could only reply that "nothing was said in our draft on this point," and the proposal collapsed.[52]

49. Foreign Office Memorandum, June 12, 1939. *B. D.*, VI, 39.
50. Seeds to Halifax, Moscow, June 16, 1939. *Ibid.*, VI, 85–86.
51. Halifax to Seeds, F.O., June 19, 1939. *Ibid.*, VI, 104–05.
52. Seeds to Halifax, Moscow, June 22, 1939. *Ibid.*, VI, 140–41.

Again the British were disheartened (as *The Times* lamented on July 5, "the negotiations now stand like an iceberg: the eight-ninths that is agreed lies submerged and at times forgotten; the ninth still defying agreement sticks out in a remarkably craggy formation") and "several members of the Government" doubted the wisdom of continuing the negotiations.[53] In the press and Parliament agitation persisted. The *Manchester Guardian* (June 24) expressed the almost universal feeling when it deplored the "interminable delay" and chided both sides for acting like "two bankrupt horse-brokers engaged in the sale of an unsound nag," instead of two countries with common interests discussing the best way to meet a common danger. Duff Cooper, writing in the *Evening Standard,* was more pointed in his reference to British hesitation:

> When a man is attacked on a dark night by a couple of gangsters and there comes round the corner a powerful looking individual who seems inclined to render assistance, the man who is so attacked will not pause to inquire whether his potential ally is a Roman Catholic or a Plymouth Brother, nor even will he insist on testing his muscles before accepting his help.[54]

In the Commons, Chamberlain was subjected to incisive questioning almost daily,[55] frequently in none too genial terms. "Does the Prime Minister not realize," Hugh Dalton asked on June 12, "that these very long delays . . . are causing disquiet in the country and . . . doubt as to whether His Majesty's Government really mean business in this matter at all? Are they not spinning out time until they can wriggle back again to the Munich policy?"[56] "In what year does the Prime Minister expect Mr.

53. Templewood, *Nine Troubled Years,* pp. 361–62.
54. Quoted in Duff Cooper, *The Second World War,* p. 294.
55. Laborite Hugh Dalton took it upon himself to question Chamberlain about the negotiations at least once, and sometimes twice, a week. This, Dalton hoped, would help to quicken the British replies to Russia, since Chamberlain would prefer to answer that "the ball was in the Russians' court and that he was awaiting a reply from them." Dalton, *The Fateful Years,* p. 246.
56. *Parl. Debs., HC,* June 12, 1939, vol. 348, 881–82.

Strang's visit to be concluded?" asked W. Leach on June 21.[57] Other comments were as caustic. In addition, the demand that a Cabinet minister go to Moscow to negotiate was expressed with increasing frequency. But Chamberlain refused to countenance such a mission, dismissing its suggestion with curt, quixotic replies, even denying that the Russian Government had ever asked for the visit of a British minister, despite the fact that, on June 12, Maisky had invited Halifax to Moscow, though admittedly "when things were quieter."[58]

The "enormous interest" of the British public in the Moscow negotiations is attested by the German Ambassador in London. Optimistic announcements, Dirksen recorded, were greeted with loud cheers; Molotov's cold pronouncements with "disciplined disappointment." In his view, it was the "political public" which, by its "doggedness, fanaticism, almost hysteria," urged on the negotiations and "compelled the Government to make greater and greater concessions in order that the pact might be concluded as speedily as possible."[59]

Contemporary British writers shared Dirksen's view. "The friendship between His Majesty's Government and the Soviet Union has only ripened in the forcing house of a very warm public opinion," wrote Wedgwood Benn in the *Contemporary Review* (July, 1939),[60] while the divergence of opinion between the British people and the Government was spelled out by M. Wolf in the *Nineteenth Century* (June, 1939):

> The British nation, with an almost unanimous voice, de-

57. *Ibid.*, June 21, 1939, vol. 348, 2204.

58. Halifax to Seeds, F.O., June 12, 1939. *B. D.*, VI, 50–51. Halifax doubted whether his going to Moscow would serve any good purpose. He felt that since Molotov was obliged at every stage to consult his Government, the same would apply to any British representative. Campbell-Johnson, *Viscount Halifax*, p. 531. He may also have felt that the risk of failure was too great. But later he expressed regret that he had not made a warmer response to Russian overtures, despite his doubt that anything the British or French could have done would have changed the outcome of the negotiations with Russia. Birkenhead, *Halifax*, pp. 438, 440.

59. Dirksen, *Moscow, Tokyo, London*, p. 221; Dirksen's Survey of His Ambassadorship to London, September, 1939. *Dirksen Papers*, pp. 173–74.

60. Wedgwood Benn, "The Prospect for European Peace," *Contemporary Review*, CLVI (July, 1939), 4.

> mands a Pact with Russia as an indispensable condition of the country's safety. . . . Public opinion . . . has swung decisively over to the view that only a marshalling of all the forces that are willing to oppose aggression in a solidly built peace front can save peace. In this the opinion of the public has far outdistanced that of the Government.[61]

So it was that at the end of June, the British Government, disposed to tell Russia "to go jump into the Baltic Sea or any other sea they can find, except that they have been under constant pressure from all their friends who say that the failure of a Russian pact would be psychologically bad for England" (so Halifax told Joseph Kennedy)[62] continued the negotiations with Russia.

Britain notified Russia on July 1 that she was willing to agree that the alliance should operate in the event of aggression against "another European state whose independence or neutrality the contracting country concerned felt obliged to defend against such aggression." Molotov thought it necessary to give this new British draft precision by adding a roll of the countries to be defended. Britain agreed on the condition that Holland, Luxemburg, and Switzerland be included, but Molotov refused, arguing that this introduced a "new element" which Russia could not accept: these states did not recognize the Soviet Union. Further, Molotov insisted that the agreement provide for cases of "indirect aggression," which he defined as "an internal *coup d'état* or the reversal of policy in the interests of the agressor."[63] This was "completely unacceptable" to the British, to whom aggression "is to be understood as covering action accepted by the State in question under threat of force by another power and involving the abandonment by it of its independence or neutrality."[64] Molotov rejected this definition, offering a new one of his own: "Action accepted by any of the above-mentioned States under threat of force by another Power, or without any

61. M. Wolf, "The European Situation," *Nineteenth Century,* CXXV (June, 1939), 646, 648.

62. Kennedy to the Secretary of State, London, June 29, 1939. *U.S. For. Rel.,* I, 276.

63. Seeds to Halifax, Moscow, July 1, 4, 1939. *B. D.,* VI, 230–31, 249–50, 251.

64. Halifax to Seeds, F.O., July 6, 1939. *Ibid.,* VI, 277.

such threat, involving the use of territory and forces of the State in question for purposes of aggression . . . and consequently the loss of, by that State, its independence or violation of its neutrality." He further declared that the agreement would include Holland and Switzerland only "if, and when, Poland and Turkey conclude pacts of mutual assistance with the Soviet Union."[65]

Again the British objected, maintaining that such a formula would "undermine our whole moral position in Europe." On July 17 they re-submitted their formula of July 8; Molotov again rejected it. The British then proposed a new draft protocol omitting Holland and Switzerland and providing for consultation only "in the event of aggression by a European Power against a European State not named in the foregoing list." Without rejecting this proposal, Molotov raised a new point: his Government would also insist upon a military agreement, without which "the political part would have no existence."[66]

By this time the negotiations had begun to drag to such an extent that even some sections of the press began to lose heart. The *Manchester Guardian* declared on July 13: "It is coming to be realised here that Russian procrastination is methodical." *The Times* (July 19) observed that after twelve weeks the negotiations had become "a dispiriting theme, lacking now even the joy of the chase."

Yet the spirit of hope and urgency had not disappeared. The *Daily Herald* (July 6), the *Manchester Guardian* (July 6), and the Cardiff *Western Mail* (July 8) concurred in the view that Britain and Russia should sign the mutual assistance pact upon which they were in apparent agreement; then, with the development of greater trust and confidence, negotiations on "wider matters" could proceed from there. "No more delay!" demanded the *Sunday Pictorial* (July 9). "What about that pact?" asked the

65. Seeds to Halifax, Moscow, July 10, 1939. *Ibid.*, VI, 310–11.

66. Halifax to Seeds, F.O., July 12, 1939; Seeds to Halifax, Moscow, July 18, 1939. *Ibid.*, VI, 333, 375–76. Halifax had earlier suggested that it might be proposed to Russia that if she would accept the British definition of aggression, Britain would agree to the simultaneous signature of political and military agreements. But upon the objection of the French, this compromise formula had been momentarily abandoned. Halifax to Seeds, F.O., July 11, 12, 1939. *Ibid.*, VI, 319–20, 337.

News Chronicle (July 29); it still must be pursued "boldly and resolutely" until "signed, sealed, and delivered." "The sands are running out," warned the *Leeds Weekly Citizen* (July 28) in an editorial entitled "To Be Or . . .?" For the *Statist* (July 8), the adhesion of Russia was still the primary need of the peace bloc; for the *National Review* (July), Russia was as indispensable to Britain in 1939 as she had been in 1914. A Russian alliance was essential to convince the world that Britain was willing and able to resist further aggression, echoed the *New Statesman and Nation* (July 1) and the *Economist* (July 8).

Throughout the month of July intensive questioning of the Government on the Russian negotiations—including the advisability of sending a Cabinet minister to Moscow—continued in the House of Commons, the Prime Minister usually replying with "I do not know"; "that does not depend on me"; or "I am not in a position to say more." On July 12 Noel-Baker, intensely annoyed by Chamberlain's evasive answers, asked whether, in view of three and one-half months of fruitless negotiation and Russia's early willingness to come to some agreement, the Government would consider publishing all the proposals which had been put forward on both sides "in order that public opinion might assist towards a solution . . . upon which the peace of the world probably depends." To this earnest inquiry, the Prime Minister gave the irritatingly simple reply: "No, Sir."[67]

The continued pressure on the Government to hasten the conclusion of the Russian negotiations was acknowledged by Strang in a July 20 letter to Sir Orme Sargent of the Foreign Office. "We are being urged by our press and by our public to conclude an agreement quickly," he wrote, "and the Russians have good reason to assume that we shall not dare to face a final breakdown of the negotiations." This made it certain that if Britain wanted an agreement, "we shall have to pay their price or something very near to it." A treaty of mutual assistance appeared to Strang as the best solution for "giving satisfaction to our public" and for deterring a possible aggressor. Looking backward, he suggested: "We should have perhaps been wiser to pay the Soviet price . . . at an earlier stage, since we are not in a good position

67. *Parl. Debs., HC,* July 12, 1939, vol. 349, 2212–13.

to bargain, and since, as the international situation deteriorates, the Soviet price is likely to rise."[68]

By mid-July a demand of considerable proportions had developed in Britain for the inclusion of Churchill in the Cabinet. Since he was among the foremost advocates of a binding alliance with Russia, it is not unreasonable to suppose that this demand was in part an expression of the continuing desire for the completion of the Russian negotiations. The "We Want Churchill" campaign was by no means new. It had found intermittent expression in the press ever since Munich. By mid-1939 it had reached new heights. Many newspapers reflected this surge of opinion. The *News Chronicle* (July 10) observed that the British public was "virtually unanimous" in desiring Churchill's presence in the Cabinet, while the *Observer* (July 16) held that his exclusion was "repugnant to the average man's notions of national common sense." The *Leeds Weekly Citizen* (July 14) indicted Chamberlain, whose Cabinet was a "collection of duds," for being "stupidly bent" on keeping the best brains, even of his own party, out of the Government. The *Daily Telegraph* (July 3), which had earlier found Churchill's judgment on foreign policy wanting, now extolled his "unrivalled practical knowledge," his "vision, energy, and popular appeal," and the *Manchester Guardian* (July 21) declared that Chamberlain's acceptance of Churchill's services would be "proof that he is determined to carry his policy to success." Even the *Daily Mail* (July 5) believed that Churchill's "drive and ability" would be "an asset to the country."

Nor was the Churchill campaign limited to the press. Posters appeared in London demanding "Churchill Must Come Back," and placards bearing similar slogans were carried up and down before the House of Commons.[69] But Chamberlain was utterly unwilling to entertain such a notion, and in his stubborn refusal, Sir Samuel Hoare sees "a fault of his qualities." He resented outside pressure; therefore the more the press clamored, the less

68. Strang to Sargent, Moscow, July 20, 1939. *B. D.*, VI, 422–26.
69. Churchill, *The Gathering Storm,* p. 358. Churchill declares that he was surprised by this and had nothing to do with it, though he would have joined the Government had he been invited.

likely Chamberlain was to listen. Still "sure of himself and his program"—whatever at this point that may have been—"he was . . . opposed to changes that might spoil his carefully laid plans."[70]

In addition to the implications of the Churchill campaign, the course of events in Danzig, where tension grew daily, added weight to the necessity for concluding the Russian agreement at the earliest possible moment. During July the Germans proceeded to remilitarize the city, alleging that it was a purely defensive measure in anticipation of a Polish attack. This explanation fooled no one, least of all the Poles, who were also aware that arms were being smuggled into the city. For its own protection, the Polish Government reinforced its customs inspectors with a number of frontier guards. By way of reprisal, it also took certain economic measures of a nature prejudicial to the trade of Danzig. Thus the ingredients for a formidable explosion were gathering.[71]

Referring to this situation in the Commons on July 10 (in a speech drafted in part by Halifax[72]), Chamberlain recognized that recent events in Danzig had inevitably given rise to fears that Germany intended to settle the city's future status by "unilateral action, organised by surreptitious methods, thus presenting Poland and other Powers with a *fait accompli.*" If that occurred the issue could not be considered a purely local matter, but would raise graver issues affecting Polish national existence and independence. Britain had guaranteed assistance to Poland in the case of a clear threat to her independence, and she was "firmly resolved to carry out this undertaking."[73]

70. Templewood, *Nine Troubled Years,* p. 387.

71. Henderson, *Failure of a Mission,* pp. 251–52; Shepard to Halifax, Danzig, July 19, 1939. *B. D.,* VI, 391–94.

72. Campbell-Johnson quotes Halifax as declaring a month later that he had a hand in drafting this speech for Chamberlain. This meant, apparently, that Sir Horace Wilson no longer enjoyed a virtual monopoly over the drafting of Chamberlain's speeches and letters to Hitler; instead, the Prime Minister had been restored to his official advisers. *Viscount Halifax,* p. 536.

73. *Parl. Debs., HC,* July 10, 1939, vol. 349, 1788. Henderson reminded the German Government on several occasions that Britain would assist Poland should she feel compelled to resist German unilateral action in

Chamberlain's statement was heartily greeted by the press, which had constantly held that Britain's word was pledged and that if German threats to Danzig affected Polish independence, the British must stand by their word. The Bradford *Yorkshire Observer* (July 11) complimented the Prime Minister on his "firm resolve" to back the Poles, and the *Glasgow Herald* (July 11) welcomed Britain's "readiness to honor her pledge." So did the *Financial News* (July 11), which urged that Chamberlain quickly define the point at which the German military infiltration would become a threat to Poland. In the *Daily Herald's* (July 11) view, "if Poland is at war, Britain is at war." It was for something far bigger than Danzig that British pledges had been given and would, if the challenge came, be honored, it had earlier declared (July 4). All that the Government need do now was to "stand four square by its public statements," asserted the *News Chronicle* (July 11), which later (July 19) warned that "the British Government has pledged itself to the utmost, and will be held to that by the unwavering resolve of the British people." The *Spectator* (July 14) rejoiced that "Mr. Chamberlain has realised that a halt must be called." Perhaps the Cardiff *Western Mail* (July 11) best expressed the prevailing sentiment: German agitation in Danzig was only a pretext for the destruction of Poland. "We shall be forced . . . to arrest this madness sooner or later, and, having tried all methods of appeasement in vain, we had better arrest it now before we lose our allies and are weakened by further humiliating concessions to a ravenous and insatiable Power."

It was this state of public feeling in Britain to which Dirksen referred in a dispatch to Berlin on July 10:

> It may be stated that hostility toward Germany is growing, that the readiness to fight has become more pronounced, that there has been a stiffening in the feeling: We must not tolerate any more nonsense, our honour is at stake; we must fight; the Government must stand pat. . . . This

---

Danzig. He impressed that upon Weizsäcker on July 14. Henderson to Halifax, Berlin, July 15, 1939. *B. D.*, VI, 363.

> attitude of the British public . . . must be taken as a serious reality, especially in a country like Britain, where public opinion plays so decisive a role.[74]

It was this state of public feeling to which Nevile Henderson referred when he told Bonnet that Chamberlain would not be able to do "now" what he had done "last September": the movement of opinion in Britain against the dictators, and against Hitler in particular, was so violent that if the Prime Minister should go to Germany, he would be swept away immediately by Parliament.[75] The British Government was, in effect, a prisoner of its own public opinion. It could not escape from the commitment to Poland even had it wished to do so.

Within the Government, it was generally recognized that to retreat from the guarantee would merely land Britain back in the difficulties from which she originally sought to extricate herself. Chamberlain did not, apparently, harbor any notion of trying again what he had done the previous September. He wrote his sister in mid-July that a solution to the Danzig question along the lines of Munich was "not good enough." In fact, he doubted "if any solution, short of war, is practicable at present." Yet he still believed that "if dictators would have a modicum of patience . . . a way could be found of meeting German claims while safeguarding Poland's independence and economic security."[76] And events in London during the third week of July

74. Report of German Ambassador in London Dirksen to the German Foreign Office, London, July 10, 1939. *Dirksen Papers,* p. 65. In his later survey of his ambassadorship in London, Dirksen noted three strata of public sentiment in Britain in July, 1939: a numerically small, but politically influential group which was anxious for an adjustment with Germany; a broader stratum of determined anti-Germans composed of the Churchill-Eden-Cooper circle and the newspaper group around the *Daily Chronicle* and the *Manchester Guardian;* and the general public, who felt no hatred toward Germany but were tired of the "eternal interruptions of peaceful development" for which they held Germany responsible. Their sentiments could best be expressed in the words: "If there is to be a fight, let us have it now." *Ibid.,* p. 180.

75. Bonnet, *Défense de la Paix,* II, 254–56. For still further evidence of the state of opinion in Britain in July, 1939, see Eduard Benes, *Memoirs of Dr. Eduard Benes* (Boston, 1953), pp. 81–84.

76. Feiling, *Life of Neville Chamberlain,* p. 407.

indicated that he had not abandoned all hope of reaching a peaceful agreement with Germany.[77]

Helmut Wohltat, a leading official of Göring's economic staff, visited London as a delegate to an International Whaling Conference. He was approached almost at once by Sir Horace Wilson, who discussed with him a program for Anglo-German cooperation which embraced a non-aggression pact embodying the renunciation of aggression in principle, a limitation of armaments, and economic arrangements. Colonial questions were also considered, and Wilson spoke of a project for the formation of an extensive international African colonial zone.[78] That Chamberlain approved the plans Wilson presented, and perhaps had even worked them out himself, is suggested by Wilson's proposal that Wohltat meet the Prime Minister "then and there" for an endorsement of the program. (Wohltat declined, perhaps feeling uncertain as to how his intrusion into high politics would be viewed in Berlin.) The general objective of Wilson's proposals was a broad Anglo-German agreement on all major questions. In that way issues of such great importance would be raised and settled that the deadlocked eastern European questions, such as Danzig and Poland, would be pushed into the background. The conclusion of a non-aggression pact would ease Britain's commitments to Poland and, as a result, the Polish problem would lose much of its acuteness.[79]

Wohltat also met with R. S. Hudson, the British Minister for Overseas Trade, who developed far-reaching plans for Anglo-German cooperation in world markets. Hudson spoke in detail of

77. The "double line of British policy towards Germany" consciously pursued by the Government in the summer of 1939 is fully developed in Toynbee, *The Eve of War, 1939,* pp. 204–24.

78. Amery writes that Chamberlain seems almost to the end to have thought that Hitler's demands against Poland might be bought off by concessions in Africa. *My Political Life,* III, 250.

79. See Record of conversation between Sir H. Wilson and Dr. Wohltat on July 18, 1939. *B. D.,* VI, 389–91; Memorandum by an Official on the Staff of the Four Year Plan, Berlin, July 24, 1939. *G. D.,* VI, 977–83; Memorandum of German Ambassador in London Dirksen regarding Wohltat's Conversations with Wilson and Hudson, July 21, 1939. *Dirksen Papers,* pp. 67–72; Dirksen, *Moscow, Tokyo, London,* pp. 224–25; Hesse, *Das Spiel um Deutschland,* pp. 168–71. For a secondary account based on the pertinent documents, see Toynbee, *The Eve of War, 1939,* pp. 215–17.

a delimitation of German and British spheres of interest and the avoidance of deadly competition in common markets, and mentioned the possibility of a British loan to Germany.[80]

Word of the Hudson-Wohltat meeting leaked to the press,[81] and the *Daily Express* (July 24) printed a report of an interview with Hudson in which he had outlined the proposals discussed with Wohltat. The *Daily Mail* (July 24), representing the more excited portion of the press, at once proclaimed that Chamberlain should lose no time in dissociating the Government in "the most precise terms" from any connection with the supposed offer of a loan to Germany. Britain would never be in favor of buying peace from Germany, it declared (July 25); "the Danegeld policy has been tried once," and "its discreditable memory has lasted nearly a thousand years. Britain has no desire to return to that chapter in her history."

Other newspapers deplored the incident, but discussed it with moderation. Although the *Daily Herald* (July 24) carried a bold headline about the conversation, its editorial comment was restricted to the sentiment that Chamberlain must ensure that the Foreign Office "shall not again be embarrassed . . . by the private and personal conversations of junior Ministers." The *News Chronicle* (July 25) felt that Hudson's action was a "grave disservice to peace" for it would lead Germany to believe that Britain was weakening. "A little like Munich appeasement again," said the *Liverpool Daily Post* (July 25). Anything which would give the British and German people the idea that Britain was prepared to buy Hitler's good will would be "most unfortunate." Germany must be made to appreciate the singleness of Britain's purpose;

80. See Record of a conversation between Mr. R. S. Hudson and Dr. Wohltat, July 20, 1939. *B. D.*, VI, 407–10; Memorandum by an Official on the Staff of the Four Year Plan, Berlin, July 24, 1939. *G. D.*, VI, 977–83; Memorandum of German Ambassador in London Dirksen regarding Wohltat's Conversations with Wilson and Hudson, July 21, 1939. *Dirksen Papers,* pp. 67–68; Dirksen, *Moscow, Tokyo, London,* p. 225; Hesse, *Das Spiel um Deutschland,* pp. 169–70. For a secondary account based on the pertinent documents, see Toynbee, *The Eve of War, 1939,* pp. 217–18.

81. Exactly how is not certain, but according to a statement by Dirksen to Sir Orme Sargent, the leakage did not come from Wohltat or the German Embassy.

therefore, individual or unofficial approaches which might be misconstrued should be carefully avoided. The *Glasgow Herald* (July 25) agreed that Hudson's action was "politically improper." The very formulation of a "peace plan" by a member of the British Government was liable to be interpreted in Germany and elsewhere as indicating a duality of purpose in British policy not in accord with ministerial pronouncements and actions over the last few months.

The Cardiff *Western Mail* (July 25) warned that the Foreign Secretary was the minister to undertake conversations on "larger issues." In view of the acute complexity of Anglo-German relations, Hudson's conversation with Wohltat "ranged over too wide a field in the absence of a reliable guarantee of its strict privacy." The Bradford *Yorkshire Observer* (July 25) saw nothing in the incident to warrant fear that the Government was going back on its March declaration of policy. Doubt about the wisdom of the talk sprang from the fact that Germany had given no encouragement for the adoption of a conciliatory attitude towards her, but there was no harm in throwing out "unofficial feelers," provided that the importance of doing nothing that could be misconstrued by those who now saw "eye-to-eye" with Britain was clearly recognized. The *Manchester Guardian* (July 25) actually came to Hudson's defense, declaring that neither he nor anyone else in the Government was proposing a loan to Germany; "but this sort of talk always gets out." In the future, if any minister contemplated such talks, it would be wise to confer with the Foreign Secretary first, then speak less informally and less privately. That would at least decrease the danger of misunderstanding.

The press' relative composure in the face of this revelation of an approach to Germany is probably due to a number of factors. When the news "broke," Hudson immediately explained that he had spoken to Wohltat only as President of the Board of Overseas Trade, not as a representative of the Government, had discussed only the kind of economic and financial cooperation with Germany which might be possible once political difficulties were solved, and had not made any loan proposal to Germany. This seemed to relieve the tension. Had the Wilson-Wohltat conversations been known publicly, the excitement engendered surely would have been much more intense. But they remained unknown.[82] It is also possible that there was a growing sense of responsibility in the press because of the grave international situation, and a feeling that affairs in Europe had reached such a pass that any attempt to alleviate the strain was better greeted with reasoned scrutiny than with noisy expressions of distrust. Had not the Government repeatedly declared in recent weeks its intention to stand firm against the dictators? Perhaps most important was the fact that the news of the conversation leaked out over a weekend, and before the press could become too aroused, Chamberlain denied in the House of Commons (early Monday afternoon, July 24) the possibility of a loan to Germany and declared that as far as he knew Wohltat's mission had not extended beyond questions arising out of the Whaling Conference and European refugee problems.

Chamberlain told the Commons that Wohltat, in the course of other visits to Britain in recent years, had met with a number of officials concerned with trade and economic questions as part of his normal duties. Thus it was "in no sense unusual" that he and Hudson should meet to discuss subjects in which they were mutually interested and for which they were responsible in their official capacities. In reply to a question from Greenwood, Chamberlain said that the Cabinet knew nothing about the conversation, nor did any minister except Hudson. It was not the intention of the Government to initiate any discussions in order to buy peace.[83] Chamberlain was technically correct in explaining that Wohltat's mission did not extend beyond questions arising out of the Whaling Conference and refugee problems, but his statements —and what he left unsaid—in view of the Wilson-Wohltat conversations, illustrate the art of dissembling at its best.

Nothing came of the Wohltat visit to London. Germany did

82. Dirksen reported to Weizsäcker that the publicity given the Hudson-Wohltat meeting was "perhaps quite a good thing since, as a result, the really serious and significant part of his [Wohltat's] talks here—namely his two conversations with Sir Horace Wilson—has to some extent been kept in the dark; therefore the possibility of continuing them remains." Ambassador Dirksen to State Secretary Weizsäcker, London, July 25, 1939. *G. D.*, VI, 1001.

83. *Parl. Debs., HC,* July 24, 1939, vol. 350, 1026–27.

not pursue the contact further.[84] But the incident is significant as evidence that the new British policy adopted after Prague did not rule out entirely the hope of reconciliation with Germany. Previously, the British Government had pursued appeasement publicly while occasionally warning Hitler in private; after March, 1939, it warned him publicly and clung to a faint hope for appeasement in private.

Meanwhile, in Moscow, the Anglo-Russian negotiations continued. Although the British preferred to settle the outstanding political points before agreeing to military talks, Molotov rejected further political discussions without military conversations as "a needless waste of time." In a sudden reversal of position—perhaps inspired by some knowledge of the events in London or calculated to stimulate a further German offer to Russia—the Soviet Foreign Minister foresaw no "insuperable difficulties," so the political questions could be settled during the military conversations. Consequently, the British, who had already decided to pursue military talks if a breakdown in the political conversations seemed imminent, agreed on July 27 to undertake immediate military conversations.[85]

After months of intense questioning in Parliament, Chamberlain was finally able to make a definite statement with regard to the Russian negotiations on July 31, announcing that military talks would begin in Moscow "as soon as possible." The debate which followed served as a sounding board for reaction to the new development in the Russian negotiations, the German threat to Danzig, and the Hudson-Wohltat conversation. Sinclair feared that Chamberlain was still inclined toward appeasement and called for a clear, firm, and spirited declaration by the Prime

84. Wohltat reported his conversations with Wilson via Göring to Ribbentrop, and Dirksen submitted additional reports to the German Foreign Office. But before going on leave in mid-August, Dirksen had received no indication of how Wohltat's reports, or his own, were viewed in Berlin. In fact, Dirksen claims that he applied for leave because it was clear to him that only a personal explanation in Berlin would give weight to his reports. *Moscow, Tokyo, London,* p. 228.

85. Seeds to Halifax, Moscow, July 24, 1939; Halifax to Seeds, F.O., July 21, 1939; Seeds to Halifax, Moscow, July 28, 1939. *B. D.,* VI, 456–60, 427–29, 521.

Minister of his intention to resist aggression. At what point did Britain intend to resist aggression in Danzig? Arms had been pouring into the city from East Prussia for weeks, and unless Germany was told at what point Britain would take action, she would not stop until Danzig was absorbed. Britain also stood in urgent need of reassurance about the negotiations with Russia; a man of "the highest political standing" should be sent to Moscow. Dalton blasted the Government's "diplomatic dawdling" and "gross procrastination" in the Russian talks. He felt that Halifax should go to Moscow; in fact, it would do no harm if Chamberlain himself were to exchange views with Stalin. Any kind of talks with Germany were quite out of place until a real peace front had been established. Indeed, before Britain even considered conversations with Germany there should be an end to the arms race and a complete German evacuation of Prague.[86]

Chamberlain replied that the Government's willingness to send a military mission to Russia before the conclusion of the political conversations already constituted a move without precedent in such negotiations. Britain held back because she did not want to encroach upon the independence of other states. Anyway, there was no reason for undue concern about Danzig. This failed to satisfy Liberal P. L. Horabin, who observed in the Government "an infirmity of purpose" and asked it to ponder the words of Cromwell used in that House: "I beseech you, by the bowels of Christ, to believe that you may sometimes be a little wrong." Britain should make it clear to the Nazis that it was her settled policy to encircle Germany, not to impair the national existence of the German people, not to carry out offensive action, but in order to protect the rest of the world from the horrors of Nazi rule. Further, Britain should not contemplate negotiations with Germany until she had returned to the frontiers agreed upon at Munich.

Concentrating on the Russian problem, Eden regretted that

86. Significantly, Dalton, like Sinclair, separated Halifax from the rest of the Government. Halifax's colleagues had "kept him in chains," he declared. It was "quite beside the point" to ask whether Labor had confidence in the Foreign Secretary, but in the rest of the Government, Labor could express no reliance.

the Government had not made up its mind two months earlier to send "the most authoritative mission to Moscow," including some official who could negotiate directly with Molotov. But as for the present—why not send a political mission along with the military mission and attempt to finish the whole thing in one week? A direct approach was more likely to produce results than any other method; since Germany appeared to be using the same technique in Danzig that she had employed in Czechoslovakia, the rapid conclusion of an agreement with Russia was all the more essential. Haden Guest, Wedgwood, and Gallacher spoke to the same effect, the former urging "the addition to the military mission of a number of representatives of all parties in this House" with a view to gaining "a greater understanding of the peoples of the Soviet Union in order to bring the negotiations . . . to a successful conclusion." Wedgwood suggested sending part of the British fleet to the Baltic as a sign of British determination and good will, while Gallacher flatly denied the genuineness of Chamberlain's desire for a pact with Russia since he had neither sent a Cabinet minister to Moscow nor invited Molotov to London. Gallacher was also disturbed by Chamberlain's comment that the Polish Government was showing "admirable restraint." Why should Poland show admirable restraint he asked. "Why is it that it is always those who are being attacked who have to show admirable restraint and that we allow the aggressors to go on from one stage to another?" In his view, it was about time for Britain to encourage Poland to adopt a different attitude toward the aggression in Danzig.

From the Labor bench, F. J. Bellenger opposed any talk of a conference with Germany and urged that the Prime Minister simply stick to his recent declarations; "although hon. Members may think some of us require a lot of convincing, we cannot forget past events, and it will be a long time before they can be eradicated from our minds." Conservative A. C. Crossley joined in Bellenger's sentiment, proposing that Britain's motto should be: "Not an inch further, and no discussion with the German Government except on our own terms." Waxing poetic, he concluded with a few lines which he felt "absolutely apt." After recalling the "years of appeasement," he continued:

Those years are gone. Now England stops to think,
Fear of this war has brought us to its brink.
The climax comes. The silly speeches cease.
Within a month we shall have war or peace.
Let Hitler choose. But ours it is to show
Not one yard further shall this tyrant go.
That way lies peace, perhaps. The other way
Lies shame, disintegration and decay.[87]

Colonel Wedgwood found Crossley's performance "most remarkable." Referring to him as "one of the worst of the appeasers," he now welcomed him as "a Daniel come to judgment."[88]

There was no motion on the floor during this debate. The entire international situation was under general discussion, and the conclusions toward which the discussion tended were quite distinct: the Russian negotiations should be pressed forward speedily; Britain must stand firmly behind Poland in the event of German aggression in Danzig; there must be no thought of conversations with Germany, at least until the peace front (agreement with Russia) was firmly established.

The British press generally was pleased with Chamberlain's announcement of the military mission to Moscow, but the wearisome and abortive course of the political conversations had dulled some of the earlier enthusiasm. The *Manchester Guardian* (Aug. 1) expressed what seemed to be the general feeling, hoping that the dispatch of the mission would soften whatever political difficulties remained. The British Government was not entirely to blame for the long delays, but any further delay on its part which could be avoided would be inexcusable. There was surprisingly little comment in the press on the composition of the mission. Although it did not include any of the Chiefs of Staff,[89] no dissatisfaction was evident. The *Liverpool Daily Post* (Aug. 1) did suggest, however, that a "prominent member of the Gov-

87. *Parl. Debs., HC,* July 31, 1939, vol. 350, 2062–63.
88. *Ibid.,* July 31, 1939, vol. 350, 1993–2100.
89. It was deemed advisable for them to remain in Britain because of the international situation. Templewood, *Nine Troubled Years,* p. 358. The mission was headed by Admiral Sir Reginald Plunkett Ernle-Erle-Drax.

ernment" should accompany the mission "to make the occasion all the more impressive."

On August 2 the House of Commons engaged in heated debate on the question of summer adjournment. The Opposition frankly distrusted the Government and feared that if the House adjourned until October 3, as Chamberlain proposed, it might return to appeasement. Greenwood, therefore, moved adjournment until August 21. Some members were especially anxious about the Russian negotiations. "What guarantee have we," asked Greenwood, "that when our backs are turned the Government will not throw in their hands on this question of a triple alliance?" These negotiations are so important, Sinclair asserted, that "I do not think we ought to rise before they are completed." Tinker, Gallacher, and Sexton joined in expressing concern with the way the Government, as Sexton put it, "has dawdled and diddled along the road to a peace bloc with Russia." Some dissident Conservatives (including Churchill, Law, Crossley and others) also spoke for Greenwood's motion. The dictators had always struck when the House was adjourned, Churchill observed. Therefore, it should continue to sit at short intervals as an indication of the resolution and strength of the British Government. Just before Chamberlain rose, Amery implored him to give a lead in expressing the sense of national unity which animated all sections of the House. But the Prime Minister saw the Opposition's motion only as "another form of the usual vote of no-confidence," and announced: "I confidently expect my right hon. Friends to defeat it." And defeat it they did, by a vote of 132 to 250.[90]

Again, however, the cold statistics of the vote tell only an incomplete story. "I could feel the dismay on all sides of the House at [Chamberlain's] complete misjudgment of the atmosphere," Amery records in his memoirs.[91] The "general feeling," according to Amery, was then conveyed by Geoffrey Mander (Liberal), who said that the Prime Minister had missed one of the greatest opportunities of his career, and by young Ronald Cartland (Conservative), who passionately deplored Chamber-

90. *Parl. Debs., HC,* August 2, 1939, vol. 350, 2425–522.
91. *My Political Life,* III, 317.

lain's failure to ask for confidence as leader of the country and not merely of his party. Cartland's regret was echoed by others, but the issue was decided and the Commons broke up in a dissatisfied and unhappy mood. Chamberlain could still command the support of a disturbingly sullen and "well-behaved" majority when the need arose, but he could inspire little confidence among his more alert and perceptive colleagues in the Parliament.

While Chamberlain argued with the Commons over adjournment, Halifax addressed the Lords with notable calm and resolution. Expressing the hope that the military mission would afford the "best evidence of the bona fides and determination" of the British Government and facilitate a quick and successful conclusion of the Russian negotiations, he concluded:

> There can, I think, be no mistake now as to where the country stands. We have taken our own precautions, and we have done everything, by organising the forces of peace, to strengthen the deterrents of war. It only remains for us . . . to keep calm and, as far as we may, to keep united, to avoid exaggerated attention to rumour and to be neither over-confident nor over-pessimistic. For I suggest that a united nation which both knows exactly where it stands and knows itself to be strong can meet the future, whatever it may hold, with confidence.[92]

As Members of Parliament went their various ways, all eyes turned toward Russia, where the last act in the Anglo-Russian tragi-comedy was about to be staged.

92. *Parl. Debs., HL,* August 3, 1939, vol. 114, 864–65.

CHAPTER TEN

The Descent to War

THE BRITISH AND FRENCH military missions journeyed to Russia by sea,[1] arriving there on August 11, 1939, more than two weeks after military conversations had been agreed upon. They received a favorable welcome and the talks began auspiciously. As a result, Admiral Drax, leader of the British mission, requested permission to depart from his original instructions to "go very slowly" and to discuss British plans more openly.[2] The French mission had already received such authority, and there was a danger that the Russians might become suspicious of British motives—as indeed they already were.[3]

The British delegation was immediately put in an awkward position when Admiral Drax had to confess that he had no written credentials (he received them, eventually, on August 21) and was empowered only to negotiate, not to sign a military conven-

1. They traveled via the Baltic Sea on the British liner *Exeter,* said to have been capable of a speed of only thirteen knots. Many reasons have been put forward for going by sea, among them the idea that Russia was in no great hurry, the need of the two missions to compare notes before arriving in Moscow, and reluctance to fly officers on active duty across Germany by military airplanes in peacetime. See Toynbee, *The Eve of War, 1939,* p. 480; Templewood, *Nine Troubled Years,* p. 358.

2. The British mission had been instructed to "go very slowly" and "treat the Russians with reserve" until the political agreement was concluded, the decision as to how far British intentions and views should be disclosed to depend upon the general attitude of the Russian negotiators. Of the nineteen points of "general policy" included in the mission's instructions, eleven specified subjects which should not be discussed with the Russians or information which should not be given them. Instructions to the British Military Mission to Moscow, August, 1939. *B. D.,* VI, 762–64.

3. Notes by Mr. Roberts on Anglo-Franco-Soviet Military Conversations; Seeds to Halifax, Moscow, Aug. 13, 1939. *Ibid.,* VII, 558; VI, 682.

tion.[4] On August 14, the third day of the conversations, the Russians asked whether, in the event of German aggression, they could move Soviet troops across Poland and Rumania. Here was the crucial question. The British were unable to answer because according to their instructions the Soviet Government should pursue that matter directly with Warsaw and Bucharest. But Russia insisted upon a definite reply before proceeding further.[5] The talks were adjourned, never to be resumed except to reach agreement on indefinite adjournment.

Britain reluctantly, and France more eagerly, pressed in Warsaw for agreement to the passage of Soviet troops,[6] but the Poles refused, suspicious of Russian intentions, fearful lest the Soviets were "attempting today to reach in a peaceful manner" what they had "attempted to obtain by force of arms in 1920."[7] No inquiry was made of Rumania.

Meanwhile, no progress had been made in the political conversations. On August 17 Halifax submitted to Seeds four alternative proposals for dealing with indirect aggression.[8] But they were withheld pending the resumption of the military talks and consequently never reached Molotov.

Events had far outrun the course of the Anglo-Russian conversations. On August 23 the Russians revealed to the world their astounding nonaggression pact with Germany—an eventuality which the British had not completely ignored but apparently had never taken seriously.[9] The British and French missions

4. Minutes of the First Meeting of the Anglo-Franco-Soviet Military Delegations, Aug. 12, 1939. *Ibid.*, VII, 563.

5. Minutes of the Fourth Meeting of Anglo-Franco-Soviet Military Delegations, Aug. 14, 1939. *Ibid.*, VII, 571–75.

6. See *Ibid.*, VII, 69–91. For additional evidence of the pressure put upon the Poles, see Bonnet, *Défense de la Paix,* II, 275–84; Paul Reynaud, *La France a suavé l'Europe* (Paris, 1947), I, 586 ff.; Leon Noël, *L'agression allemande contra la Pologne* (Paris, 1946), pp. 420 ff.

7. Kennard to Halifax, Warsaw, Aug. 20, 1939. *B. D.*, VII, 85–86. The Polish Chief of Staff, Smigly-Rydz, explained: "With the Germans we risk losing our liberty. With the Russians we lose our soul." Kennard to Halifax, Warsaw, Aug. 20, 1939. *Ibid.*, VII, 91; Bonnet, *Défense de la Paix,* II, 284.

8. Halifax to Seeds, F.O., Aug. 17, 1939. *B. D.*, VII, 42–44.

9. Strang testifies: "It was always present to our minds that the Russians might, as an alternative, come to an understanding with the Germans."

lingered in Moscow for several days thereafter, but only to recover from the shock and arrange for the journey home.

Whatever emotions the British experienced following the news of the Nazi-Soviet Pact, recrimination was not among them. Though staggered and perturbed by the contradictions of the past, only the needs of the future claimed attention. The Government issued a communique declaring that the Nazi-Soviet agreement would in no way affect the British obligation to Poland,[10] and Chamberlain addressed a personal letter to Hitler, informing him of certain precautionary measures[11] Britain was undertaking because of military movements which had been reported from Germany and because the Nazi-Soviet Pact apparently was taken in some quarters in Berlin to mean that British intervention on behalf of Poland was a contingency that needed no longer to be reckoned with. "No greater mistake could be made," the Prime Minister warned.

> Whatever may prove to be the nature of the German-Soviet Agreement, it cannot alter Great Britain's obligation to Poland which His Majesty's Government have stated in public repeatedly and plainly, and which they are determined to fulfill.

It has been alleged that if His Majesty's Government had

Home and Abroad, p. 196. The British Government did not have full information about the Nazi-Soviet contacts during the summer of 1939; neither was it totally ignorant of them. See *Ibid.,* pp. 194–96. The Kordt brothers hinted to English friends that Hitler was about to get the better of them in Moscow. Weizsäcker, *Memoirs,* pp. 189–90; Erich Kordt, *Nicht aus den Akten,* pp. 313–19. Even more important, Washington was informed of the entire negotiation, the American Embassy in Moscow having received full reports from members of the staff of Count von der Schulenburg, the German Ambassador in Moscow. Because of the source of information, it was considered inadvisable to impart much of this intelligence to the British, but "broad hints" were occasionally dropped to members of the British Embassy in Washington. Langer and Gleason, *The Challenge to Isolation,* pp. 124–25. And A. J. P. Taylor writes that the British were warned of a possible Nazi-Soviet agreement by Seeds, by Daladier, and even indirectly by Göring. *The Origins of the Second World War,* p. 229.

10. *The Times,* Aug. 23, 1939.

11. These included the assembling of anti-aircraft defenses, the requisitioning of twenty-five merchantmen for conversion to armed merchant cruisers, the calling up of 6,000 reservists for overseas garrisons and 24,000

> made their position more clear in 1914, the great catastrophe would have been avoided. Whether or not there is any force in that allegation, His Majesty's Government are resolved that on this occasion there shall be no such tragic misunderstanding. If the need should arise, they are resolved and prepared to employ without delay all the forces at their command, and it is impossible to foresee the end of hostilities once engaged.[12]

Chamberlain felt that direct German-Polish negotiations, resulting in a settlement that would be guaranteed by other powers, was the only way to avoid plunging Europe into war.

This determination to honor Britain's pledge to Poland rang from all sections of the press. Britain must stand together with France for human dignity and freedom, reasoned the Conservative *Daily Telegraph* (Aug. 23). They had fought side by side twenty-five years before, and "so long as freedom has not perished from the earth, that alliance will instinctively endure." Whatever the terms of the Nazi-Soviet Pact, the Conservative *Daily Mail* (Aug. 23) wrote, Britain's pledge would be "observed to the hilt." "There will be no retreat," proclaimed the Conservative *Financial Times* (Aug. 25) with calm resolve; Britain had pledged herself to Poland in order to end Germany's attempt to submit the Western world to the "jack-booted domination of Berlin." The pro-Government *Times* (Aug. 21) wrote clearly and simply: "This country has given a specific pledge from which it will not and cannot recede."

For the Liberal *Manchester Guardian* (Aug. 23) Britain's position was clear: she had given her pledge to Poland before Russia was even approached, so her position remained unchanged. The Labor *Daily Herald* (Aug. 23) joined in warning that Britain's pledge was not conditional upon Russian support and asserted (Aug. 24) that, although Labor had strongly criticized the Government's record, no one should make the mistake of thinking that this would mean a division in British ranks in

---

air force reservists, and the concellation of all leaves throughout the fighting services. Churchill, *The Gathering Storm,* p. 395.

12. *British War Blue Book,* pp. 125–27.

the event of war. The leaders and members of all parties were determined to stand by Poland. If the Poles elected to fight, the Liberal *News Chronicle* (Aug. 23) declared, Britain and France would fight. The Liberal *Liverpool Daily Post* (Aug. 23) agreed, proclaiming resistance to aggression and the upholding of international justice the supreme task of Britain. The Liberal Bradford *Yorkshire Observer's* view was expressed clearly in the title of its lead editorial on August 23: "Honouring Our Bond."

In standing firmly by Poland, Britain was not defending Danzig or Polish independence, the independent *Glasgow Herald* (Aug. 24) observed; she was meeting a challenge ultimately directed at herself, an attempt at world domination by a barbarous regime. The independent *Sunday Pictorial* (Aug. 27) put it another way: if Britain had to fight, she would be fighting "for the preservation of those principles the destruction of which would involve the destruction of all possibilities of peace and security in the world." Or as the independent *Financial News* (Aug. 23) reasoned, nothing would encourage Hitler more than the suggestion that Britain was prepared to break an engagement rather than stand against him. The radical *New Statesman and Nation* (Aug. 26), the independent *Time and Tide* (Aug. 26), and the independent *Economist* (Aug. 26) all shared the view that Britain must stand firm, the *Economist* again striking the core of the issue: "If war comes, it will not be fought for Danzig or Poland. It will be fought for the right to live in peace, to pursue the ends of human welfare untroubled by the constant necessity to divert resources and attention to the sterile purposes of defence."

In assessing the attitude of the press during the week which followed August 23, there is little need to distinguish among various journals on the grounds of political affiliation or sentiment. There was virtually unanimity on the point that the Nazi-Soviet Pact should in no way alter Britain's commitment to Poland, and wide recognition that what was now at stake was not territorial adjustment but the security of Europe and broader principles of international justice. Even those journals most amenable to the idea of appeasement earlier clearly recognized that appeasement as an ideal and appeasement as a game of give-away which violated all standards of justice and human decency were two vastly different things. There could be no question now as to which of the two concepts was involved. Certain of the Labor and Liberal journals took pains to make it clear that Britain's commitment to Poland was not contingent upon Russia's position—apparently concerned lest the Government take Russia's changed status as an excuse for altering its own. The Conservative and some independent journals put greater emphasis on the need to recognize and defend a principle vital both to European security and human decency. Whatever the primary emphasis, the ultimate conclusion was the same: Britain must stand by Poland, and she must do so not only for the sake of Poland, but because that "something bigger" which Chamberlain had never quite perceived in the Czechoslovak situation was indeed at stake.

When the House of Commons reconvened in special session on August 24, it was at once evident that its feeling toward the international situation was also one of firm resolve. Major-General Sir Edward Spears, a Conservative M. P., records that the members seemed to be on the watch to detect, and resent, any sign of weakness in the Prime Minister's statement.[13] Chamberlain graphically traced the German-Polish dispute up to the Nazi-Soviet Pact and reaffirmed that Britain's obligations remained unaltered. If, despite all her efforts for peace, Britain was forced to embark upon a struggle fraught with untold misery and suffering, he explained, she would be fighting not for the "political future of a far away city in a foreign land," but for the preservation of those principles of justice and freedom for which Britain had always stood.

Speaking for Labor, Greenwood expressed keen disappointment that the peace front had not been strengthened by the addition of Russia, but he did not propose "to rake over the embers of the days that are behind us." Rather, he wished to make clear the position of the Opposition. He read to the House a declaration issued earlier by the National Council of Labor to the effect that the obligations undertaken by Britain in defense of the independence of Poland should be honored in full and concluded:

13. Major-General Sir Edward Spears, *Assignment to Catastrophe* (New York, 1954), I, 13.

> The peril of war comes not from us. No democratic country will make war, but Britain, with others, will defend their own liberties and the liberties of those who are threatened by force, realising that a threat to the liberty of one is a threat to the liberties of all. The aggressor must know that in our view liberty, like peace, is indivisible. That is the lesson that ought to go from this Chamber today to the potential aggressor.[14]

In a moving speech, Sinclair appealed for an impressive demonstration that when Britain's vital interests, the moral values of civilized life, and the peace of the world were menaced by brutal force, the people of Britain would stand firm. If Britain yielded on Danzig, she would be faced with further demands, and she would have to face those demands weakened and discredited by her betrayal of the Poles.

> We should be a nation upon whom our best friends and closest allies would hesitate to rely. With diminishing power and in increasing loneliness, incapable of appealing to the conscience of the world in the name of freedom, law and justice, for which we should have proved ourselves unwilling to make sacrifices, we should have to await the onslaught of the dictatorships on the power and wealth of the British Empire and on the homes and liberties of our people.[15]

Anthony Eden agreed. It took two to make a quarrel; it took two to make a peace, and Britain could look in vain for any sign of reciprocity, however far she had gone to meet German demands. The only result of concession was more unjust and ruthless demands. Having given her pledge, Britain could not turn back, for

> Step by step and stage by stage the subjugation of Poland has been the object, and if that process is continued, if we do not join with others to resist it now, who can doubt that there will be yet another victim next year? While it is fearful to have to contemplate the use of force, I am convinced

14. *Parl. Debs., HC,* August 24, 1939, vol. 351, 13–14.
15. *Ibid.,* August 24, 1939, vol. 351, 14–15.

that the attitude of a large and overwhelming majority of the House endorses that determination as the only means by which at this late hour we may save Poland, and also save our children from what some of us went through in the years gone by.[16]

While a few speakers used this opportunity to criticize Chamberlain's policy toward Russia, most of them agreed that this was no time for recrimination. The mood of the House was unmistakable: Britain must honor her obligation to Poland if the occasion arose; that very act would constitute a defense of international good faith, freedom, and justice. The virtual unanimity of the Commons was perhaps best expressed in the passing of a motion to turn to a consideration of a bill to confer emergency powers upon the Government, 427 to 4.[17]

Despite the pointed statements in the press and Parliament, the clearest reaffirmation of Britain's pledge to Poland appeared on the afternoon of August 25, when Halifax and Raczynski, the Polish Ambassador in London, signed the formal Agreement of Mutual Assistance between the two countries. The first article of that pact stipulated that: "Should one of the Contracting Parties become engaged in hostilities with a European Power in consequence of aggression by the latter . . . the other Contracting Power will at once give . . . all the support and assistance in its power."[18]

One week separated the signing of the Anglo-Polish Pact and Hitler's blitzkrieg against Poland. Those days were filled with fruitless efforts on the part of British diplomacy to avert the

16. *Ibid.*, August 24, 1939, vol. 351, 24.
17. *Ibid.*, August 24, 1939, vol. 351, 59–60.
18. Great Britain. *Agreement between the Government of the United Kingdom and the Polish Government regarding Mutual Assistance, London, August 25, 1939.* Command Paper 6144 (London, 1939). This pact had some effect upon Hitler. After conferring with Ribbentrop and Keitel, the Chief of Staff, he cancelled the orders for "Operation White," the plan of attack on Poland, which had been set to go into effect on August 26. See Wheeler-Bennett, *Munich,* p. 421; Langer and Gleason, *The Challenge to Isolation,* p. 197. It is probable that a letter from Mussolini on the same day, announcing that Italy would not be able to take part in a war at that time, also contributed to Hitler's decision.

imminent calamity. The main lines of that story have been analyzed in detail elsewhere.[19] It remains to show the British attitude during those days of crisis. After the signing of the Nazi-Soviet Pact, British efforts were devoted toward two ends: to induce the Germans and Poles to negotiate, and to leave no shred of doubt in Hitler's mind that in the event of a German attack on Poland, Britain would honor her engagement. This did not necessarily mean that Chamberlain had at last abandoned all hope of reaching an accommodation with Germany.[20] It is highly unlikely, however, that any program other than the one pursued would have been tolerated by the British public, which, as Dirksen reported to Berlin, was tired of being described as weak, unreliable, and degenerate, and was determined to fight rather than to retreat again.[21]

Chamberlain's letter to Hitler evoked an outburst of rage and invective against the Poles, and against the British for backing them, but the Führer promptly gave Sir Nevile Henderson a written reply outlining his position. Germany was prepared at first, he wrote, to settle the questions of Danzig and the Corridor by negotiation on the basis of a proposal of "truly unparalleled magnanimity." But the British guarantee to Poland, among other things, had dispelled the Polish inclination to negotiate; Polish atrocities against the German inhabitants of Poland were intolerable; Poland's numerous breaches of her legal obligations toward the Free City had initiated a process of economic strangulation. Thus the questions of the Corridor and Danzig "must and shall be solved," and if Britain mobilized, Germany would mobilize also.[22]

Then on August 25 there suddenly occurred one of those striking changes which were so formidable a part of Hitler's

19. See Toynbee, *The Eve of War, 1939,* Part VI; also Namier, *Diplomatic Prelude,* Chapter VIII.

20. Lord Ismay testifies that the Prime Minister still clung to such a hope. *Memoirs,* p. 98.

21. Letter from German Ambassador to London Dirksen to Secretary of State in the German Foreign Office Weizsäcker, Gröditzberg, Silesia, Aug. 19, 1939. *Dirksen Papers,* pp. 138–39.

22. Henderson to Halifax, Berlin, Aug. 24, 1939. *B. D.,* VII, 177–79.

temperament. Summoning Henderson to the Chancellery early in the afternoon, he suggested that once the urgent Polish situation were settled, he would be glad to approach Britain with a "large comprehensive offer." He was prepared, so he said, not only to pledge himself personally to the continued existence of the British Empire, but to place the power of Germany at its disposal "in any part of the world where . . . help might be needed"—on the conditions that his colonial claims be met in due course and that his obligations to Italy remain unaltered. But this, he asserted, was his last offer.[23]

What had happened to Sir Horace Wilson's proposals made to Helmuth Wohltat a month earlier? According to Fritz Hesse, who claims to have gotten his information from Ribbentrop and Hewel, the liaison officer between Hitler and Ribbentrop, Hitler was convinced at the time those proposals reached him that Britain would not fight. Wilson's program was looked upon only as a contrivance to keep Hitler from recovering Danzig. The discussions with Russia apparently thrust the British offer into the background, for Hitler felt he could solve the Polish problem with Stalin without considering Wilson's conditions.[24] Dirksen confirms this view. Visiting Weizsäcker in mid-August, he inquired about the effect of his dispatches concerning Wilson's proposals. Weizsäcker shrugged his shoulders and made a movement with his hand as if brushing something off of the table. Wilson's offer simply had been thrown in the wastepaper basket. Ribbentrop, too, was convinced that Britain would not go to war over Poland, and Dirksen's reports, as well as Wohltat's, had been taken only as a further sign of British weakness.[25]

Upon receiving Hitler's proposals, Henderson reminded him that the Russian pact in no way altered Britain's attitude toward Poland. She could not go back on her word, and this German offer would not be considered unless it meant a negotiated settlement of the Polish question. Hitler refused to guarantee that on the ground that Polish provocation might at any moment render German intervention to protect German nationals inevitable. In

23. Henderson to Halifax, Berlin, Aug. 25, 1939. *Ibid.*, VII, 227–29.
24. Hesse, *Das Spiel um Deutschland*, pp. 183–90.
25. Dirksen, *Moscow, Tokyo, London*, pp. 228–29.

his report, Henderson ventured the opinion that, whatever view the Government took of Hitler's offer, he regarded it as an indication that Hitler still wished to avoid world war. He advised that it be treated seriously and proposed that he fly to London the next morning in order to avoid giving the impression in Berlin of any "off-hand rejection."[26]

Britain's reply to Hitler apparently received almost continuous consideration in the Cabinet for two days. During that time Halifax was in communication with Warsaw, where he sought and obtained Colonel Beck's consent to inform Hitler that Poland was ready to enter at once into direct discussion with Germany.[27] Henderson submitted the British reply to Hitler on the evening of August 28. It held that everything turned upon the nature of the settlement with Poland and the method by which it was reached. It also emphasized Britain's determination to carry out her undertaking to Poland and declined to discuss Hitler's grandiose offer of collaboration with the British Empire, stating: "His Majesty's Government could not, for any advantage offered Great Britain, acquiesce in a settlement which would put in jeopardy the independence of a State to whom they have given a guarantee." Britain proposed as the next step the initiation of direct negotiations between Poland and Germany "on a basis which would include . . . the safeguarding of Poland's essential interests and the securing of the settlement by an international guarantee." If such discussion led to agreement, the British note added guardedly, "the way would be open to the negotiation of that wider and more complete understanding between Great Britain and Germany which both countries desire." It concluded with the unequivocal words:

> A just settlement of these questions between Germany and Poland may open the way to world peace. Failure to reach it would ruin the hopes of better understanding between Germany and Great Britain, and would bring the two coun-

26. Henderson to Halifax, Berlin, Aug. 25, 1939. *B. D.*, VII, 229–30, 235. Henderson arrived in London on the morning of August 26. Henderson, *Failure of a Mission*, p. 272.

27. Kennard to Halifax, Warsaw, Aug. 28, 1939. *B. D.*, VII, 328.

tries into conflict, and might well plunge the whole world into war. Such an outcome would be a calamity without parallel in history.[28]

Hitler received the British note with surprising calm, although he was uncompromising in his verbal statements, claiming the entire Corridor and rectifications in Silesia. He promised to give it careful consideration and to reply next day. According to Paul Schmidt, Hitler's interpreter, "he appeared to be interested in some way in the British proposal."[29]

While these official communications passed between Britain and Germany, Hermann Göring was actively engaged in efforts to keep Britain from going to war over Poland. Wishing not to fight Britain but to employ her once more in obtaining concessions for Germany, Göring sent Birger Dahlerus, a Swedish engineer and manufacturer, shuttling back and forth between Berlin and London carrying unofficial messages, the ultimate aim of which was to detach Britain from Poland. Halifax at first tried to redirect these contacts into regular diplomatic channels, but later (August 26) sent a personal message, devoid of concrete contents, to Göring.[30] Dahlerus continued his zealous endeavors, carrying notes from Göring to London with Hitler's

28. Halifax to Ogilvie-Forbes, F.O., Aug. 28, 1939; Henderson to Halifax, Berlin, Aug. 29, 1939. *Ibid.,* VII, 330–32, 348.

29. Henderson to Halifax, Berlin, Aug. 29, 1939. *Ibid.,* VII, 348; Schmidt, *Hitler's Interpreter,* p. 148. It is interesting to note that when Henderson arrived to make his communication to Hitler, no effect was omitted by the Germans which might emphasize the importance of the occasion. Henderson was greeted with a guard of honor in the forecourt of the Chancellery, a roll of drums announced his arrival, and he was greeted on the steps by several German officials. Henderson, *Failure of a Mission,* p. 276. It seemed that every attention was to be paid to Britain's envoy in the hope that the reply he carried would announce Britain's willingness to abandon Poland to her fate.

30. In essence, Halifax wrote that time was necessary for both sides to understand clearly the implications of the messages passing between the two governments. Meanwhile, both sides must work to avoid further inflammation of the already dangerous situation. See Minute by Mr. Roberts, F.O., Aug. 26, 1939. *B. D.,* VII, 283. In his memoirs Halifax mentions an invitation to Göring (issued in response to a "cryptic message" from Germany) to visit Chamberlain secretly in Britain on August 23. But nothing came of this, apparently because Hitler put a stop to it. *Fullness of Days,* pp. 212–13. See also Birkenhead, *Halifax,* p. 444.

knowledge, until the outbreak of the war.[31] The sum total of his story shows Britain determined to stand by her guarantee to Poland, but at the same time tolerating this distasteful form of negotiations lest there be in it a remote chance of preserving peace.

The House of Commons met again on August 29. Chamberlain spoke of Hitler's professed desire for an Anglo-German understanding but explained that, while the Government would welcome an opportunity to discuss issues, everything depended upon the manner in which the immediate German-Polish differences were settled. He then traced the ways in which Britain was preparing for war. Her air defense had been placed in readiness, the Royal Air Force had been brought up to war strength, the coastal defenses were ready and manned, the navy was in an advanced state of preparedness, and civil defense measures were being worked out. "The issue of peace or war is still undecided," he concluded, "and we still will hope, and still will work, for peace; but we will abate no jot of our resolution to hold fast to the line which we have laid down for ourselves."

Major General Spears records that the Prime Minister's speech caused some uneasiness among the "anti-Munichers." Alert to anything savoring of further surrender to Hitler, to any indication that Hitler was to be believed, they were not reassured by Chamberlain's remarks concerning the conversations between Hitler and Henderson.[32] Skepticism was immediately evident in the response of Arthur Greenwood, who reiterated his party's "inflexible determination" to defend liberty and uphold the rule of law and asserted that "Poland will not be allowed to follow to the grave those nations that were martyred by the aggressors." Threats and open aggression must come to an end, and "he who today, whether on those benches opposite or outside in this country, or abroad, would dishonour the pledges which have been given, endorsed, re-endorsed and endorsed again, would be a traitor to the peace and freedom of the world."

31. Dahlerus tells his story in *The Last Attempt* (London, 1947). See also Namier, *Diplomatic Prelude*, pp. 417–33; Halifax, *Fullness of Days*, p. 212.

32. Spears, *Assignment to Catastrophe*, I, 14–15.

On this occasion, however, Sinclair was unusually solemn. He noted the "pleasure" with which the House had listened to Chamberlain's assurance that the Government was standing firm in its obligation to Poland. He also expressed gratitude that the Prime Minister, working within the framework of British determination, was seeking every possibility of a peaceful solution. "In that way Britain finds herself in harmony with world opinion. . . ." Sinclair knew of nothing that the Government had left undone to make it possible for Hitler to speak the word of negotiation and peace. There was but one road barred to the Government: surrender to demands based on no higher sanction than the alleged national will of a single nation backed by the threat of force.[33]

Throughout the last days of August, 1939, the press remained calm and resolute. The *Daily Telegraph* (Aug. 30) pronounced the British people ready for any sacrifice they might be called upon to make. Upon the national determination to keep its pledge there could be no going back; "no government could survive for twenty-four hours the sense of our whole people that its faith had been forsworn." In an editorial "Ready and Steady," the Bradford *Yorkshire Observer* (Aug. 30) expressed Britain's "inflexible determination" to defend liberty. She could no longer afford to pay blackmail for the sake of a temporary truce, proclaimed the *Glasgow Herald* (Aug. 28). The *Daily Mail* (Aug. 29) wrote: "Our course is clear before us; our purpose is plain to ourselves and to the world." The *Manchester Guardian* (Aug. 30) agreed; the world had merely to wait for Hitler to decide the issue of war or peace. If Germany chose war, declared the *Daily Herald* (Aug. 30), Britain was ready. That sentiment was duplicated in the *Liverpool Daily Post* (Aug. 30), the *News Chronicle* (Aug. 31), the non-partisan *Spectator* (Aug. 25), and a number of other journals. It was to this overwhelming unanimity of opinion to which William Duns referred when he wrote in the *Nineteenth Century:*

> If war should break out, we should be fighting . . . for no other purpose than to repel danger; danger to ourselves, to our lives, our security, our property, our national existence,

33. *Parl. Debs., HC,* August 29, 1939, vol. 351, 111–22.

our Empire, and . . . our freedom. All these things are in danger. It is this realisation which has produced the most remarkable example of a united nation in our history.[34]

When Sir Nevile Henderson visited Hitler on the evening of August 29 to receive his reply to the British note, he found a very different atmosphere from that which he had left the night before. Hitler, now cold and uncompromising, held no hope for the success of direct negotiations with Poland; yet he would accept them solely out of a desire to ensure lasting friendship with Britain. A Polish representative with full plenary powers must arrive in Berlin on the next day (August 30). Henderson protested that as tantamount to an ultimatum, but both Hitler and Ribbentrop assured him that it was only intended to stress the urgency of the moment when two fully mobilized armies were standing face to face.[35]

Acting upon instructions from Halifax, Henderson called on Ribbentrop a few hours later (4 a.m., August 30) to tell him that it was unreasonable to expect the British Government to produce a Polish representative in Berlin in twenty-four hours. Indeed, Henderson had made that observation to Hitler earlier and had received the reply that one could fly from Warsaw to Berlin in one and one-half hours.[36]

The British found it difficult to advise Poland to accept the procedure demanded by Germany, and the message which Henderson conveyed to Ribbentrop at midnight, August 30, recommended instead the use of normal diplomatic channels. When the German proposals were ready, the Polish Ambassador should be handed a copy for transmission to Warsaw with a view to the immediate opening of negotiations. Ribbentrop's only reply was to read very rapidly (in German) a list of Germany's demands

34. Williams Duns, "If War Comes," *Nineteenth Century,* CXXVI (September, 1939), 258.

35. Henderson to Halifax, Berlin, Aug. 29, 30, 1939. *B. D.,* VII, 374–75, 388–90; Henderson, *Failure of a Mission,* pp. 277–80. In view of reports of upwards of thirty German divisions moving toward the Polish frontier, Poland took measures on August 24 involving mobilization of two-thirds of the Polish Army. Kennard to Halifax, Warsaw, Aug. 24, 1939. *B. D.,* VII, 189.

36. Henderson to Halifax, Berlin, Aug. 30, 1939. *B. D.,* VII, 400–01.

on Poland. When Henderson asked for a copy of these proposals, which included the return of Danzig to the Reich and the holding of a plebiscite in the Corridor,[37] Ribbentrop declared that it was now too late; the Polish representative had not arrived in Berlin by midnight.[38] Henderson then charged that the German request for a Polish representative on August 30 did indeed constitute an ultimatum, but Ribbentrop dismissed that as a figment of Henderson's imagination. When Henderson asked why, then, the Polish Ambassador was not summoned and handed a copy of the proposals, Ribbentrop raged that he would never ask the Ambassador to visit him. If the Ambassador asked for an interview, that would be different. On that note the two men parted.[39]

Not until the evening of August 31 did Henderson receive the German proposals in writing. Even then he was more fortunate than the Polish Ambassador who, in the course of a visit to Ribbentrop that same evening, received no such document. By the time Henderson received the proposals, however, he had already been informed by Weizsäcker that, since the German Government had waited two days in vain for the arrival of a Polish negotiator, it regarded its proposals as having been "neglected."[40]

At dawn, September 1, 1939, the German Army opened its

37. Other German proposals provided for an extra-territorial German traffic zone to East Prussia in the event of the Corridor going to Poland; a similar Polish zone to the port of Gdynia if the Corridor went to Germany; the demilitarization of Danzig, Gdynia and the Peninsula of Hela; the settlement of minority complaints, including compensation for damage done since 1918, by an international committee of inquiry; a guarantee of "free development and practical application of their nationality" to the minorities remaining in each country; and demobilization on both sides if an agreement was reached on the basis of these proposals. Henderson to Halifax, Berlin, Aug. 31, 1939. *Ibid.,* VII, 459–62.

38. Paul Schmidt, who interpreted at this meeting, records that at the moment Ribbentrop refused to give Henderson a copy of the German proposals, "I understood that Hitler's high-sounding proposals had been produced only for show, and were never intended to be put into effect. The refusal to hand the document over to Henderson was made for fear that the British Government would pass on the proposals to the Poles, who might well have accepted them." *Hitler's Interpreter,* p. 153.

39. Henderson to Halifax, Berlin, Aug. 31, 1939. *B. D.,* VII, 432–33.

40. Henderson to Halifax, Berlin, Aug. 31, Sept. 1, 1939. *Ibid.,* VII, 459–62, 457–58, 468–69.

assault on Poland. A few hours later the mobilization of all British forces—which Hore-Belisha and others had been urging in the Cabinet for a week[41]—was ordered. After a meeting of the full Cabinet that afternoon, Halifax dispatched to Henderson an urgent note warning Germany that the invasion of Poland had "created conditions . . . which call for the implementation by the Governments of the United Kingdom and France of the undertaking to Poland to come to her assistance," and that unless the German Government suspended "all aggressive action against Poland and are prepared promptly to withdraw their forces from Polish territory, His Majesty's Government . . . will without hesitation fulfill their obligations to Poland." The note was to be regarded as a warning, not an ultimatum, but for Henderson's own information Halifax added that if the German reply was unsatisfactory, "the next stage will be either an ultimatum with time limit or an immediate declaration of war."[42]

The House of Commons met at 6 p.m. "The time has come when action rather than speech is required," Chamberlain began. "Eighteen months ago in this House I prayed that the responsibility might not fall upon me to ask this country to accept the awful arbitrament of war. I fear that I may not be able to avoid that responsibility." Those words conveyed a world of shattered illusions. Gone was the faith that he, a simple, direct businessman, had discovered a new approach to diplomacy. Chamberlain told the House that Britain would oppose force by force and read the document which Henderson had handed to the German Government, explaining: "If a reply to this last warning is unfavorable, and I do not suggest that it is likely to be otherwise, His Majesty's Government's Ambassador is instructed to ask for his passports." Although he went on to declare that Britain must enter the struggle with firm determination to see it through to the end, his words concerning "this last warning" left the House puzzled.[43] The plain fact was that by the terms of the agreement with Poland, Britain should by now have come to her aid.

Greenwood at once questioned the "loophole" which the Prime

41. See Minney, *Private Papers of Hore-Belisha,* pp. 217–25.
42. Halifax to Henderson, F.O., Sept. 1, 1939. *Ibid.,* VII, 485–86, 488.
43. See Spears, *Assignment to Catastrophe,* I, 16.

Minister had left open to Hitler. "His communication gives the German Government an opportunity of withdrawal. There can be no withdrawal, and in any event this nation is in honour bound." But Greenwood was careful not to be critical of, or hostile to, the Government. He evidently intended that no words of his should leave Hitler in any doubt that Britain was at one in her undertakings. The same was true of Sinclair, who felt that Chamberlain had spoken for the entire nation and urged "vigorous action" by Britain and her allies to sustain the common cause of freedom.[44]

In the House of Lords, September 1, the feeling that Britain must act was just as definite. Halifax gave a damning indictment of the perjured intrigue of the German leaders and spoke with an air of finality. Of Germany's doings the world would judge, but Britain's conscience was clear, he declared. Lord Snell warned that Britain could not allow the people of Poland to bear the whole brunt of the German assault, and the Archbishop of Canterbury asserted that Britain was contending for a clear and simple moral issue and accepting a challenge which, if it were not met, would be fatal to civilization itself. At the end of his brief, but particularly moving remarks the Archbishop noted:

> In this dark and confused world, it is given to man only to see some clear line of duty and to do his best to follow it. I shrink indeed from linking our broken lights and our fallible purposes with the Holy Name of God, yet I honestly believe that in this struggle, if it is forced upon us, we may humbly and trustfully commend our cause to God.[45]

September 2 was a day of acute suspense, and the tension was reflected in the Commons. The House had been restive the day before in the absence of positive action by the Government, and the uneasiness grew as the hours passed. General Spears records that in his long experience covering many critical moments, he had never seen the Commons so stirred, so profoundly moved, as it was that afternoon. It was dawning upon even the most uncritical Government supporters that Britain's honor was in danger.

44. *Parl. Debs., HC,* September 1, 1939, vol. 351, 130–37.
45. *Parl. Debs., HL,* September 1, 1939, vol. 114, 917–19, 923.

Something else was happening, too. Winston Churchill was obviously advancing to the center of the political scene. The more the Cabinet vacillated, the more eyes turned toward him. Everyone was aware that he saw clearly the path to follow while others were still groping. As the weary afternoon dragged on, members moved from group to group, in the smoking-room, on the terrace, back to the lobbies. All anxiously awaited a statement from the Prime Minister.[46]

At 7:45 p.m. the House assembled to hear Chamberlain. All were keyed up for the announcement that war had been declared, but as the Prime Minister spoke they listened with amazement, then stupefaction, then exasperation. He reported that no reply to the British note of September 1 had yet been received from Germany. The delay might have been caused, he explained, by an Italian proposal that hostilities should cease and that there should be an immediate conference among Britain, France, Poland, Germany, and Italy.[47] Britain could not take part in a conference while Poland was being subjected to invasion, he continued, and if the German forces were not withdrawn from Polish territory, Britain would be bound to take action. The Government was in communication with France as to the limit of time within which it would be necessary for the German Government to consent to such a withdrawal. But if Germany agreed to withdraw her forces, then Britain would be willing to regard the situation as being the same as before the German forces crossed the Polish frontier.

When Chamberlain finished the House was silent. Then there was a kind of ripple. Someone was being betrayed. It was incon-

46. Spears, *Assignment to Catastrophe,* I, 17–19.

47. Ciano had called Halifax at 12:50 p.m., August 31, to suggest a conference of the five powers "for the revision of the clauses of the Treaty of Versailles which are the cause of the present troubles in the life of Europe." Before the British replied, Hitler's troops entered Poland. Ciano was then informed that while Britain appreciated Italy's efforts, the German action rendered impossible any action along the proposed lines. Halifax telephoned Ciano on the afternoon of September 2 and told him that the withdrawal of German troops from Poland was the essential condition of any conference. Minute by Viscount Halifax, F.O., Aug. 31, 1939; Halifax to Loraine, F.O., Sept. 1, 1939; Minute by Mr. Jebb, F.O., Sept. 2, 1939. *B. D.,* VII, 442, 477, 518–19. Since Britain stood by that condition, and German troops were never withdrawn from Poland, the conference proposal lapsed.

ceivable that anyone should believe that Hitler meant to turn back. It was unbelievable that anyone not bent on surrender should be prepared to treat now with the Germans, who would only negotiate to gain further military advantage. Arthur Greenwood rose slowly. There was another moment of silence, and then an astonishing thing happened. L. S. Amery stood up on the Government side and shouted across to Greenwood: "Speak for England!" His meaning seemed clear: the Prime Minister had not spoken for England; then let the Opposition do it. Those three words constituted a cry of defiance which meant that the House and the country would neither surrender nor accept a leader who might be prepared to trifle with the nation's pledged word.[48]

Greenwood, acting with great patriotism and statesmanship, then made a remarkable speech—remarkable neither for eloquence nor for dramatic effect, but for the transparent sincerity which pervaded it. In clear, simple terms he declared:

> An act of aggression took place 38 hours ago. The moment that act of aggression took place one of the most important treaties of modern times automatically came into operation. There may be reasons why instant action was not taken. . . . That delay might have been justifiable, but there are many of us on all sides of this House who view with the gravest concern the fact that hours went by and news came in of bombing operations, and news today of an intensification of it, and I wonder how long we are prepared to vacillate at a time when Britain and all that Britain stands for, and human civilisation are in peril. We must march with France.[49]

The Prime Minister, Greenwood demanded, must tell the House when it met at noon "tomorrow" (September 3) whether Britain's promises were in the process of fulfillment. Every minute's delay imperilled the foundations of Britain's national honor; there

48. See Amery, *My Political Life,* III, 324–25; Spears, *Assignment to Catastrophe,* I, 20–21; Duff Cooper, *Old Men Forget,* p. 259; Dalton, *The Fateful Years,* pp. 264–65; Minney, *Private Papers of Hore-Belisha,* p. 226. [illegible]explains that his call to Greenwood was motivated by fear of a [illegible]rtisan speech."

[illegible] *Debs., HC,* September 2, 1939, vol. 351, 282–83.

must be no more devices for dragging out what had already been dragged out too long.

The words evoked universal cheers, particularly from the Conservatives. They had listened to their own leader in embarrassed silence and, according to Hore-Belisha, they would have supported Greenwood had he turned upon the Government.[50] Before the cheers had subsided, Sinclair was on his feet proclaiming: "This meeting will not have been in vain if it demonstrates to the world that the British Parliament will not tolerate delay in the fulfillment of our honourable obligations to Poland." The House was evidently in so furious a mood that Chamberlain felt it advisable to rise again. He hoped his statement had not betrayed the slightest weakening on the part of the Government—though, indeed, that was the distinct impression it gave—and he assured the House that he would have been very glad had he been able to announce that the French and British Governments were agreed on giving the Germans the shortest possible time in which to accept or reject their warning. But there were difficulties in co-ordinating action between the two Governments.[51] He felt certain that he would be able to make an announcement on the next day which, save for a miracle, would be a declaration that Britain was at war.

50. Minney, *Private Papers of Hore-Belisha,* p. 226. There were, of course, (in the words of Conservative Earl Winterton) a few "foolish virgins" on the Conservative side who even on September 2 were adverse to war with Germany. Winterton, *Orders of the Day,* pp. 249–50.

51. France had raised unexpected difficulties. She tended to favor a conference as proposed by Italy without the conditions Britain had insisted upon, and sought a delay in presenting an ultimatum to Germany on the ground that she needed more time to complete her mobilization. The British pressed for immediate action at the Quai d'Orsay. Phipps to Halifax, Paris, Sept. 1, 2, 1939; Halifax to Phipps, F.O., Sept. 1, 1939. *B. D.,* VII, 471, 504, 501. Sir Samuel Hoare claims that Britain's delay was caused entirely by the French hesitation; the time was consumed in trying to persuade France to act quickly with Britain. For that reason, he declares, the suspicion that Chamberlain was contemplating another surrender is unwarranted. *Nine Troubled Years,* pp. 393–94. Halifax supports the latter point. *Fullness of Days,* p. 215. A full account of the diplomatic maneuvering of September 1–3 is presented in Namier, *Diplomatic Prelude,* Chapter XI. The French side is presented in: Reynaud, *La France a sauvé l'Europe,* I, 597–602; Bonnet, *Défense de la Paix,* II, chapters XIX-XXI; Pierre-Etienne Flandin, *Politique Francaise, 1919–1940* (Paris, 1947), part Chapter VIII.

Again Chamberlain sat down without a cheer. "The feeling was astonishing," Duff Cooper later wrote in his diary. Eden was urged to speak by those sitting around him, but the honor eventually fell to John Wardlaw Milne, an old Conservative, Chairman of the Conservative Committee, and a loyal supporter of the Government, whose apparent indignation led the Duff Cooper-Eden-Amery group to believe it would be particularly effective if he addressed the House. When Wardlaw Milne rose, he argued that Britain's pledge to Poland was Britain's, not France's. Twenty-four hours had passed since the British note had been delivered to Berlin. If Germany had any intention of complying with it, she would have stopped the devastation in Poland by now. He felt compelled to say so much because "the whole country is nervous about this continual delay in carrying out our pledges." Thereafter the House adjourned amid mingled feelings of hostility and dismay.[52]

Chamberlain's statement had left even Cabinet members "aghast" (Hore-Belisha's word). Earlier that afternoon, in an angry and exasperated mood, they had agreed unanimously on an ultimatum to Germany, to expire at midnight irrespective of French action, and they were unaware of the last-minute appeals from Paris which had led the Prime Minister to make so halting and ambiguous a statement. Consequently, some of them (Hore-Belisha identifies ten) huddled in the Chancellor's room and, staging a kind of "sitdown strike," agreed to press for another Cabinet meeting at once. Simon was deputed to seek out the Prime Minister, who then received them at Downing Street. There these "scruffy and smelly" men (as one of their own number described them) demanded that a statement should be made forthwith, regardless of the French, and, adjourning back to Simon's room, sent a letter to Chamberlain repeating their points.[53]

Later that evening a small group of dissident Conservatives,

[52]. *Parl. Debs., HC,* September 2, 1939, vol. 351, 281–86; Spears, *As-[illegible]ent to Catastrophe,* I, 20–22; Duff Cooper, *Old Men Forget,* p. 259. [illegible]ng to Duff Cooper, Churchill wished to speak in this debate, but [illegible]een invited to join the War Cabinet on the previous day, he re-[illegible]ling himself almost a member of the Government.

[53]. [illegible]y, *Private Papers of Hore-Belisha,* pp. 226–27; Amery, *My* [illegible] III, 324–25; Birkenhead, *Halifax,* pp. 446–47.

including Eden, Duff Cooper, Robert Boothby, Brendan Bracken, and Duncan Sandys, met at Churchill's apartment. All of them, Duff Cooper records, were in a state of "bewildered rage." Boothby was convinced that Chamberlain had lost the Conservative Party "forever" and that it was in Churchill's power to "break him" and take his place. The group talked long into the night: was it better to split the country at this critical moment, or to bolster Chamberlain? Eventually they received news of what was to occur next day in the House of Commons, and the heated discussion cooled.[54]

Public opinion throughout England was bewildered and disturbed—and determined that there must be no retreat.[55] As *The Economist* (Sept. 2) summarized it: "The British people, with a . . . resolution as strong as anything in their history, have determined that it is better to fight a war than to yield an inch on a principle that has become one of national honor and national safety."

Even before the unscheduled meeting with his irate Cabinet, Chamberlain was painfully aware of the unpleasant feeling running against him. Calling Halifax to Downing Street about 8:30 p.m., he reported that his statement had infuriated the House and doubted, unless the Government could clarify its position, that it would be able to maintain itself when it met Parliament next day. The warning of the Chief Whip had made this clear. Halifax recalls never having seen Chamberlain "so disturbed." There followed a conference with Cadogan, the Permanent Undersecretary at the Foreign Office, and M. Corbin, the French Ambassador; then an hour of frantic telephoning to the French Government with the object of obtaining agreement on giving the Germans as short a time-limit as possible; and then a two-hour (11:30 p.m.–1:30 a.m.) Cabinet meeting, at which it was eventually agreed the ultimatum to Germany should expire at 11 o'clock the next morning.[56]

54. Duff Cooper, *Old Men Forget,* pp. 259–60.

55. This was evident in the press, and various Government officials attest to it. See, for example, Minney, *Private Papers of Hore-Belisha,* p. 225; Kirkpatrick, *The Inner Circle,* p. 144.

56. Halifax, *Fullness of Days,* p. 214; Minney, *Private Papers of Hoare-Belisha,* pp. 227-28; Birkenhead, *Halifax,* pp. 446–47; Kirkpatrick, *The Inner Circle,* p. 144. Halifax records that the "last straw" for him was a

Another brief meeting of note also took place late that night. Fritz Hesse called on Sir Horace Wilson at 11 Downing Street bearing an offer from Hitler. According to Hesse, he had been reached earlier that afternoon by Ribbentrop, who told him that Hitler was ready to withdraw from Poland and to offer reparation for the damage done, on condition that Germany would receive Danzig and the road through the Corridor and that Britain would act as mediator in the German-Polish conflict. Hesse was empowered to submit this proposal to the British Government and begin negotiations immediately. He thereupon arranged the conference with Wilson through George Stewart, the press officer at 10 Downing Street.

When Hesse saw Wilson about midnight, September 2,[57] he begged him to submit Hitler's proposals to the Cabinet. Wilson replied (presumably reflecting Chamberlain's opinion, for he had conferred with the Prime Minister after receiving Hesse's communication) that he saw no way for Chamberlain to turn back, and anyway he, Wilson, did not believe that Hitler had changed his mind. Would the Führer, Wilson asked, be prepared to make a public apology? He alone was responsible for the present situation; if he wanted to get out of it, he must show that he had learned his lesson. As the two men talked, a servant knocked on the door and handed Wilson a note. He read it several times, then burned it. Turning to Hesse, he said that since the invasion of Poland things had happened which made it impossible for any Englishman to consider Hitler's proposal. News had come that France was prepared to declare war with Britain. The British

chance meeting with "a prominent member of the Labour Party" (identified elsewhere as Hugh Dalton) outside the Foreign Office just after the Cabinet meeting. When asked "Foreign Secretary, can you give me any hope?" Halifax replied, "If you mean hope of a war I think I can promise you a certainty for to-morrow"; to which there came the reply, "Thank God."

57. Hesse was taken to Downing Street by Stewart, whom he had met at the sentry box on the Horse Guards Parade. According to Hesse's account, rain was falling in torrents, and the night was so black he could not see his hand before his eyes. Stewart greeted him only by saying, "What a dramatic night." Upon their arrival at Downing Street, Hesse was shown into a room dimly lighted by two candles. It was there that he met Wilson. *Das Spiel um Deutschland,* p. 211.

could not allow a foreign power to wield hegemony over the Continent without destroying the foundations on which the British Empire and its prestige in the world rested. In that situation, Hitler's proposals could not be laid before the Cabinet; no Englishman could evade the inevitable war.[58]

Three and one-half hours after the Cabinet meeting (5 a.m., September 3), Henderson was instructed by Halifax to convey to the German Government a note which, after repeating the warning of September 1, declared:

> Although this communication was made more than twenty-four hours ago, no reply has been received but German attacks upon Poland have been continued and intensified. I have accordingly the honour to inform you that unless not later than 11 a.m., British Summer Time, today September 3, satisfactory assurances to the above effect have been given by the German Government and have reached His Majesty's Government in London, a state of war will exist between the two countries as from that hour.[59]

Henderson executed Halifax's orders, according to a pre-arranged schedule, at 9 a.m. Paul Schmidt received the communication on Ribbentrop's behalf.[60]

Chamberlain addressed the House of Commons at six minutes past noon. He informed the members of the final note that Britain had sent to Berlin and stated simply: "No such undertaking was received by the time stipulated, and, consequently, this country is at war with Germany." He assured the Commons that Britain was ready and concluded:

> This is a sad day for all of us, and to none is it sadder than to me. Everything that I have worked for, everything that I

58. *Ibid.,* pp. 211–16. Although the British sources contain nothing on this episode, there is no apparent reason to doubt its authenticity. Halifax, in his memoirs, describes the relief he felt that Hitler did not produce, at the last moment, some "specious terms which would appear superficially very reasonable, but which the Poles would feel bound to reject." *Fullness of Days,* pp. 215–16. But so general a reference hardly precludes Hesse's account.

59. Halifax to Henderson, F.O., Sept. 3, 1939. *B. D.,* VII, 535.

60. Henderson to Halifax, Berlin, Sept. 3, 1939. *Ibid.,* VII, 536.

> have hoped for, everything that I have believed in during my public life, has crashed into ruins. There is only one thing left for me to do; that is, to devote what strength and powers I have to forwarding the victory of the cause for which we have to sacrifice so much. I cannot tell what part I may be allowed to play myself; I trust I may live to see the day when Hitlerism has been destroyed and a liberated Europe has been re-established.[61]

War had begun. Appeasement was dead.

61. *Parl. Debs., HC,* September 3, 1939, vol. 351, 292.

CHAPTER ELEVEN

Appeasement and the Critics

DURING THE TWO YEARS 1938–1939, crises capable of shattering the peace of Europe occurred with disconcerting frequency and regularity. Prime Minister Neville Chamberlain, firmly convinced that his policy of appeasement would contribute to the lessening of international tension, and in that way assure peace for Europe, pursued his adventure with untiring devotion. His aim was admirable, his method open to question. Some members in all parties consistently held that the policy of concessions to the dictators would lead Britain to eventual disaster and urged upon the Government an alternative policy, usually referred to as collective security.

Those in Britain, and particularly those Members of Parliament, who opposed appeasement were a politically heterogeneous group. In fact it is misleading to speak of them as a group at all. They included the Labor Party, members of the Liberal Party, a number of dissident Conservatives, and men independent of any political affiliation. The Labor Party had adopted collective security—support for the League of Nations—as its set policy in foreign affairs and had persistently supported the policy since 1931. The Liberal Party had done likewise. The Conservatives who opposed appeasement were those members of Chamberlain's own party who were alarmed by Hitler's increasing power in Germany and were convinced that Britain, in close collaboration with France, must stand by the rule of law in international affairs; concessions to dictators only whetted their appetites and encouraged them to make ever larger demands.

Although the Labor and Liberal Parties in the Parliament worked together during these years, it was undoubtedly detrimental to the general cause of opposition to appeasement that little or no cooperation was ever effected between those parties and the dissident Conservatives. It is true that they stood on similar ground in the Parliamentary debates, but in the practical everyday operation of politics the dissident Conservatives and the Labor-Liberal group each went their own way. Eden, after his resignation from the Foreign Office, refused to indulge in factious opposition to the Government, though he did not hesitate to criticize its policy. Churchill, whose ability in debate brought vigor and keen criticism into the House of Commons and whose call for a "grand alliance" in March, 1938, gave definite form to the vague Labor-Liberal demand for a return to collective security, was hardly amenable to the general cause of the Left. The leaders of the Labor Party lacked national stature, and their general socialistic policy had not yet fired the popular imagination. In short, the Opposition groups which had come together on the issues of diplomacy and were essentially agreed that the Government's policy lacked both principle and, except in the shortest run, expediency, were too divided in their creeds, philosophies, and programs to undertake an effective cooperative effort.

The one attempt to create a Popular Front was that made by Sir Stafford Cripps, and it was doomed from the start because of the lack of interest of both the dissident Conservatives and the Laborites. Labor was unwilling to compromise its chances of returning a pure Labor government in the near future, and Eden and Churchill, while anxious to see a reconstructed National Government with perhaps themselves and the Labor leaders included, were certainly not willing to enter a government of the Left. Thus there was never any serious threat to the Chamberlain Government. Though the denunciations of its policy were often loud and long both in Parliament and the press, it was able to pursue appeasement as it wished—at least until March, 1939—without fear of endangering its political position.

Some of the public distrust of Chamberlain's policy which might have showed itself in votes and speeches was quite probably driven into silence by the tactics of the Labor Party, which had framed its indictment, both inside and outside of Parliament, in terms calculated to frighten rather than to attract the section of "middle opinion" which was disquieted by Chamberlain's policy but had not gone so far as to believe that the Laborites were heaven-sent diplomatists. Anxious Conservatives in the constituencies were by no means ready to accept the nostrums of socialism in order to get a new foreign policy—which leads one to wonder how the history of appeasement might have been altered had Chamberlain been anything but a Conservative Prime Minister, or had the alternative for the English voter been anything but Laborite leadership.

Labor's reluctance to sanction British rearmament certainly damaged its appeal for a firmer foreign policy. The country, in fact, was faced with an astonishing paradox. The Conservatives were in favor of armaments on the understanding that they would not be used, and the Labor Opposition was in favor of using armaments on the understanding that they were not to be provided. It was because of this contradiction in Labor policy that the opposition to appeasement of the dissident Conservatives appears to have been more logical, and, in fact, more influential in the country.

During the entire period the Government enjoyed the support of an overwhelming majority in the House of Commons. There were 365 Conservatives in the assembly that Baldwin had brought about in 1935, and all but 25 or 30 followed Chamberlain unflinchingly. No Prime Minister could have asked for more unquestioning allegiance. Few of the party, outside of Cabinet members, spoke with conviction in the House, or even outside it. In the Parliamentary debates Opposition speakers, including dissident Conservatives, almost invariably equalled and usually surpassed the Government-supporting speakers both in number and intensity of argument. But when divisions occurred, the votes revealed consistently large, unimperilled Government majorities. Even as late as May, 1940, when the crisis over Norway finally brought Chamberlain down, he still had a majority of eighty. But he fell, still holding that majority, for (according to A. L. Rowse, an admittedly biased but able English historian-politician) the "vast majority in Parliament never represented the situation in the country."[1]

The practice of the Conservative back-benchers of remaining silent while the Government did its own talking, allowing the critics to have their say without much interruption or rebuttal, then confidently overwhelming the Opposition in any vote that was taken, cannot be described as unusual in English politics. Yet the fact that it occurred week after week and month after month in 1938–1939, without so much as the slightest murmur of doubt (except on March 16 and September 2, 1939) about anything the Government proposed or did in foreign affairs, raises a point concerning Chamberlain's Parliamentary followers which is less than comforting. This is especially so in view of Chamberlain's own unabashed retort to a respected colleague who once suggested that he might bring some younger and more vigorous talent into the Cabinet: "Survey the back benches? The material available is meagre in the extreme, and I don't remember any time when there was so little promise among the younger men in the Government and on the back benches."[2] It might be that Chamberlain simply did not recognize any talent that fit into his scheme, or that potential talent was subdued by the Prime Minister's heavy-handed leadership. Yet the impression that there existed a "mass" of Conservative members devoted only to blind followership, wherever that might lead, is difficult to avoid.

Of course, a number of Conservatives were in sincere sympathy with the announced policy of the Government. Some were blind to the unannounced policy, the part which lay beneath the surface (the use of secret diplomacy and, critics would say, chicanery, to bring the new policy into effect) and could not, therefore, be reached effectively in debate. In addition, many Conservatives who had misgivings about Chamberlain's policy were unwilling, either because of fear for their own political lives or a genuine belief that it was not in the best interests of the country, to con-

1. Rowse, *Appeasement,* p. 53.
2. Feiling, *Life of Neville Chamberlain,* pp. 386–87. Note Macleod's biography (*Neville Chamberlain,* p. 200) for a statement on Chamberlain's Victorian outlook and its effect on his relations with younger men.

tribute to a vote which, if passed, might have caused the downfall of the Government and possibly the elevation of the Labor leaders to power. Consequently, Chamberlain, who took almost every challenge as a personal affront and looked upon almost every division as a vote of confidence, had an effective body of "yes-men" in the Commons.[3]

The practical effect of all this was that, for a time, the House of Commons was excluded from positive participation in foreign policy. Yet its indirect influence was inevitably significant in that the innumerable questions and frequent debates revealed more and more clearly to the British people that the Prime Minister's policy was dangerous and even at odds with the nation's conscience. So it was that, despite their own shortcomings and the apparent invincibility of the Government, the heterogeneous Opposition elements were able to subject the Government to continual and searching criticism, to put forward a coherent and constructive alternative policy, and, as the vertiginous course of international affairs placed Britain's security in an ever more tenuous position, to gain an increasing hearing from the British people.

During the first months of Chamberlain's ministry, the British press reacted to his policy on strict party lines. Labor and Liberal journals opposed appeasement on the same grounds as the Labor and Liberal Parties within Parliament, the Conservative journals favored his new departure, or at least expressed a willingness to let him give it a trial, and the independent journals ranged anywhere in between, tending more and more to oppose appeasement as time progressed. After Munich, however, the press can hardly be categorized. All sections expressed relief that war had been averted, but the humiliation and dishonor of the whole affair was reflected in journals of all political hues. The weight the newspapers tended to give each of those considerations did not necessarily follow party lines. A growing skepticism and anxiety

3. On this point see Kenney, "The Role of the House of Commons in British Foreign Policy During the 1937–1938 Session," pp. 144, 180–85. This writer explains with regard to foreign policy (and with specific reference to 1938) that for all practical purposes, Britain was not a democracy but an oligarchy, in which Chamberlain functioned almost dictatorially—something quite possible under the English electoral system.

was evident in the press as a whole, and Hitler's occupation of Prague was a bombshell which touched off a vigorous and unrelenting demand for a firmer policy toward the dictators. That demand continued in one form or another until the outbreak of the war.

In essence, Chamberlain's appeasement policy was directed towards the re-establishment of a concert of Europe which should be directed by the four great powers: Britain, France, Germany, and Italy. This meant the exclusion of Russia from Europe, and the abandonment of the whole concept of collective security and the League of Nations which Britain had followed since the end of the World War. In addition to considerations of power politics, certain moral issues were involved. Abandonment of collective security and the League of Nations would eliminate whatever progress had been made in the development of a peaceful system of international relations. If Germany and Italy were promoted to full participation in the hegemony of Europe, would it not mean that immorality and ruthlessness were being rewarded? And if the violations of international law by Germany and Italy were condoned, would it not be useless to expect permanent cooperation among the four powers? For all these reasons Chamberlain's policy was an adventure, and as such met some resistance from the very beginning.

At the time of Eden's resignation, the question of international morality was the major point raised by the critics. Italy had given no evidence of good faith in international dealings; in fact, she was engaged in active support of the Nationalist side in the Spanish Civil War in direct violation of her adherence to the Non-Intervention Agreement. An agreement with Italy implied a willingness on the part of Britain to recognize the Italian conquest of Abyssinia. Chamberlain was, however, prepared to ignore the question of international morality and to go out of his way to befriend the unscrupulous Italians. In so doing, he was motivated in part by the hope of separating Italy from Germany, thus making it easier to deal with the Reich. The outburst in the press and in Parliament against approaching Italy under such circumstances did not deter the Prime Minister in the least. He was too frequently told, and quite willingly believed, that a fresh initiative towards the dictators would yield lasting results, and that he was the only man in all the world to make it.

When the Czech crisis developed during the summer of 1938, the critics of appeasement stood firmly against any solution arrived at by force or the threat of force. They interpreted Munich as just that—as a national humiliation for Britain—and as time passed, the realization of the great sacrifices made there rapidly spread. The British people generally were relieved, but with relief came the uncomfortable (and almost sub-conscious) idea that perhaps they should have fought. Indeed, it was the very shock of their own relief which set more British people to hard thinking, and it was at this point that concessions made in the name of expediency—a word not wholly anathema in Britain—began to bother the conscience of the British people. Yet, peace had been preserved, and for Chamberlain (who seemingly could not persuade himself that more was at stake than a local quarrel between tiresome Czech factions) and a majority of the British people, this was still the most important thing.

When Chamberlain combined the policy of rearmament at home with appeasement abroad, the attitude of the country seemed to be one of suspended judgment. The period from Munich to Prague was particularly one of mingled emotions. Alarmed at the totalitarian challenge to democracy and the interests of the Empire, the British people were relieved that the dogs of war were still leashed. Thankful for the respite which the Prime Minister had won, shocked by the inadequacy of Britain's defenses, longing for the peace which appeasement sought and yet skeptical that such a policy could indeed secure it, the nation seemed to be asking for a lead without knowing from where a lead was to come. There was dissatisfaction with the personnel of the Chamberlain Government, which as a whole was unimpressive. Yet the nation was as far removed as ever from a belief in socialism or the policy with which Labor until recently had been identified—the policy of pugnacity from weakness.

By one act Hitler changed the whole situation. His occupation of Prague struck the illusions from the minds of millions. The mask fell from the face of Nazi Germany and the hideous features were disclosed. The frequently repeated protestations of satisfied ambitions were omitted as having served too often their purpose of deceiving the gullible. The solemn assertion of desiring to include only Germans within the Reich was exposed as lying humbug. The British people realized at last that they were faced by a power that sought European and perhaps even world domination and which could be prevented from obtaining it only by force. The critics had been right; the dictators could not be trusted. Hitler must be stopped!

Harold Nicolson testified that "the average Englishman . . . [would] adopt almost any expedient rather than face realities which might disturb his equanimity." He could endure almost anything except "cerebral discomfort," and "when faced with conditions involving tremendous and most unpleasant mental effort, he escaped from that effort by pretending that these conditions were easily remediable, or much exaggerated, or actually non-existent." He was, in such circumstances, the victim of "extreme mental absenteeism." But his absence of mind could be shaken by the intrusion of instinct, notably self-preservation and wounded pride.[4] If the British instinct of self-preservation had been aroused from slumber by the sudden distribution of gas masks and the digging of pitiable ditches in London parks at the time of Munich, it was the instinct of wounded pride which was wrenched from the soft mud of the sub-conscious on the Ides of March. It was borne in upon the British people that they had now been exposed by the dictator powers to intolerable affronts, and a great tide of injured dignity rose from the depths of the British character.

The resulting clamor in Parliament and press for vigorous action to meet the emergency was only stimulated by Chamberlain's uninspired announcement in the Commons on March 15 that Britain must not be deflected from her course. Serene statements of this sort were no longer enough. European democracy, peace, and British security were in grave danger. The demand for action was not confined to the Opposition in Parliament. Most Conservatives now realized the danger, and all sections of the press joined in the call for firm and vigorous measures. The

4. Harold Nicolson, "Is War Inevitable?" *The Nineteenth Century*, CXXVI (July, 1939); 2–4.

demand became so intense that it is not unreasonable to suppose that had Chamberlain ignored it, it might well have meant the collapse of his Government. His Birmingham speech followed, and later the Government's guarantee to Poland—a somewhat abortive diplomatic maneuver which nonetheless committed Britain to crying halt to Hitler whatever the consequences. Appeasement apparently lay in ruins.

Chamberlain's indignation after Prague was undoubtedly genuine. He had been duped by Hitler. He had been made to look a fool in the eyes of Europe. This certainly helps to account for his change of opinion and his departure from appeasement. So does the influence of Halifax, who, never as enthusiastic about the results of Munich as the Prime Minister, was quick to see the implications of Hitler's Prague *coup* and from that moment on began to assume some stature as Foreign Secretary rather than remaining Chamberlain's messenger. But the fact remains that the stiffening of Britain's attitude did not originate with the Government. It originated with Parliament, with the press, and with the now very politically-conscious public. It was this sort of thing to which Kurt von Schuschnigg, the Austrian Prime Minister, once referred when, in discussing Britain's European policy, he observed that the British Government sometimes "makes an about-face in the last moment . . . because it is not the master, but the servant of the country."[5]

The change of policy was not necessarily final or decisive. There was still a hope (as A. J. P. Taylor so aptly puts it) "of conciliating Hitler under the determination to resist him just as previously there had been an inclination to resist under the top layer of appeasement." From that point on, however, "the appeasers were on the defensive, easily distracted from their work and hardly surprised at their own failure."[6]

There can be little doubt that Britain "quibbled" too much during the early stages of the negotiations with Russia,[7] just as there can be no doubt that Russia, enabled to do so by her

5. von Schuschnigg, *Austrian Requiem,* p. 164.
6. *Origins of the Second World War,* p. 204.
7. Strang admits in his memoirs that the Government was "unreasonably slow" in accepting the principle of a three-power alliance. *Home and Abroad,* p. 166.

simultaneous conversations with Germany, bargained unscrupulously in an effort to sell her support—or at least her neutrality—to the highest bidder. Nothing could have been less engaging than the way in which the Russians conducted the negotiations, snubbing and disparaging British efforts to meet their declared wishes, refusing to compromise, and raising new points and difficulties. But it was also a mistake on the part of the British Government to treat the Soviet Union like a suppliant and to begin the conversations with suggestions which were both ludicrous and humiliating; it was a further mistake to go on haggling about every concession, thus rendering Britain unconvincing; it was a third mistake to send a junior official to Moscow to buoy the sagging negotiations.[8]

It can be argued, as does Sir Ivone Kirkpatrick[9], that the outcome of the Anglo-Russian negotiations was decided the moment the Germans began to talk with the Russians, for they simply had more to offer. It can also be held, as does Lord Vansittart[10], who was anything but an advocate of appeasement, that Britain would probably have been double-crossed by the Soviets even had there been some agreement on Anglo-Russian cooperation. Yet the former argument only emphasizes the importance of timing; the latter involves speculation from hindsight on a question which is by nature moot.

It may be asked why the Government was so concerned about the "feelings" of Poland and Rumania—it had had so little concern for Czechoslovakia in September, 1938. Why was the Prime Minister, who had been so oblivious to violations of international morality in dealing with Hitler and Mussolini, so insistent upon "principle" in dealing with Russia? The Government obviously doubted Russia's motives; it feared lest it be drawn into a purely Nazi-Soviet quarrel over the Baltic states; as the

8. Strang claims that his mission was only a "routine assignment" for a junior Foreign Office official, and that the Russians never showed resentment that he, rather than a major official, had come to Moscow. *Ibid.*, pp. 158–59. But it certainly did nothing to inspire Russian confidence in British sincerity.

9. *The Inner Circle*, pp. 142–43.

10. "A Morally Indefensible Agreement," *The Listener*, XL (November 4, 1948), 676.

alleged protector of the small states in Europe, it could hardly force upon them the acceptance of conditions to which they strenuously objected. Even beyond this, it is impossible to escape the conclusion that Chamberlain did not fully appreciate the danger of the German threat to Europe. Pursuing a policy which tacitly assumed that Britain had nothing to fear for herself, and that she still had the power to assert herself as the arbiter of Europe whenever the need arose, he neither shared nor understood Russia's fear of a German invasion—a war in which Russia might have to fight alone and receive the German attack on Russian soil instead of going out to meet it in the Baltic states, Poland, and Rumania. Chamberlain could not believe that the rantings of *Mein Kampf* were a practical manual of daily conduct from which Hitler would not deviate, nor did Chamberlain ever seem quite able to convince himself that detached reasonableness might not have any influence with Hitler.[11] But if he ever had a serious notion of breaking off the talks with Russia, he was never given the opportunity, for the pressure on him from Parliament, press, and even some members of his own Cabinet was relentless.

Despite Chamberlain's deep resentment over Prague, his inability to reach an agreement with Russia, combined with his long-held distrust of the Soviets, led to a reaction which seems to account for Sir Horace Wilson's approach to Helmut Wohltat in July, 1939. Chamberlain was still a "man of peace"—a rather meaningless cliché inasmuch as most men are—and he was determined to allow no opportunity for preserving it to slip away unheeded.

Sir Samuel Hoare maintains that Chamberlain was never fooled by Hitler. The Prime Minister referred to him on various occasions as a paranoiac, and was certain from the first that Hitler was partially mad.[12] Credence is lent to that view by the constant reference to Hitler in the Inner Cabinet, especially dur-

11. For a fuller critical evaluation of Britain's part in the Anglo-Russian negotiations, see Rock, "Grand Alliance or Daisy Chain: British Opinion and Policy Toward Russia, April–August, 1939," pp. 330–37. See also Taylor, *Origins of the Second World War*, pp. 223–30. For the Soviet view, see Maisky, *Who Helped Hitler?*, passim.

12. Templewood, *Nine Troubled Years*, p. 378.

ing September, 1938, as "the madman." In this light Chamberlain's policy seems all the more foolhardy. Is it logical to attempt to construct a basis for peace in Europe on friendship with a madman? Perhaps in his ardent desire for peace Chamberlain just did not have the courage to face his inner conviction. The critics, and especially Churchill, saw Hitler as a dangerous, unpredictable creature and did not hesitate to say so. But Chamberlain approached the dictators as reasonable men—a misjudgment all the more serious in that he continued to regard them as such, or at least acted as if he did, in spite of strong evidence to the contrary. For him, there indeed seemed no dividing line between hope and belief.[13]

Perhaps the most cogent criticism of Chamberlain's policy is that he sacrificed *Realpolitik* to his own ideals. While down to March 15, 1939, the opponents of appeasement might have been unable to substantiate their belief that Hitler was aiming at world domination, it was equally impossible for Chamberlain to verify his own contrary conviction that Hitler had limited aims which could be met by peaceful negotiation. That Hitler might have sinister designs against Britain seems never to have entered the Prime Minister's mind before the occupation of Prague. Chamberlain's fault was that on so open a question on which alternative answers—including the baleful one which subsequently proved to be the truth—were being given, he deliberately kept his eyes closed to unpalatably pessimistic views conflicting with his own, even though these views were held, and were convincingly expounded, by British statesmen with greater experience and understanding of foreign affairs than his own, and by official advisers who constitutionally had the first claim on the Prime Minister's attention on questions of foreign policy. As early as January, 1938, Chamberlain had branded the Foreign Office "not sincere" in its approach to the dictators, and all its expert knowledge was cast aside because knowledge seemed in conflict with hope. Moreover, he not only ignored or stubbornly over-

13. Halifax writes that, after Munich, "the dominant constituent" in Chamberlain's thought was "hope rather than faith." *Fullness of Days,* p. 207.

rode weighty dissenting opinions, but took immense and indefensible risks on the strength of his belief in the superiority of his own judgment.

In this way Chamberlain was, perhaps, his own worst enemy. Assuming an exalted attitude in the Commons, refusing to acknowledge that he might ever be a little bit wrong, deriving keen delight from sticking barbs in his critics (for whom he had very little respect), resenting outside pressure, setting his own pace in everything so as to appear on no account to be yielding to ill-advised agitation, responding to honest questioning by anxious elements of the Opposition as if, a Labor peer once charged, he had been "weaned on a pickle," calling upon the loyalty of his Conservative colleagues to sustain him in every Parliamentary division—in short, constantly exercising an almost incomprehensible obstinacy which sprang from his confidence solely in himself and his own ideas (which even his most ardent defenders recognize[14])—the Prime Minister was simply incapable of "the generous gesture." It was for this reason that able men like young Ronald Cartland, a Conservative M. P. (who lost his life in France during the early part of the war), were convinced that

> he represents so much that . . . is wrong in modern politics. The world has progressed beyond what he stands for—the people are asking for something 'bigger' in every meaning of the word. You can't hold the Empire without ideals—you can't run this country without vision—you can't lead the people of England without generosity of mind and soul.[15]

It is sometimes argued in Chamberlain's defense that he could not move more decisively because of the "peace phobia" of the British people. But in a sense this contributes as much or more to the indictment of the Chamberlain Government as to its defense. What is the purpose of political leadership? Is not one of its important functions that of keeping the nation informed and warning it of the dangers which it must face? Yet the reality

14. See Templewood, *Nine Troubled Years,* p. 387, for example.
15. Barbara Cartland, *Ronald Cartland* (London, n.d.), p. 140.

of the German peril was never exposed to the British electorate until late in the game, and the historian is left to wonder how any government could have deliberately closed its eyes and those of the nation to so clear and imminent a peril. The magnitude of German preparations for war, the ruthless speed with which they were pushed ahead, and the vast scope of German ambitions were all well known to those in positions of leadership. They seemed to leave the Government largely unmoved. In consequence, the ignorance of the public was complete—and the argument that Chamberlain was deterred by the drag of his own people inevitably raises the question wherein the responsibility for this ignorance ultimately lay.[16] The ineptness of British foreign policy in the period 1938–1939 may well be due more to the drag of the Government upon public opinion than to the drag of public opinion upon the Government.

If one accepts Harold Nicolson's description of the "average Englishman's" approach to unpleasant problems[17], it would appear that Chamberlain and his colleagues qualify as "average Englishmen." In fact, a strong case can be made for this point, and it is perhaps the best explanation why Chamberlain was able to carry the public with him as far as he did along the path he followed.

It has been said in Chamberlain's defense (and Halifax takes this view in his memoirs) that the "big thing" he did was to unite Britain and the Commonwealth[18] in the belief that "every

16. On this point, see Kirkpatrick, *The Inner Circle,* pp. 81, 132; Rowse, *Appeasement,* p. 58.

17. See p. 328 above.

18. The effect of Commonwealth opinion on British foreign policy during 1938–1939 is, unfortunately, not very clear. Halifax explains that the Commonwealth "would certainly not have been united for war in 1938" as it was in 1939 (*Fullness of Days,* p. 208), and John Wheeler-Bennett writes that the Dominions would not have approved the abandonment of appeasement at the time of Munich (*King George VI,* p. 408). But what effect, if any, this had on British policy is questionable. In September, 1938, Joseph Kennedy reported to Washington his impression that Dominion opinion had little influence on British policy. He seemed to think it something of a crutch which the Government used when necessary to explain away some of its actions—saying in effect that "public opinion in this country and in certain of the Dominions" would not allow otherwise. *U.S. For. Rel., 1938,* I, 577–78. Some pertinent materials on Commonwealth opinion may be found in Nicholas Mansergh, *Survey of British Commonwealth Affairs: Problems of External Policy, 1931–1939* (London, 1952);

conceivable effort had been made to find the way of sparing Europe the ordeal of war, and that no alternative remained."[19] This contention does not take into consideration the possibility that the same end could have been reached by other means which might well have afforded a greater chance for success along the way, and is, in any event, a depressingly negative result. Admittedly, statesmen sometimes find themselves confronted with problems to which there seem to be none but the most unpleasant solutions. But this does not invalidate the question whether other courses of action, undertaken earlier, could have prevented these problems from arising or at least have minimized their effect. Here is the central question in any appraisal of Chamberlain's diplomacy. Few have ever doubted that Chamberlain was sincere and well-meaning. The fact remains that sincerity and good intentions alone are no guarantee that a man may not sometimes be wrong.

From the original violation of the Treaty of Locarno in 1936, when Britain was forced to admit that she had put her name to a treaty which she could no longer maintain, to Hitler's occupation of Prague, there was a fundamental lack of leadership in Britain which resulted in a complete failure on the part of the British public to realize how far their vital interests lay in Europe. The people of Britain did not want to face hard facts, and, far from being deterred in their blindness by alert leadership, they were actually encouraged by Government leaders whose views were based on hope rather than fact—who seemed, indeed, to derive a sort of sanctimonious satisfaction from believing in the good intentions of the fascist dictators despite all the evidence to the contrary.

There were, however, some who were not afflicted with political myopia and who constantly tried to combat the ailment in the others. Those were the critics of appeasement, the most realistic of whom were the dissident Conservatives. They recognized the ruthless and unscrupulous dictators as a menace to the peace of

---

Nicholas Mansergh (editor), *Documents and Speeches on British Commonwealth Affairs, 1931–1952,* 2 vols. (London, 1953), I; and Gwendolyn M. Carter, *The British Commonwealth and International Security: The Role of the Dominions, 1919–1939* (Toronto, 1947).

19. Halifax, *Fullness of Days,* p. 201.

Europe and the security of Britain; they saw that a threat to the peace of any one country was a threat to Britain. By persistently advocating their cure, they led most of the afflicted ones, when the ailment had become alarmingly serious, to accept their prescription. It was on the basis of their program that collective resistance to aggression was eventually attempted. It was around their policy that the British people finally rallied when it had become evident that appeasement had dismally failed.

APPENDIX ONE

The Semantics of Appeasement

APPEASEMENT WAS A TERM used by a fairly wide range of British policy-makers midway through the 1930's. It was a respectable word, freely accepted in the currency of political discussion. But its meaning was never really defined, much less agreed upon, and as efforts were made to implement the "policy of appeasement" in the second half of the decade, it became a diversely-interpreted and much-disputed concept.

Appeasement defied precise definition in part because it involved a psychological reaction against the severities and inconsistencies, perhaps even absurdities, of the Treaty of Versailles. It was "an affair of the heart, intuitive, not taught; a strong emotion, not an academic speculation."* The term generally was taken to mean the reduction of international tension in Europe and the world by the methodical removal of the principal causes of friction among nations. More specifically, it meant the promotion of conciliation through the redress of legitimate grievances of the defeated powers of the World War. Exactly how all this should be done, however, and in what circumstances, was always open to debate, and it was from this fact primarily that widely-varying interpretations developed.

In the hands of Neville Chamberlain and his associates the policy came to mean, in practice if not in theory, the making of timely concessions to disgruntled powers—who may have been disgruntled for good reasons—in the hope that this would alleviate their grievances, reduce their tendency toward aggressive action, and open the way to lasting international peace and harmony. This policy was so reasonable that it was difficult to see

* Gilbert and Gott, *The Appeasers,* p. 23.

how anyone could possibly oppose it. To Chamberlain's opponents, however, appeasement came to mean cowardly surrender to aggressive and unscrupulous powers, mainly from motives of fear, indolence, or simple indifference. Invariably the concessions were made at the expense of some weaker nation. The appeaser himself sacrificed nothing; in fact he usually acted out of the desire to avoid sacrificing anything of value. This policy was so dangerous that it was difficult to see how anyone could possibly espouse it.

Appeasement took on divergent meanings in response to specific events in Europe; consequently, the definitions hardened gradually. For many Englishmen, no clear definition ever emerged, and there was always a "mass" of opinion which stood somewhere between the two poles, sometimes accepting (consciously or unconsciously) portions of this or that definition, and thus forming a rather broad field of indecision and flexibility. This made the debate over appeasement all the more intense and meaningful.*

* The subject of these paragraphs is almost inexhaustible. For further discussion, see Gilbert and Gott, *The Appeasers,* pp. 21–38; Wheeler-Bennett, *Munich,* pp. 3–8; Rowse, *Appeasement, passim.*

APPENDIX TWO*

Party Representation in Parliament

As of January 1, 1937, representation in the British Parliament was as follows:

House of Commons

Government		
Conservative	383	
Liberal National	33	
National Labor	9	
Independent Nationals	4	
		429
Opposition		
Labor and Independent Labor	161	
Liberal	20	
Independent	4	
Communist	1	
		186

Note: The Liberal National Party was originally composed of a group of Liberal Members of Parliament who believed that the National Government should have complete freedom in approaching national problems without restraint of party views. A separate party was formed in 1933 after the Liberals supporting Sir Herbert Samuel had gone into opposition.

The National Labor group was originally formed of those Labor ministers and members, and their supporters, who helped in 1931 to establish the National Government.

* The data given here is taken from *Political Handbook of the World: Parliaments, Parties and Press, as of January 1, 1937*. Edited by Walter H. Mallory. (New York, 1937), pp. 82–86.

The Independent Labor Party was a small group which advocated the use of more direct and definite action to ensure "Socialism in our time."

House of Lords

Party alignment in the House of Lords is not certainly fixed, but of the total membership of 772 (including 126 members whose politics were not stated, such as archbishops and bishops, and 26 minors not seated), 517 were listed as Conservatives.

APPENDIX THREE*

Newspapers and Periodicals

Name of Paper	*Political Affiliation*	*Proprietor, Editor, etc.*
Daily Herald (London) (2,000,000)	Labor	Odhams Press, Ltd. and Trade Union Congress (Props.) Francis Williams (Ed.)
Daily Mail (London) (1,602,209)	Conservative	Viscount Rothermere (Controlling shareholder) (Assoc. Newspapers, Ltd.) (Prop.) S. L. Head (Ed.)
Daily Telegraph (London) (630,000)	Independent Conservative	Lord Camrose (Prop.) Arthur E. Watson (Ed.)
Evening Standard (London) (388,040)	Independent; Conservative tendency; Imperialist	Lord Beaverbrook (Controlling shareholder) Frank Owen (Ed.)
Financial News (London)	Independent	Financial Newspaper Proprietors, Ltd. (Prop.) Eyre & Spottiswoode (Controlling shareholders) J. Maurice Green (Ed.)
Financial Times (London)	Independent	Lord Camrose (Controlling interest) A. Chisholm (Ed.)

* The data given here is taken from *Political Handbook of the World: Parliaments, Parties and Press, as of January 1, 1939*. Edited by Walter H. Mallory. (New York, 1939), pp. 83–85. Also very useful is Viscount Camrose, *British Newspapers and Their Controllers* (London, 1947).

Name of Paper	*Political Affiliation*	*Proprietor, Editor, etc.*
Glasgow Herald	Independent Conservative; moderate	George Outram & Co., Ltd. (Controlling shareholders) H. P. Haddow (Ed.)
Liverpool Daily Post	Liberal and independent	John Macleay (Ed.)
Manchester Guardian	Advanced Liberal; influential newspaper; well-informed on foreign affairs	W. P. Crozier (Ed.)
News Chronicle (London) (1,384,253)	Opposition Liberal	News and Westminster, Ltd. (Cadbury interests) and United Newspapers, Ltd. (Inveresk interests) (Props.) Gerald Barry (Ed.)
Observer (London)	Independent; Conservative; influential	Viscount Astor (Controlling shareholder) J. L. Garvin (Ed.)
Reynolds News (London)	Coöperative	S. R. Elliott (Ed.)
Sunday Graphic (London)	Independent	Lord Kemsley Group (Props.) R. Simpson (Ed.)
Sunday Times (London)	Independent; Conservative; influential	Lord Kemsley (Controlling shareholder) (Allied Newspapers, Ltd.) (Prop.) W. W. Hadley (Ed.)
Times (London) (196,977)	Very influential; independent; moderate Conservative; supports any Government so far as possible; correspondence from men of all parties	Major J. J. Astor, J. Walter (Controlling shareholders) Geoffrey Dawson (Ed.)
Western Mail (Cardiff)	Conservative	J. A. Sandbrook (Ed.)

Name of Paper	*Political Affiliation*	*Proprietor, Editor, etc.*
Yorkshire Observer (Bradford)	Liberal	S. Oddy (Ed.)
Economist	Independent, moderately Liberal; favors free trade; more financial and statistical than political	Shares so distributed between Financial Newspaper Proprietors, Ltd., and individual shareholders as to ensure editorial independence. Geoffrey Crowther (Ed.)
Fortnightly	Independent	W. Horsfall Carter (Ed.)
National Review	Imperialist; Conservative	Viscountess Milnor (Prop.)
New Statesman and Nation	Independent; radical, with Labor tendency	Kingsley Martin (Ed.)
Round Table	A review of the politics of the British Commonwealth	H. V. Hodson (Ed.)
Spectator	Non-partisan; Conservative tendency	H. Wilson Harris (Ed.)
Statist	Financial and economic	Patrick FitzGerald (Ed.)
Time and Tide	Independent; non-party	

Bibliographical Note

THE MATERIALS on which this study is based fall into four main categories: government documents; memoirs, diaries, and private papers; newspapers and other organs of opinion; and secondary works. Without any attempt at exhaustive coverage, remarks about some materials in each category follow.

1) Documents

The publication of documents for the years preceding the outbreak of the Second World War has provided ready access to basic materials vital to any study of the kind attempted in this volume. Especially useful in providing the framework of diplomatic activity are the *Documents on British Foreign Policy, 1919–1939,* published by the British Government, and the *Documents on German Foreign Policy, 1918–1945,* translated and published through the joint efforts of the American, British, and French governments. Both projects are still in process, but documents for the years 1938-1939 are among those in print. The *Foreign Relations of the United States* provide useful observations on the British scene by Joseph Kennedy, the American Ambassador in London. The papers of Herbert von Dirksen, German Ambassador in London, published by the Soviet Government as one volume of *Documents and Materials Relating to the Eve of the Second World War,* contain periodic commentaries on Anglo-German relations. Essential to this study, of course, is the record of everything said about British foreign policy in both houses of Parliament in 1938–1939, contained in the *Parliamentary Debates* (Fifth Series).

2) Memoirs, Diaries, and Private Papers

A number of Englishmen and others connected in some way with British foreign policy during this period have written memoirs. They vary greatly in depth of coverage, directness of approach, and consequent usefulness. The most thorough treatment, indeed defense, of the Government's position and actions is Viscount Templewood's *Nine Troubled Years.* Lord Halifax's account in *Fullness of Days,* defensive in nature but not vehemently so, is sketchy. The work of Sir John Simon, *Retrospect,* is disappointingly superficial. The Labor side is presented most thoroughly in Hugh Dalton's *The Fateful Years,* while Lord Citrine's *Men and Work* and Clement Attlee's *As It Happened* provide some useful insights in the context of summary treatment.

Partly because of the vantage-point from which they wrote, dissident Conservatives have produced some of the most useful memoirs for this study. Sir Winston Churchill's *The Gathering Storm* contains important material for the whole period, by one who was a consistent critic of appeasement. Of Anthony Eden's volumes, *Facing the Dictators* is especially helpful on the events which surrounded his resignation from the Foreign Office in February, 1938. *Old Men Forget,* by Duff Cooper, includes a revealing account of the British Government in the Czech crisis, while Leo S. Amery's *My Political Life* (vol. III) provides the useful viewpoints of one who first supported Chamberlain's policy and then turned against it.

Also noteworthy are the accounts of Sir William Strang, *Home and Abroad,* in which the negotiations with Russia in 1939 are discussed by one of the key participants, and Sir Ivone Kirkpatrick, *The Inner Circle* in which the events of September, 1938, are thrust into bold relief by one who was present to assist the Prime Minister at Godesberg and Munich. *Moscow, Tokyo, London,* the memoirs of Herbert von Dirksen, include observations on the British Government and its critics throughout the period. Fritz Hesse, press attaché at the Germany embassy in London, describes Anglo-German contacts after Prague in *Das Spiel um Deutschland. The Ciano Diaries* and *Ciano's Diplomatic Papers* contain the views of the Italian Foreign Minister on a wide variety of matters; Jozef Beck's *Final Report* reveals the outlook and role of the Polish Foreign Minister; Georges Bonnet's *Défense de la Paix* contains the appeasement-bent recollections of the French Foreign Minister; and *The Last Days of Europe* is an account of events in 1939 as seen by Grigore Gafencu, Rumanian Foreign Minister.

3) Organs of Opinion

A study of this kind necessarily depends heavily on newspapers and other organs of opinion. Especially valuable because of their constant awareness of and concern for the issues of appeasement are the pro-Government *Times* (London), the Conservative *Daily Telegraph,* the Labor *Daily Herald,* the Liberal *News Chronicle,* and the Liberal *Manchester Guardian.* But a wide variety of other journals were almost equally concerned and rank closely behind those mentioned in terms of usefulness in gauging press opinion on specific matters.

4) Secondary Works

Secondary works which touch on some facet of this subject are numerous, diverse, and wide-ranging. Sir John Wheeler-Bennett's *Munich*: *Prologue to Tragedy* is one of the first full accounts of the ups and downs of appeasement in the 1930's, and it has stood the test of time exceedingly well. The relevant volumes in the *Survey of International Affairs* (Laffan, *The Crisis Over Czechoslovakia*; Toynbee and Ashton-Gwatkin, *The World in March, 1939;* and Toynbee, *The Eve of War, 1939*) provide perhaps the most detailed accounting of the pertinent events of 1938–1939. All were written with the benefit of published British documents. Keith Eubank's *Munich* is a thorough account of the Czechoslovak problem in 1938. *The Origins of the Second World War*, the controversial work of A. J. P. Taylor, is the most thought-provoking treatment of the years preceding the outbreak of war. Keith Feiling's *The Life of Neville Chamberlain,* the official and sympathetic biography of the Prime Minister, includes material from Chamberlain's papers which is available nowhere else. The general outlook and approach to foreign policy of those who promoted appeasement is ably presented in Gilbert and Gott, *The Appeasers,* and Margaret George, *The Warped Vision.* The series of eight articles which appeared in *The Listener* in the autumn of 1948 under the general title "A Munich Survey," presents the views of eight noted Englishmen as they reappraise that general episode of their history ten years later.

Bibliography of Works Cited

I. Primary Sources

A. Documents

The British War Blue Book: Documents Concerning German-Polish Relations and the Outbreak of Hostilities Between Great Britain and Germany on September 3, 1939. (New York, 1939).

Documents on American Foreign Relations. 1938–1939 edited by S. Shepard Jones and Denys P. Myers. (Boston, 1939).

Documents on British Foreign Policy, 1919-1939. Edited by E. L. Woodward and Rohan Butler. Third Series (London, 1949–1955).

Documents on Events Preceding the Outbreak of the War. Compiled and published by the German Foreign Office, Berlin, 1939. (New York, 1940).

Documents on German Foreign Policy, 1918–1945. Series D (Washington, D.C., 1949–).

Documents on International Affairs. Issued under the auspices of the Royal Institute of International Affairs. 1938–1939 (London, 1943, 1951, 1954).

Documents and Materials Relating to the Eve of the Second World War. Published by the Ministry of Foreign Affairs of the Soviet Union. 2 vols. (New York, 1948).

Documents and Speeches on British Commonwealth Affairs, 1931–1952. Edited by Nicholas Mansergh. 2 vols. (London, 1953).

Foreign Relations of the United States: Diplomatic Papers. 1938–1939 (Washington, D.C., 1955–1956).

The French Yellow Book: Diplomatic Documents, 1938–1939. (New York, 1940).

Great Britain. Agreement between the Government of the United Kingdom and the Polish Government Regarding Mutual

Assistance, London, August 25, 1939. Command Paper 6144. (London, 1939).

———. *Agreement between the United Kingdom and Italy, Consisting of a Protocol with Annexes and Exchange of Notes,* Rome, April 16, 1938. Command Paper 5726. (London, 1938).

———. *Statement Relating to Defence, Presented by the Prime Minister to Parliament by Command of His Majesty, February, 1938.* Command Paper 5944. (London, 1939).

———. *Parliamentary Debates, House of Commons* (Official Report). Fifth Series.

———. *Parliamentary Debates, House of Lords* (Official Report). Fifth Series.

League of Nations, Official Journal. 1938 (London, 1938).

Nazi Conspiracy and Aggression. 8 vols. (Washington, D.C., 1946).

Nazi-Soviet Relations, 1939–1941: Documents from the Archives of the German Foreign Office. (Washington, D.C., 1948).

Trial of the Major War Criminals Before the International Military Tribunal. 42 vols. (Nuremburg, Germany, 1947–1949).

Trials of War Criminals Before the Nuernberg Military Tribunals Under Control Council Law No. 10. 14 vols. (Washington, D.C., 1950–1952).

B. Memoirs, Diaries, Papers, and Speeches

Amery, L. S. *My Political Life* (3 vols.) (London, 1955).

Assmann, Kurt. *Deutsche Schicksalsjahre, Historische Bilder aus den zweiten Weltkrieg und seiner Vorgeschichte* (Wiesbaden, 1950).

Atholl, Katharine, Duchess of. *Working Partnership* (London, 1958).

Attlee, Clement. *As It Happened* (New York, 1954).

Avon, Earl of. *The Memoirs of Anthony Eden: Facing the Dictators* (Cambridge, 1962).

———. *The Memoirs of Anthony Eden: The Reckoning* (Cambridge, 1965).

Bartlett, Vernon. *And Now, Tomorrow* (London, 1960).

Beck, Colonel Jozef. *Final Report* (New York, 1957).

Benes, Eduard. *Memoirs of Dr. Eduard Benes* (Boston, 1953).

Birchall, Frederick T. *The Storm Breaks* (New York, 1940).

Bonnet, Georges. *Défense de la Paix* (2 vols.) (Geneva, 1946–1948).

Chamberlain, Neville. *In Search of Peace* (New York, 1939).

Churchill, Winston S. *The Gathering Storm* (Boston, 1948).

———. *Step by Step, 1936–1939* (New York, 1939).

———. *Blood, Sweat and Tears* (New York, 1941).

The Ciano Diaries: The Complete Unabridged Diaries of Count Galeazzo Ciano, Italian Minister for Foreign Affairs, 1939–1943. Edited by Hugh Gibson. (New York, 1946).

Ciano's Hidden Diary, 1937–1938 (New York, 1953).

Ciano's Diplomatic Papers. Edited by Malcolm Muggeridge. (London, 1948).

Citrine, Lord. *Men and Work: An Autobiography* (London, 1964).

Coulondre, Robert. *De Staline á Hitler: souvenirs de deux ambassades, 1936–1939* (Paris, 1950).

Dahlerus, Birger. *The Last Attempt* (London, 1947).

Dalton, Hugh. *The Fateful Years: Memoirs, 1931–1945* (London, 1957).

Davies, Joseph. *Mission to Moscow* (New York, 1941).

Dirksen, Herbert von. *Moscow, Tokyo, London: Twenty Years of German Foreign Policy* (Norman, Oklahoma, 1952).

Duff Cooper. *Old Men Forget: The Autobiography of Duff Cooper* (London, 1953).

———. *The Second World War* (New York, 1939).

Eden, Anthony. *Foreign Affairs* (New York, 1939).

———. *Freedom and Order: Selected Speeches, 1939–1946* (Boston, 1948).

Flandin, Pierre-Etienne. *Politique Francaise, 1919–1940* (Paris, 1947).

Francois-Poncet, André. *The Fateful Years: Memoirs of a French Ambassador in Berlin, 1931–1938* (New York, 1949).

Gafencu, Grigore. *Last Days of Europe: A Diplomatic Journey in 1939* (New Haven, 1948).

Gamelin, General Maurice. *Servir: Le Prologue du Drame (1930–Aout 1939)* (Paris, 1946).

Halifax, Lord. *Fullness of Days* (New York, 1957).

Henderson, Sir Nevile. *Failure of a Mission: Berlin, 1937–1939* (New York, 1940).

———. *Water Under the Bridges* (London, 1945).

Henderson, Alexander. *Eye-Witness in Czecho-Slovakia* (London, 1939).

Hesse, Fritz. *Das Spiel um Deutschland* (Munich, 1953).

Hitler, Adolf. *Mein Kampf* (New York, 1939).

Ismay, General Lord. *The Memoirs of General Lord Ismay* (New York, 1960).

Jones, Thomas. *A Diary with Letters, 1931–1950* (London, 1954).

Kemp, Lieutenant Commander P. K. *Key to Victory: The Triumph of British Sea Power in World War II* (Boston, 1957).

Kirkpatrick, Ivone. *The Inner Circle* (London, 1959).

Knatchbull-Hugessen, Sir Hughe. *Diplomat: In Peace and War* (London, 1949).

Kordt, Erich. *Nicht aus den Akten, Die Wilhelmstrasse in Frieden und Krieg Erlebnisse, Begegnungen, und Eindrücke, 1928–1945* (Stuttgart, 1950).

Low, David. *Low's Autobiography* (New York, 1957).

Maisky, Ivan. *Who Helped Hitler?* (London, 1964).

Mander, Geoffrey. *We Were Not All Wrong* (London, 1944).

Maugham, Viscount. *At The End of the Day* (London, 1954).

Meissner, Otto. *Staatssekretär unter Ebert-Hindenburg-Hitler, Der Schicksalsweg des deutsches Volkes von 1918–1945, wie ich ihn erlebte* (Hamburg, 1950).

Minney, R. J. *The Private Papers of Hore-Belisha* (New York, 1961).

Noël Léon. *L'agression allemande contre la Pologne* (Paris, 1946).

Papen, Franz von. *Memoirs* (New York, 1953).

Putlitz, Wolfgang zu. *The Putlitz Dossier* (London, 1957).

Reynaud, Paul. *La France a sauvé l'Europe* (2 vols.) (Paris, 1947).

Ribbentrop, Joachim von. *Zwischen London und Moskau: Erinnerungen und letze Aufzeichnungen* (Leoni, Germany, 1954).

Samuel, Viscount (Herbert). *Memoirs* (London, 1945).

Schmidt, Paul. *Hitler's Interpreter* (New York, 1951).

Schuschnigg, Kurt von. *Austrian Requiem* (New York, 1946).

Selby, Sir Walford. *Diplomatic Twilight, 1930–1940* (London, 1943).

Simon, Viscount (John). *Retrospect: The Memoirs of The Rt. Hon. Viscount Simon* (London, 1952).

Slessor, Sir John. *The Central Blue: The Autobiography of Sir John Slessor, Marshal of the RAF* (New York, 1957).

Spears, Major-General Sir Edward. *Assignment to Catastrophe* (2 vols.) (New York, 1954).

Speeches on Foreign Policy by Viscount Halifax. Edited by H. H. E. Craster. (London, 1940).

The Speeches of Adolf Hitler, April 1922–August 1939. Edited by Norman H. Baynes. (2 vols.) (London, 1942).

Strang, Lord. *Home and Abroad* (London, 1956).

Templewood, Viscount (Sir Samuel Hoare). *Nine Troubled Years* (London, 1954).

Vansittart, Lord (Robert). *Lessons of My Life* (New York, 1943).

———. *The Mist Procession: The Autobiography of Lord Vansittart* (London, 1958).

Wedgewood, Rt. Hon. Josiah C. *Memoirs of a Fighting Life* (London, 1941).

Weizsäcker, Ernst von. *Memoirs of Ernst von Weizsäcker* (Chicago, 1951).

Winterton, The Rt. Hon. Earl. *Orders of the Day* (London, 1953).

Woolton, The Earl of. *The Memoirs of The Rt. Hon. The Earl of Woolton* (London, 1959).

C. Newspapers

The Daily Herald (London).
The Daily Mail (London).
The Daily Telegraph (London).
The Evening Standard (London).
The Financial News (London).
The Financial Times (London).
The Glasgow Herald
The Leeds Weekly Citizen
Liverpool Daily Post
The Manchester Guardian
The Herald Tribune (New York).
The New York Times
News Chronicle (London).
The Observer (London).
Reynolds News (London).
Sunday Graphic (London).
Sunday Pictorial (London).
The Sunday Times (London).
The Times (London).
The Weekly Scotsman (Edinburgh).
Western Mail (Cardiff).
The Yorkshire Observer (Bradford).

D. Periodicals

The Economist
The Fortnightly
The National Review
The New Statesman and Nation
The Round Table
The Spectator
The Statist
Time and Tide

II. Secondary Sources

A. Biographies, Histories, and Special Studies

Anderson, Mosa. *Noel Buxton: A Life* (London, 1952).

Birkenhead, The Earl of. *Halifax: The Life of Lord Halifax* (London, 1965).

Broad, Lewis. *Anthony Eden: The Chronicle of a Career* (New York, 1955).

Campbell-Johnson, Alan. *Sir Anthony Eden* (London, 1955).

———. *Viscount Halifax: A Biography* (New York, 1941).

Camrose, Viscount. *British Newspapers and Their Controllers* (London, 1947).

Carter, Gwendolen M. *The British Commonwealth and International Security: The Role of the Dominions, 1919-1939* (Toronto, 1947).

Cartland, Barbara. *Ronald Cartland* (London, n.d.).

Connell, John. *The "Office": A Study in British Foreign Policy and Its Makers, 1919–1951* (London, 1958).

Cooke, Colin. *The Life of Richard Stafford Cripps* (London, 1957).

Craig, Gordon A. and Gilbert, Felix (eds.). *The Diplomats, 1919–1939* (Princeton, 1953).

van der Esch, P. A. M. *Prelude to War: The International Repercussions of the Spanish Civil War (1936–1939)* (The Hague, 1951).

Estorick, Eric. *Stafford Cripps: Master Statesman* (New York, 1949).

Eubank, Keith. *Munich* (Norman, Oklahoma, 1963).

Feiling, Keith. *The Life of Neville Chamberlain* (London, 1947).

Furnia, Arthur H. *The Diplomacy of Appeasement: Anglo-French Relations and the Prelude to World War II, 1931–1938* (Washington, D.C., 1960).

Gathorne-Hardy, G.M. *A Short History of International Affairs, 1920 to 1938* (London, 1939).

George, Margaret. *The Warped Vision: British Foreign Policy, 1933–1939* (Pittsburgh, 1965).

Gilbert, Martin and Gott, Richard. *The Appeasers* (London, 1963).

Goerlitz, Walter. *History of the German General Staff, 1657–1945* (New York, 1954).

Graves, Robert and Hodge, Alan. *The Long Week-End: A Social History of Great Britain, 1918–1939* (London, n.d.).

Hadley, W. W. *Munich: Before and After* (London, 1944).

Higham, Robin. *Armed Forces in Peacetime: Britain, 1918–1940, A Case Study* (Hamden, 1962).

The History of The Times. 4 vols. (New York, 1952).

Hodgson, Stuart. *Lord Halifax* (London, 1941).

Jenkins, Roy. *Mr. Attlee: An Interim Biography* (London, 1948).

Jordan, W. M. *Great Britain, France, and the German Problem, 1918–1939* (London, 1943).

Keith, Arthur B. *The Causes of the War* (London, 1940).

Kenney, Marion L., "The Role of the House of Commons in British Foreign Policy During the 1937–38 Session," in Norton Downs (ed.), *Essays in Honor of Conyers Read* (Chicago, 1953).

Laffan, R. G. D. *The Crisis Over Czechoslovakia, January to September, 1938* (London, 1951). (Volume II, for year 1938, of *Survey of International Affairs,* edited by Arnold Toynbee.)

——— et al. *Survey of International Affairs, 1938,* III (London, 1953).

Langer, William L. and Gleason, S. Everett. *The Challenge to Isolation, 1937–1940* (New York, 1952).

Macleod, Iain. *Neville Chamberlain* (London, 1961).

Madge, Charles and Harrison, Tom. *Britain by Mass-Observation* (Harmondsworth, Middlesex, England, 1939).

Mansergh, Nicholas. *Survey of British Commonwealth Affairs: Problems of External Policy, 1931–1939* (London, 1952).

McKenzie, R. T. *British Political Parties: The Distribution of Power Within the Conservative and Labour Parties* (New York, 1955).

Medlicott, W. N., "Neville Chamberlain," in *British Prime Ministers: A Portrait Gallery Introduced by Duff Cooper* (New York, 1953).

Micaud, Charles A. *The French Right and Nazi Germany, 1933–1939: A Study of Public Opinion* (Durham, North Carolina, 1943).

Mowat, Charles Loch. *Britain Between the Wars, 1918–1940* (Chicago, 1955).

Namier, Lewis B. *Diplomatic Prelude, 1938–1939* (London, 1948).

———. *Europe in Decay: A Study in Disintegration, 1936–1940* (London, 1950).

———. *In the Nazi Era* (London, 1952).

Postan, M. M. *British War Production* (London, 1952).

Reynolds, P. A. *British Foreign Policy in the Inter-War Years* (London, 1954).

Rock, William R., "Grand Alliance or Daisy Chain: British Opinion and Policy Toward Russia, April–August, 1939," in Wallace, Lillian P. and Askew, William (eds.), *Power, Public Opinion and Diplomacy* (Durham, North Carolina, 1959).

———, "The Munich Agreement of September 29, 1938: Its Enforcement and Results." Unpublished M.A. thesis, Duke University, 1953.

Rowse, A. L. *Appeasement: A Study in Political Decline, 1933–1939* (New York, 1961).

Seton-Watson, R. W. *A History of the Czechs and Slovaks* (London, 1943).

Strauss, Patricia. *Cripps: Advocate Extraordinary* (New York, 1942).

Tansill, Charles C. *Back Door to War: The Roosevelt Foreign Policy, 1933–1941* (Chicago, 1952).

Taylor, A. J. P. *Englishmen and Others* (London, 1956).

———. *The Origins of the Second World War* (New York, 1962).

Toynbee, Arnold J. *Survey of International Affairs,* 1938, I (London, 1941).

——— and Ashton-Gwatkin, Frank (eds.). *The World in March 1939* (London, 1952). (Volume I, for years 1939–1946, of *Survey of International Affairs.*)

——— and Veronica (eds.). *The Eve of War, 1939* (London, 1958). (Volume X, for years 1939–1946, of *Survey of International Affairs.*)

Wedgwood, C. V. *The Last of the Radicals, Josiah Wedgwood* (London, 1951).

Wheeler-Bennett, John W. *King George VI: His Life and Reign* (New York, 1958).

———. *Munich: Prologue to Tragedy* (London, 1948).

———. *The Nemesis of Power: The German Army in Politics, 1918–1945* (London, 1953).

Williams, Francis. *Ernest Bevin: Portrait of a Great Englishman* (London, 1952).

Windrich, Elaine. *British Labour's Foreign Policy* (Stanford, 1952).

Wolfers, Arnold. *Britain and France Between Two Wars: Conflicting Strategies of Peace Since Versailles* (New York, 1940).

Wrench, John Evelyn. *Geoffrey Dawson and Our Times* (London, 1955).

Young, G. M. *Stanley Baldwin* (London, 1952).

B. Articles

Ashton-Gwatkin, F. T. A., "The Personal Story of the Runciman Mission," *The Listener,* XL, 595–97.

Brailsford, H. N., "The Tory Policy of Peace," *Political Quarterly,* IX, 325–33.

Burns, C. Delisle, "Top Dog Diplomacy," *Fortnightly,* CL, 693–701.

Carroll, E. Malcolm, "Recent German Publications and German Foreign Policy, 1933–1945," *American Political Science Review,* XLVI, 525–41.

Carter, W. Horsfall, "Reconnaissance on the Home Front," *Fortnightly,* CL, 12–22.

Charlton, Air-Commodore L. E., "The Mischief in the Mediterranean," *Fortnightly,* CXLIX, 282–90.

Davies, (?), "The Anglo-French Alliance," *Contemporary Review,* CLIV, 544–51.

Dell, Robert, "Abyssinia Unconquered," *New Statesman and Nation,* XV, 597–98.

Duff, S. Grant, "Germany and Czechoslovakia," *Contemporary Review,* CLIII, 182–89.

———, "British Policy and Czechoslovakia," *Contemporary Review,* CLIV, 147–53.

Duff Cooper, Rt. Hon. Sir, "A Cynical Act of Cold-Blooded Butchery," *The Listener,* XL, 757–58.

Duns, William, "If War Comes," *Nineteenth Century,* CXXIV, 257–60.

Emrys-Evans, P. V., "Facing the Issues," *Fortnightly,* CL, 679–85.

Falls, Cyril, "Should the Democracies Have Fought in 1938?" *The Listener,* XL, 717–18.

Fitzsimons, M. A., "The Masque of Uncertainty: Britain and Munich," *Review of Politics,* XII, 489–505.

Garnett, Maxwell, "The Future of the League," *Contemporary Review,* CLIII, 402–10.

Gedye, G. E. R., "Austria—The Curtain Falls," *Contemporary Review,* CLIII, 543–54.

Gooch, G. P. "The Grouping of the Powers," *Contemporary Review,* CLIV, 129–38.

Headlam-Morley, Agnes, "Was Neville Chamberlain's Policy Wrong?" *The Listener,* XL, 551–53.

Hobhouse, Charles E., "The International Situation," *Contemporary Review,* CLIII, 513–21.

———, "The New Deal in Europe," *Contemporary Review,* CLIV, 651–58.

Liddell Hart, B. H., "Strategy and Commitments," *Fortnightly,* CXLIX, 641–49.

Lockhart, Sir Robert Bruce, "September Crisis—and After," *The Listener,* XL, 635–37.

Lothian, Lord, "The Issues in British Foreign Policy," *International Affairs,* XVII, 360–77.

Mowat, R. B., "The Crisis in Central Europe," *Nineteenth Century,* CXIII, 394–404.

Namier, L. B., "Munich Survey: A Summing Up," *The Listener,* XL, 835–36.

Nicolson, Harold, "British Public Opinion and Foreign Policy," *Public Opinion Quarterly,* I, 53–63.

———, "The Commons and the 1938 Crisis," *The Listener,* XL, 795–96.

———, "Is War Inevitable?" *Nineteenth Century,* CXXVI, 2–4.

Parker, Robert, "The Czech Crisis: The Background," *Fortnightly,* CL, 398–406.

Powers, Richard H., "Churchill's Parliamentary Commentary on British Foreign Policy, 1935–1938," *Journal of Modern History,* XXVI, 179–82.

Rowse, A. L., "Reflections on the European Situation," *Political Quarterly,* IX, 334–50.

Samuel, Viscount, "The Choice Before Us," *Nineteenth Century,* CXIII, 641–55.

Seton-Watson, R. W., "Czechoslovakia After the German Coup," *Contemporary Review,* CLIII, 522–32.

———, "Munich and After," *Fortnightly,* CL, 526–39.

Spender, J. A., "Munich—Before and After," *Contemporary Review,* CLIV, 513–22.

Steed, Wickham, "British Interests," *Contemporary Review,* CLIII, 385–95.

Tower, Charles, "Business As Usual," *Nineteenth Century,* CXXIV, 643–57.

Toynbee, Arnold J., "The Issues in British Foreign Policy," *International Affairs,* XVII, 307–32.

Vansittart, Lord, "A Morally Indefensible Agreement," *The Listener,* XL, 675–77.

Index